SHAKESPEARE,
THE MAGICIAN AND THE HEALER

"In *Shakespeare, the Magician and the Healer*, Annie-Paule de Prinsac offers an original and quite remarkable account of Shakespeare's plays and poems. Her interpretive strategy is to assess the meaning and method of his work by means of mannerist (and also baroque) æsthetics, but her wide-ranging knowledge of continental and, especially, French literature and culture also broadens and enriches her perspective. It is unlikely that anyone will agree with everything she says, but almost everyone will here find insights into Shakespeare's works that both challenge and enhance their own insights — which is the purpose of literary criticism."

— R.V. YOUNG, author of *Shakespeare and the Idea of Western Civilization*

"This volume should interest anyone intrigued by recent claims that William Shakespeare was a life-long Catholic and that his religious beliefs directly and fruitfully affected both his art and his artistry. It should also interest readers who are curious to learn more about artistic 'Mannerism' and how that important aesthetic movement may have intricately influenced Shakespeare's works. Finally, the author's personal familiarity with French culture and literature allows her to see Shakespeare from an unusual and fresh vantage point."

— ROBERT C. EVANS, I. B. Young Professor of English, Auburn University at Montgomery

"Annie-Paule de Prinsac has given us a terrifically revealing, necessary, and exciting reading of Shakespeare — 'healer and magician' indeed — along with rich servings of cultural history and artistic contexts from Renaissance Italy to the Baroque. Risking the religious jeopardies of his own time, we see the crypto-Catholic poet deploying the misdirections of mannerist tools (a fresh mode of 'unusual couplings giving birth to surprise') throughout the entire range of his poems and plays (*Cymbeline* will never be the same). This project, ever-beguiling and quite deliberate, united manner and matter as no other and probably saved his life."

— JAMES COMO, author of *C. S. Lewis: A Very Short Introduction* and *Mystical Perelandra*

"'What religion wilt thou be of next?' Malvole asks Pietro in John Marston's Elizabethan play, *The Malcontent*, which is itself a fantasy of recusant Catholics in England. That question haunts the whole of the great age of English drama, especially in the life and work of William Shakespeare. In this ambitious and energetic study, Annie-Paule de Prinsac not only argues for the Catholic formation of Shakespeare's dramas but also for their coded mannerism, wherein the Catholicism proscribed in the playwright's England still finds voice and expression — voice and expression in the greatest plays of all time, Shakespeare's late masterpieces."

— JAMES MATTHEW WILSON, author of *Saint Thomas and the Forbidden Birds*

"Shakespeare scholarship is emerging from its own dark age, and Annie-Paul de Prinsac's detailed and extensive analysis of the Bard's works is a bright star in that new constellation of analysis. Deftly weaving threads of theology, history, and aesthetics into her tapestry, de Prinsac provides a portrait of Shakespeare as an adroit conjuror whose spells reveal ever-new depths of religious and anthropological riches."

— **STEPHEN MIRARCHI**, Chair and Associate Professor, Benedictine College

"In the recent and growing body of criticism that examines Shakespeare as a Catholic author, this book considering the Bard through a Mannerist lens provides a fresh and intriguing perspective. Shakespeare's Mannerism, the author argues, arose from the extreme religious and political complexities of his time, a moment in history that, given his Catholic sympathies, necessarily called for a style that conceals even as it reveals. I highly recommend this elegantly written work."

— **MARY REICHARDT**, Professor of Literature Emeritus, University of St. Thomas; editor of *Encyclopedia of Catholic Literature*

"*Shakespeare, the Magician and the Healer* is a provocative and enlightening contribution to Shakespeare studies. Annie Paul de Prinsac situates Shakespeare fully in the shifting and complex religious and cultural milieu of Early Modernity, forthrightly exploring the contested question of Shakespeare and Catholicism. The book's unique contribution lies in connecting Shakespeare's elusive religious convictions to emergent European aesthetic developments in painting, music, opera, architecture, and sculpture which emphasize indirection and competing perspectives. It is equally valuable as a compendium of brilliant, close readings of Shakespeare's individual works sure to illuminate both the uninitiated and advanced student of the Bard."

— **AARON URBANCZYK**, Professor of English, Franciscan University

"Annie-Paule de Prinsac's *Shakespeare, the Magician and the Healer* explores the religious tensions inhabiting the soul of the incognito Catholic William Shakespeare and his delicate sojourn through the politically and religiously dangerous ages of Elizabeth I and James VI and I. Along the way, she guides us through the psychology of England's greatest playwright in a manner both edifying and illuminating."

— **MICHAEL MARTIN**, author of *Sophia in Exile* and *Mythologies of the Wild of God*

"The elegantly written *Shakespeare, the Magician and the Healer* blends deep scholarship with fascinating insights into the individual plays and the moral and stylistic currents that run through the long arc of Shakespeare's works. It is a significant addition to the body of Shakespeare criticism."

— **RICHARD BLUMENTHAL**, Former Head, International School of Boston

Shakespeare

THE MAGICIAN
&
THE HEALER

❈

ANNIE-PAULE DE PRINSAC

Foreword by Joseph Pearce

Angelico Press

Book and cover design
by Michael Schrauzer

For Guillaume, Sébastien, and Gaultier
my three beloved sons

But all the story of the night told over,
And all their minds transfigured so together,
More witnesseth than fancy's images,
And grows to something of great constancy;
But howsoever, strange and admirable.
                    —*A Midsummer Night's Dream,* V i 23–27

CONTENTS

FOREWORD
BY JOSEPH PEARCE

*T*IMES HAVE CHANGED AND IN SOME WAYS THEY HAVE changed for the better. This is certainly the case with respect to Shakespeare scholarship. There was a time, not so long ago, when few voices of reason, or even sanity, could be heard amidst the maelstrom of malevolent and maladroit nonsense that passed for scholarship on Shakespeare and his work. The nonsense continues, of course; such are the nonsensical times in which we find ourselves. The Bard is still beset by those who claim him as a fellow queer theorist or radical relativist, or by those who declaim him as a nihilistic proponent of deconstruction— centuries ahead of his time—or by those who denounce him for being a misogynist or a racist. But these voices, insofar as they are aware of the broader and deeper scholarly conversation, are now on the defensive. The tide is turning.

Recently published works have concentrated on the evidence for Shakespeare's Catholicism and on the Catholic dimension of his work, or on his Christian humanism and his place within the tradition-oriented conversation which constitutes Christian civilization. No longer do we find ourselves in the dark days at the end of the last century in which Peter Milward ploughed a lonely furrow as the lone scholar advocating the Catholicism of Shakespeare's plays. In the past ten years, a host of new books have been published, each of which illustrates that the works of Shakespeare are Catholic theologically and philosophically, either formally or at least in spirit. Clare Asquith followed her earlier book, *Shadowplay: The Hidden Beliefs and Coded Politics of William Shakespeare* (2005) with *Shakespeare and the Resistance: The Earl of Southampton, The Essex Rebellion, and the Poems that Challenged Tudor Tyranny* (2018). The great German scholar, Hildegard Hammerschmidt-Hummel, has published some groundbreaking volumes but perhaps her crowning achievement is *The Life and Times of William Shakespeare* (2007), in which she shows the abundance of evidence for Shakespeare's Catholicism within the historical context of his life and times. Three significant books were published in 2022 alone — *Christian Humanism in Shakespeare: A Study in Religion and Literature* by Lee Oser; *Shakespeare and the Elizabethan Reformation: Literary Negotiation and Religious Difference* by Dennis Taylor; and *Shakespeare and the Idea of Western Civilization* by R. V. Young. Last and hopefully not least are my own contributions to this scholarship — *The Quest for Shakespeare: The Bard of Avon and the Church of Rome* (2008); *Through Shakespeare's Eyes: Seeing the Catholic Presence in the Plays* (2010); and *Shakespeare On Love: Seeing the Catholic Presence in Romeo and Juliet* (2013). As a means of indicating the extent of good scholarship related to the topic of Shakespeare's Christian faith and philosophy, I provided at the end of *The Quest for Shakespeare* a five-page selected bibliography of other books connected to the topic.

The happy fact is that scholarship on Shakespeare's religion, especially that which shows the abundance of evidence for his abiding Catholicism, has moved from the margins to the mainstream. This was made evident in an anecdote related personally to me by someone who had attended a talk by the director of the Shakespeare Theatre Company in Washington DC. During the questions following the talk, the director was asked what was known about Shakespeare's religion. He answered that many people seem to believe that he was Catholic. The fact that this is the answer which instantly sprang to mind when the unexpected question was raised illustrates that the evidence for the Bard's Catholicism is now more widely accepted than at any time since the decades immediately following his death.

This acceptance of Shakespeare's Catholic sympathies and sensibilities animates the present volume, the author of which has enjoyed a lifelong love affair with the Bard, which is evident in the breadth and depth of her understanding of the man, his works and his times. What is unique about her approach is the way in which she places Shakespeare amongst the advocates and practitioners of mannerism, an aesthetic movement that straddled the period between the late Renaissance and the Baroque. As with the Baroque, it was an expression of the Catholic Counter-Reformation's response to the austerity and aesthetic minimalism of the Protestant Reformation. The author argues that Shakespeare was a mannerist by both taste and necessity, mannerist technique enabling him both to reveal and conceal religious elements in his works with finesse and subtlety, both of which were necessary in the religious tensions of Elizabethan and Jacobean England. In essence, Shakespeare disguised himself and his meaning in a mannerist mask which simultaneously and paradoxically revealed truths indirectly and allegorically which would be illegal for him to reveal candidly. As the author explains, "Shakespeare could not displease the absolute power which provided for his and his company's living, yet he could, by using indirections, various kinds of artistic contortion and subterfuge, manage to say what he meant and offer the audience a critical view which could at all times be deniable." In other words, to put the whole matter and manner in blunt idiomatic form, Shakespeare felt contracted morally to telling the truth but told it in such a way that he always had a plausible get-out clause. Such an approach, such a manner of speaking, was a life-preserving necessity, not a nicety, in the perilous times in which he and his audience lived.

Concluding with my own get-out clause, I would say that I am not always in agreement with the author's reading of some of the plays. I also question her reading of the historical context on occasion. Nonetheless, I am pleased to be able to raise the curtain on this fine addition to the burgeoning body of new and true Shakespeare scholarship. ♣

INTRODUCTION

*T*HE WORD AND IDEA OF METAMORPHOSIS FIRST inspired my exploration into Shakespeare's plays. It contained within itself the diversity of his poetry, the astonishing shapes of his theater and the wisdom of a philosophy of life, which still fascinates audiences four hundred years later. Like Montaigne, who said, "I describe not the essence, but the passage;"[1] Shakespeare enjoyed having characters, plots, words, and situations reverberating upon each other, eluding answers to questions that were never put directly, but constantly hinted at, visualized, stretched out like the spiral of a Baroque torso column that pretends to be what it is not while feigning not to be what it is. For the poet, as for his clown Feste, "A sentence [was] but a cheverel glove to a good wit, how quickly the wrong side may be turned outward."[2] Scholars have, for more than four hundred years, attempted to capture the nature of this sleek Proteus and of his work, but more often than not, they remained mystified by what they considered contradictions. Whereas the Ovidian tales and inspiration that had nourished him as a schoolboy gave him some of the keys to develop his ability as a poet, Shakespeare's style encompasses so many different influences, his imaginative range is so vast, that few critics have managed to do justice to the totality of his oeuvre until now. To the schoolgirl I was, nurtured by French classical drama with its extremely rigid rules, which restrained a play to one action in one location, on one day[3], here was a dramatist who systematically broke them all. As for propriety and verisimilitude such as they were defined by seventeenth century French society, they did not apply at all. To French classical drama, Shakespeare was the quintessence of political-incorrectness. Was he indeed the inspired barbarian described by Voltaire? It required study. I spent hours of my life reading his plays (aloud), inventing imaginary performances, pondering over their poetry and dramatic structure with an ever-renewed sense of wonder. I scrutinized his words and characters, imagined his staging, trying to express the "precious marrow" or "substantifique moelle"[4] of his plays

---

[1] "Je ne peins pas l'estre, je peins le passage." Montaigne's *Essays*, Bk. III, chap. 2, trans. John Florio (London: The Folio Society, 2006).
[2] *Twelfth Night*, III i 11–13. The text of the Oxford University Press Shakespeare has been generally used, in the edition of The Folio Society, 2007.
[3] "Qu'en un lieu, qu'en un jour, un seul fait accompli / Tienne jusqu'à la fin le théâtre rempli." Nicolas Boileau, *L'Art Poétique* (Paris: Hachette Livre Bnf, 2013).
[4] From Rabelais's Prologue to the First Book of *La vie très horrificque du Grand Gargantua* (Paris: Jean de Bonnot Editeur, 1973). It can also be translated as "the very substance."

without ever locking them into any preordained grid. I entered his world on tiptoe, full of the spirit of adventure and discovery of the traveler who sets foot on a *terra incognita*. I was amazed and never satiated, and like Jaques in *As You Like It*, I could only say, "More, more, I prithee, more" (II v 9). This sense of wonder never abated.

As time went on, however, all those stories and the complexity of their manners ended up witnessing much more than "fancy's images," and I had to recognize "something of great constancy" in the purpose as well as the overall style of the author. Over the years, I had written essays on individual plays, which marked the progress of my investigations, but I somehow felt that I owed more to William Shakespeare than a fragmented appraisal of his plays. You can indeed be misled if you omit to consider each play within the totality of the poet's work, notwithstanding the fact that plays are, by essence, like musical scores: they must be interpreted, each performance infusing it with a variety of new meanings. It suddenly became vital for me to gather all these pieces of writing together and to attempt to give them the coherence they deserved.

Shakespeare's universality, which is the consequence of his essential elusiveness, has too often been the pretext to make him say absolutely anything, especially in the theater. Having tried on several occasions to convince my friends of his "greatness" by inviting them to see a play, I failed miserably, betrayed by unconscionable stage productions, as vulgar as they were unjustified by the text itself. Yet, unlike Coleridge, I believe in the necessity of performance to obtain the full effect of what Shakespeare was trying to do. It entails an appropriate understanding of the historical and aesthetic contexts in which he worked. Shakespeare's plays can certainly be turned into postmodern revolutionary happenings, but one should be aware that he did not create them for that effect.

MY FIRST CHAPTER FOCUSES ON THE TROUBLED HISTORICAL context which marked Shakespeare's childhood and youth. One cannot hope to understand his plays, if one does not take into account the reality of the time. The difficulty, as always, lay in the mystery surrounding his own life and education. The William Shakespeare I encountered at University was definitely England's child prodigy; he was the national poet and dramatist, the man who wrote *Henry V*, whose political and religious ideas must therefore conform to Tudor politics. There is as yet, it is true, no letter, no document that could be credited one way or another. Yet, William Shakespeare was born into a Catholic family, in a still profoundly Catholic county, and we have absolutely no evidence that he ever recanted his faith. To overlook these facts was like deliberately altering the reality that shaped his mind, but we never mentioned the subject, never even talked of religious wars, and my education in secular France somehow kept me from broaching the subject.

The revelation came with Clare Asquith's *Shadowplay,*[5] which opened my eyes to the hidden strings behind the whole. She meaningfully linked her experience of censure in Moscow during the Soviet era with Elizabethan politics, revealing how the constraints of censorship could in fact foster ingenuity and the art of circumvention. I discovered that Merry Old England was in fact an age of terror and persecution, surveillance and brutal executions. There was no room for dissidence and people lived in fear of denunciation. A free mind could only resist such oppression, all the more if he was born in the camp of the victims. Like Ben Jonson and John Donne, Will Shakespeare could probably have abandoned Catholicism and officially opted for the new faith, but there is no trace that he did.[6] If he wanted to succeed and yet remain true to himself, he surely had to follow Polonius's advice and "by indirections find directions out" (*Hamlet,* II i 65). Shakespeare was such a self-aware artist, constantly reflecting on his art, outwitting and toying with his audiences, he could not have written plays completely disconnected from his time. And he did not. According to Clare Asquith, he simply hid his comments and beliefs using all kinds of indirections and the codes covertly used by dissident writers in the sixteenth century. One may not agree with all of her argument, but her beautifully written book is a thought-provoking thriller. The realization that William Shakespeare must have been at heart a resisting Catholic suddenly made sense, highlighting the most complex obscurities, mirror plays and indirections of his theater. It also somehow threw light on the obscure corners of his life, providing plausible reasons for his lack of a university education as well as for his opting for the freedom of the theater in a world which barred him from the most rewarding jobs anyway.

The immediate consequence for me was that Shakespeare's mannerist style was made even more relevant once his Catholic background and faith were recognized. Suddenly, content and style, or matter and manner to use contemporary words, threw light upon each other. Shakespeare found many mannerist devices convenient for his purpose; they suited the complexity of the time and the necessity of covering up one's tracks. For some reason, however, which may be the same reasons as before mentioned,

---

[5] Clare Asquith, *Shadowplay* (New York: Public Affairs, 2005).
[6] Shakespeare's constancy differed greatly from Donne's tormented soul and inner division, which, as John Carey argues, were provoked by his apostasy: "when he abandoned Catholicism he lost an irreplaceable absolute." John Carey, *John Donne: Life, Mind and Art* (London: Faber, 1981), 30.

mannerism as a style did not seem applicable to a man everyone wanted
to see as the quintessence of the English artist. It would have entailed
forbidden ties and protections in a kingdom resolutely separated from
the cultural evolution of the rest of Europe. Even though Shakespeare's
work answered many requirements of mannerism, few, before the twenty-
first century, dared grant him such a controversial appellation.[7] Besides,
it seemed easier to look for higher-born substitutes among the nobility
than to accept the fact that a country boy without a university education
could have had access to such extensive knowledge and such a mastery
of style and matter. Notwithstanding, William Shakespeare spent his life
trying to refine the tools that would enable him to raise the theater to
the level of the greatest arts and eventually to reach, through mannerist
artifice, the spirituality of the Baroque. Such a man also mastered the
various artistic theories of his time, whose trends and rivalries he was
to reproduce, and occasionally mock, in his plays. When he felt he had
achieved his esthetic and moral purpose, he even discreetly left the name
of the artist who inspired him in his plays. But critics generally missed
the mark and overlooked his manifesto.

At first, the young playwright hardly concealed his anger and disgust,
and the violence of his early plays tends to focus on rape, usurpation,
and exile. He obviously launched into the War of the Roses with Tudor
England in mind, and as he went through the chroniclers, the questions of
legitimacy and rivalry within the realm became a lifelong obsession. That
it was linked to Henry VIII betraying his position as "Defender of the
Faith"[8] and to the dissolution of the monasteries is made visible through
the imagery of rape in the plays and poems.[9] The moral quality of the
ruler would remain a major concern of the playwright until his death.
The recurrent themes and characters of his plays also reveal his everlasting
concern with intercession and healing, with those people who, in time of
distress, are there to mediate between the afflicted soul and the divine.
The emptiness left by the religious Reformation called for a renewal of
representations. Churches had been whitewashed, but you could create
moving images with words. The Counter-Reformation had developed

---

[7] With the notable exception of Professor Gisèle Venet, whose enthusiasm was a great
incentive. "Shakespeare, maniériste et baroque?" in XVII–XVIII. *Bulletin de la société
d'études anglo-américaines des XVIIe et XVIIIe siècles* 55 (2002), 7–25.

[8] A title conferred on him by Pope Leo X on October 11, 1521, as a reward for the king's
pamphlet *Assertio septem sacramentorum adversus Martinum Lutherum* ("Declaration of
the Seven Sacraments Against Martin Luther"). This is a title that "neither he nor his
Protestant heirs have ever relinquished." Richard Marius, *Thomas More* (New York:
Alfred A. Knopf, 1984), 276.

[9] See in particular *The Rape of Lucrece* (705–28) and *King Edward III*, ed. Giorgio
Melchiori (Cambridge: Cambridge University Press, 1997), II i 229–93.

the idea of the incarnation of divine representations, especially statues. Shakespeare's theater gradually seems to have absorbed those ideas and emerged as the place where incarnated *Logos* could be made manifest. He needed to find a style that would implement both the profound political and religious crisis of the time and the aesthetic structures necessary for a sensitive representation of a now missing spirituality. Yet, he also had to cover his own tracks and confuse the issue so that anything he said could also be denied.

As an artist, and a Catholic, he naturally turned toward Italy for inspiration. Connected as he was with the Earl of Southampton, Shakespeare not only came across famous Italian figures such as John Florio, the translator of Montaigne in English, but he had access to the best libraries of the time. And there was also Emilia Bassano, the mysterious Dark Lady of the Sonnets, who gave William pleasure, headaches, and useful connections.[10] I tried to show Tasso's influence on his comedies and his use of pastoral. The success of *A Midsummer Night's Dream* was evidence that Shakespeare's imagination was roaming far and wide. It was "a dramatic conjuring trick that must have induced awe at the extent of Shakespeare's virtuosity and at his astonishing self-assurance."[11] The play of perspectives in a play designed like a set of Russian dolls provided endless reverberations, blurring any dangerous content since anything that was said could be unsaid, each level of reality offering contradictory or ironical comment on the other. Shakespeare brilliantly bandied literary and philosophical references without ever losing control of his subject: the sacred and undefinable reality of true love.

The turn of the century was eventful with the Earl of Essex's failed riot and death, followed shortly by the Queen's death, King James's accession, and the Gunpowder plot. In Shakespeare's own life, death had intruded too, first his son Hamnet in 1596, then his father in 1601. He had narrowly escaped the dire consequences of the Earl of Essex's plot;[12] he had probably hoped like many Catholics that James would keep his word and restore at last a kind of peace for Catholics, but the Gunpowder Plot ruined all that. His plays became accordingly gloomier, more sarcastic too, but the overall purpose had not changed. He had now found the manner, in particular an irreverent mixture of the comic and the tragic in what are traditionally

---

[10] Peter Bassano, *Shakespeare and Emilia: The Untold Story* (n.p.: Giustiniani Publications, 2022).

[11] Asquith, *Shadowplay*, 107.

[12] *Richard II* had been performed on the very night preceding the Essex Rebellion, the Lord Chamberlain's Men being specially commissioned by some of Essex's friends for forty shillings more. They risked being accused of treason, which would have entailed the most atrocious death.

called the "problem plays," the matter being more than ever the representation of the whirligig of the time, using multiple perspectives, shifting
emphasis as he does repeatedly in *Troilus and Cressida,* until it becomes
impossible to say who's right and who's wrong. "The systematic use of
ironic counterpointing verging on automatism is a distinctive feature of
the play,"[13] writes Jean-Pierre Maquerlot, who infers that in those years
the poet devoted himself more intensely to a search for themes and form.
I personally believe that he never ceased to do so, but the pressure of the
time did provoke a new wave of disgust in him, which gradually produced
a new focus on morals and an acute awareness of the passing of time and
of the necessity of faith.

Shakespeare's relentless effort to find a balance between extremes, to
have harmony spring up between opposites, eventually led him to the
wonderful mannerist apotheosis of the last plays, in which he was to
weave all the threads of tragedy and comedy together in what seems to
be a final testament as well as a manifesto for Shakespeare's art. Where
he got such lofty ideas of the theater remains debatable, but he certainly
did not apprehend them suddenly by being a boy actor. Within the range
of possibilities that have been traced over the years by scholars and biog-
raphers, those that best explain the coherence of his work are worth
investigating.

Now, creation rarely proceeds directly from will to product, even sup-
posing the will had been clear from the beginning. Beside books, young
William must have encountered a few significant characters in real life,
people who left a lasting impression on his mind, so that the son of
Stratford's glove maker decided not to pursue his father's calling, which,
after all, was a fashionable one in Elizabethan England. We are told that
he had the opportunity to see touring drama companies in Stratford
and, like many children, fell under the spell of the theater. Whether it
was sufficient to give him the knowledge and motive to launch into a
lifetime adventure at a time when actors were mostly considered vagrants
is doubtful. It would moreover entail a difficult time with his father, who
could not have seen it as a rewarding future. Did William reject, or worse,
betray his father? It does not look like it. Shakespeare never seems to
be the overtly rebellious sort and the way he subsequently managed
his "career" reveals his strong desire to set things right, to revenge his
father's bad fortune, and give him the Coat of Arms he had claimed for
himself in the first place. He was invested by more than immediate personal desire to succeed and his choice of the theater must have initially

---

[13] Jean-Pierre Maquerlot, *Shakespeare and the Mannerist Tradition: A Reading of Five Problem Plays* (Cambridge: Cambridge University Press, 1995), 132.

received higher blessings. He may have met someone who gave him the assurance that he not only had the talent, but that drama was the golden medium through which he could delight, teach, and persuade — in a word, make the world a better place to live in. This, of course, implies that what he saw around him was rather distressing and that he had a youthful ambition, which sometimes looks more like a mission, to improve things. My purpose here is to try and link manner and matter together, to show the pertinence, singularity, and constancy of Shakespeare's design throughout his life.[14] ❧

---

[14] Unlike Jean-Pierre Maquerlot, whose book *Shakespeare and the Mannerist Tradition* focuses on five problem plays (*Julius Caesar, Hamlet, Troilus and Cressida, Measure for Measure* and *All's Well That Ends Well*), denying the plays that came before and after the appellation "mannerist," I think that mannerism applies to all of Shakespeare's plays. But Shakespeare's faith and desire for coherence also eventually make him a Baroque artist, which does not contradict mannerist aesthetics, as both became fused at the beginning of the seventeenth century.

1. Troubled Times

*W*HEN SHAKESPEARE WAS BORN IN APRIL 1564, ELIZ-
abeth had been queen for five years; she had succeeded her
Catholic sister Mary and imposed a return to her father's Reformed religion.
Within thirty years, the English people had been ordered to deny one
faith and adopt another on pain of death at least three times. Religion had
become a commodity depending on the whim of the ruler. Only a little
imagination will suffice to tell us that it could not have gone smoothly.
We could even speak of revolution, were it not that Tudor propaganda
worked very hard at papering things over for history's sake.

The Counter-Reformation was officially barred from England, depriving the country of the artistic wealth that blossomed in Europe with its
religious renewal; freedom of speech was restricted, and printing presses
were placed under control — a bad time for young Shakespeare to begin
a career as a dramatist, yet a very good time for a Fool to develop his
variable talents and exert his freedom of speech.[1]

Pondering the events that Will Shakespeare must have witnessed as an
adolescent is mind-boggling. No wonder he had to be both cunning and
careful. Of late, a number of scholars have applied themselves to reconsider
the dark side of Elizabethan history and the impact it may have had on the
author. Even allowing for personal likings, the facts and writings are there:
the reign of Elizabeth looks like a sinister and hypocritical game in which
the golden image of the Fairy Queen aptly conceals the Machiavellian
spying schemes of the Cecils. It is impossible to read this new version
of Elizabethan history without acquiring a different perspective on the
unknown protean genius who became England's greatest writer and rare
philosopher — an enigma which, for four centuries, has fed the imagination of thousands of people all over the world. Could the man who wrote
some thirty-seven memorable plays not exist at all? Shakespeare's identity
has given birth to the most fantastical conjectures, some arguing over his
nonexistence, others his lack of education, many opting for one of his
many avatars and pondering over insoluble questions about his decidedly
nonclassical dramaturgy, rather than granting him the shadow of a thought
on his own art, which necessarily entailed placing the man within a specific

---

[1] Because they were innocent of their irreverence, fools were generally tolerated and
therefore enjoyed a considerable freedom to speak and act in ways for which others
would have been punished. It is easy to see the potentially subversive element that
the fool represented in the midst of a society which nonetheless countenanced him
because he didn't know better.

time in history. That the most popular dramatist of the time remains such a mystery today is naturally puzzling, something difficult to understand in an age when the media pry into everybody's lives and the call for openness forces politicians and artists to spread details of their lives on the front page. An enigmatic queen and a ghost dramatist, how strange and thrilling! Isn't it in itself revelatory of the iron rule of William Cecil, who had evidently acquired a powerful, fatherly influence over the young Elizabeth?

Couldn't there be meaning in this very absence?

Montaigne's purpose in his *Essais* was to paint himself, but for lack of a coherent whole, he was led to describe minutely his own fantastic diversity and metamorphoses, eventually painting a very mannerist portrait of himself, not so different perhaps from Arcimboldo's astonishing compositions. Shakespeare, on the contrary, eludes us, his own self disappearing, drowned in the fantastic diversity and metamorphoses of the characters he creates. Who can boast of knowing him unless he takes all his characters into account? The few facts we have, however, seem to attest to his great confidence. Professor Greenblatt shows him as not exactly a "maverick" but someone who obviously had a very high purpose in mind and would not be distracted. Referring to Robert Greene and the University Wits, he writes that Shakespeare "did not enter into their literary controversies, just as he seems to have been kept — or kept himself — outside their raucous social circle. This is, after all, a man who soon went on to manage the affairs of his playing company, to write steadily (not to mention brilliantly) for more than two decades, to accumulate and keep a great deal of money, to stay out of prison and to avoid ruinous lawsuits, to invest in agricultural land and in London property, to purchase one of the finest houses in the town where he was born, and to retire to that town in his late forties. This pattern of behavior did not suddenly and belatedly emerge; it established itself early, probably quite soon after the turbulent, confused, painful years that led up to his escape from Stratford and his arrival in London."[2] This is hardly the life of a timid, hesitating, or lazy man. If he therefore decided to conceal himself behind the many characters he created, he certainly had a good reason for it.[3] If, unlike Ben Jonson, he never bothered to have his work published, was it carelessness, humility, or precaution? Why would a

---

[2] Stephen Greenblatt , *Will in the World* (New York: Norton & Company, 2004), 209.
[3] The very difference of manner between Montaigne and Shakespeare, who otherwise seem to share many similarities of judgement, can probably be explained by the very different political atmospheres of their respective countries. In France, Catholics and Protestants, whether openly at war or not, could maintain their separate spiritual identity, whereas in England Catholics were forced into "Elizabeth's crucible," thus denying their faith and betraying their consciences. Such peace was tyranny, which only the utmost cunning could evade.

well-known man want to leave as few traces as possible? What could impel him to make himself as discreet, as invisible as possible? Or, like Homer's Proteus, to acquire the ability to escape all attempt at capturing him? Why would he write such an epitaph for himself, cursing those who might move his bones?[4] Who did he fear could wish for his bones to disappear? At the same time, what force could be strong enough to drive him to write an average of two masterpieces per year for over twenty years? If he had been fueled by ambition, he would certainly have taken care to have his plays published and immortalized. The answers to those contradictions must necessarily be momentous, and what better way to find the true Shakespeare than study the words he wrote and the time he lived in?

I wondered what shock, what profound trauma was likely to have impacted his life and launched him on a lifelong quest for meaning, a quest that started with a few years' disappearance during which he must have acquired abilities and refined his purpose.

Why did Shakespeare, who had early acquired a name as a poet and could have wished for no better reputation, choose drama, a profession notoriously of ill repute, at a time when the puritanical London City Council were trying their best to reform unruly and dissolute manners in the theater? Presumably because there, he could reach a wider audience. Because drama allowed him more characters and more action, too. Most of all because it erased his authorship, his many characters translating for him his now "untraceable" voice. Anything they said could be deniable. The freedom of the Fool! Shakespeare managed to say anything he wanted for more than twenty years without ever being harassed, whereas many of his fellow dramatists went to prison for lines now long forgotten. And what he said was sometimes harsh and rebellious. For a young man to start his "career" rewriting and reinterpreting some three hundred years of English history was not insignificant. If to emulate Marlowe's talent in *Tamberlain* was the initial incentive, Shakespeare obviously had a much wider purpose in mind, revealing a beautiful aspiration, but also a strong dissatisfaction with the way things were and a will to change them, as if to settle some unspoken score. What better means at the time than the public theater, which touched most Londoners and competed attractively with

---

4   "Good friend for Jesus sake forbeare,
     To dig the dust enclosed here.
     Blessed be the man that spares these stones,
     And cursed be he that moves my bones."
Joseph Pearce suggests that the reason for such a warning may have been the way recusant Catholics were buried with two shrouds, the second, outer shroud containing earth properly consecrated by a Catholic priest. Thus wrapped, the corpse could be officially buried in a Protestant churchyard, in agreement with the laws of the realm. Joseph Pearce, *The Quest for Shakespeare* (San Francisco: Ignatius Press, 2008), 169–70.

the pulpit now held by stern Puritans? His voice could be heard, without being fixed. The written text could indeed become a monument against time, but Shakespeare apparently knew all too well that it could also be held against you, that you could be hunted down and put to death for seditious printed matter. The live voice, however, suited the metamorphoses of the life it commented upon and was not (yet) recordable. The voice required listeners, who reacted, exchanged. It could evolve, it could change.

This suggests that Shakespeare was more intent on reaching the hearts of men than on establishing his own fame. It suggests that he was not merely writing for success but had a message, a philosophy of life to pass on. Year after year, he would polish his instrument, using all the means available to him in order to mirror life, but also to mend it.

Now, do you acquire learning and a talent for poetry simply by being an apprentice in a troop of traveling players? Clearly not. The more we know about Shakespeare, the more we have to accept the evidence of some more fundamental imprint on his youthful mind. First, for the Stratford boy to choose to become a dramatist could seem paradoxical at a time when artists, especially players, needed patrons to be allowed to practice their art. Yet the suggestion that in 1580 he went to Lancashire as a tutor to the recusant family of Alexander Hoghton, and then became a player in the latter's neighbor Sir Thomas Hesketh's company, has the merit of being a little more convincing than other theories.[5] It may just be the way he found a patron. That he might have met the brilliant rhetorician Edmund Campion while there, is also conjecture of course, but one that subsequently renders his interest in the spoken word perfectly relevant. That the sudden and horrific death of Campion might have shocked and revolted him to the point of launching his career as a dramatist is psychologically sound, all the more so if we consider the raw violence of some of his first plays. Campion had written dramas while in Prague[6] and drama was a central element of Jesuit education,[7] a fact that may indeed be more relevant to Shakespeare's youthful years than we imagine. We

---

[5] E. A. J. Honigmann, *Shakespeare: the "lost years"* (Manchester: Manchester University Press, 1985).

[6] Thomas M. McCoog, S. J., ed., *The Reckoned Expense: Edmund Campion and the Early English Jesuits* (Woodbridge: The Boydell Press, 1996).

[7] "The fortnightly and monthly debates that were usual in the schools were an excellent antidote for muddled expression and for stage fright; constant drill in declamation must have led to some ease in voice control, some juvenile grace of gesture and carriage, and not a little education in emotional interpretation; the occasional dialogue and scene before audiences of their fellows would have developed in the boys an elementary grasp of stage behaviour; and lastly, training in actual composition of such scenes and playlets, even the planning of complete tragedies, would have awakened a sense of dramatic values." William H. McCabe, S. J., *An Introduction to the Jesuit Theater* (Saint Louis, MO: The Institute of Jesuit Sources, 1983), 34.

know that at least two of the Stratford schoolmasters had been trained at Oxford and had "surprisingly strong Catholic connections."[8] Surprisingly, because the town council that hired them also proceeded to replace the Catholic curate in order to conform to the State's reformed Protestant policy. Chamberlain John Shakespeare, Will's father, had to oversee these actions, and we can surmise that like many of his fellow men, he tried hard to find a compromise between the State's orders and the requirements of his own conscience.[9] He probably also used his position to get the best possible teachers for his children. It is interesting to learn that the headmaster of Eton was paid only £10 a year, whereas Stratford's schoolmasters received £20.[10] No doubt, besides Latin, William learnt very early from his own father the usefulness of seeming and doublespeak. Simon Hunt, his first teacher, left Stratford in 1575 in order to attend the Catholic seminary at Douai and become a Jesuit. He took with him Robert Debdale, a schoolboy who lived in Shottery, and was six or seven years older than William. Such a drastic decision must have fed the local talk among neighboring Catholic families. Could William Shakespeare have been the next promising candidate? Would the prospect of a good education at Douai have tempted him, since, as a Catholic, he could not have studied at Oxford or Cambridge unless he swore the oath of allegiance? Stratford authorities did not hesitate to choose another Oxford Scholar to be their next schoolmaster, Thomas Jenkins, recommended by the Catholic founder of Saint John's College, Sir Thomas White, who had also protected Campion. Jenkins would have known and would probably have studied with Campion, himself a fellow at Saint John's. He stayed at Stratford for four years[11] and must no doubt have brought lasting memories to the young William, who could then have befriended the next Oxford graduate appointed at the school, John Cottam, another young man from Lancashire, whose brother Thomas had gone abroad to become a Catholic priest. He secretly returned to England in June 1580 as part of the Jesuit mission led by Edmund Campion and Robert Persons, but was betrayed and imprisoned. He, and later Debdale, would meet the same horrible fate as Edmund Campion and his fellow missionaries. In Stratford, there may have been the feeling that the enemy was closing in and the utmost care was necessary. John Cottam resigned from his position and went back to quieter, strongly Catholic Lancashire. Was he the

---

8 Greenblatt, *Will in the World*, 96.
9 John Shakespeare appears on a list of papist recusants established by the Warwickshire Commission in 1592. See Pearce, *The Quest*, 50.
10 René Weis, *Shakespeare Revealed, A Biography* (London: John Murray, 2007), 104.
11 This is contradicted by Pearce who asserts that Jenkins only spent one year as a schoolmaster at Stratford (See Pearce, *The Quest*, 62–63).

connection who provided William Shakespeare with his first job there? Honigmann certainly provides strong evidence for it.

As Stephen Greenblatt suggests, Cottam could have been asked by the Hoghtons, a nearby prominent Catholic family, "to recommend a promising young man to be a teacher to their children — not a licensed schoolmaster, someone who would have to be certified as a Protestant by the local bishop, but a private tutor for a large household. He could have proposed Will Shakespeare, who had just left school and who, since his father's financial difficulties precluded his attending university, was looking for employment."[12] In his will and testament, Alexander Hoghton, in turn, recommended both "Fulk Gyllome and William Shakeshaftes now dwelling with me" to his brother Thomas or, if he did not want to maintain players, to Sir Thomas Hesketh, "to help them to some good master." After his death in August 1581, it is therefore likely that Shakespeare found employment with Hesketh's powerful neighbor, "Henry Stanley, the fourth Earl of Derby, and his son Fernandino, Lord Strange," who employed a talented group of players with whom Shakespeare would later be associated.

What is of particular interest is the presence of Edmund Campion in Lancashire "from Easter (March 26) to Whitsun (May 14)" of the year 1581. Gerard Kilroy provides a very detailed account of his movements and of the people he visited. "Since Campion later wished to retrieve his books from Lancashire, and since the Privy Council early gave orders to search 'especiallie the house of Richard Houghton, where it is said the said Campion left his books,' he must have taken his notebooks (with quotations culled from Luther and Calvin in Munich) from Mount St John, and finished the *Rationes Decem* at Park Hall, the house of Richard Hoghton, on the banks of Yarrow Water."[13] This Richard Hoghton of Park Hall was a half-brother of Alexander and Thomas Hoghton of Hoghton Tower. Since the Hoghtons, with the Heskeths and the Stanleys, represented Catholic resistance in the North, it is unlikely that they did not communicate, and even less likely when such an orator as Campion was at hand. Young William Shakespeare would not have missed such an opportunity, and if he played in the local company, he may even have had Campion for an occasional audience. In that case, Campion would have been happy to give him his view on the importance of drama. Gerard Kilroy remains on the side of prudence, however, and simply concludes his findings with these

---

[12] Greenblatt, *Will in the World*, 103–4. The reason Shakespeare did not go to University remains conjectural, his father's financial difficulties being equally questionable. One evident cause for Shakespeare's lack of a University education remains his Catholic upbringing, which is certainly related to his father's being fined as a recusant.

[13] Gerard Kilroy, *Edmund Campion, A Scholarly Life* (London and New York: Routledge, 2015), 196.

words: "The impulse to put the iconic Catholic martyr under the same roof as the nation's bard may express the desire on all sides, to heal, four centuries later, a profound cultural dislocation; some decisive document may yet be found."[14]

If Shakespeare never met Campion, which cannot be proved, he indeed had ample opportunities to learn about him and acquire some of his talents. As his plays testify, he had certainly made Saint Ignatius's *Spiritual Exercises* his study at some point in his youth. As Professor Greenblatt very perceptively delineates, Shakespeare's life in Lancashire would have been "a peculiar compound of theatricality and danger."[15] The Stanleys, like the Hoghtons, were feudal lords who had managed to retain their ancient prerogatives far from the centralization of the Tudor monarchy, but they also provided refuge to persecuted priests who could hide their devotional objects in secret places within the household. The danger of betrayal was constant and the need for utter secrecy absolute. It could have provided young Shakespeare a remarkable training in the subtle and efficient ways to use language.

It may well be that his extraordinary self-confidence came from some inner certainty, his faith in something greater than the petty theories of university wits. I would be tempted to say that only an encounter with someone as charismatic as Campion could have given young William the encouragement to step forward. William McCabe makes an interesting comparison between Shakespeare and Catholicism (even though his study centers on drama at Saint Omer's English College founded by Persons in 1592), summing up a certain vision of life shared by the Bard: "Catholicism teaches that man cannot take a step in the direction of his destiny without a special divine help called grace. Yet even with this help, man retains his freedom. A delicate adjustment of the two factors, grace and liberty, is required… A philosophy of life which throws into relief man's liberty of will impresses us with a notion of responsibility for his acts."[16] This is of course essentially Shakespeare's vision,[17] who occasionally and discreetly mocked the idea of predestination.[18] He also shared with the Jesuits his

---

[14] Ibid., 357.

[15] Greenblatt, *Will in the World*, 105.

[16] McCabe, S. J., *Jesuit Theater*, 153–54.

[17] A vision he retained until the very end as testified in the emblematic unveiling of Ferdinand and Miranda playing chess in *The Tempest* (see later).

[18] See *King Lear*, I ii 96–107. Luther's belief in Predestination rendered freedom impossible. As Richard Marius puts it, "Luther's world swarmed with demons and witches, and in all this darkness the individual tended to be left alone with his faith in God." "Those who passionately embrace predestination are nearly always those overcome by the apparent meaninglessness of things and by the apparent inability of individuals to make the difference. To these bruised souls, predestination comes as a

disregard of Aristotle's legislation "written in the Pagan Age of Pericles, not amid the splendour of Christianity."[19] If he met Campion, this "kindred spirit," he might have managed to absorb and digest his most attractive human qualities, his knowledge and talents as an orator, while keeping at arm's length the religious "fanatic." Campion's martyrdom, just as a little later, that of the Jesuit poet Robert Southwell,[20] certainly gave him matter to think about, matter that he may have tried to explore with his Joan of Arc character in 1 Henry VI, without succeeding in finding the harmony between the beautiful, saintly dream and the disgusting, despicable end.

For centuries, critics have omitted or forgotten or been strongly pressured to drop — perhaps because Shakespeare himself seems to stay well away from the subject — the historical-religious background of their beloved dramatist. Now, the sixteenth century was a time of fierce religious wars in England as well as on the Continent. The inner division that occurred in 1533 following the decision of Henry VIII to get a divorce with or without the Pope's consent, was even more of a national trauma than the Saint Bartholomew killings in France. Since the Pope did not consent to the divorce, Henry had himself proclaimed Supreme Head of the Church of England, he repudiated his queen to marry his mistress Ann Boleyn, and ordered the dissolution of the monasteries, whose wealth would enrich the crown and the king's best friends.[21] This dark side of the Tudor era has now been sufficiently studied and explored to reveal the unspeakable tragedy of a people forced "within a month" to deny their Faith, their traditions and beliefs. Speaking of a Cambridge doctor, John Gerard writes in his autobiography: "He was known to have changed his religion three or four times to suit the change of ruler, Catholic and Protestant."[22] Elizabeth, for all

---

sublime consolation, a liberation from the oppressive compulsion to succeed in or to be responsible for a world that moves in its own relentless way, beyond our control." Marius, *Thomas More*, 273, 266.

[19] McCabe, S. J., *Jesuit Theater*, 154.

[20] Robert Southwell was born in 1561 and died in 1595 a martyr at Tyburn, following in the steps of his blessed predecessor, Edmund Campion. Robert was a Jesuit and a poet, loosely connected to the Wriothesleys, the family of Shakespeare's patron. Christopher Devlin, in his biography, even shows a remote connection between Robert and William Shakespeare through the Vaux family (264), which impels him to suggest that a dedication "to his loving cousin," originally written "To my worthy cousin, Master W. S. [from] Your loving cousin, R. S." was actually meant to be William Shakespeare, there being no other W. S. interested in poetry and the stage around him. He was urging him to show "how well verse and virtue suit together," which could explain the sudden change of tone between *Venus and Adonis* and *The Rape of Lucrece*. Christopher Devlin, *The Life of Robert Southwell Poet and Martyr* (Harlow, U. K.: Longmans, Green and Co, 1956).

[21] See Clare Asquith, *Shadowplay*, chap. 1, for a brief evocative summary of this sacrilegious dismantling of the nation.

[22] John Gerard, S. J., *The Autobiography of a Hunted Priest* (San Francisco: Ignatius Press, 2012), 23.

her enlightened mind, did not tolerate Catholic extremists who challenged her authority, especially after the pope excommunicated her in February 1570. His *Regnans in Excelsis* bull absolved Catholics from their duty to their sovereign, *ergo* they now became traitors and were barred from all positions of power and influence. Priests, especially the new generation of seminary priests returning from the Jesuit Colleges of the Continent, and their supporters were hunted down, put to torture and executed. It was the England in which William Shakespeare was born and bred, in a Catholic family, in Warwickshire, a still widely Catholic county. His first sixteen years saw the gradual hardening of William Cecil's Machiavellian policy against Catholics and whatever raid, fine, capture, or torture was happening was not only the talk of his town, but often taking place in its immediate vicinity, when it was not directly linked to his family.

The fact that this troubled time of his adolescence corresponds with the landing into England of undercover Jesuits sent from Rome on a mission cannot be too much emphasized. Edmund Campion and Robert Persons hoped to help believers, preach the gospel, say Mass, and give sacraments to those who desired them. They were not supposed to meddle in politics, yet made use of a secret printing press to publish pamphlets and books which were widely disseminated underground. However, the period was particularly ill-chosen[23] and William Cecil's government could not abide such a threat under their nose. The books and pamphlets were very quickly confiscated. Within a year, Edmund Campion was betrayed, arrested and imprisoned in the Tower of London. He stayed there for five months, being racked as well as granted fake debates to justify himself. His death on December 1, 1581 was a great scandal to all Catholics in England and abroad, where, like Thomas More before him, he was known for his scholarly accomplishments, his faith and honesty. Hanged till nearly dead, then disemboweled and quartered—who could imagine worse punishment for one wrongly accused of treason, who could dream of worse barbarity at the heart of the enlightened cultural era launched by Queen Elizabeth I? As Campion put it on dying, to kill the Catholics amounted for the English to denying their ancestors, their past, and their kings. Had not all Protestants been Catholics to begin with? No one could change religion overnight, and the breach, even though artfully concealed by Tudor propaganda, remained painful for many a Christian soul long afterward.

William was seventeen, then, and must of necessity, if only by hearsay, have followed Campion's Way of the Cross from Lyford Grange to the Tower of London. What kind of trauma was it for him, we can only guess.

---

[23] The why and the how are minutely delineated in Kilroy, *Edmund Campion, A Scholarly Life*.

If he had met him, as Peter Milward also suggests,[24] if he had even had time to study a little with him while in Lancashire at the Hoghtons, he must have been impressed by the man's charisma, his well-known rhetorical talent, and his love of drama, too. He may even have heard from him of the wonders of Bohemia and of Rudolf's lenient and learned court. Campion would have been equally impressed by young Shakespeare, who shared many characteristics of his ideal student. What would have happened if he had lived, we can never know, but the shock and horror of his untimely, unfair death could have profoundly distressed the young man and may explain his inextinguishable search into the human soul. It possibly also accounts for Shakespeare's apparent familiarity with this other remarkable Jesuit, Robert Southwell, who five years later followed in Campion's footsteps and managed to publish beautiful religious poetry and prose until he, too, was finally caught, prosecuted for treason and brutally executed on February 20, 1595. All this probably also explains why saints, ideological heroes, or fanatics, as Professor Greenblatt calls Campion, do not belong to Shakespeare's many forms of male heroism. Knowing his ever present double-consciousness, Shakespeare would have been able to appreciate the measure of folly in Campion's and Southwell's noble enterprise. As a Catholic, he must naturally have felt deeply concerned, torn apart, and threatened. Simply imagine the fear weighing people down in a country newly dedicated to Protestantism where Catholics, originally everybody, and in 1580 still a great part of the population whether openly or secretly, were hunted like traitors and submitted to horrific tortures. Shakespeare never speaks of exile but feelingly, and the theme runs throughout his work. The sad prospect that one could be suddenly deprived of one's property, and cut off from one's language and family, was obviously part of his inner landscape.[25] The utmost care was required, and Shakespeare succeeded so well in eluding attacks that to this day critics hesitate to grant him some religious belief. If he had belonged to the victors, surely, such caution would have been unnecessary. Shakespeare's mystery exists precisely because he did not feel altogether in harmony with his time. Our secular civilization is reluctant to talk about religion and critics like to think of Shakespeare as one of us, but applying our vision of the world to his world is also a gross distortion of reality. That he never openly engaged in debates on the subject does not mean that he was not a true believer, with the doubts that it entails. He was a poet, not a theologian and as a poet, he kept well away from religious controversy. Notwithstanding,

---

[24] Peter Milward, *Shakespeare the Papist* (Florida: Ave Maria University Press, 2005).
[25] Who knows if this general feeling of insecurity does not explain William Shakespeare's desire to own property and ensure his family's rootedness in Stratford-upon-Avon?

Shakespeare's comedies are full of benevolent friars, whose advice seems straight out of Saint Ignatius's *Spiritual Exercises*,[26] his ghosts emerge from purgatory, confession is for him a virtue, young people are encouraged to look for a good priest to marry them, and there are many prayers said for the living and the dead in his work, all things that were, together with beads, crucifixes, and images, officially prohibited in Elizabethan England. These signs reveal the believer and should not be discarded on the evidence of a few unprincipled prelates among his characters. Shakespeare's keen moral sense could distinguish between politics and true faith. The only thing which he recurrently denounces and mocks is extremism, whether it be Catholic, Protestant or Jewish. Overzealous Jesuits are not spared any more than Puritans. The subtle equivocation of the former, the hypocrisy of the latter—no one escapes the sharp pen of the poet.

WHO CAN REALLY MEASURE THE IMPACT THAT THE CONSTANT necessity of evasion may have had on Shakespeare's talent and philosophy? Elizabeth (who may herself have been equivocating and always kept near her the Catholic chapel master Thomas Tallis, and his famous pupil William Byrd, who converted to Catholicism) was intelligent enough not to silence her favorite dramatist, the man who always showed a protean agility in creating characters and debates which eluded any possibility of knowing what he himself really thought. The wisest sentences might be pronounced by the most unlikely characters, and the greatest Shakespearian characters are diabolical actors constantly manipulating the entire cast including themselves, playing with words too—so much so that they sometimes lose themselves in the act. As Peter Milward put it, Shakespeare "had to be like Hamlet, spying upon his enemies, even while being spied upon by them, striving to keep one step ahead of their devices by means of no less ingenious devices of his own."[27] As mentioned earlier, to my mind, the most daring book to date on these "obliquely topical indications of political doublespeak" certainly is Clare Asquith's scholarly *Shadowplay,* which manages to give a very compelling, integrated vision of Shakespeare in his own time. More recently Stephen Alford summed up the situation this way: "The Elizabethan story would be a peculiar one: a strange aberration in English history when, against prevailing patterns of royal dynasty and

---

[26] The new Society of Jesus, created by Ignatius de Loyola, grouped itself round "a scheme of devotion" embodied in his *Spiritual Exercises* (created c. 1522). "It is a manual of instructions for those who make or direct a certain sort of religious retreat ... intended to have a transforming effect upon life and character." A. G. Dickens, *The Counter Reformation* (London: Thames and Hudson, 1968), 78. The first edition of the *Spiritual Exercises* was published in Rome in 1548.
[27] Milward, *The Papist*, 17.

religion in Europe, England struggled alone as an isolated pariah state for nearly thirty years . . . . The weapons they used were espionage, relentless interrogation, surveillance, the suppression of dissent, robust treason law, torture and propaganda."[28] We cannot possibly be fair to Shakespeare without recognizing the religious and political forces weighing upon artistic creation in the Elizabethan and Jacobean periods.

Given this explosive background, in which truth killed truth and anyone could be accused of conspiracy, Shakespeare knew that whatever he did, he had to use indirections and a lot of ingenuity to speak his mind without seeming to. The ten years that followed Campion's death must for so many reasons have been years of gestation-maturation. William probably started his theatrical career with Lord Strange's company, but at the beginning of 1582 he was back home where he met Anne Hathaway, whom he was to marry before the end of the year, possibly on Saturday December 1, 1582, which was, as Weis points out, "the first anniversary of Campion's martyrdom in London."[29] There were, as everyone knows, "biological imperatives" behind this expedited wedding, but who knows if William's hasty engagement and marriage a few months after the horror of Campion's death were not a healthy reaction and a way to ward off the frightful vision of martyrdom, a way to restore his faith in life too? And if Campion's fate had managed to make Shakespeare think twice about following in Campion's footsteps to Douai, was this not the best way to shelve the idea once and for all? Soon he would be a father of three and part of his energy would subsequently be employed in earning money to support his family. Shakespeare's youthful life had made him aware of the horrendous cost of dissidence, as Weis suggests, and this is probably why he would never join Marlowe or any of the University Wits in their delinquent escapades. Marlowe's brilliance certainly motivated Shakespeare to outshine him. There was mimetic rivalry between those two gifted poets, who both started with momentous historical political works (*Tamberlain* and *Henry VI*), followed by "strikingly similar history plays"[30] (*Edward II* and *Richard II*) and long erotic poems (*Hero and Leander* and *Venus and Adonis*). Marlowe's untimely, violent death would eventually prove Shakespeare right.

He would therefore need to shape his own tool, invent his own dramatic practice to seem what he was not and be found untraceable. The theater was the best place to throw words into the wind. He, in fact, must have taken great care not to leave any trace behind, so that we don't even have

---

[28] Stephen Alford, *The Watchers, A Secret History of the Reign of Elizabeth I* (London: Allen Lane, 2012), 11.

[29] Weis, *Shakespeare Revealed*, 57.

[30] Greenblatt, *Will in the World*, 256–57.

a letter from him. If it reveals one thing in the man, it is the spiritual seriousness of his design. Just think about it: a stupendous energy was developed over twenty-two years to produce a bulk of work which, for all its variety of stories and plots, "More witnesseth than fancy's images, / And grows to something of great constancy" (*Midsummer Night's Dream*, V i 25–26). Somehow, one has the feeling that the poet was impelled to write, sometimes a little too fast perhaps, but his work denotes an urgency, a sense of moral duty, which somehow ceased only when he believed he had, at last, reached his goal, or more sadly perhaps, when he was "silenced."[31] He did not need to look for words;[32] they rather poured forth like lava from some boiling magma, sometimes even preceding his ideas. Once he launched into his dramatic production, it seems that nothing could keep him from exploring at greater length the evil of human nature and its beauty. All the plays are linked by very subtle threads which eventually make a complete world of the whole, and what a world, what a mirror to life indeed! It stands like a gem of its own, as an art which nobody even thought of trying to continue after him.

Regardless of fashions, of contemporary codes and rules, Shakespeare created his own means to reach his own end, looking for inspiration every-where, but particularly in Italy where a whole host of artists at Rome, Florence, Mantua, and Ferrara inspired him technically as well as theo-retically.[33] The Folio division into comedies, tragedies, and histories is certainly confusing and does not reflect much of the boiling work that went on in the creation of most plays. Shakespeare occasionally showed that he could respect Aristotelian rules, but most of the time, the matter dictated the manner, and the content being the representation of life, no means were expressive enough, short of life itself. The very fact that he could be working simultaneously on a comedy, a tragedy, and a history, or else a problem play — if by "problem" is meant that there is no ready-made answer to the life situation created by the characters, what play by Shakespeare is not a problem play, I wonder — reveals that the author was on a quest, looking for the best means to interpret what he wanted to transmit. Hence the importance of not considering plays as separate entities, of relating them together and although we may lack an absolute chronology, of trying our best to follow the progress of Shakespeare's creative genius in time.

---

[31] Asquith, *Shadowplay*, chap. 16.

[32] I personally find astonishing the critical debates that try to trace each and every word he wrote to some unknown predecessor, as if Shakespeare had consciously plodded away at his desk, looking for words.

[33] See for instance, Michèle Marrapodi, ed., *Shakespeare, Italy, and intertextuality* (Manchester: Manchester University Press, 2004).

MANNERIST ESTHETICS

For four hundred years, Shakespeare has curiously been denied any real esthetic standards, his plays being conveniently used to feed each and everyone's fancy. Studies of art and politics in the English Renaissance generally avoid coming close to him, perhaps because he does not fit any recognizable category. Like the crocodile of Egypt, he can only be tautologically explained by himself.[34] A man for all time, he was repeatedly denied any temporality of his own, locked up in the self-referential myth of the Stratford boy providentially turned the greatest poet of all time. This vision was enhanced by the persistence of another myth: the happy reign of *Gloriana*, propitious for poets and musicians and liberal to dramatists, who enjoyed the reality of successful public theaters in London. This was partially true and a great wonder if we compare the English stage with what took place elsewhere in Europe. Queen Elizabeth I did love her people, whom she wanted happily entertained, an aspect of her willful nature which could not displease her devoted secretary Robert Cecil, whom many considered the true king of England. "Whatever aesthetic requirements Elizabethan drama fulfilled, a large part of the visual appeal of the spectacles was surely directed toward satisfying middle-class aspirations,"[35] whereas the masque, a favorite of James's court, would present "the triumph of an aristocratic community."[36] Stephen Orgel is here using the well-known opposition between two forms of theater, which Shakespeare never actually pitted against each other. He regularly used the form of the masque to enhance his intention, and the figure of Prospero, "the royal illusionist, derives from a profound understanding of court theater, and the quintessentially courtly theatrical form of the masque."[37] Throughout his career, Shakespeare catered for all tastes, subtly interweaving popular and courtly styles. His plays were directed toward satisfying a motley audience as socially and politically varied as the population of London. His first characteristic surely was stretching the rules of genre and decorum and his plots often introduced three or four interwoven "concurrent affairs" which were "resolved in a polyphonic manner."[38] This was of course particularly true of the pastoral, as Shearman suggests, but Shakespeare extended it to all genres. The musical metaphor is not gratuitous. Shakespeare's

---

[34] "Lepidus: What manner o' thing is your crocodile?
Antony: It is shaped, sir, like itself; and it is as broad as it hath breadth. It is just so high as it is, and moves with his own organs. It lives by that which nourisheth it, and the elements once out of it, it transmigrates." *Antony and Cleopatra*, II vii 40–44.
[35] Stephen Orgel, *The Illusion of Power: Political Theater in the English Renaissance* (Berkeley: University of California Press, 1975), 8.
[36] Ibid., 40.
[37] Ibid., 45.
[38] John Shearman, *Mannerism* (London: Penguin, 1990), 92.

plots often appear to have been conceived more by a musician than by a playwright. His innate sense of balance and harmony is often more at stake than cold reason and recognized rules of composition. It may be interesting to note that Lomazzo, the famous author of *Trattato dell'arte della pittura, scoltura et architettura*, published in 1584,[39] was conversant with music theory, which played an essential role in his esthetic development. Surely, anyone who has studied Shakespeare closely will have noticed the prominent part played by music in whatever theatrical form used by the playwright in the twenty years he reigned over the theater in London. The closest structural analogy I can find is the musical Variation form, which was developed during the sixteenth century. It is said to have derived "from the practice of improvising embellishments in successive strophes of songs and dances,"[40] a practice which seems to have been the very foundation of much creation at a time when imitation and improvement on the model were the basis of literary inspiration. Shakespeare seems thus to have excelled at creating variations upon genres, themes, plots, and characters, just as Bach was master at manipulating "texture, motifs, register, and playing techniques."[41]

Take the revenge tragedy, take the pastoral, the tragicomedy or any other genre invented or debated at the time, Shakespeare was a master at it, used it, debunked it, turned it upside down, then moved to a more comprehensive art, which imitated life more closely, an art which came closer in its conception and realization to what was being discussed and imagined in Italy than to anything as yet propounded in England. By so doing, he was not at all an isolated poet in some postromantic idea of inspired, godly creation, which is the way he has been studied since the nineteenth century, but he fully belonged to his time, when technical virtuosity, performance, and style in the service of an idea were praised and admired.

As an artist, William Shakespeare turned toward Italy for inspiration, the novella providing a wealth of stories to be transformed, and the pastoral a very malleable genre, whose main aim was rebirth. Italy would have been naturally attractive for a Catholic and a lover of art, but William also crossed the path of a beautiful dark lady, who made him giddy for a while: Emilia Bassano. It is the opinion of her "first cousin, twelve times removed," Peter Bassano, that Emilia, who was a musician and a poet

---

[39] Lomazzo's treatise was partly translated into English by Richard Haydocke as early as 1598. *Giovanni Paolo Lomazzo, A Tracte Containing the Artes of Curious Paintinge, Caruinge & Buildinge, translated by Richard Haydocke*, ed. Alexander Marr, Tudor and Stuart Translations, 1598.

[40] Alison Latham, ed., *The Oxford Companion to Music* (Oxford: Oxford University Press, 2002), 1324.

[41] *The Oxford Companion to Music*, 1325.

and the daughter of a Venetian, and by all accounts, a remarkable character, "aroused Shakespeare's interest in Italy." She quite possibly inspired some of his most attractive women characters and it is most probable that she was the Dark Lady of the Sonnets, involved with both the poet and his patron, Henry Wriothesley. Peter Bassano has been hunting all the details from his memorable relative's life and he goes on to assert that her three cousins, Arthur, Andrea and Jeronimo, who were court musicians, befriended Shakespeare and took him on a three month trip to the North of Italy in the autumn of 1593.[42] The reasons given, although not literary, sound nonetheless very convincing: they needed an expert on calfskins. The son of a glove maker, who had spent his childhood watching and helping his father, would be a huge asset for the Bassano brothers when they received a license to export "six thousand dickers of calfskins." The Bassanos were not mere musicians, they were instrument makers and "records show that the Bassanos distributed the instruments that they built in London, throughout the Hapsburg Empire, as far south as Toledo in Spain."[43] Leather was used as strips to cover the wooden cornetti and for the shaped hides in the manufacture of instrument cases, lute and viol cases, for instance, and the export of skins could obviously be a lucrative complementary business. Shakespeare shows a very good knowledge of music and instruments throughout his work. He also "possessed the experience in dealing with the production of leather that the Bassano family lacked. The closure of the London theaters was a good time to seek his assistance in a mercantile trip to Venice."[44] Such a mercantile trip was not to displease a man, who, as we know, never denied his origins nor did he lose track of his own family interests.[45] The four men would have left London by the end of summer in 1593 and were gone for at least three months, through the Po valley to Veneto, which Shakespeare often refers to in his plays. The most likely route would have gone through Milan, Bergamo, Verona, and Padua, which is only twenty-five miles from Venice. They could have returned via Mantua, where the Bassanos "may have been strongly motivated to seek out the twenty eight year old composer,

---

[42] Bassano, *Shakespeare and Emilia*, xi.

[43] Ibid., 184.

[44] Ibid.

[45] In spite of its rather sloppy edition, Bassano's book offers a wealth of details and references that every Shakespeare lover cannot easily ignore. We naturally tend to omit the image of Shakespeare as "the kill-cow champion of the three brethren," as a man who always kept farming contacts in and around Stratford and who bought farm land when he had the available cash, rather than some fancy place in the capital (185). Bassano takes Thomas Nashe's quotation in his *Strange News* of 1593 (3.1.5) mostly directed at Gabriel Harvey, for "more than a hint of the veracity of a connection between the poet and the Bassano brothers" (184).

Claudio Monteverdi, employed at the Gonzaga court."[46] It would also give us a very good source for Shakespeare's knowledge of Giulio Romano, who was the main architect of the city and of Palazzo Te, just a few miles away. Before returning however, they would have stopped in Venice and gone to Bassano del Grappa, the city whose name was adopted by his friends, originally named Piva, when they moved to Venice. The city certainly aroused Shakespeare's imagination with its murals depicting naked ladies, goats, and monkeys,[47] images that were prohibited in puritanical England and which fill Othello's imagination. As a matter of fact, the city is also the only place in Italy where there were Otellos, one of whom owned an apothecary's shop, which would explain why Shakespeare links Othello to drugs and medicines. In Bassano, another popular apothecary was known as *the Moor* because of the Moor's head hanging outside his shop. It is moreover interesting to learn that silkworms were cultivated in Bassano and that the Bassano family coat-of-arms displayed three silkworm moths and a mulberry tree. All this undoubtedly "more witnesseth than fancy's images, And grows to something of great constancy." Peter Bassano never fails to draw parallels with Shakespeare's text and there are plenty. We can even surmise that it is along the road from Venice to Bassano that William's mind created Belmont, out of his own admiring wonder when he reached the city at the foot of the Trentino Alps.[48] The Baroque beauty of Italian cities could not but lastingly impress the young man from Warwickshire. There is such detailed inside knowledge of Bassano and Venice in both *The Merchant of Venice* and *Othello* that it cannot have come from books or informants. Let those who need to touch in order to believe persist in doubt, some documents may one day resurface bearing the proof of Shakespeare's journey. As Peter Bassano explains, he looked for, but did not find, any passport for any of the brothers, or Shakespeare. The armigerous Bassanos were gentlemen and as such were granted travel documents "which allowed them to take horses and be accompanied by servants." Shakespeare would conveniently have travelled as a servant, so needed no travel document in his name.

For those who are willing to believe in the existence of such a journey, which also throws light on Shakespeare's knowledge of Italian waterways,[49] Shakespeare's knowledge of Giulio Romano now acquires context.

---

46 Ibid., 186.

47 The fresco with its wall was eventually transported to the city museum, "Dal Corno frescoe."

48 Name given to the Dolomites, which are a mountainous massif of the southeastern Prealps that rises in Italy between Trentino and Venetia.

49 "He knows that nearly all the chief cities, such as Padua, Verona, Bergamo, Mantua, and Milan are accessible by water, and are commonly reached in this way by ship. The

If he had gone to Rome, he might more readily have referenced Raphael, but in Mantua, Giulio Romano was wonder enough for the young man. This documented trip offers answers to many questions about the source of Shakespeare's knowledge. Where did he get his obviously thorough understanding of anamorphoses, what painters influenced some of his most beautiful descriptions, and what readings shaped his mind and his method of composition? Peter Bassano asserts that "between 1592 and 1594 Shakespeare studied the works of several Italian poets in the original, and used them freely as sources for his plays. He borrowed much from Tasso's *Aminta*, and was influenced by Boiardo's *Orlando Innamorato* and Ariosto's *Orlando Furioso* as he wrote *Love's Labour's Lost*. Perhaps these works were owned by the Italian speaking Bassanos."[50] Such a journey would have inflamed the poet's imagination, it would have given him the manner he was looking for, not to mention a lot of exotic names and decors.

In England, which was so evidently closed to the main continental artistic influences, Shakespeare ceaselessly quoted knowledge that seemed to be barred from England, or reserved to aristocratic circles, which he was not supposed to know,[51] and he fearlessly deepened his mastery of an art which only he possessed to such a degree. Such variety, for a long time attributed to recklessness or lack of taste, especially in France, not only makes Shakespeare a mannerist artist in his own right, but also reveals, through the complex layers of texture, a manner with an ethical purpose, "something of great constancy," which underlies all his work. The artist's technical mastery of his chosen medium certainly improved over the years, but the message seems to have been there all along for us to decrypt. Now, what if the message had conditioned the manner? What if the very prohibitive nature of its content had made the detours and sophisticated designs of mannerism a necessity?

The word mannerism has had a very troubled history through the centuries, and was not recognized as the prevailing artistic practice of the

---

thirty principal tributaries of the Po were all navigable, and were then linked by an extensive system of canals." Bassano, 188.

[50] Bassano, 188. I had not read Bassano when I wrote my chapter devoted to the influence of Tasso.

[51] Reading David Howarth's remarkable study of art in the reigns of the Tudors and the Stuarts, I had the curious impression that Charles I and the Bard somehow had missed each other, and that Charles would have loved having Shakespeare to grace his court. Now, who influenced whom? Charles was born in 1600 and as a young prince must have had more than one occasion to attend Shakespeare's plays. His brother, Prince Henry, was hailed as patron of arts and literature by all those who wanted England to change. Unfortunately, typhoid took him away too soon and Shakespeare died before Charles could ascend the throne and, a few years later, acquire the Gonzaga Collection.

sixteenth century until the end of the twentieth century. Actually coined toward the end of the eighteenth century by the historian Luigi Lanzi, who transferred into Italian the French word *maniériste,* the word was used in a derogatory manner to qualify technical facility. It was applied sometimes a little erratically to all paintings which did not fit in recognized categories such as Gothic, Renaissance, or Baroque, hence its negative connotation. For three centuries, moreover, mannerism was studied by art historians almost exclusively in relation to painting and sculpture. But as John Shearman later demonstrated, the idea of *maniera* had been developed very early in Renaissance Italy, where it became the equivalent of *style.*[52] Vasari called the new manner of his time *bella maniera,* involving qualities such as harmony and measure (*regola, ordine, mesura, disegno*), imagination and fancy (*fantasia*). It expressed perfectly the ideal of courtesy and refinement of the sixteenth century such as Baldassare Castiglione defined it in his *Libro del Cortegiano* (translated by Thomas Hoby in 1561[53]): the search for beauty and grace went hand in hand with that of perfection, expertise, virtuosity, and elegance. Mannerism became the lingua franca of the Europe of the Arts, permeating not only the arts of design (architecture, painting, and sculpture), but also the arts called "minor" like furniture and cabinet making, interior design, gardens, garments, and even social behavior with the cult of good manners and this specially mannerist virtue, "sprezzatura."[54] It goes without saying that literature and the performing arts together with music were equally concerned, each developing its own particular features. Scholars are still in the process of rediscovering Leonardo's passion for theater decors, stage design, costumes, and music in creations that must have been the first opera performances, almost a century before Monteverdi.[55] Unfortunately, but for da Vinci's drawings and scores, the very mutability of stage designs and the ephemeral quality of live performances has rendered almost impossible a fair appraisal of the artistry and special effects of the whole until now. A lot of what we call mannerism was esthetically permeated with theatrical effects. It is difficult for us today to understand the fascination it exerted then, unless we take into account the new magic exerted by perspective and movement, which had long attracted Leonardo. This sense of movement is of course at the heart of Shakespeare's art together with a talent for finding the right tempo

---

[52] Shearman, *Mannerism,* 17.
[53] It is interesting to note that Thomas Hoby used the exact same route to Bassano del Grappa and Venice as the Bassanos and Shakespeare, in his well-documented journey to Italy in May 1554.
[54] "[A] kind of well-bred negligence born of complete self-possession," Shearman, 21.
[55] Olivier Lexa, *Léonard de Vinci: L'invention de l'opéra* (Paris: Les Editions du Cerf, 2019).

for lasting, fascinating effects.[56] Daniel Arasse calls mannerism the artistic expression of the sixteenth century.[57]

Originally an Italian style, Shearman tells us that "wherever it appears outside Italy it represents the adoption of Italian standards," (24) which were very often superposed on to local elements of late-Gothic style, especially in Northern Europe, as is the case of the painters known as "Antwerp mannerists." The facts are that between 1550 and 1650, mannerism had become an overall European style, with Emperor Rudolf II of Bohemia's court as its hub, which is especially interesting for us in the ties it entertained with the courts of Elizabeth and James I.

Technically, mannerism also expressed the attraction of the time for new discoveries and unlikely wonders, whether natural or manmade. Rudolf was undoubtedly the greatest patron and art collector of the time; he gathered around him an international Areopagus of artists and scientists, regardless of their religious faith. It is interesting of course to note that among the many people who visited him were diplomats such as Sir Philip Sidney and Henry Wotton, adventurers like Sherley, magicians like John Dee and Edward Kelley, the Protestant traveler Fynes Moryson[58] as well as the Jesuit Edmund Campion. The paradoxes of mannerism evidently reflected the moral and religious questioning of a tumultuous time in which received beliefs were jeopardized. Rudolf himself, a Catholic who did not like Spain, was more committed to art and alchemy than to any particular faith. It appears that James I entertained similar interests, which may explain the numerous exchanges between them. Reluctant to engage in any religious crusade whatsoever, both men equivocated in matters of religion, while encouraging some aspects of pansophic learning around them. "The painter's vision and the poet's insight overlapped with the experiments of the scientist and the speculations of the philosopher. Therefore it was not surprising to a contemporary that one person should embrace several of these disciplines; no clear line of division could be drawn."[59] Mannerism was in many ways a response to the spiritual and religious questioning of the time, its "turbulent disharmony always

---

[56] Had Shakespeare lived in the twentieth century, there is little doubt that he would have been a great film director.

[57] Daniel Arasse, and Andreas Tönnesmann, *La Renaissance Maniériste* (Paris: Gallimard, "L'Univers des Formes," 1997).

[58] In 1592 Moryson recorded having the opportunity of "free speech with the Jewes and to enter their Synogoges at the tyme of divine service." Quoted by Joaneath Spicer, "The Star of David and Jewish Culture in Prague around 1600, Reflected in Drawings of Roelandt Savery and Paulus van Vianen," *Journal of the Walters Art Gallery* 54 (1996), 203–25.

[59] R. J. W. Evans, *Rudolf II and His World: A Study in Intellectual History, 1576-1612* (London: Thames and Hudson, 1997), 255.

threatening the embattled islands of classical certainty and calm"[60] as well expressed by John Donne:

> 'Tis all in pieces, all coherence gone;
> All just supply, and all Relation:
> Prince, Subject, Father, Sonne, are things forgot,
> For every man alone thinkes he hath got
> To be a Phoenix, and that there can bee
> None of that kinde, of which he is, but hee.[61]

Beyond the endless discussions over particulars, Shearman outlined a number of "characteristic forms" adopted by, or to be found in most arts, like the *figura serpentinata*, the pastoral conventions, polyphony and the madrigal, intermezzi and set-pieces or *meraviglie*, marvels which were displayed in "cabinets of curiosities" all over Europe.[62] Even though most analyses primarily referred to the visual arts, scholars gradually turned to the study of literature and music, evolving the adequate vocabulary for each form, which could not simply be compared subjectively to painting. How do you give a fixed form to movement or metamorphosis in a certain place, or how do you make movement or metamorphosis happen in a fixed form?[63] How do you paint the "passage"? The formal characteristic found for these years in literature is the figure of contradiction. They dominate French poetry between 1556 and 1610, but they are also found in great number in Petrarch and Shakespeare, and they represent the basic principle of the Baroque metaphors which Jean Rousset defines as "unusual couplings giving birth to surprise."[64] The *oxymoron* is a particularly interesting figure of style which Rougé compares to the *contrapposto* in visual art. In this "yoking of incompatibles"[65] can be found the juncture where the oxymoron

---

[60] Ibid., 256. "It was precisely the breakdown of this secure harmony in face of a new naturalism and a particularizing pursuit of the empirical during the earlier seventeenth century which threw the unquestioned axioms into sharp relief and aroused conscious defence of them" (265).

[61] John Donne, *The Complete Poetry of John Donne*, ed. John T. Shawcross (New York: Doubleday, "The Anchor Seventeenth-Century Series," 1967), "An Anatomy of the World, The First Anniversary," ll.213–18.

[62] The Rudolfine *Kunst-und-Wunderkammer*, as well as the *Kunstschränke* (cabinets of virtù) remain the epitome of such a phenomenon. They featured an impressive collection of paintings and *objets d'art*, supposed to "reproduce the divine creative purpose for material things." Evans, *Rudolf II and His World*, 177.

[63] I refer here to the interesting article of Bertrand Rougé, "*Oxymore et contrapposto*, Maniérisme et Baroque: sur la figure et le movement, entre rhétorique et arts visuels," *Etudes Epistémè* 9 (2006).

[64] From Jean Rousset, *La Littérature à l'âge baroque. Circé et le paon* (Paris: Corti, 1953), 188; "des accouplements inhabituels d'où naît la surprise."

[65] An expression borrowed from Michael Fried, "New York Letter," *Art International* (Feb. 1963), 60–63.

presents and generates movement. The oxymoron is a figure of contraposition. Placing a term against its contrary, it makes them lean against each other in order to produce a figure which does not flow, but which makes us wonder. A figure that inclines to doubt, too. The juncture of the oxymorons, like the *flexus* of the *contrapposto*, moves the viewer. It does not represent movement, it creates it. Shakespeare very early understood what effects he could obtain from this basic rhetorical as well as esthetic principle in an art which, unlike painting, had movement and time at its heart.

Moreover, we must never forget that for sixteenth-century artists the world was made of analogies — that poetry was painting with words and music was asked to translate the feelings expressed in poetry. In the vision of sixteenth-century intellectual humanists the world was still represented as an integrated whole, the microcosm reflecting a perfectly ordered and wonderfully varied macrocosm. The theater, which represented the world, was naturally the art which best concentrated all these features.

The image of the *theatrum mundi* was not new but fitted perfectly the Baroque[66] state of mind. When the theater reflected the world, it was actually reflecting the theater. The stage is the reflection of a reflection. Thus do we lose reality. "Lost in the infinite replicas of this game of mirrors, the Baroque consciousness reaches the haunting question: is there anything behind the reflection? Is it possible to arrive at something that is not a mockery?"[67] This is clearly Shakespeare's questioning, which, as I will try to show, he eventually answered with confidence in time and faith. By holding up a mirror to nature, the theater reveals its own paradoxical nature, which is to be both illusion and the image of a reality, which is illusion too, unless you believe in a higher spiritual reality. The theater deceives us, yet it represents us. To the science of painters was added that of engineers in order to translate on the stage all the metamorphoses of this vision of the world. Thus, the questioning reverberates into a *mise en abyme*,[68] an infinite flight down the length of time: the absolute *trompe-l'oeil*.

---

[66] Didier Souiller, *La littérature baroque en Europe* (Paris: Presses universitaires de France, 1988). His study covers the period from 1580 to 1640, that is to say roughly the historical period spanning the reigns of Elizabeth I, James I, and Rudolf II. It is technically difficult to disentangle mannerism from the Baroque which succeeds it, borrowing most of its canons. If mannerism expresses the confusion born of the religious and intellectual crisis of the sixteenth century, the Baroque may be seen as an attempt to ward off such distress by recreating the lost correspondences between heaven and earth. Contrary to mannerism, which is often infused by skepticism, the Baroque renews with faith and upward aspiration.

[67] "Perdue dans les répliques à l'infini d'un tel jeu de miroirs, la conscience baroque rejoint aussi la lancinante question: qu'y a-t-il derrière le reflet? Peut-on atteindre autre chose qu'un simulacre?" (my translation); Souiller, *La littérature baroque*, 251.

[68] *Mise en abyme*: a term for a self-reflexive repetition in a text (mirror effect or infinite regression), such as a dramatist inserting a play into another play which is very similar.

MANNERISM AS A STYLE IS STILL PROBLEMATIC FOR SOME art historians and my purpose is not to enter yet another debate over its validity as an art form. John Shearman's return to the original concept of *maniera* revealed the universality of its applications to arts and crafts as well as social manners, together with the license in discipline (*nella regola una licenzia*) allowed to each artist striving to emulate High Renaissance art. Far from being an alienated artistic expression, *la maniera* was perceived as an improvement upon the Masters.[69] Giulio Romano, the only artist mentioned by Shakespeare, was Raphael's best pupil and disciple. He never meant to break away from the perfection of the style in which he had become a master, but added movement to it, strange perspectives and *trompe-l'oeil*. He added irony and wit to the formality and seriousness of his master. Mannerism perfectly corresponded to a century of "self-fashioning" in which the rise of individualism led artists to differentiate themselves more and more from their competitors in an attempt to secure high patronage or better commissions. *La maniera* expressed an artist's virtuosity and also an indirect way to react to political-historical tensions in a patron-centered model of creation. The artist who expected patronage had to please and satisfy the wishes of his patron, without sacrificing his own self-conscious art. Mannerism may register sometimes "as an art of complacency, an ornament of power,"[70] and Shakespeare has often been accused of serving and reflecting the foibles and mores of the patriarchal power he served. However, those opinions are often due to very superficial or biased readings of his plays. As Stephen Greenblatt puts it, "Shakespeare was a master of double-consciousness;"[71] he could say one thing and the reverse with equal force, just as he could pay for a coat of arms and mock Malvolio for his pretentiousness. He defended order, yet at the very same time, his plays sound so daring in their appraisal of monarchy, some of his judgments on power are so critical that it is a wonder that he did not end at Tyburn. Shakespeare could not displease the absolute power which provided for his and his company's living, yet he could, by using indirections, various kinds of artistic contortion and subterfuge, manage to say what he meant and offer the audience a critical view which could at all times be deniable. Stephen J. Campbell appropriately sums up the question of mannerism "as a practice that points to a cleavage between its own processes of making meaning, its own internal theoretical concerns,

---

[69] The High Renaissance Masters such as Raphael, Leonardo da Vinci and Michelangelo, had established such high standards that they were thought to be unsurpassable.
[70] Stephen J. Campbell, "Counter Reformation polemic and Mannerist counter-aesthetics: Bronzino's 'Martyrdom of St Lawrence' in San Lorenzo," *Anthropology and Aesthetics* 46 (2004), 98–119, 100.
[71] Greenblatt, *Will in the World*, 155.

and the political and religious institutions it is designed to serve. While artists might affect a posture of courtly or academic subordination before tradition and authority, the self-consciousness that operates in their work might be regarded as an 'other' self, one that confronts the viewer with unauthorized meanings, and where alienation might have a critical potential."[72] Campbell is here speaking of painting and of Bronzino's later art in particular, but the artistic conditions met by Shakespeare in Elizabethan England were in many ways similar to that of Bronzino at the court of Duke Cosimo de Medici in Florence. There was a similar cleavage, only much more dramatic since the religious isolation of England maintained it far from European artistic influences. Whereas the Baroque style was emerging in Italy, the England of Elizabeth looked backward and revived some aspects of its medieval culture, with jousting knights celebrating the Fairy Queen on Accession Day.[73] It was obviously necessary for her government to stress some kind of continuity and legitimacy between the present monarch, and those of the past, even though to obtain legitimacy as a monarch of divine right would require a singular sleight of hand.

When Henry VIII decided to break from Rome and to claim his own authority over the Church, he probably never imagined the disastrous consequences it would have on the visual arts in his kingdom. The Puritans disapproved of images in general; while the great Renaissance Popes, Julius II and Leo X, stimulated and funded the great artistic geniuses of the time, England was busy destroying its religious heritage and whitewashing sacred images in churches. Major studies of the arts under the Elizabethan and Jacobean regimes[74] agree about the absence of interest of those monarchs for the arts. "Stylistically England was a backwater, for Gloriana's reign had been a rock against change."[75] The Tudor reigns were particularly poor in visual arts, apart from very emblematic portrait painting destined to mirror

---

[72] Campbell, 100.

[73] During Queen Elizabeth I's reign, her accession day was declared a holy day by the Protestant church, in imitation of the Catholic saints' days: a "Form of Prayer and Thanksgiving" to be used in churches on the anniversary of the queen's accession was published in 1576 and used until 1602. In 1568, the tenth anniversary of Queen Elizabeth's accession was marked with the ringing of bells and November 17 became known as "Queen Elizabeth's Day" or "Queene's Day." As her reign progressed, it was celebrated with increased fervor and, long after her death, it continued to be observed as a day of Protestant rejoicing and expression of anti-Catholic feeling. The observances included triumphal parades and processions, sermons against superstition, and the burning of the pope in effigy. The Accession Day is still celebrated today, even though its date and meaning vary with the circumstances and character of the new monarch.

[74] Roy Strong, *Henry Prince of Wales and England's Lost Renaissance* (London: Pimlico, 2000); David Howarth, *Images of Rule, Art and Politics in the English Renaissance, 1485–1649* (London: Macmillan Press, 1997).

[75] Strong, *Henry Prince of Wales*, 65.

the power of the sovereign. And Elizabeth did not share her father's luck in the presence of a talented international painter at court. Holbein had settled in London in 1532, just as Van Dyck would settle there a century later. Both immortalized the king they served, even though they probably "compromised their artistic integrity and ambitions"[76] in the process. Painting Henry as King Solomon, Holbein never shied from propaganda dedicated to the new state religion, which was seen as casting off "a thousand years of servitude." Portraits were political tools used to negotiate royal marriages, or whole territories. But illusionism was not their primary virtue. Howarth notes that "the imagery of the second half of the sixteenth century addressed the mind rather than the eye." It was often didactic. Elizabeth controlled her own image and any reproduction had to follow the pattern of an approved portrait. Hence a very symbolic, heavily coded image, with jewels, clothes, animals, and objects furnishing emblems to be deciphered. Her portraits were as far from life as possible. "By Vasarian standards, and they remain the dominant methodology in art history today, the portraiture of Elizabeth is inept, timid, confined."[77] Illusionism was not wanted, Howarth concludes, denying the fact that England's isolation may have had something to do with it. The reign of Elizabeth, so often praised as a great cultural blossoming, is singularly lacking in those arts, which Vasari put first: painting, sculpture, and architecture. There were indeed good painters in Protestant countries, so religion is not the cause, but could not the necessity of asserting her power on a divided country where a good number of aristocratic families remained secretly attached to the old faith have motivated such rigidity and didacticism in a woman who measured up her frailty and the threat of chaos within the realm? The dirty work was very conveniently left to William and Robert Cecil, who served both Elizabeth and James with complete devotion. Whatever the reason that made her choose the look of a "powdered Pharaoh,"[78] Elizabeth unwittingly favored the word and the talent of her best dramatist for *ekphrasis*. She obviously loved the secrecy of the mask, which she seems to have worn from age twenty to fifty in her portraits. She probably enjoyed playing with her appearance like any theater lover, and she may even be the reason why the supreme art of Elizabethan England was not painting or sculpture as in most Catholic countries, but drama. To hold a mirror up to human nature and to teach men to reflect on their behavior was certainly a very attractive agenda for the queen, and could hardly have been opposed by her ministers.

---

[76] Howarth, *Images of Rule*, 77.
[77] Ibid., 105.
[78] According to Horace Walpole.

Shakespeare may have benefited from his sovereigns' personal ambiguity of allegiance; after all, Elizabeth always kept a Catholic Kapellmeister and James would honor his Catholic mother (Mary Stuart) as late as 1612, transferring her body to Westminster Abbey, in a chapel opposite the tomb of Elizabeth. Shakespeare's position certainly gave him plenty of opportunities to come across learned foreign visitors, to listen to them profitably and widen his own knowledge accordingly. Critics generally agree on the fact that Prince Henry (whose brother would become Charles I)[79] brought the first light of a possible dawn. Roy Strong, who believes the prince was a staunch Protestant, turns him into the lost patron of the arts for whom everyone was waiting. Clare Asquith makes much of the inspiration the young prince gave Shakespeare, whose last plays were, according to her, directed to him. Yet, Shakespeare, who is not found among the artists surrounding the prince, had explored the subtleties of mannerism long before Henry became Prince of Wales. That the young prince raised the hopes of many for greater toleration and patronage in the future was true however, and Shakespeare in his last plays certainly outdid himself with mannerist mechanical devices and stage tricks, which would please the young man, who, unlike his father, is said to have been more attracted by natural philosophy, riding, and shooting, than by learning.

As Malcom Smut very correctly points out, the prince's entourage and his education were at all times supervised by the king himself, and "James's actual policies were always more complex and devious than his image as Rex Pacificus suggested."[80] Protestant James ascended the English throne in 1603 with promises of religious toleration to the Catholics, many of whom had been faithful supporters of his mother, Queen Mary Stuart. However, the honeymoon did not last long and the Gun Powder Plot, in November 1605, put a brutal end to those hopes. It gave Robert Cecil a perfect opportunity to increase his own influence over the king, by reviving the penal laws against Catholics.[81] However, if only to comply with his queen, Anne of Denmark, who had converted to Catholicism in 1600, James had to be somewhat personally accommodating. Which means that both father and

---

[79] James I and Anne of Denmark had eight children, among whom only three lived long enough to be known: Henry Frederick Stuart (1594–1612) became Prince of Wales, his sister Elizabeth (1596–1662) became Electress Palatine and Queen of Bohemia, and Charles (1600–1649) became King Charles I of England in 1625.

[80] Malcolm Smuts, "Prince Henry and his World," in Catharine MacLeod, *The Lost Prince: The Life and Death of Henry Stuart* (London: National Portrait Gallery Publications, 2012), 19–31.

[81] "On the pretext that Catholics had taken liberties with the concessions offered by the king, £20 a month was again exacted, backdated to include the date of suspension. The slightest default in payment incurred forfeiture of all goods and chattels and two-thirds of any property." Asquith, *Shadowplay*, 187.

son were courted by both Catholics and Protestants (in particular Puritans), each party trying to secure any form of advantage or relaxation in the law that constrained them. Prince Henry received a Protestant education, which might help explain why Shakespeare does not appear among his favorites. Yet his mother was a Catholic and he admired Henry IV of France, whom he considered his second father. As a burgeoning diplomat, the prince would discover that some Catholics, like the Duke de Guise, who approved of toleration for Protestants, were ready to look for James's alliance against the regency government of Catholic Marie de Medicis that had negotiated an alliance with Spain.[82] Religious affiliation could be a tricky matter and the world was not, nor has it ever been, black and white.

Speaking of Queen Elizabeth's godson Sir John Harington, Gerard Kilroy writes: "Harington's own refusal to be identified as either Protestant or Catholic or Puritan, should make us wonder whether these historical labels are preventing us responding to the large body of men and women in early modern England whose resistance to the State sprang from a sense of justice and a love of freedom."[83] In a world of untruth, where legions of informers made it necessary for dissenters to put on masks and disguise their meanings under elaborate stylish turns and figures, it was not only difficult to discern whose side some people were on, but also necessary "to read between the lines, probe beneath the surface and hold the paper up to the light"[84] in order to discover the truth. If, as Kilroy insists, the only positive consequence was the enrichment of language, it is surely not unreasonable to admit that Shakespeare must have known, better than most, how to manipulate it. As Harington and Tresham[85] both experienced, since "untruth was corrupting the individual's relations with the state and with his neighbour ... the passion for truth, the desire for secrecy and the absolute life-saving need for complexity forced men to find ways of expression which preserved the 'heart of the mystery' and yet answered their need to utter the truth aloud, on paper or in stone."[86]

Or on the stage.

---

[82] When Henri IV was assassinated in 1610, Marie de Medicis, who may have had a hand in the assassination, ruled the kingdom of France in the name of her son, Louis XIII, who was only eight years old.

[83] Gerard Kilroy, *Edmund Campion: Memory and Transcriptions* (London: Routledge, 2016), 2.

[84] Ibid.

[85] Sir Thomas Tresham was a prominent recusant Catholic landowner in Elizabethan Northamptonshire, who immortalized his faith and his memory of Edmund Campion in the complicated, arcane, symbolic architecture of Rushton Triangular Lodge. Gerard Kilroy grants a learned fifth chapter to "the interior life of Sir Thomas Tresham" and the elucidation of his Lodge's spiritual meaning.

[86] Kilroy, *Edmund Campion: Memory and Transcriptions*, 5.

As it happens, although England remained for political and religious reasons officially apart from the main European influences, many characteristics of mannerism are to be found in Shakespeare's work. There we find deliberate distortions, visual *contrapposti*, plays on perspectives and genres, and the twisting of plots and characters, in order to translate in the most subtle fashion his differing perspective in a country torn apart by religious divisions. The influence of Italy, of its arts and intermezzi, pervaded his plays long before Prince Henry had grown old enough to make them his study. For evident reasons, we miss much of the way his plays must have been staged, and modern productions, depending, as they generally do, on the whims of the directors, often give a very foggy idea of what the original plays must have been like when performed. From the empty space of a bare stage to the visual and technical richness of indoor theaters, it seems that Shakespeare enjoyed a whole range of possibilities, which he certainly did not hesitate to use whenever he needed them. Our post-Cartesian rational minds like to erect rigid barriers between styles and traditions, but this was not the way it worked then, and Shakespeare, more than any one, always evaded labels, keeping himself, as it were, on the edge, "one foot in sea, and one on shore" (*Much Ado About Nothing*, II iii 55). The oxymoron, which is essentially a Baroque figure, the verbal equivalent of the contrapposto in painting, runs through all of his work, creating the most unlikely combinations, joining contradictory terms together, yoking light and darkness together in his own paradoxical vision of humanity. ♣

2. Youthful Rage:
THE ROOTS OF EVIL

*C*ONSIDERING SHAKESPEARE'S FIRST WRITINGS, ONE senses a deep feeling of rage in the young man aroused by two elements which never cease recurring in his work: his dejection at the schism, the division, or what he calls the "civil wound" which is destroying England, coupled with the gross indecency and lack of loyalty of men who think their power justifies their deeds. In most of his plays, Shakespeare underlines the mimetic violence that animates his characters and wreaks havoc around them.[1] The cycle of revenge that seemed to rule English history obviously disgusted him and led nowhere unless it was to more senseless violence. Rape appears to be a major theme in his work, both literally and allegorically. With a little power, proud men are ready to rape women, like cities, countries or monasteries, without realizing the psychic and spiritual damage this entails. For that matter, *The Rape of Lucrece*, where Lucrece assimilates herself with the city of Troy and Tarquin with the false Sinon, is a case in point useful to understand the dramatist's treatment of Lavinia and Titus's blindness. A little earlier, the Henry VI plays had sketched a first picture of England's decay and Shakespeare had felt the need to add a first part to the whole in which he pointedly chose to stage the mimetic rivalry between Talbot and Joan of Arc.[2] Most critics swiftly pass over "the *Pucelle*" ("the Maid") as a mere farcical addition to the play. I believe there is much more to it than is often admitted, and Shakespeare's Joan suffers from the aforementioned cleavage between his own vision and the requirements of the political and religious institutions he served. And more generally, there are already present in those works the mirroring effects and contrasting inclusions which point to a new esthetic vision.

THE PARADOX OF JOAN OF ARC

The *Henry VI* trilogy shares with *Titus Andronicus* the same conflicting violence born of mimetic rivalry. They both depict rising chaos in the land and a glaring absence of justice. Within the realm of England where

---

[1] René Girard's work on the subject is of course invaluable and has been a great inspiration to me throughout my life. Shakespeare, who had not read Girard, had perfectly understood the underlying mechanisms of rivalry. René Girard, *La Violence et le sacré* (Paris: Grasset, 1972).
[2] *1 Henry VI* was written after part II and III.

the house of Lancaster and the house of York have been competing for the throne ever since Bolingbroke usurped the crown of Richard II, the victorious campaign on the part of Henry V to recover his lost French possessions helped keep the internecine quarrels at bay, until his early death revived the conflicts both inside and out. France swiftly recovered her lost provinces, while the rival lords pursued their reciprocal hatred over their sovereign's coffin. It is particularly so in 2 and 3 *Henry VI*, where a deep sense of general chaos can never be contained by young, devout King Henry VI. His meekness and moral isolation turn him into a Christ-figure, without the strength and support that might have tipped the scales of power. With the character of Henry VI, Shakespeare seemed to acknowledge a measure of incompatibility between ruling a country and serving Christ. Was he thinking of Campion? At some point the poet must have read about Joan of Arc and decided to add a first part to his plays, possibly clarifying the message he had in mind.

In both *1 Henry VI* and *Titus Andronicus*, Astraea, the Goddess of Justice, has forsaken the land. But she is given a strongly paradoxical role in *1 Henry VI* since it is Joan of Arc who is greeted by the Dauphin of France as "Divinest creature, Astraea's daughter," (I viii 4) turning her into the innocent shepherdess of the Golden Age with stalks of wheat woven into her hair, who became the divine and imperial warrior, dispenser of the law, sent by heaven to bring order back to earth. It is a surprising persona which, for many people at the time, would have evoked the Virgin Queen, whose task was to reunify the kingdom of England. From the moment of her accession, Elizabeth had indeed been hailed by poets and courtiers as Astraea the Virgin, a persona that had not ceased to grow, in particular after the defeat of the invincible Armada in 1588.[3] An etching from Thomas Cecil dated 1630 even features the queen in armor, riding side saddle and gathering her troops against the Armada.[4] We do not know for sure if the queen ever wore the armor, but we know from her speech at Tilbury that her desire was to be among her men as their general. That an English dramatist should praise Joan of Arc thus, using the symbolic persona of the queen, even if Joan is praised by her own countrymen, may have sounded strange and risky. It was certainly daring, especially at a time of great suspicion against the old

---

[3] Frances A. Yates, *Astraea, The Imperial Theme in the Sixteenth Century* (London and Boston: Routledge and Kegan Paul, 1975), 59.
[4] Stephen Orgel, *Impersonations, The performance of gender in Shakespeare's England* (Cambridge: Cambridge University Press, 1996). The image by Thomas Cecil of "Elizabeth in Armor," c. 1630, the Mansell Collection, can be found on page 101. It may reference the queen's famous speech to the troops at Tilbury, August 9, 1588 and *1 Henry VI* is supposed to date from 1592.

faith, especially soon after the English learnt of their hero Talbot's defeat in the play. The play keeps insisting on the fact that these English defeats are due to brawls and betrayals within their own camp rather than to the superiority of the French. The English may be the best, but the seeds of evil are within. Bedford, who is the regent of France, makes bombastic threatening speeches against the Dauphin, whom he swears he will hale "headlong from his throne," (I i 149) whereas the next scene, viewed from the French side, brings from Alençon a eulogy of their opponents, who just won the day:

> Froissart, a countryman of ours, records
> England all Olivers and Rolands bred
> During the time Edward the Third did reign.
> More truly now may this be verified,
> For none but Samsons and Goliases
> It sendeth forth to skirmish. (I iii 8–13)

It is such mythic giants that Joan is sent from heaven to fight and drive "forth the bounds of France." Now, as a character, she appears straightforward and to the point. She will not be fooled, is quick to respond to any challenge, and swiftly retorts to those men who taunt her. "And while I live, I'll ne'er fly from a man," (I iii 82) she tells the Dauphin before fighting him, which brings her more mythic epithets; she is an Amazon, another Deborah. In the 1965 Peter Hall RSC Production, Janet Suzman was her perfect impersonation. Joan of Arc actually is the first heroic woman staged by Shakespeare, his first witty girl clad in men's garments, too.

The structure of the first three acts of the play are built on the mimetic rivalry and the parallelism of both heroes, Joan for the French and Talbot for the English. Both are greater than nature, adored by their allies like gods and accused of witchcraft by their enemies. The author multiplies mirror effects between the two superheroes, which he does not try to differentiate. The same words are used in turn to describe each of them, the same wonder is occasioned by them in their country and abroad, and the same hateful epithets are used by their enemies. The French call Talbot a devil whereas the English call Joan a witch. This is fair game. And until Talbot's death at the end of Act IV, the play remains fair to both heroes, whose courage and loyalty stay far above the jarring rivalries of the English court and the betrayal of the French king by Burgundy. Joan is not only God's chosen messenger to save the realm of France, she also happens to speak well and convincingly, as does Talbot, naturally. When she decides to conquer Burgundy, his heart is immediately crushed and he has to surrender like a fortified city:

I am vanquished. These haughty words of hers
Have battered me like roaring cannon-shot
And made me almost yield upon my knees. (III vii 78–80)

The military term "batter" reveals the power and obstinacy of the *Pucelle*, who strikes with words as she does with weapons. We can already feel adumbrated in her the audacity and persuasion of a Rosalind or a Helen.

So when later in the play, Joan suddenly metamorphoses into a witch consorting with fiends, and worse still, a disloyal whore who denies her parents' blood, one has the feeling that a stranger's hand, with no understanding of the poet's design, is hastily giving the popular audience a version of the character more in keeping with the official tradition. Shakespeare's creation is literally whitewashed, like church frescoes. The Chroniclers, and Holinshed in particular, were not tender to the *Pucelle*, and most critics accept the idea that Shakespeare was simply following them. How else could the English have justified the atrocious end of the maiden? The grotesque image of the witch of France, such as it suddenly appears at the end of the play, however, is completely out of character. There is no way a rational mind can step from Astraea's daughter to the sorceress of Act V. It does not correspond to anything Shakespeare ever does with his characters, even the least likable ones. In order for the play to be successful on stage, as the Hall production was, it has to undergo a few alterations and Joan is made to mention "her spirits" early enough in the play to justify the end, which nevertheless remains unconvincing. Act V, scene iii is a grotesque farce little in keeping with the character and the atmosphere which have been developed throughout the preceding acts. An anonymous joker must have found Shakespeare's Joan a little too idealized, or too heretically convincing as a saint, for her to survive as such on the English stage. Or did Shakespeare receive a threat and angrily choose to deface his own character? The hellish hag from France probably attracted her share of jocund applause and dirty names on the London stage and must have been quite a success. Admittedly, for an English playwright to give Joan of Arc such an aura at a time of bitter religious struggle was a daring choice. As a loyal subject of the queen, how could he, in the person of Astraea, praise the woman who was the leader of her enemies, a Catholic and a martyr, moreover?

In Act V, Shakespeare's saintly Joan has somehow disappeared and her executioners even manage to clear themselves by having her so-called father ask for her death: "O burn her, burn her! Hanging is too good" (V vi 33). This indeed "goes far beyond anything found in Hall or Holinshed or in the Burgundian chronicler Monstrelet,"[5] as Professor Bullough remarked, except this cannot be Shakespeare.

Let us turn the problem the other way around: Why on earth would Shakespeare, who is supposed to have found his inspiration in Holinshed and Hall, start by giving Joan the stature of a goddess? Charles, who hails Joan as a divine creature, also praises the courage with which she makes real her promises. Her virginity naturally adds to the wonder she arouses. Did Joan really succeed in keeping men at bay? They themselves certainly don't believe it and her enemies spend a lot of time in jokes. "A maid? And be so martial?" says Bedford. To which Burgundy retorts:

> Pray God she prove not masculine ere long.
> If underneath the standard of the French
> She carry armour as she hath begun. (II i 21–24)

There's nothing here that we do not find much later in *Antony and Cleopatra*. A woman in men's garments was unnatural and suspicious to some. Her body's shapes were not made to fit in armor and she could hardly hope to have the strength to compete with the best of warriors. Besides, she was unlikely to keep her maidenhead in an army corps. Men wanted to believe in women's natural modesty, but they did not want to bear the responsibility for the enticement a feminine body represented for them. Establishing a moral code that made women responsible for the desire they aroused was more comfortable — both Richard III and Proteus in *The Two Gentlemen of Verona* use this argument to exonerate themselves. If she was not a goddess, the *Pucelle* could only be a whore, and her masculine garment in that case was further evidence of her freedom, her easy ways (a masculine prerogative), and her dangerousness.

Shakespeare, however, unlike Holinshed, does not stress this point about Joan. The men, English or French, may mock the maid, he does not. The eulogy made to Joan of Arc, and the comparison with Astraea, even if it came from the French Dauphin, could certainly seem surprising and wholly unconventional on the English stage. As a woman of courage who could with panache equal the best warrior (Talbot), Joan could shock and certainly had to be debunked. Now the interesting question is of course: where did Shakespeare's Joan come from? Where did he find his inspiration and what did he mean by drawing such a character?

It would seem that in the Spring of 1580, at the university of Pont-à-Mousson (Lorraine), was performed a play *L'Histoire tragique de la Pucelle*

---

[5] Geoffrey Bullough, *Narrative and Dramatic Sources of Shakespeare* (New York: Columbia University Press, 1966), 3:41.

de Dom-Rémy. It was written by a Jesuit, Fronton du Duc.[6] Throughout
the tragedy, God's power is of course what inspires the heroine's eloquence,
until the end where, instead of the curse we find in *1 Henry VI*, we have
a mirror image with a prophetic benediction for France:

> Ah! Do not weep, my friends, she said,
> But rather praise God for the good news
> Of my death, for before the Heavens have granted
> The Sun seven vast circles around this land of France,
> You will see the English people hunted down.
> Then your leaders will feel light and free from the yoke
> With which their harsh injustice had burdened them [my translation].[7]

There too, naturally, she is silenced by the executioner "[Il] Lui a d'un fer
tordu bride la bouche" (v. 2314), since her tongue has proved as dangerous
as her arm:

> For she has beguiled with such pleasant tricks
> The princes' minds that she made them believe
> That God's voice was in everything she said.[8]

Richard Hillman asserts that only two texts at the time stage the Chinon
meeting as a dialogue, Shakespeare's (I ii 87–93) and Fronton du Duc's
(v. 526–29):

> Now I know whence comes the wisdom, which has astonished us,
> To exceed your sex: it would not be possible for her to know this.[9]

There are strange verbal correspondences within a few lines concerning
the same characters:

---

[6] Fronton du Duc, S. J., *L'Histoire tragique de la Pucelle d'Orléans* (London: Forgotten
Books, 2018). The original 1581 title was *L'Histoire tragique de la Pucelle de Dom-Remy,
aultrement d'Orléans*. "La Pucelle de Dom-Rémy" is Joan's recognized French appellation.
[7]   Ah! Ne me pleurez point, mes amis, disait-elle,
    Mais plutôt louez Dieu d'une bonne nouvelle
    Que vous donne ma mort car avant que les cieux
    Aient fait au soleil son cercle spatieux
    Recommencer sept fois de la française terre
    Vous verrez déchassé le peuple d'Angleterre.
    Lors vous verrez vos chefs du dur joug allégés
    Que leur grave injustice a si longtemps chargés. (v. 2289–96)
[8] My translation.
    Car elle a endormi de ruse si gentille
    Des princes les esprits que croire leur faisait
    Etre la voix de Dieu tout ce qu'elle disait. (v. 1949–51)
[9] My translation.
    Maintenant je connais
    D'où la sagesse vient, dont tu nous étonnais,
    Pour surpasser ton sexe: il serait impossible
    Qu'elle cogneu cecy... (v. 526–29)

"Tu nous étonnais" / "Thou hast astonish'd me"
"surpasser ton sexe" / "exceed your sex"
"Impossible" / "possible"....

It is difficult not to accept Hillman's suggestion that Shakespeare had read the Jesuit's play. We will probably never have any absolute evidence, but Hillman's argument convincingly relates Pont-à-Mousson to London via Scotland where Edmund Hay, SJ, who had been rector of the University of Pont-à-Mousson since its foundation in 1572, had been sent on a diplomatic embassy concerning a marriage between young James of Scotland and the Duke of Lorraine's daughter, Christine de Lorraine. Fronton du Duc had composed his play while Hay occupied this position and perhaps Hay did not leave France without one or two copies of the new play in his bag. It would be surprising if Walsingham had not sent his spies to Pont-à-Mousson, as he already had to Reims, also a foundation of the Cardinal de Lorraine. There were intense negotiations between the Ambassador of Scotland and the Duke of Guise, who was also Governor of Champagne and as such had transferred the English College of Douai to Reims in 1578. The purpose of Guise was of course to support Catholicism, reinforce its educational bulwark via Jesuit Colleges and, incidentally, to invade England and free Mary Stuart.[10]

The text of La Pucelle could have reached London, or Stratford, in the luggage of Huguenot printer Thomas Vautrollier, who happens to have traveled twice to Scotland between 1580 and 1582 and between 1584 and 1586 to sell books to the king that would counter the Jesuit propaganda. English translations of du Bartas were among his productions, one of them being the king's work. Du Bartas was a Huguenot diplomat and soldier, and his own visits to Scotland were not solely literary. His Judit could almost be seen as an anti-Joan, making of the Duke de Guise's assassination in Orleans a miraculous liberation of the people of France. Whatever purpose Vautrollier was meant to reach, he may well have brought back to London a copy of La Pucelle. His apprentice, Richard Field, was Shakespeare's friend and as such gave him access to his rich library.

Now what did Shakespeare intend by such an eloquent, and politically engaged, portrait of La Pucelle? Admittedly, the praises of Joan are made by the French, and the playwright could always pretend to be fair to his sources. Still, when one has read Shakespeare, one can only be surprised by certain similarity of character between Joan and Lavinia, the assurance and pride, the courage and resoluteness, qualities that are also to

---

[10] After the deaths of Pope Gregory XIII in 1585 and of Mary Stuart in 1587, the Scottish Seminary at Pont-à-Mousson lost much of its importance and would be eventually transferred to Douai in 1591.

be found in a number of Shakespearean heroines like Beatrice, Rosalind, Helen, Cleopatra, and Imogen. Joan is not only his first woman warrior, she seems to be the blueprint for many a Shakespearean woman character. The bow, or wink, to Queen Elizabeth, via Astraea's daughter, presumably meant that she, too, could become England's savior by putting an end to the religious war that was tearing her people apart.

What Shakespeare had not quite fathomed perhaps was the degree of fanaticism, or nationalism of his audience. Of course the text of a play, and what is made of it in certain contexts are two different things. Shakespeare's *1 Henry VI* says things that may never totally appear in a performance that has chosen to play Joan as a mad witch from the start. Anticlerical France would not be the last to put on such tomfoolery and the audience would love it! That would explain the metamorphosis of the last act.

Who would not dream of laying hand on the original manuscript? As it is, we can only wonder at Shakespeare's intent and original design. That Richard Field was working for the Protestant cause naturally does not imply that his friend Shakespeare was a Protestant.[11] We discover an arch Proteus in him, with a remarkable ability to elude labels and definitions. One thing is certain: he refused to condone internecine wars, be they religious or political. His message was always clear: the sovereign was responsible for the welfare of his people, all of them, not just a faction upheld by the vanity of a few great lords. By 1456, Joan of Arc had been officially exonerated and declared a martyr. In 1581, England made such another martyr in the bloody inhuman execution of Edmund Campion. You did not have to be Catholic or Protestant to feel that such bloodshed among men who all called themselves Christians was unholy.

Joan's end having turned, by necessity or compliance, into a farce, Shakespeare would find another way to arouse tears and say what he meant to say. Diving further into the past in Roman history was one way to erase all risk of being accused of being a recusant. *Titus Andronicus* probably followed *1 Henry VI* closely, together with *The Rape of Lucrece*.

TITUS: THE GOOD MAN WHO TURNS HIS OWN LAND INTO A SLAUGHTERHOUSE

Titus Andronicus in particular demonstrates a kind of butchery that many have refused to accept as belonging to Shakespeare, unless we should perhaps see it as an outlet for the pent-up rage and grief he felt at the time. That there are so many lopped, hewed limbs in the play seems indeed like a gross

---

[11] The homage that Shakespeare certainly pays him in *Cymbeline* through the name Richard du Champ would tend to prove, on the contrary, that Protestants and Catholics could work profitably together and be friends.

caricature of Elizabethan London where for whatever reason or no reason at all, you could not simply be condemned to death; you had also to be hacked to pieces and disemboweled, your body parts thrown into a boiling cauldron. Those barbarous methods are not so different from Macbeth's witches cooking their magic brew, possibly another indirect sarcastic comment.

In *Titus Andronicus*, however, we are supposedly in an archaic world where men have no qualms, no moral questioning, and no conscience. Men have no more value than a worm or a piece of meat; human sacrifices are practiced and killing seems to be the handy solution to all problems. Titus, who is called *Pius,*[12] surprisingly begins by denying all gesture of mercy to Tamora, the foreign queen who is submitted to the shame of the Roman triumph, which Cleopatra later fears so much that she kills herself to escape. Tamora's speech already heralds Portia's plea in *The Merchant of Venice*:

> Andronicus, stain not thy tomb with blood.
> Wilt thou draw near the nature of the gods?
> Draw near them then in being merciful.
> Sweet mercy is nobility's true badge,
> Thrice-noble Titus, spare my first-born son. (I i 116–120)

But if Titus has a sense of duty, he does not show mercy. Tamora's first-born son's limbs "are lopped / And entrails feed the sacrificing fire" (I i 143–144) as a revenge for the death of Titus's own sons in the war. Good and evil are obviously not what they seem at the beginning of the play. As Titus later ironically says to his followers, "Terras Astraea reliquit." Ovid's passage reads, "Victa iacet pietas et virgo caede madentis, / Ultima caelestum, terras Astraea reliquit" (I 149–150).[13] Justice has fled the earth, following piety! Is not Shakespeare here pointing to a very English problem? Since Astraea was also Queen Elizabeth's title, there is little doubt that this verse and Titus's acts in general refer to the barbarous events taking place in England, and against whom, if not the Catholics?

So, this noble Roman is the first to deny pity and justice to his prisoners. Between blood and Tamora's tears, he chooses blood, leading the way to chaos and the torrents of effluvia and body fluids of the play. In a world deprived of mercy and forsaken by justice, what remains to be destroyed or possessed but the integrity of bodies, hence a sad story of

---

[12] Should we see a covert reference to Pope Pius V, who issued the Bull *Regnans in Excelsis* which excommunicated the queen in 1570 and in that case is it an indirect comment on his lack of mercy?

[13] "Piety lay vanquished, and the maiden Astraea, last of the immortals, abandoned the blood-soaked earth." Ovid, *Metamorphoses*, trans. Frank Justus Miller, revised by G. P. Goold (Cambridge, MA: Loeb Classical Library, Harvard University Press, 1916), 1. 149–50.

rupture, rapine, robbery, and rape. The mother is refused her son's life, the prince, his bride. Titus unfeelingly gives his own daughter to the emperor and does not hesitate to kill his own son when the latter tries to stop him. Eventually Emperor Saturninus chooses to marry Tamora, the outraged mother, and rejects Titus from the new court. The proud leader becomes the supplicant in his turn. The irony of the situation is matched only by the hard-heartedness and lack of pity of the characters.

One feels a fierce jocundity in young Shakespeare's writing. What better way to sublimate his own grief and disgust? Titus is Hamlet's "engineer / Hoised with his own petard" (*Hamlet*, III iv 207). Titus next invites the emperor and his queen to "hunt the panther and the hart," (I i 492) offering a great metaphor to the murderous impulse of this animal world. Unfortunately, Lavinia herself becomes the doe at bay, the Philomel who will, according to Aaron, lose her tongue and chastity. Before this Ovidian reference applies however, Lavinia has had time to reveal herself a strong-minded woman, with a saucy tongue toward the queen. One already feels a hint of future Shakespearian heroines and the stoicism of some Roman ladies like Portia, Brutus's wife. She seems so assured of her moral superiority that she does not hesitate to provoke and abuse the woman who now is her empress (II iii 66–88). She sounds so sanctimonious that one wonders whether she would show more pity than her rival if their parts were reversed. It seems that in the first two acts, Shakespeare makes a point of showing the shared violence of the opposing parties. Titus, the eponymous hero, is proud and cruel and does not seem to be touched by emotions.

The sudden flood of tears that drown him when he learns of Lavinia's fate therefore seems strange and unexpected, the scene looking like a sudden Baroque tableau carved on the hard marble of the Roman world. The moment Lavinia is discovered by Marcus, the tonality of the play abruptly changes. Eugene M. Waith points to "an excess of refinement, or an overloading with classical allusions," which make it "impossible to see a meaningful relationship between action and style."[14] He finds fault with the Ovidian narrative intrusion which takes over in Marcus's florid description of Lavinia's mutilated body, "the presence of live actors" making it impossible for "the poetry to perform the necessary magic."[15] The question, of course, is whether Shakespeare is trying to evoke magic, or is he not rather trying to say something else? Is he not willingly pitting Ovid's poetry against the reality of Lavinia's maimed body, drawing the audience's attention upon the clash, commenting indirectly on another destruction?

[14] Eugene M. Waith, "The Metamorphosis of Violence in *Titus Andronicus*," *Shakespeare Survey* 10 (1957), 39–49.
[15] Ibid., 48.

Clare Asquith finds the passage "strongly reminiscent of a lament in one of the Jesuit plays for the vandalism of a statue of the Madonna." [16] And surely, it is. Time slows down and the picture of vandalized Lavinia is anatomized, Marcus insisting on every gruesome detail only to produce the negative image of what she no longer is. This is "life imprisoned in a body dead," and surely Lucrece would find her wronged in having "so much grief, and not a tongue." [17] "Poor instrument," quoth she, "without a sound, / I'll tune thy woes with my lamenting tongue" (*The Rape of Lucrece* 1464–1465). Shakespeare is obviously trying to make a point: What Marcus sees is so lamentable that he can only wail upon the mutilation and loss of such beauty in a long, lyrical complaint. The dramatic action, the speed and violence of preceding events, is suddenly suspended and we face another genre, a freeze on a frame, on a tragic tableau. The author wants the spectator to be shocked into thinking. He creates an image which will jolt some among his audience into remembering events they might have witnessed at Tyburn, the dismembered bodies of some of the most promising young men of the nation, tortured and mutilated for the lust of a single man. For Titus is very close to *The Rape of Lucrece* in which the seeds of most of Shakespeare's ideas are sown. One stanza is particularly evocative of a meaning which obviously goes far beyond Lucrece's own plight:

> Why should the private pleasure of someone
> Become the public plague of many moe?
> Let sin alone committed light alone
> Upon his head that hath transgressed so;
> Let guiltless souls be freed from guilty woe.
> For one's offence why should so many fall,
> To plague a private sin in general? (*The Rape of Lucrece* 1478–1484)

Those lines apply to Lavinia as much as to Lucrece, but even more so to all the Catholic families that had been and were being systematically destroyed for the lust and arrogance of a king, father to a queen who had forgotten the meaning of her namesake Astraea. In a very mannerist manner, Shakespeare wants to shock and move his audience as much as educate them. The attempt is dangerous, and he has to use whatever means at his disposal to point to his meaning.

Lavinia's mutilated body, mocked and derided by her assailants, becomes the monument on which they carve their domination, while the fluids flowing out of her (blood and tears) trigger, empathetically, a storm of passions in Titus.

---

[16] Asquith, *Shadowplay*, 93.
[17] *The Rape of Lucrece*, 1455, 1463.

> Is not my sorrows deep, having no bottom?
> Then be my passions bottomless with them. (III i 215–216)

From now on, the mute presence of this mutilated body on stage is both obsessional and unbearable. This is no martyrdom. The viewer cannot escape into any form of worship; it is pure abomination. Like Titus, he can only wish for the end of this torment. There is no sublimation of atrocities for Shakespeare, who turns his play into a manifesto against strength and violence as the prerogatives of virility and power. Titus who has brought this paroxysm on himself pays dearly for his own brutality, which is not quenched by his pain. When he has shed all the tears of his body, he becomes stone, for tears without the spiritual blessing of forgiveness have no healing power. The final carnage is the stage image of the violent loss of differentiation within the group in a world which does not know mercy, as has been propounded by René Girard in his exploration of mimetic violence.[18] The play actually offers a condensed version of the theme which is equally at the heart of the *Henry VI* trilogy, and its philosophical outcome. Without justice and compassion, man is but a predator on man. In such a world, Shakespeare tells us, strong men aren't heroes. They are tigers.

The bloody body of Lavinia on stage provokes in her and around her a flood of tears. It is the immeasurable pain provoked by the horrible vision, which gives the best painting of the unspeakable rape and the torture suffered by the young woman. Shakespeare already knew and tested here a mannerist technique which he would bring to perfection in his last plays. Horror, just like beauty, could best be represented and felt by the reactions they triggered, in the characters first, and in the audience by mimeticism.

---

[18] For René Girard, the imitation of others (what he calls mimetic desire) is what drives all human impulses. Unfortunately, it almost inevitably leads to rivalry and conflict, as his study of human rites and rituals, myth as well as history and literature, testifies. In the course of his huge intellectual enterprise, Girard discovered the "scapegoat mechanism," i.e., whenever "human violence cannot expend itself against the creature which originally inspired its fury, it will find a surrogate victim. The surrogate victim has committed no offense. It is simply vulnerable as well as available." Richard J. Golsan, *René Girard and Myth* (New York: Routledge, 2002), 30. "If one surrogate or group of surrogate victims can become the focus of all the hostilities of the larger group, then that one victim . . . will deflect or channel internal dissensions outside the group. Once this occurs, social harmony is reestablished and the development of culture becomes possible" (31). The violent crisis that precedes is called the "sacrificial crisis" or crisis of distinctions: it "entails the collapse of social hierarchy and the loss of difference within the group." The mimetic process tends to erode differentiation among individuals. With the loss of degree, rivalry erupts into violence, which transforms antagonists into violent doubles. In his study of the Gospels, Girard is led to reassert the unique position of Jesus as "the only being capable of rising above the violence that [has], up to that point, absolutely transcended mankind." René Girard, *Things Hidden Since the Foundation of the World* (Redwood City, CA: Stanford University Press, 1987), 214.

The moment Marcus sees Lavinia, a stream of tears carries blood, sperm, and vomit in a purifying verbal flow. Nothing can contain these "bodily floodings." It may be, according to Pascal, "the flood of passions necessary to move great souls." [19] Love itself is nothing but tears and the father and daughter embrace through a cosmic metaphor:

> I am the sea. Hark how her sighs doth blow.
> She is the weeping welkin, I the earth.
> Then must my sea be moved with her sighs,
> Then must my earth with her continual tears
> Become a deluge overflowed and drowned,
> For why my bowels cannot hide her woes,
> But like a drunkard must I vomit them. (III i 224–230)

There is something deeply sexual in this metaphor of the sky and the earth, the loving of two characters mingling, melting into each other in a reversal of bodies, projecting the inside outside, while the outside itself melts and crumbles.

The heart of this Roman play is nothing but twisting and flowing passions, a kind of gaping wound in the middle of a world of stone.

The style chosen by the Bard, obviously far from the traditional revenge tragedy, is meant to express his inner heart about a situation which we can recognize as that of Elizabethan England. In a world of lies and spies, only indirections could lead to truth, and mannerism was Shakespeare's way to cut through the well-received tradition.

If there is any heroism in Lavinia's body, it is by suffering, like Christ's suffering body, ill-treated, humiliated by men's folly. But Lavinia is a collateral, unwilling victim of human violence. As noted above, she belongs to the same pitiless world as the others. Her body is heroic in spite of herself, or rather thanks to the tears shed on it. As Charvet puts it, tears reveal what man keeps secret and allow silence to have its say. [20] They also show us what is not seen in a woman. It is when the tear escapes from the body that it signifies, that it gives it significance. [21] Lavinia's tears are what remains from her body to express her suffering. That this half-sensitive, half-sensible element, traditionally attributed to women whose grief and pain as well as grace they usually demonstrate, should become the link

---

[19] My translation. Jean-Loup Charvet, *L'éloquence des larmes* (Paris: Desclée de Brouwer, 2000), 31. Those "inondations corporelles" may be "l'inondation de passions nécessaire à l'ébranlement des grandes âmes."

[20] "[L]es larmes nous révèlent ce qui se tait dans l'homme, et donnent son temps de parole au silence." Charvey, *L'éloquence*, 14.

[21] "C'est quand la larme s'échappe de notre corps qu'elle signifie, qu'elle *le* signifie le mieux." Ibid., 17.

uniting father and daughter, that this flood of tears should be essentially shed by the man whom nothing until now, not even his son's death, had managed to move, is not banal. Because we can't suspect Titus of being womanish, we have to see something of a different order in the event, a "precipitate of thought" or "précipitation de pensées" as Pascal put it in chemical terms, some kind of revelation. It is undoubtedly the birth of some new esthetics, debunking the heroic ideal, twisting it, melting it with compassion. Titus, the Roman stoic hero literally becomes a new Niobe, and before Hamlet, before Antony, melts, collapses, emptying himself of his own substance.

"The play ends with an assurance that rescue will come from abroad," says Clare Asquith, but measured against the butchery of the final act, this assurance is indeed very slight and distant, and unnatural in so far as banished Lucius,[22] like Coriolanus, has had to "beg relief among Rome's enemies" (V iii 105). There is neither mercy nor pity in the last scene and only the presence of the boy Lucius may herald a new, kinder age blessed by tears and memory that may help re-member a dismembered family. But this means two generations at the least. Shakespeare was already aware of the importance of time as a means to assuage and restore what had been broken. No proper ending could be possible in a twenty-four-hour tragedy! Time and patience were of the essence, a fact that he would try gradually to embody within his plays.

IF WE CAN DRAW AN EARLY CONCLUSION FROM *TITUS Andronicus* and *1 Henry VI* concerning the character of the hero, it is that the courageous, fearless warrior does not necessarily look like Hercules. Or rather Hercules, as displayed in Renaissance iconography was himself an androgynous creature, often pictured dressed in Omphale's garments and serving her. Shakespeare would ceaselessly come back to this very mannerist image of the hero. It is moral greatness that makes a hero, not strength or power. Talbot makes it clear to the Countess of Auvergne that he is but the shadow of himself, his substance being made of his men ready to die for him. Talbot is the perfect character of the army leader, the traditional hero warrior, ready to die for his King and country, proud and brave, waxing poetical when he finds himself face to face with his fair son. The stichomythia of lines 34 to 46 (IV v) enhance both the mirror effect and the confrontation of both Talbots. Neither of them will save his life leaving the other behind. Unfortunately, the regent is not so principled and breaks his word. Without such cohesion and brotherhood, the hero's

---

[22] Note that Shakespeare uses the name again in *Cymbeline*, where another Lucius more adequately represents the "light" his name suggests.

life is brittle and Talbot, for all his valor, dies on the corpse of his own son, betrayed by their own party.

> Come, come, and lay him in his father's arms.
> My spirit can no longer bear these harms.
> Soldiers, adieu. I have what I would have,
> Now my old arms are young John Talbot's grave. (IV vii 29–32)

IF SIR WILLIAM LUCY'S PREDICTION IS TO BE TAKEN SERI-ously,[23] it might point to Talbot's descendants in Shakespeare's time, a bow to the Montague family with such men as Lord Strange and Henry Wriothesley, who were the flower of the Catholic resistance in England. It might also indirectly warn them to unite as there was dissension even among their ranks. Talbot's last exhausted words, which in many ways herald Antony's own dissolution when he believes he has been forsaken by his love, no doubt would also inspire Falstaff's questioning of honor.

As for Titus, whose moral severity isolates him from his sons from the beginning, we are made to perceive the weakness of the iron man, pierced open by his own daughter's torture.

Titus Andronicus and the *Henry VI* plays make much of mimetic rivalries, constantly frustrating the superiority one group or faction might feel over the other. Titus reveals himself to be as bloodthirsty and pitiless as Tamora, and the bloody war for power between the houses of York and Lancaster finds no excuse, especially when it weakens the kingdom and forsakes those who fight for it abroad. Saintly King Henry VI seems to express Shakespeare's thoughts when he wonders:

> Good Lord, what madness rules in brainsick men
> When for so slight and frivolous a cause
> Such factious emulations shall arise? (IV i 111–113)

Factious emulations among men seem indeed to be, throughout Shakespeare's plays, the evil core of most of his plots, reflecting the world at large. Shakespeare's first plays already display the subjects, the themes, and the characters that will haunt him all his life. Not surprisingly, the solutions and the hope are here too adumbrated.

LUCRECE'S RAPE

When he wrote his long symphonic poems, those poetic rhapsodies that launched him as a major poet of the Elizabethan world, Shakespeare was already experimenting with a great creative freedom and certain mannerist

---

[23] "I'll bear them hence, but from their ashes shall be reared / A phoenix that shall make all France afeard." *1 Henry VI*, IV vii 92–93.

effects which he would later expand in his dramas. Thus, the reflection of Lucrece's sad plight in a painting — Priam's Troy assaulted by the Greeks, artfully detailed in the manner of Philostrates — is certainly one of its most curious, and least classical elements. After the violent rape which she suffered, Lucrece spends the hours of the night wailing and debating with her own conscience about how to react so that no one should doubt her purity of mind, least of all her husband Collatine, whom she does not want betrayed. Having failed to "read" Tarquin's deceit in his looks, she realizes that appearances, like words, require interpretation and that whatever she says next can be misconstrued just as her own tears may be thought to express her remorse after yielding. The main perpetrator having vanished, appearances are against her.

The aforementioned painting suddenly emerges like a memory image in her mind. She remembers all its details with a curator's expertise, praising the painter's art along the way. Even though the painting does not appear to be connected in any way with her fate Lucrece finds in it support as well as matter for clarifying her doubts. By lending her "lamenting tongue" to Hecuba, she manages to transform her own private wound into a public cause: both of them suffering the consequences of men's lust and deceit. "Why should the private pleasure of someone / Become the public plague of many moe?" (1478–79), she asks, returning to the argument she had developed as a plea to Tarquin to refrain from staining his own honor as a king. The duty of a king, as it could be read in countless treatises on the education of princes at the time, was to be in all things an example: "For princes are the glass, the school, the book / Where subjects' eyes do learn, do read, do look" (615–16). How could his people behave properly if he himself projected an image of evil and crime? How could the law be enforced if he himself broke the law? Lucrece's language then, which sounds like that of a political counsellor, may seem surprising, but reveals itself highly significant of Shakespeare's underlying meaning. To say, like Burrow, that it is male language is to forget that a woman was Queen of England, and that Shakespeare's heroines generally have beautifully articulated minds. Lucrece is a remarkable woman and her analysis of the painting of Priam's Troy reveals great psychological abilities. There is no doubt that Shakespeare's Lucrece is also a Renaissance lady with the education that this implied. She had certainly read her More and her Erasmus and her Castiglione! When at last she lays eyes on the figure of Sinon, she is confirmed in her idea that appearances can lie, that the most beautiful men can beguile "with outward honesty" and defile "with inward vice." From Sinon's appearance, Lucrece's own sense of guilt draws a likeness to the way Tarquin behaved toward her. She decides therefore to kill herself, adding action to words to prove the truth of her tearful appearance (an attitude not unlike More's adamant insistence on acting in accordance with his faith).

Paradoxically, beholding the carnage at the end of *Titus Andronicus*, a Roman lord wonders "what Sinon hath bewitched our ears, / Or who hath brought the fatal engine in / That gives our Troy, our Rome, the civil wound" (V iii 84–86). Who, indeed, unless it is great Titus's own rigid code of honor and lack of mercy, his own arrogance and wish to please his new emperor by organizing the hunt that will ironically be fatal to his daughter? In a similar way, it is Collatine's boastful assurance that calls Tarquin's attention to his beautiful wife and ironically kindles the fire that will destroy Collatine's life. Shakespeare must have meant a lot by this alteration of the original character[24] since he would resort to the same "trick" many years later in *Cymbeline*, showing once again how arrogance and a lack of humility in men always took their toll.

Shakespeare's dramatic and rhetorical talents seem to overflow the poem's limits and Lucrece appears as the first of a long line of beautiful, thoughtful feminine characters abused by ruthless and thoughtless males. The poem is obviously too narrow a vehicle for him to express the full extent of his meaning. The interweaving of plots and themes, the clever use of mirrors and perspectives, of paintings or plays-within-plays, to explore the reality behind appearances, the complexity of motives which give birth to action — all of these are already found like seeds in his poems, which give sufficient evidence of the artist's awareness and of his early search for the best means to express his ideas. No doubt, through *Lucrece*, Shakespeare realized that drama was the best means to express himself, combining together image, voice and action in order to delight, teach, convince, and offer the best mirror to nature. He would never cease to explore and improve on it, appropriating critical theories for his own purpose, and raising the theater to as great and meaningful an art as painting and sculpture were at the time.

In his poetical attempt however, being less exposed to the public, he could perhaps express more clearly ideas that would be dangerous elsewhere. The connection between Priam's Troy and Lucrece's rape enables him to blur the English reference, which no doubt every one of his readers among the Earl of Southampton's circle would have perfectly understood. Indeed, what king chose to privilege lust and "dishonour in his name" and,

---

[24] Clare Asquith suggests that Collatine here calls to mind Wolsey's arrogant and boastful attitude which "drew attention to the riches of the church, inflaming the king's lust for its holdings." Clare Asquith, *Shakespeare and The Resistance* (New York: Public Affairs, 2018), 80. Shakespeare's own discretion concerning his personal life certainly testifies to his humility and prudence.

by choosing a "strumpet" over his rightful queen, triggered a fratricidal war in his kingdom, but Henry VIII? And whom did he rape but the Catholic Church? The vocabulary used to describe "holy-thoughted Lucrece," who is compared to a virtuous monument, is very explicit. The way she visualizes herself as a "sacred temple spotted, spoiled, corrupted, / Grossly engirt with daring infamy" (1172–73), her soul deprived of her natural abode (mansion), naturally recalls the dissolution of the monasteries, a barbarous assault which reverberates on the perpetrator "That through the length of times he stands disgraced / Besides, his soul's fair temple is defaced" (718–19). "Ruins," "battered down consecrated wall" form an eloquent lexicon which metaphorically applies to the soiled characters, both victim and assailant, as well as literally to the fate of the Church in England, its "bare ruined choirs"[25] and devastated abbeys. The symbolic and metaphysical meaning would be there throughout Shakespeare's career as a dramatist, particularly revived in the last plays where he would strive toward some kind of epiphany. In this poem already, there is a faint hope of resurrection, phoenix-like, from shame's ashes, which necessarily entails Lucrece's death if she is to be revived. Self-slaughter, naturally, might be held against her, though she clearly accuses Tarquin of being responsible for her death, which eventually appears as the inescapable consequence of the rape. If Shakespeare is alluding to the state of things in contemporary England, it is a sad vision at this stage and there seems to be only one action left for believers: the postmortem vindication required by Lucrece from Collatine.

Astraea, injustice, and rape seem to be the hallmarks of Shakespeare's first artistic productions. There are hardly any filters there and he dared express what was on his mind almost openly. Too openly perhaps, which might explain Joan's metamorphosis and Titus's twisted design. Shakespeare must have quickly understood that his indirections had to be even more indirect, that the design of his plots had to be more complex, that he needed to harmonize the whole without renouncing the purpose. These were precisely the tricks of mannerism: How do you express your mind subtly in a world where you depend upon the generosity of an absolute monarch for your living—or your very life? He tried his hand at comedy, or rather, he invented a comic counter-hero in the midst of a history play.

A FRIENDLY BASTARD

King John, often presented as a piece of Reformation propaganda, is a real conundrum which "highlights a wide range of forbidden subjects"[26] without taking sides with any of them. Only a mannerist sleight of hand could enable

---

[25] Sonnet 73.
[26] Asquith, *Shadowplay*, 79.

the author to say what he wanted without seeming to. *King John* veers danger-
ously close to aspects of contemporary Elizabethan politics, with an openly
rebellious King John being excommunicated for his refusal to submit to
the pope's choice of Stephen Langton as the new archbishop of Canterbury.
His subjects are encouraged to break their allegiance to their now heretic
king, whose murderer, says Pandolf, would be "canonized and worshipped
as a saint" (III i 103). John's reaction to Pandolf's question is a sudden flow
of abuse that would have satisfied many reformers even though the play
shows him exclusively motivated by his own capricious will and arrogance:

> What earthy name to interrogatories
> Can task the free breath of a sacred king?
> Thou canst not, Cardinal, devise a name
> So slight, unworthy, and ridiculous
> To charge me to an answer, as the Pope. (III i 147–151)

Shakespeare's Elizabethan audiences would have no difficulty linking the
situation to that of their own Queen, whose legitimacy was questioned by
the supporters of Mary Stuart, and who had been excommunicated in 1570
by Pope Pius V, thereby relieving English Catholics from their oath of allegiance to their monarch. But in the play, John is portrayed as a usurper, all
the more evil as his natural opponent is presented as a child (Shakespeare's
transformation). By ordering his death, John comes closer to the villain
Richard III than to Elizabeth. The question of his legitimacy, which even
his own mother is doubtful about, is indeed a prominent theme, which
cannot be separated from the problem of succession. However, Shakespeare
subtly displaces the debate onto the conflict between Robert and Philip
Falconbridge, which certainly is "a complex and impressive overture to
the dynastic struggle between John and Arthur,"[27] politically drawing
attention away from the King. The Bastard Falconbridge, by blood and
character, has so much more dramatic presence than John, to whom he
nevertheless vows allegiance, that he quickly upstages him. John's anti-papal
declarations merely isolate him, revealing a wrathful, duplicitous character
whose words cannot be shared by Shakespeare, who spends a whole scene
underlining the foolishness and dire consequences of such rash decisions
on international alliances. The perplexity of the King of France appears
through a long speech in which he laments Pandolf's demand of a breach
of faith between both their kingdoms, which had just reached a difficult
peace by agreeing to the marriage of their children:[28]

---

[27] A. R. Braunmuller, Introduction to *The Life and Death of King John* (Oxford University Press, 1989), 60.
[28] The King of France appeared like an obedient puppet to the Cardinal's order in the
earlier *The Troublesome Raigne of John, King of England* — of ambiguous authorship.

And shall these hands, so lately purged of blood,
So newly joined in love, so strong in both,
Unyoke this seizure and this kind regret,
Play fast and loose with faith, so jest with heaven,
Make such unconstant children of ourselves,
As now again to snatch our palm from palm,
Unswear faith sworn, and on the marriage-bed
Of smiling peace to march a bloody host,
And make a riot on the gentle brow
Of true sincerity? O holy sir,
My Reverend Father, let it not be so. (III i 239–249)

Once again, Shakespeare makes an oblique use of France, whose language is permeated with the same grace and devotion as that of *Romeo and Juliet*, in order to impart his deep thoughts on the vagaries of papal politics.[29] By asking him to break from newly excommunicated England, the pope risks no less than new disorders, bloody wars, and treachery. By then, however, Shakespeare knew that he could not turn France into his own spokesman. The Bastard appears to be "both a reader of the text of history and part of that text,"[30] created by Shakespeare to comment upon a constantly vacillating history and to mediate between the actors of history and their responsibilities in the general chaos. Is he not after all an illegitimate heir proving by his wit and bravery more loyal to his kingdom than any nobleman? Thus by indirections, Shakespeare raises important questions to which he carefully provides no answer, the initial debate on legitimacy eventually leading nowhere, as if to suggest that the important thing is the ability and moral character of the ruler rather than his legitimacy. Similarly, the religious question is evoked, then subverted by "commodity," the bias of the world, as the Bastard very perceptively calls it. Pandolf is very diplomatically riding on it, making and unmaking alliances for the sake of power rather than any argument of faith, while King John, in a similar way, defies the pope and plunders the monasteries from sheer expediency. He changes sides as soon as it is expedient to do so, just as he orders Arthur's death, then revokes that order when he fears his lords' disapproval. Shakespeare carefully manages to defuse the dangerous topicality of his subject by creating a fictional character, whose position and behavior cut across classes and genealogies. The Bastard is both a Fool and a villain, a hero and a trickster, a commentator and an

---

[29] King Philip's pejorative reaction in *The Troublesome Raigne* hardly seems in character and the use of "Romish rytes" does not square well with the general tone of the playwright in such a context.
[30] Braunmuller, Introduction, 71.

actor, a character whose loyalty to his king and country recalls Talbot's and who will later inspire both Falstaff and Enobarbus among others. He is Shakespeare's only friendly bastard, kept away from the stain of John's evil decisions by having his sacking of the Church off stage, and since Pandolf appears more of a diplomat than a priest, it is impossible to fault Shakespeare's personal religious position. The plot owes so little to these elements and there is so much ambiguity in the way the characters interact with each other, that the religious background is submerged by the will to power of the warring parties who are finally all bypassed by the irony of fate. Prince Henry, who has been kept away from the general wrangling, appears at the end of the play, like a *deus ex machina*, solving the question of succession and legitimacy. This is surely another indirect way to point to the missing heir who would have solved many tensions in Elizabeth's reign.

COMEDY AS A PLEASANT SCREEN

The Comedy of Errors, written at the same time, strangely begins with the same mimetic rivalry between the cities of Syracusa and Ephesus. In each city, identical laws have been enacted to apply the same "rigorous statutes" against their rival city's merchants. Needless to say that the penalty applied to Egeon for setting foot in Ephesus, i.e., a heavy ransom or death and the confiscation of his goods must have reminded attentive listeners of the fate endured by many a Catholic recusant disembarking in England.[31] The fact that Shakespeare includes such grisly precisions at the beginning of a comedy certainly is another indirect way to state plain facts under the guise of mockery. When the abbess at the close of the play reveals herself to be Egeon's lost wife and the mother of the twins, we do have a farcical comedy wrapped not so much in "a setting of emotional earnestness and ethical normality," as Professor Bullough has it, as in a contemporary setting of internecine strife, now deprived of the benevolent solutions provided by the priory. No audience could be blind to the hints provided by this nearly tragic framework imposed on the comedy, which evolves rapidly to complete chaos until it reaches an apex with the tragic rejection of Egeon by one he thinks is his son Antipholus, who does not know he has a twin, and his impending death at the hands of Duke Solinus. Shakespeare goes as far as drawing his audience's attention to "the melancholy vale," "The place of death and sorry execution, / Behind the ditches of the abbey here" (V i 120–122). They were probably attending the performance on the spot, at the newly built theater, hence the "here" added by the merchant. They would have been sensitive to this evocation of a recent past, the theater

---

31 Asquith, *Shadowplay*, 55–61.

having been built on the land formerly belonging to Holywell Priory, in Shoreditch. The convent still comprised fourteen nuns together with a prioress when the priory was dissolved in 1539 after four hundred years of existence, being sold to the crown as a dwelling house for the queen's noble parentage. The priory had been replaced by Holywell gallows standing in the shadow of Shakespeare's playhouse. The people had lost a quiet, benevolent surrounding, not to speak of the care, sacraments and holy waters, provided by the nuns, and even the actors of Shakespeare's company would soon suffer from the meaning of 'private property' when owner Giles Allen refused to renew the twenty-one-year lease of the theater. Why would the author have inserted this echo of England's grim past in a comedy unless he meant to suggest that with the dissolution of the priory, it was now his responsibility to keep on with the spiritual tradition?

After the confusion of mistaken identities which lead the comedy to almost complete chaos, peace is ultimately brought back thanks to the practical wisdom of the abbess, who hides and heals one of the distraught twins with herbs and rest, and provides matronly advice to Adriana, the other's wife. No doubt, Shakespeare still had her in mind when he created Desdemona's Emilia, and later Paulina, his benevolent, witty, generous matrons. The abbess is a holy woman and the fact that she is finally happy to go back to married life is not contradictory with her benevolent act and the vital right of sanctuary which allows Antipholus of Syracusa the possibility to escape from his pursuers, and the time for the different threads of this complicated plot to be tied together. This sacred right of asylum too was greatly diminished by the Reformation of Henry VIII. It is as if Shakespeare lost no opportunity to drop some reminder, a memory image, of the not so far away time when England must indeed have been old and merry. The double twin plot of *The Comedy of Errors* is Shakespeare's first attempt to expand the confusion of senses and actions aroused by the tricky appearances of twins who have lost track of each other in a wreck at sea. The thematic seeds of exile, of loss and rebirth, of self and other were sown.

A CONCEITED AND LAMENTABLE TRAGEDY

Warring parties and the irony of fate equally happen to be the frame and backcloth of *Romeo and Juliet,* the playwright's first attempt at a tragedy of youthful love crushed by an unexplained "ancient grudge." There, however, he structurally subsumes the social and political feuds to the overall paradox of the *coincidentia oppositorum* (the "coincidence of opposites" or the harmony between things opposed), consistently pitting the beauty and truth of the lovers' feelings against the meanness and rigidity of their environment. Thus, *Romeo and Juliet* is probably Shakespeare's first attempt at creating harmony and concord out of division and rivalry. As the play opens, we are made to understand that the inevitability of such enmity has almost become a comic game in Verona, which is periodically made bloody by violent skirmishes. The two patriarchs don't shy away from brandishing their swords in spite of their wives' disapproval. Words are bandied about for sheer malicious pleasure, witnessing to the superficiality of Verona's social world. Tidying and streamlining his source, Shakespeare has taken great care to build a very formal world, full of parallelisms and antitheses, in which the characters engage in rhetorical contests and battles of wit, bandying oxymora and paradoxes as easily as they draw their swords and daggers. The young generation is sophisticated enough to speak sonnets and love by the book. It is a city world reflecting the meaninglessness of words and manners in a society which has evidently lost its spiritual *raison de vivre*. Only the surface glitters. Against such a background, the beautiful love-at-first-sight of Romeo and Juliet is suddenly given a tangible reality. As Rosalie Colie puts it, "set against the artificiality and unreality of Romeo's self-made love for Rosaline; its conventionality is forgotten as it is unmetaphored by action."[32] The sonnet shared by both lovers is enacted before our eyes, its religious content turning them into pilgrims of faith, holy palmers. What it tells us is that words of love must find their true embodiment in reality. From this moment on, the rich poetry of Romeo and Juliet's language is no longer metaphorical or hyperbolic, it sounds true because it is true. It has the intransigence and absolute quality of faith, pitted against the worldly wisdom and fickleness of feelings of Verona's society.

Shakespeare manages such a revelation by literally twisting the official genres of drama, turning the comic conventions of plot, character and style to fit tragedy, whose subject matter is equally transformed from heroic saga to love story. He deliberately plays with the artificiality of conventions and language, setting the bawdiness of the opening scene and Romeo's affected Petrarchan codes against the truth of Christian love, polishing his play into a well-wrought poetic jewel. The shortening of the dramatic time makes love and death happen almost simultaneously, so that the play can almost be seen as the lovers' deliberate choice of death as the inevitable end of their love. For there is a congruence in their fated love and their willed submission to a passion which, right from the beginning, means death. When they meet in the balcony scene, Juliet is immediately concerned by the risks incurred by Romeo's transgressing Verona's social codes:

---

[32] Rosalie L. Colie, *Shakespeare's Living Art* (Princeton: Princeton University Press, 1974), 145.

How cam'st thou hither, tell me, and wherefore?
The orchard walls are high and hard to climb,
And the place death, considering who thou art,
If any of my kinsmen find thee here. (II i 105–8)

When Romeo replies with the metaphor of "love's light wings" (even though he had serious misgivings when he entered the Capulet's palace), she obstinately pursues: "If they do see thee, they will murder thee" (i 113). Death appears to be a real, concrete risk at the outset, both young people being fully apprised of the socio-political tensions of their city. The death penalty is upon their love, yet they choose to embark on this dangerous course of life, straight away opting for the sacredness of a religious marriage, "for better, for worse, till death do us part." This is the deliberate choice of a martyred Christian love. We are very far from the *Liebestod* of romantic myth, which is self-inflicted death for the desperate love of a deified other, far from a modern love story where the lovers would have met secretly by night without renouncing the freedom and selfishness of their celibacy. Romeo and Juliet's love, by comparison, becomes a metaphor of Christian love, of the faith and spirituality attached to it. There would be no tragedy if they were not secretly willfully religiously tied to each other, which of course dooms Romeo the minute he kills Juliet's kinsman, and threatens Juliet with perjury should she marry a second time while her husband is alive. It is their zeal and purity that illuminate the play and push them to extreme action, Romeo in his effort to maintain peace, Juliet in her desire "to live an unstained wife" (IV i 88) to her love. And it is also their faith and innocence that prevent them from running away together. They want to do things well and both trust Friar Lawrence completely.

Close to Shakespeare's surroundings, it may have alluded to a few couples separated by religion or social conventions, sometimes exiled, as recusant Roger Line[33] was from his wife Anne, whom he never saw again. She would remain faithful to him, becoming a martyr to their religion. Shakespeare was clearly not writing a play about the romantic or post-Freudian death wish; he was writing about Catholic marriage and the true meaning of faith. Like Lucrece, Juliet interprets literally the meaning of marriage and is determined to be faithful. For this, she is ready to embark on a fearful death-like experience, feigning death as a way to resist and overcome death. Esthetically, the play offers us an extraordinary *danse macabre*, a very Baroque visualization of its horror and fascination, of its *jouissance* too, in a most mannerist representation. After Friar Lawrence has delineated for

---

[33] Martin Dodwell, *Anne Line, Shakespeare's Tragic Muse* (Leicestershire: Book Guild Publishing, 2013).

her the effects of his potion,[34] Juliet, not without some misgivings, tries to strengthen her resolution "to live an unstained wife to my sweet love," (IV i 88) by painting in her mind the frightful scene of her waking among dead bodies in the Capulet's tomb,

> —what with loathsome smells,
> And shrieks like mandrakes torn out of the earth,
> That living mortals, hearing them, run mad—
> O, if I wake, shall I not be distraught,
> Environèd with all these hideous fears,
> And madly play with my forefathers' joints,
> And pluck the mangled Tybalt from his shroud,
> And, in this rage, with some great kinsman's bone
> As with a club dash out my desp'rate brains? (IV iii 45–53)

Of all his plays, this is probably the one in which Shakespeare applies most feelingly the method of intense visualization of Saint Ignatius's *Spiritual Exercises*, first conjuring up for his audience a mental image of death before producing the interior of a tomb on stage. Saint Ignatius's *Exercises* appear to be a manner of staging a series of mysteries, of creating within oneself a kind of solitary theater where the plays of one's soul and mind will be performed. Ignatius's representations are by no means mere pictures, they have depth and all the measurements of architecture. They are not restricted to sight alone, they use all the senses, so that in a meditation on hell, you have "to hear, the wailing, the screaming, cries and blasphemies," you have "to smell the smoke, the brimstone, the corruption, and rottenness." You have "to taste bitter things, as tears, sadness" and "with the sense of touch to feel how the flames surround and burn souls."[35] It is naturally tempting to think that Shakespeare himself must have been a particularly imaginative student. Whether it be in the tracking of human sins and foibles or in the painting of love and death, he was excellent. And whoever convinced him that such a method could create great drama surely deserves our blessings. A little later, the attempt by Richard II to recreate the world he misses in his mind also owes a lot to the *Exercises*. Incarnation was not merely a word for Ignatius, it was the flesh and blood of faith. Shakespeare changed many details from his source, but indulged in the ghastly descriptions, which he refined to the effect that both Juliet and Romeo seem to be as fascinated by death as they are by love.

That the text of the play should hide some discreet references to Edmund Campion becomes all of a sudden very plausible. The nurse's

---

34 See further down, *Shakespeare's Healers*.
35 Saint Ignatius, *The Spiritual Exercises*, trans. Anthony Mottola (Garden City, NY: Image Books, 2014), 59.

rambling memories of Juliet as a toddler not only point to Saint Ignatius de Loyola's feast day, Juliet's birthday on July 31, but repeatedly insists on her memories of July, eleven years before, when she weaned the little girl "sitting in the sun under the dove-house wall" as the "earthquake" struck, which was the year 1580 when Campion and Persons set foot in England. The dove-house also recalls the fated "pidgeon house"[36] which initiated the search at Lyford Grange, where Campion was arrested on Monday July 17, 1581.[37]

When he created *Romeo and Juliet*, Shakespeare was obviously still divided between his admiration for such forms of "suicidal resistance,"[38] which corresponded to his inner conviction, and his sense of absolute waste. He loved life too much to tolerate its complete annihilation, even though it might be in a Bosch-like phantasmagoria. The humanist streak in him was stronger than the sense of martyrdom. He would later come back to a *Romeo and Juliet* type of relationship in *Cymbeline*, but his purpose would be life and pardon. Meanwhile, this youthful "conceited" tragedy esthetically represented a great step forward in Shakespeare's work. For the first time he experimented with the "Baroque oxymoron" linguistically, structurally, as well as philosophically. He managed to integrate and harmonize the whole into a play whose luminous darkness remains awe-inspiring to this day. ♣

[36] Kilroy, quoting Elyot, *A Very True Report*, in *Edmund Campion, A Scholarly Life*, 232.
[37] Asquith, *Shadowplay*, 75–76.
[38] Ibid., 75.

3. Circumscribing Evil

*E*LIZABETHAN ENGLAND WAS A COUNTRY WHOSE INHAB-
itants had to wear masks for fear of being denounced and accused of
treason. Seeming was of the essence. How could they be certain that their
friends would not inform against them? Anyone could become a spy for
a substantial reward; your own household servants could witness against
you. Such was the "traitor" George Eliot, who procured Campion's arrest,
after having been employed by the Ropers (Sir Thomas Roper, grandson
of Thomas More) and by the Brownes (Viscount Montague), who had
discharged him for insolence.[1] Who could trust any in this world of lies?
Circumscribing evil would be Shakespeare's ceaseless task, which he very
early linked to his own artistic explorations. Whether it came through his
research on comedy, or through his love of words and what they meant for
a man of faith is difficult to tell, but King Henry VI was perhaps the first
to point to this link between his own destiny and the stage. Facing Richard
of Gloucester in the tower, he is the first to call him Roscius (a reference
to skillful acting),[2] thus laying the ground for the demonic character of
Richard III. And who better than Thomas More linked together the stage
and political life, and first saw evil in Richard's protean linguistic ability?

THOMAS MORE AND SHAKESPEARE: PERSPECTIVES ON RICHARD III

The portrait of Richard III, which posterity inherited from More, is
particularly interesting, not only because it is very probably founded on
contemporary oral testimonies, but also because it is remarkable for its
keen observation and subtle irony, none of which was lost upon Shakespeare.[3] True, the *History* he writes, which bears on the government of the

---

[1] Walsingham had given "Elyot royal authority to seek out all those plotting against
the Queen [...] The 'smylinge' Elyot must have been sufficiently plausible to work
his way through three major Catholic houses. The combination of impudence, social
resentment and raw cunning, allowed him to denounce many Catholic families"
(Kilroy, *Edmund Campion*, 224).

[2] "What scene of death hath Roscius now to act?" (3 *Henry VI*, V vi 10).

[3] Shakespearean critics generally overlook More's *History* (the 1513 version being
officially the best one), later included in Edward Hall's *Chronicles* (1548), and recopied
by Raphael Holinshed in 1578. However, these Chronicles written for the glory of the
Tudor government spread the idea that More's portrait of Richard III, immortalized by
Shakespeare's play, was gross Tudor propaganda for the benefit of Henry VII against
York, his unlucky predecessor, which is unlikely. Thomas More harboured strong
resentment against Henry VII for the unjust way he sought revenge against John More,
for a speech made in Parliament by his son Thomas, 26, against new taxation. John

city and the role of the prince, partakes of a long tradition going back to Plato's *Republic* and Aristotle's *Politics*. The Renaissance saw the awakening of the humanists' interest in the education of princes. 1513 was marked by Machiavelli's *The Prince* and 1516 by Erasmus's treatise on *The Education of a Christian Prince* dedicated to young Charles V (the future head of the Holy Roman Empire). Meanwhile a first edition of Castiglione's *Cortegiano* was circulating among authoritative circles in Rome and More's *Utopia* answered Erasmus's *In Praise of Folly*.

Shakespeare does not comment, he stages, but the character of Richard III he creates strangely resembles the one described by More. Thanks to structured parallelisms and mirror effects, the author simply enlarges the locus of monarchy to the more fundamental opposition of being and seeming already suggested by More.

More begins with a sensitive portrait of the dead king Edward IV, painting the ideal image of a peace which was about to be reversed. Without ambiguity, he situates the tragedy in the monstrous deformation of nature which, in Richard, knows neither blood ties nor human pity. The violation of the royal children's rights, their imprisonment, followed by their murder, are presented like the paradigms of chaos, which More ascribes without hesitation to Richard's character. His style, however, is completely dispassionate, it has the precision and the subtlety of the lawyer's, scrupulously contemplating several options when they exist, refraining from asserting anything unless he can consciously do it. A master in the art of irony, the author of *Utopia* skillfully handles litotes and understatements, providing Shakespeare with richly paradoxical material which Shakespeare masterfully uses.

> Hee was close and secrete, a deepe dissimuler, lowlye of counteynaunce, arrogant of heart, outwardly coumpinable (friendly) where he inwardly hated, not letting to kisse whome hee thought to kyll.[4]

These lines conclude the description of a great dissembler and a practiced actor little graced by his physical appearance, of whom it is said ("it is for trouth reported") that he was born the wrong side up, the feet first, and his mother the Duchess "had so muche a doe in travaile, that shee coulde not bee delivered of hym uncutte,"[5] a bad omen for the reversal of values of many events during his reign. It was only natural that he should

---

More was locked in the Tower until he paid a fine of £100. Richard Marius vouches for More's hatred of Henry VII, who is said to have been a mean and avaricious character (see Marius, *Thomas More*, 50–52). His purpose in writing *The History of Richard III* seems to have been more to stage the accession of a tyrant to the throne and reveal his iniquity, than to glorify his successor.

[4] *The Complete Works of St. Thomas More*, ed. Richard S. Sylvester (New Haven: Yale University Press, 1963), 2:8.

[5] Ibid., 7.

become a Judas, the supreme traitor whose poisoned kiss was as much as a death sentence.

It is precisely in this gap between appearance and reality that truth is swallowed. If the question had merely been to describe a jealous monster, Richard III would not be the fascinating character that we know. Rather than a monster, the man is an arch actor, a skilled dissimulator, who cheats, perverts, and fascinates by his ability to pretend one thing and do another. This man bewitches Shakespeare, who from the very first line plants him there in front of the audience, brazenly telling them why he has decided to become a villain. His first monologue is a remarkable rhetorical exercise, multiplying antitheses and contrasts, first to define the spirit of the time — which after burying the weapons of war, enjoys "sportive tricks" and lascivious music — then to demonstrate logically the opposition of his ego to courtly delights. This is a disproportioned, narcissistic ego, emphasized by the recurring "I" which seems in conflict even with the forces of history. How could he, "deformed, unfinished," take pleasure in "an amorous looking-glass"? How could he enjoy beauty and love? If appearances are to be believed, could he be anything but a villain, since, nature having cheated him, he could not please, unless he made his appearance lie? Thus the most skillful liar is the most honest, and who is to blame if Edward, a righteous man, is deceived, or if the audience, informed as they are, cannot believe their eyes? Has not Thomas More already suggested the case when he so perfectly compares Richard's imposture to a play?

> And menne must sommetime for the manner sake not bee a knowen what they knowe.... And in a stage play all the people know right wel, that he that playeth the sowdayne (sultan) is percase a sowter (shoemaker). Yet if one should can so lyttle good, to shewe out of seasonne what acquaintance he hath with him, and calle him by his owne name whyle he standeth in his magestie, one of his tormentors might hap to breake his head, and worthy for marring of the play. And so they said that these matters bee Kynges games, as it were stage playes, and for the more part plaied upon scafoldes. In which pore men be but the lokers on. And they that wise be, wil medle no farther. For they that sometyme step up and playe with them, when they cannot play their partes, they disorder the play and do themself no good. (80–81)

The comparison of monarchy to a theater, with the grisly wordplay on *scafoldes,* is a recurring feature in Thomas More's writing,[6] who shares it with

---

[6] More uses the comparison again in the first book of *Utopia*: "So go through with the drama in hand as best you can, and don't spoil it all simply because you happen

Erasmus and which possibly contains all of Shakespeare's play "in a nutshell."

All those who happen to be in Richard's way or who happen to cross his destiny, all but one lose their lives. Therefore, it would seem that the Richard that Shakespeare stages is Thomas More's own, the subtle actor who brilliantly deceives everyone. Like Pope Alexander VI,[7] he is a character whose "deceptions always worked, because he knew this side of human nature so well."

A true disciple of Machiavelli, he knows that having a prince's virtues is not necessary, it is enough, and much less harmful, "to seem" to have them. In this respect, Richard is the perfect prince who is a master at deceiving crowds, a talent he shares with his accomplice Buckingham:

> *Richard*: Come, cousin, canst thou quake and change thy colour,
> Murder thy breath in middle of a word?
> And then again begin, and stop again,
> As if thou wert distraught and mad with terror?
>
> *Buckingham*: Tut, I can counterfeit the deep tragedian,
> Speak, and look back, and pry on every side,
> Tremble and start at wagging of a straw,
> Intending deep suspicion. Ghastly looks
> Are at my service like enforced smiles,
> And both are ready in their offices
> At any time to grace my stratagems. (III v 1–11)

More and Shakespeare however go further than Machiavelli in as much as the people are never taken in, not any more than Richard's main victims. All of them are perfectly conscious of the hypocrisy and of the danger they are in should they attempt to reveal it. With ironical details More knows how to uncover the treachery underlying Hastings's condemnation: "that everi child might wel perceive, that it was prepared before" (54). Further on, he shares a schoolmaster's doubts as to the length of the accusation, considering the swiftness of the execution, to which a shopkeeper replies: "It was written by prophecy" (54). Shakespeare puts the same derisive question in the scrivener's mouth: "Who is so gross / That cannot see this palpable device? / Yet who so bold but says he sees it not?" (III vi 10–12), yet he concludes that it is surely less risky not to say anything.

Thus Richard's strength is partly ascribed to the cowardice of all those who, though conscious of the deceit, yet prefer closing their eyes. Prudence, cowardice, fascination — which is the cause? How can one account for

---

to think another would be better." Thomas More, *Utopia, A Norton Critical Edition* (New York: W. W. Norton and Company, 2011), 26.

[7] Niccolò Machiavelli, *The Prince*, trans. Tim Parks (New York: Penguin Random House, 2009), chap. XVIII, 70.

Richard's power over men, unless it is the pleasure they feel at fooling themselves? As a Christian and a lawyer, More considers the Londoners with kindness and even suggests through his comparison that they have little more power than children. His comments are not without irony when we think of the fate that awaited him! Shakespeare knows and understands the people but does not credit them with more greatness than their leaders. As Girard demonstrates, it is perhaps because violence is mimetic and Richard's adversaries as corrupted as he is that his villainy sometimes appears heroic in Shakespeare's play. The theatrical metaphor points to the heart of a matter that seems to have haunted More as much as Shakespeare: the power of illusion, man's will to lie to himself and to prefer the fables of his imagination to the evidence of reality. Reality is so improbable that the spectators welcome the scene with fascination and incredulity, as they would at any performance of some mannerist wonder. In the theater as in life, it is here appropriate not to doubt appearances and to pretend not to know what one knows.

Like More, Shakespeare takes great care to have Richard and Buckingham masters in the art of rhetoric, and like him, he questions a devalued rhetoric which has only the appearance of reason and has lost contact with truth: "a tale," as More appropriately names it. In the past, Plato had attacked Sophists, those speech experts who could with equal success demonstrate a truth or a lie. He was already making the distinction in his *Republic* (382a) between the true lie, which cheats on the nature of things and a lie in words, a mere fiction devoid of ontological consequence. More would take up again this subtle distinction in his "Letter to Peter Giles" prefacing his *Utopia*: "potius mendacium dicam, quam mentiar"—I had rather make a mistake or say something wrong, than say a lie—drawing the reader's attention on the theological difference implied, a difference which is of course at the heart of Shakespeare's own experience of the theater. This allows us to understand Richard's true nature, an imposture committed by nature itself through him. He is lie personified, deceiving and perverting the soul about the very nature of truth. Nothing seems to hinder his march forward and one even gets the impression that each of the characters is eager to be deceived. The truth is that true lie works thanks to men's fascination for this other lie, which is called fiction.

In his conquest of power, Richard goes far beyond Machiavelli's Prince, who is advised to be feared rather than loved, the two hardly agreeing together (Ch. xvii, 65). Richard manages to take up this new challenge since he succeeds in conquering the love of the victim who hates him, the woman whose husband and father-in-law he has murdered, as she is weeping over the latter's corpse. Shakespeare seems to have been the only instigator of this scene, which is certainly the most staggering seduction scene in all literature and which, better than any other, gives dramatic form to the evil reversal engendered by Richard. In this confrontation with Lady Anne, his grotesque presence displays the antagonistic forces of life and is all the more fascinating as it scoffs at the human mind. Better than any other scene, it stages the mechanisms that allow Richard to seduce and win the game for so long — until he provokes destiny and the corpses of two children become his stumbling block.

The little princes' death, which is historically presented as the symbol of Richard's monstrosity, is only reported in its supreme horror through the unexpected reaction of the murderers, two hardened knaves, "bloody dogs," who, like Titus, break into tears like children. This evil climax is also what brings about a reversal in Richard's rising trajectory and heralds the "catastrophe," since it draws away from him his most loyal confidants. This unnatural monster, who has denied all human ties, is also rejected by his own mother and from now on will never know peace. Words have turned into empty shells with no reality: too many dead, too much blood reveal the lie in the most perfect rhetoric and tear the veil of illusion. Words are now left to the mothers' curses.

If truth and the coherence of the world depend on the cohesion between signifying and the signified, Richard is a "corrupter of words" infinitely more malicious than Feste, because he does not simply play with words but empties them of their meaning and then transcribes this emptiness into acts. He turns them inside out like gloves and availing himself of nature's betrayal, gives them the logical sense demanded by his original monstrosity. Order becomes disorder. Love in a monster is turned to hatred. Harmony becomes chaos. The most solemn oath is nothing but wind. With his poisoned words, he flatters Lady Anne's vanity, at the same time accusing her beauty of causing his wrongdoing. Their stichomythic exchange seems to proceed from the reflections of a warped mirror in which all proposition is reflected as its contrary: the soft-spoken monster is begging for the charity of the wrathful angel as he avows his murder, which he metamorphoses into a blessing. The spirit has turned into the letter and murder becomes redemptory. Edward was "gentle, mild and virtuous," says Lady Anne. "The better for the King of Heaven that hath him," replies Richard (I ii 104–5). Richard sent him to heaven, let him be thanked for it. Meaning is annihilated, words a mere subterfuge, a ploy hardly concealing the bestial ambition underneath. Richard plays with Lady Anne as wanton boys play with flies,[8] he will kill her for his sport when he feels like it.

---

[8] See *King Lear*, IV i 37: "As flies to wanton boys are we to th' gods; / They kill us for their sport."

What this scene reveals, beside Richard's cynicism and his unbeliev-able protean mastery as a player who revels in his own expert stunning loquaciousness, is the total inability of words to prove anything. Man has actually no means of feeling assured of the truth of a sentence unless he has faith in some concord between the word and the idea it expresses on the one hand and in the orator's honesty on the other hand. Doubt either of these and all men are turned liars:

> *Anne*: I would I knew thy heart.
> *Richard*: 'Tis figur'd in my tongue.
> *Anne*: I fear me both are false.
> *Richard*: Then never was man true. (I ii 196–99)

Richard is here expressing a truth which the play makes evident, whereas Lady Anne interprets it as a syllogism to be refuted. The trouble, as *King Lear* will later demonstrate, is that faith and loyalty are very fragile weapons against the lies and cynicism of those whose only god is their own ambition. The fools of God lose their life for believing in an unprovable truth, the murderous fools end up losing theirs because the fate they trigger always falls back on their heads.

Thomas More interrupts *The History of King Richard III* precisely when Cardinal Morton, like a perfect disciple of Machiavelli, tells Buckingham that he should now think of himself and of the kingdom. Thus, Richard's example is likely to undo him at last. Was it More's consciousness of his-tory's constant repetition, the fear, as he was writing, of seeing the same ambitions and the same lies flourish again? More did not finish; he did not even acknowledge, as did Shakespeare, Henry Tudor's victory. The continuation of this meditation on the prince's role has to be looked for in the *Utopia*, this land where the prince is elected and where a complex system of assemblies is established in order to control the least tyrannical attempt. By his death, Thomas More seems to prove that the London-ers were right in avoiding confrontation and seeming not to know what they knew all too well. The very small part allotted by Shakespeare to Richmond and the parallelism of his appearances with those of Richard seem to turn his victory into the simple reverse of Richard's fall, until the next turn of the wheel of fortune, possibly bringing with it a new cycle of mimetic violence.

Whether it be by More or by Shakespeare, it is truly difficult to believe in a glorification of the Tudor state, least of all if, as Clare Asquith suggests, Shakespeare's Richard III was secretly meant to be a portrait of Robert Cecil.

Who today would deny that the fundamental lie represented by a Hit-ler is still and always possible thanks to men's love of fiction, their deep, perhaps innate tendency to cling to their illusions rather than face the terrifying reality which is theirs? Who today would deny the pertinence of a reflection on the lies of political speeches and the people's almost total indifference when they hear the false promises of their rulers? From the psychopathic killer to the monstrous ruler, there has ever been a fascination exerted by evil and the grotesque, which certainly justified Saint Bernard's warning against such marvelous "deformed beauty and beautiful deformity"[9] likely to corrupt the soul. And if Richard's visage was truly the sensitive and intelligent face his portrait at the National Portrait Gallery shows, wasn't he even more monstrous?

The outrageous level of deceit on the part of Richard III somehow led Shakespeare backward to the origins of such devastation. He needed to understand what had brought the collapse of monarchy and of the sacred body of the King. In his second series of history plays, he went back in time as far as the fourteenth century in order to question the deposition of King Richard II. A breach had been opened that would not heal and which, in Shakespeare's work, takes the appearance of two different styles, two aesthetic visions. The influence of Italian mannerism is felt throughout the slow dissolution of Richard II. What had been adumbrated in Titus here becomes manifest. The heroic virtues have been challenged by the severed link between the letter and the spirit. In a world now devoid of sacredness, and therefore lacking the legitimacy of God's protection, man is left alone to play the tormented fool on the stage of the Globe.

MIRROR AND TEARS: IS *RICHARD II* MEDIEVAL OR BAROQUE?

Contrary to most of Shakespeare's heroes who are introduced indirectly, Richard II opens the play as a King in full majesty, prepared to render justice as God's anointed. We are about to witness the body politic of the king at work in a scene whose staging has the formal and static quality of a Medieval triptych. Accordingly, there is a tone of calm assurance in Richard's speech which is meant to impress the audience as well as the attendants. The balanced repetition of the sentences to the plaintiff and to the accused reveal the artificial quality of the ritual, which is meant to increase the distance and the sacredness of the king's word, as much as

---

[9] Saint Bernard de Clairvaux, *Apologia ad Guillelmum*, 29, ed. Leclercq III, 106. "Ceterum in claustris, coram legentibus fratribus, quid facit illa ridicula monstruositas, mira quaedam deformis formositas ac formosa deformitas. Quid ibi immundae simiae? Quid feri leones? Quid monstruosi centauri? quid semihomines? quid maculosae tigrides ? quid milites pugnantes? quid venatores tubicinantes?" "In monasteries, before the eyes of the reading brothers, what does this ridiculous monstrosity, this strange deformed beauty, or beautiful deformity do? What are these unclean monkeys doing here, these wild lions, these ugly centaurs, these half-human half-beasts, these spotted tigers, these fighting warriors, these hunters who blow their horns?" (my translation).

they put forward the rivalry of the two dukes who, through their rebellion, are about to debunk the spiritual quality of the king's body politic.[10]

The solid and immutable architecture of this lengthy scene settles the historical context as well as it provides the audience with a visualized rendering of the superiority and solitariness of the seat of majesty. Richard, from on high, insists on his prerogative and lawful authority:

> Wrath-kindled gentlemen, *be ruled by me:* ...
> *This we prescribe* ...
> Forget, forgive, conclude and be agreed. (I i 152–56)[11]

As befits a Christian king, Richard first exerts his role as mediator in order to avoid the shedding of blood. Failing to convince the two dukes, he tries more vehemently to impose his authority:

> Norfolk, throw down, *we bid;* there is no boot. (I i 164)
> Rage *must* be withstood.
> Give me his gage. *Lions make leopards tame.* (173–74)

To which Mowbray replies, "Yes, but not change his spots" (175). And suddenly a breach seems to be opening in the sacred authority of the king. Mowbray's "yes, but" questions his power to cleanse his stained honor, to redeem him, so to speak, even though his metaphor may sound paradoxical, since he likens the essence of his life to the leopard's appearance. Whether honor is Mowbray's outer garment or the essence of his life, is actually intimately linked to the interpretation of the scene as a mere show rather than a sacred judgment. The whole problem is one of words, and the meaning that is attached to them. If the king's divine body is recognized, his judgment is sacred. So are the quality of an oath and the definition of honor. If, however, the king is a mere word without a divine essence, then all the aristocratic code of honor becomes meaningless, a mere mask to

---

[10] For the legal fiction of the king's two bodies, we refer students to the excellent book of Ernst H. Kantorowicz, *The King's Two Bodies, A Study in Mediaeval Political Theology* (Princeton: Princeton University Press, 1957). This concept was a distinctive feature of Elizabethan political thought, but its ancestry goes back to the beginning of the twelfth century. According to Plowden's *Reports*, written under Queen Elizabeth: "the King has in him two Bodies, *viz.,* a Body natural, and a Body politic. His Body natural (if it be considered in itself) is a Body mortal, subject to all Infirmities that come by Nature or Accident, to the Imbecility of Infancy or Old Age, and to the like Defects that Happen to the natural Bodies of other People. But his Body politic is a Body that cannot be seen or handled, consisting of Policy and Government, and constituted for the Direction of the People, and the Management of the public weal, and this Body is utterly void of Infancy, and Old Age, and other natural Defects and Imbecillities, which the Body natural is subject to, and for this Cause, what the King does in his Body politic, cannot be invalidated or frustrated by any Disability in his natural Body"; *Commentaries or Reports* (London, 1816), 212a, quoted by Kantorowicz, 7.
[11] The italics are mine.

cover up ambition or greed. Richard will all too soon discover it for himself, whereas Shakespeare, with Falstaff in mind, may already be undermining a conception of honor that was all too often the pretext for war and violence. According to Pierre Francastel, this duality and the questioning it entails is at the root of the opposition between classicism and Baroque, which he understands as two essential aspects of a single, living reality.[12]

IN THAT SENSE, RICHARD'S TRAGEDY IS UNDOUBTEDLY A Renaissance play, gradually unveiling the different levels of consciousness and the perplexity of the Renaissance man. However, I would suggest that the character of the king himself and much of the play's esthetics belong to the Baroque trend encouraged by the Counter-Reformation. And it was certainly not haphazardly! Performed as it was, at a time of violent rebellions in a kingdom divided by religious allegiances—Richard's reign being in many ways a mirror to that of Elizabeth—it was an extraordinarily bold attempt which adroitly makes a point while diffusing meaning and responsibilities over the previous two hundred years of English history.

When Richard once again insists on his authority—"We were not born to sue, but to command" (I i 196)—we may have the feeling that he overdoes it; if the king protests too much, it is perhaps because he knows the fragility of his position in the midst of the lies and ungodliness of men. As body politic, the king is indeed "incapable of *doing* wrong," he is immortal and perfect, and his decisions "cannot be invalidated or frustrated by any Disability in his natural Body."[13] But is this legal and religious assertion lived by the man as such?

The very performance of Richard in this first scene seems to imply the reverse. The ritual and protocol are precisely meant to impart to the man the sacredness of a character he does not have naturally. Moreover, Richard is perfectly aware of the lies and flattery beneath the protests and sacred oaths of both rivals. Since they both make lofty speeches, while pretending to accuse the other of felony, one perforce is a liar. Unable to solve their quarrel and unwilling to condemn, Richard finally chooses to exile both of them, asking them to respect their oath to him and be honest in banishment. While he performs his part without flaw, we wonder whether Richard really believes that his authority comes from God and cannot be gainsaid. By punishing both men, he necessarily wrongs the innocent one, and by asking them to respect the terms of their banishment, he requires

---

[12] "La dualité de l'esprit et de la matière a entraîné la découverte et l'exploration du réel, ainsi qu'une vision dialectique de la nature, une conception du signe et du symbole qui ne ramène plus fatalement à l'unique mais à des niveaux différents de la conscience et de la vie." Pierre Francastel, "Le Baroque et nous," *Baroque, L'Arc* (1990), 11–19.

[13] Edmund Plowden, quoted by Kantorowicz, 7.

from them a loyalty he knows at least one of them does not have, in spite of their oaths.

Immediately, the rivals go on protesting and each of them voices some criticism of the King's decision. Mowbray foresees coming troubles on account of Bolingbroke whereas the latter reflects dryly on "the breath of kings" capable of cutting four years away from his punishment for the sake of his father's old age. But, as John of Gaunt himself points out, he cannot lengthen a life by a minute; "breath" refers to the living man who speaks under the guise of the king, as much as to the bubble-like quality of his decisions: mere words that can lose their air in an instant, precisely because they are voiced by one whose breath is soon smothered by death. [14]

It seems evident that a number of paradoxes underlie the theory of the two bodies of the king and that his supreme authority is liable to multiple variations of perspectives. In Act II, scene ii, the process of anamorphosis [15] is described incidentally by Bushy who tries to comfort the queen by explaining that what she sees indirectly through the lens of her tears, when "rightly gazed upon," actually is nothing but confusion, a blurring of forms and colors that mean nothing:

> Each substance of a grief hath twenty shadows
> Which shows like grief itself but is not so.
> For sorrow's eye, glazed with blinding tears,
> Divides one thing entire to many objects —
> Like perspectives, which, rightly gazed upon,
> Show nothing but confusion; eyed awry,
> Distinguish form. So your sweet majesty,
> Looking awry upon your lord's departure,
> Find shapes of grief more than himself to wail,
> Which, looked on as it is, is nought but shadows
> Of what it is not. (II ii 14–24)

---

[14] Speaking of death, Richard later uses the same word "breath" to illustrate the brittleness of the King's station.

[15] Anamorphosis, a particular technique which requires the viewer of a painting to play his part in its contemplation by reproducing the image by himself, was a developing practice by the fifteenth century. Derived from the discovery of the laws of perspective, this art was an extreme example of the subjective character of vision mechanisms. The beholder is first deceived by a scarcely recognizable image which can only be "known" from a very precise point dictated by the formal construction of the tableau. He must then straighten the distorted perspective. In order to correct the image, he has to view it through a peephole in the frame of the painting, or at a very precise angle which permits the image to emerge out of the apparent chaos. Convex mirrors, cylinders or cones can also be used to "anamorphotize" the original image. The sixteenth century saw the further development of this art which painters like Hans Holbein the Younger skillfully used to include hidden allegory in their painting. This illusionistic art was used by Shakespeare on many levels.

Bushy adroitly reverses the process for her sake, pretending that the distortion and confusion that appear to the eye when you behold the painting represent reality, albeit confused, and therefore are nothing to weep about. But the shapes that clearly appear when looked upon indirectly through warped mirrors, water, or tears, by the sophisticated use of the laws of perspective, are "things imaginary." Of course, the sequel will prove that the Queen's grief did give her the right angle from which to view their fate. For such is the nature of anamorphoses —"by indirections find directions out" (*Hamlet*, II i 65).[16]

The passage is precious, not only because it testifies to Shakespeare's knowledge of the applications of artificial perspectives to painting and to the theater—where he would actually use them in the architecture of many of his plays, and probably in their staging too—but also because we may safely assume that it gives us a subtle indication of the way we should look at Richard's tragedy as a whole.

His appearance, until Act III, is that of a king whose decisions cannot be gainsaid. As in Holbein's *The Ambassadors*, the first act shows an official portrait of the majesty of the king, keeping the lurking threat of death at bay, hiding the fragility of the man, which only the indirect perspective of tears will uncover for him.[17] The king is strong, even arrogant at times, filled with the certainty of his power. It is clear that as long as he finds support and obedience among the nobility, Richard has no fear and no real awareness of his double person. He does not see, or does not want to see, the confusing signs of disorder which fracture the seat of majesty. For the audience, however, those signs, while still unclear, are ominous, owing perhaps to the slanting perspective they have on the king. Gaunt's death and his malediction look very much like the deformed skull which figures prominently in *The Ambassadors*. Dying Gaunt, whose very name is a *danse macabre*, goes so far as to tell Richard that he, the King, is already dead, but full of youthful pride and cold arrogance, the latter does not hear.

---

[16] Shakespeare could have seen William Scrots's *Portrait of Edward VI*, 1546, just as he probably knew Holbein's *The Ambassadors*, painted in England in 1533. After Leonardo da Vinci paved the way for the development of anamorphic constructions, they became very fashionable attractions all over Europe until the eighteenth century. See Jurgis Baltrusaitis, *Anamorphoses* (Paris: Flammarion, 1996) and Fred Leeman, *Hidden Images from the Renaissance to the Present* (New York: Harry N. Abrams, 1976).

[17] In *The Ambassadors*, the elongated form in the lower foreground pierces the painterly illusion and makes it relative. When one looks at it from the top right corner, it is seen to be a skull, discreetly and ironically reminding both friends of the transitory nature of human endeavors. Hans Holbein the Younger. *The Ambassadors*. 1533. Oil on panel, 81½ inches by × 82½ inches. National Gallery, London. Under the influence of Holbein, William Scrots also used perspective means convincingly in his portrait of Edward VI, which must be viewed through a hollow in the frame in order to get the correct angle. William Scrots, *Portrait of Edward VI*. 1546. Oil on panel, 16¾ inches by 63 inches. National Portrait Gallery, London.

During the ensuing eclipse of the sun-king, which lasts a whole act, the audience is given a few tips as to some aspects of the man Richard, his "defects and imbecilities," his futility and prodigality which, according to Northumberland, raise people against him. The king is both man and god (although no saint), a complex figure with a double allegiance to God and to humanity. Shakespeare clearly points to the paradoxes of a concept that can only work as a fiction: no matter how spiritual the king, his exactions are materially consequential and are always felt in the body by his people.

WHEN THE KING REAPPEARS IN ACT III, SCENE II, HE IS STILL and more than ever the "deputy elected by the Lord" (III ii 57) and "God's substitute, / His deputy anointed in His sight" (I ii 37–38) and this glorious image of kingship, that Richard himself compares to the rising sun, whose light unveils hidden murders and treasons, is yet comforted by the presence in the heavens of a celestial host of angels. The doctrine of angels has always existed in the Catholic Church, but they certainly invaded ceilings, pillars, and paintings during the Counter-Reformation. The image aroused by Richard is that of a *trompe-l'oeil*, a Baroque ceiling made alive by the agitation of the celestial warriors swirling around their Sun King. In the world-as-theater mood of the seventeenth century such vistas could be created through poetic metaphors as well as through manipulation of volumes and lines in architecture. The audience would have no problem identifying with it, even though, in Elizabeth's reign, angels, which would have evoked either older times, or distinctly the Counter-Reformation, had been white-washed in most parish churches. The image is thus closer to the high altar at Saint Andrew of the Quirinal, whose golden rays diffuse the light of God. The passionate outburst of the king, "weeping, smiling" as he sets foot on his island again, reveals a sensitivity hardly in keeping with a medieval posture of Christian humility. Such ostentation, such expressiveness in Richard's feelings, unveils a passion (*affetti*) in the king which is far from the martial representations of the Renaissance proper and seems to herald the most sensuous postures of Baroque art.

AS BAD TIDINGS TRICKLE IN, RICHARD BEGINS TO CRUMBLE. It is as if the Godly majesty of the king was slowly fading, becoming but a shadow, a name. He who once had the power to call forth spiders and toads and lurking adders for support has dissolved in a dream and only his name remains for him to play with, like the Old Gaunt, or like Feste, "the corrupter of words." Behind the figure of the king appears the Fool, the conscience he should never have forgotten. And the king with the evocation of "three Judases" (III ii 132) ever more resembles the figure of Christ, the

God-Man. Waking up, Richard is now face to face with his mortal nature. Yet it is still a tale, somewhat unreal to him: "For God's sake let us sit upon the ground / And tell sad stories of the death of kings" (III ii 155–56). Richard manages to look at his part from a distance, becoming a spectator as well as the storyteller of his own tragedy. He visualizes himself as one among many kings whose stories probably filled the evenings of his childhood. By projecting himself in the past, as it were, he can cheat time from his own future, stopping its course for the time of a tale. Yet in Scrope's words, Bolingbroke's rage is a flood of tears that dissolves the world. Metamorphosis—dissolution—has overcome Richard's stasis. "One day too late" and time is forever running away, getting out of hand like Phaeton's horses.

Grief, which pervades the play from Act I, scene ii, with the Duchess of Gloucester's mourning, has the purifying virtue of baptism, cleansing man's soul and providing a clear perspective on the mortal reality of his human nature. Tears act repeatedly like convex mirrors restoring to the eye the true essence of the shapeless image of anamorphic reality. Having lost the body politic of the king, Richard begins a metamorphosis toward the human. Eclipsed by Bolingbroke, he manages however to hold the stage for three acts, surpassing himself in the staging of his fall. We should not forget that Richard, who exemplifies the Elizabethan theory of the two bodies of the king, is also (via his Creator) a contemporary of John Dowland, who incidentally was a Catholic.[18]

He obviously relishes his tears and distress, stages them, plays with them, visualizing his own demise with the lucidity of one following the exercises of Saint Ignatius de Loyola:[19]

> For within the hollow crown
> That rounds the mortal temples of a king
> Keeps Death his court; and there the antic sits,
> Scoffing at his state and grinning at his pomp,
> Allowing him a breath, a little scene,
> To monarchize, be feared, and kill with looks,
> Infusing him with self and vain conceit,

---

[18] John Dowland, 1563–1626. One of the most sensitive and passionate musicians of his time, remembered by the phrase "Semper Dowland, semper dolens" inscribed over one of his pavans.

[19] "It should be noted at this point that when the meditation or contemplation is on a visible object ... the image will consist of seeing with the mind's eye the physical place where the object that we wish to contemplate is present." The First Exercise, 54. Richard not only seems to visualize in his mind's eye the hidden kingship of death, he actually follows in his demise the three degrees of humility advised by Ignatius: first lowering and humiliating himself, then, divesting himself of his kingly attributes and not caring any more for the things of this world, and last striving to imitate Christ. The Spiritual Exercises of St Ignatius, The Three Modes of Humility, 81–82.

> As if this flesh which walls about our life
> Were brass impregnable; and humoured thus,
> Comes at the last and with a little pin
> Bores through his castle wall; and farewell king. (III ii 160–70)

And since death plays the fool with him, his first attempt is to visualize death in all its attributes, graves, worms, epitaphs, and the patch of barren earth that covers our bones. The setting is there, precise, for a story of the deaths of kings, all puppets to the King of Kings, death, the only victor. This meditation on the end of all things convinces Richard of his body's mortality. How can one reconcile the power of a king with the weak body of man?

Bishop Carlisle, who represents Christian faith, immediately reproaches Richard for his self-indulgence and despair, which he attributes to fear. But bad news only inflates the melancholy of Richard, who swiftly indulges in despair again, addressing Aumerle:

> Beshrew thee, cousin, which didst lead me forth
> Of that *sweet way* I was in to despair! (III ii 204–5)[20]

Just as Mowbray and Bolingbroke relished the prospect of a duel as of a feast, Richard seems to wallow into despair with a kind of "jouissance." There is a pleasure in suffering, which overcomes the pain and heralds the *pena extatica* of Theresa of Avila, so spectacularly rendered by Bernini.[21] The fear of death translated itself for her into deep anguish doubled by the infinite bliss of meeting the Lord, total alienation making for absolute desire. Theresa said, "I die of not dying." Richard is of course less explicit but seems to enjoy the very idea of dissolving. The thunder stroke, which, according to Theresa, should initiate the blissful meeting of Richard's soul with God, however, ironically turns out to be the sign of his meeting with Bolingbroke, who expects to see a fiery King encountering the watery element:

> Methinks King Richard and myself should meet
> With no less terror than the elements
> Of fire and water when their thund'ring shock
> At meeting tears the cloudy cheeks of heaven. (III iii 53–56)

It is likely that such a clash may quite dampen the fire of the king. What sounds like an Ovidian metaphor introduces a king who has not yet

---

[20] Italics are mine.
[21] Bernini, *The Transverberation of Saint Theresa*, Santa Maria Della Vittoria, Rome (1647–1652). Naturally Shakespeare did not know Bernini's art, but he could have read Teresa's own description of her ecstasy.

relinquished his majestic appearance. The *fair show* may be just so indeed, but Old York will regret it for the elevation it brought to them all. Already he has chided Northumberland for his lack of respect and protocol. His wisdom suspects that what animates Bolingbroke's party is not merely the love of England but a kind of envy, a mimetic desire that is likely to unleash endless war. Once the divinity of the king is put in doubt, once the mortal body of the man is divided from the spiritual and politic body of government, there is no way for the king ever to recover his former power.

For one more brief moment, Richard manages to play the Royal part that is his and forces Northumberland to bend his knee before him, reminding him of the punishment risked by those who profane the sacredness of the king. Like a *Leitmotiv*, the two indissoluble bodies of the king are constantly reasserted throughout the play by York, by Bishop Carlisle, and by the king himself. Altogether, they are like an ancient chorus announcing the bad omen of the coming perjury.

Though still of kingly nature, Richard is now aware of the discrepancy between his present station and the lofty words he utters. He has lost the earthly power of a king, but consciously plays at being the king: "To look so poorly, and to speak so fair?" (III iii 128). Richard is aware of his duality, of the chasm between his words and his lack of power. His pride makes him wish he were as great as his grief, and like a character who has lost his part but has no desire to leave the stage, Richard now asks for a new role to play. "What must the king do now?" (III iii 145), he asks his friend and cousin Aumerle, giving away, one by one, the attributes of majesty: his name, his jewels, his palaces and robes, his insignia and scepter, and his kingdom. Having divested himself of what made him a king to the eyes of his people, he is now naked like a beggar, now but a mortal man whose only certainty in this world is death. Richard, once more, visualizes in the most realistic and sensitive fashion his last destination, "a little, little grave, an obscure grave." But he cannot help overdoing it, his imagination working at representing his impending fate in the most realistic, frightening way possible, as if to conjure away his anxiety. Once more there is some relish in this excess, as if his imagination was intent on finding the most striking posture, to translate his absolute alienation:

> Or I'll be buried in the King's highway,
> Some way of common trade where subjects' feet
> May hourly trample on their sovereign's head. (III iii 154–56)

It would be difficult not to acknowledge the esthetics of the Counter-Reformation in this imaginative exploration of reality. The deep abjection imagined by Richard, the visualization of his people treading on his head, not only turn him gradually into a figure of Christ,[22] but also help tame the fears aroused by the prospect of death. The lower Richard sinks, the greater he becomes.

The esthetic representation of this metamorphic process obeys the fluidity of tears which, like water, are called upon over and over to shape the landscape and men's feelings. As Theresa insisted, the imaginative representation of God was originally molded by your feelings: if you were happy, you would contemplate the majesty of resurrected Christ, but if grief and suffering weighed you down, you would imagine Christ carrying his cross, until your imagination reflected upon you. Whereas Bolingbroke saw himself as raining his waters on the earth, perhaps drowning Richard's sun, Richard now fancies that he and Aumerle might dig their own graves with their tears.

> Aumerle, thou weep'st, my tender-hearted cousin.
> We'll make foul weather with despised tears.
> Our sighs and they shall lodge the summer corn,
> And make a dearth in this revolting land.
> Or shall we play the wantons with our woes,
> And make some pretty match with shedding tears;
> As thus to drop them still upon one place   .
> Till they have fretted us a pair of graves
> Within the earth, and therein laid? "There lies
> Two kinsmen digged their graves with weeping eyes?" (III iii 159–68)

The whole play seems to be permeated with the ever-changing shimmer of tears, whose constantly moving, refracted perspectives dissolve each vision into a new one. In this melting of himself, it is as if Richard were hastily conjuring up new shapes, holding on to a last remnant of sensitive life, before all of him dissolves into nothing. This almost feminine posture, "like Niobe, all tears,"[23] is later caught up by Hamlet whose desire to dissolve is almost as great as Richard's.[24]

Anticipating his demise, the king now calls Bolingbroke king, and plays with the image of Phaeton for himself, thereby throwing a new light on himself, the exalted king returning to his beloved kingdom. Since, like Phaeton, he has failed to reach the sun, he may as well mock himself, turning this time into "a frantic man," (III iii 185) whose every word lashes at the fake production of Bolingbroke. If the truth comes out of the Fool's mouth, Richard's lucidity about the force that now puts him

---

[22] Richard was thirty-three when he died, murdered in his prison.
[23] *Hamlet*, I ii 149.
[24] "O, that this too, too sullied flesh would melt, / Thaw, and resolve itself into a dew" (*Hamlet*, I ii 129–30). Antony too loses his substance and dissolves himself into "this insubstantial pageant" which is the world (see *Antony and Cleopatra*, IV xv 1–22).

down reveals how far this new Machiavellian political age has come from Christian spirituality:

> They well deserve to have
> That know the strong'st and surest way to get! (III iii 198–99)

> For do we must what force will have us do. (III iii 205)

The Fool is not fooled by the hypocritical pretense of the victors. Since Bolingbroke is now potentially the king, King Richard has to eclipse himself, even though he does so unwillingly.

The following interlude, the garden scene, seems to be a variation on the main themes. It offers a metaphor of the State, which suggests that Richard's liberalism as a ruler was the source of disorder. Authority means discipline with little sensitivity. The queen, who learns the news of Richard's deposition from the gardener — another breach of hierarchy — only adds more tears to the already flooding grief. And the gardener is left with the care of turning those tears into flowers — "Here did she fall a tear. Here in this place / I'll set a bank of rue, sour herb-of-grace" (III iv 104–5) — while pointing to the redeeming power of tears. Meanwhile, Act IV begins like Act I, with a joust of accusations, protests, oaths to honor, and insults between the nobles who support Bolingbroke and those who support Richard. Mimetic violence has increased, and chaos threatens to invade the kingdom. We are made to remember Gaunt's prophecy to Richard, and the various maledictions described by York and Carlisle, who is about to make a last, moving attempt at depicting the dire consequences of usurping the throne and judging the king like an ordinary criminal. The irony, of course, is certainly found in the repetition of the first act of the play, giving to Bolingbroke little more authority over his quarrelling lords than Richard had over him and Mowbray. Even before he actually receives the name of Henry IV, Henry's power seems contested. Having destroyed the sacredness of his position, Bolingbroke will soon find out that he is but another mortal body wearing the attributes of the king. The crown has now become the wheel of fortune.

Meanwhile, Richard is brought to judgment, which he immediately likens to Christ's betrayal and trial. The preceding impersonation of Christ's fool had already prepared us for this metamorphosis — the only kingship now available to him involves re-enacting the Passion of the Man-God. As he is slipping down the ladder of wretchedness, Richard has an increasingly clear awareness of the breach effected by his enemies in order to get rid of him. He has been betrayed by all, totally abandoned, now compelled to resign his power and crown for the sake of Bolingbroke. The symbolic image he now creates for the crown underscores the duality of the king, but also the sundering of royalty, since there are now two kings in England, one by birth and one by power.

Richard's intellectual hesitation, or rather foolish corruption of words in Feste's manner obviously annoys the hasty Bolingbroke who would like things settled quickly. But since Richard has already given away the attributes of majesty in a kind of preview with Aumerle, he now improves upon the performance by fragmenting his own body, each bodily part of the king resigning its attributes: head, hand, heart, tears, tongue, breath, refracted by the prismatic color of tears, till Richard is nothing. However, even when he calls to mind once more the earthy pit awaiting him, he opposes it to Bolingbroke sitting on Richard's throne — not once relinquishing his divine right! His wish, "God save King Henry, unkinged Richard says," has the same wry oxymoronic irony. Even "unkinged," the lawful Christian king by birth is still the king. When asked to unravel his follies, Richard however refuses, he ceases to play the Fool to impersonate Christ in his Passion:

> Though some of you, with Pilate, wash your hands,
> Showing an outward pity, yet you Pilates
> Have here delivered me to my sour cross,
> And water cannot wash away your sin. (IV i 239–42)

Richard's tears provide him with a convenient perspective, which, as they blur his sight, enables him to see clearly the truth behind appearances. Among the traitors, he places himself, who willingly surrendered his role: "For I have given here my soul's consent / T'undeck the pompous body of a king" (IV i 249–50). Pompous, of course, is the other side of sacred. Once the sacred rite has been debunked, the majesty of the king becomes pomp, mere show. Richard has lost his name, therefore his identity, and now wishes for an even more complete dissolution:

> O that I were a mockery king of snow,
> Standing before the sun of Bolingbroke
> To melt myself away in water-drops! (IV i 260–62)

A sudden coquettish whim now makes Richard require a mirror. After those multiple transformations of himself, he needs to check on his appearance, his face, to find out who he is. The mirror is of course a necessary element in this exercise on anamorphoses since it stands at their heart; as Baltrusaitis puts it: "The same laws of reflection which, on a flat, isolated surface produce similar figures, in multiple, curved mirrors variously disposed, breed deceptive and fairy visions."[25] The mirror first offered

---

[25] Jurgis Baltrusaitis, *Le Miroir*, (Paris: le Seuil-Elmayan, 1978), 12. My translation. "Les mêmes lois de réflexion qui, sur une surface plane, isolée, donnent des figures

the most perfect representation of life, but being also a double of the original, it soon became a kind of shadow, a mysterious reflection of the soul of the beholder. All sorts of mysterious beliefs attached themselves to this reflection, which should not be broken for fear of encountering the same fate as one's double. With the Christian distrust of appearances, the mirror soon acquired the paradoxical meaning of being both the truth and a lie, a simulacrum of a reality all within. Thus, the beauty of Richard belies his grief, which is all within. The reflection of his face does not yet reflect the sorrow he feels. There too, he anticipates Hamlet's reactions.[26] He throws the mirror down to destroy the now lying face, giving Boling-broke the opportunity to point out the theatrical posture, revealing how the disgraced king plays with a show of sorrow and the reflection of his face: "The shadow of your sorrow hath destroyed / The shadow of your face" (IV i 292–93). If the flat surface of the mirror is lying, what Richard breaks cannot be his face, but a mere shadow. There is more truth in the curved surface of tears than in the mirror.

Should we perhaps hear in those words a critical appreciation of the extravagant way the king turned his fall into a one-man show, eclipsing Bolingbroke even as the latter was usurping Richard's seat? Is Bolingbroke weary of Richard's act, or does the man of action in him pity the self-indulgence of the poet in Richard? Shakespeare seems to pit two styles face to face, two tendencies clashing in the sixteenth century, the Machia-vellian leader versus the humanist poet-prince, but also the soberness and severity of the Reformation facing the display of feelings and emotions of the Counter-Reformation.

Richard's tragedy becomes a successful staging of shapes and feelings that cannot help but move the audience to tears. Shakespeare has perfectly understood the power of images in Counter-Reformation art. Through the visual representation of his tortured mind, Richard reaches the spiritual intensity that was denied him as a king. He now, more than ever, succeeds in being both the spiritual and the physical body: the spirit of Christ impersonated in the body of fallen man. Somehow, Bolingbroke senses Richard's power and is suddenly in a hurry to be officially crowned, while the first plot against him is being devised in the dark.

After divesting himself of his kingly attributes, Richard now parts from his queen in moving lines that recall *Romeo and Juliet*. There is a delicacy and sophistication in their words that is in keeping with the mannerism of

---

similaires, font naître dans des miroirs multipliés et incurvés différemment disposés, des visions fallacieuses et féériques."
[26] "Seems, Madam? Nay, it is. I know not 'seem'. . . . I have that within which passeth show—These but the trappings and the suits of woe." *Hamlet*, I ii 76–86.

Richard. Ironically, the quick portrait given by Bolingbroke of the future Henry V makes him an "unthrifty," "effeminate boy" who would rather fight for whores than for his honor. Meanwhile, York entreats the new king not to pity his own son, Aumerle, who plotted a conspiracy against him with his companions. The themes of blood and pity revive the matter of Act I in a new perspective on the politic body of the king and the personal feelings of the man beneath. It seems that the paradox is complete and even though York preaches against a forgiveness that will breed more sins, Henry IV, like Richard, cannot resist the prayer of a kinsman. The Duchess of York's part, generally turned into a comic passage in the play, is a variation on the theme of human feelings, which in a patriarchal world all too often sound "effeminate." Not only does the Duchess remind her husband that, "Hadst thou groaned for him / As I have done, thou wouldest be more pitiful" (V ii 102–3), but she later insists on the visibility and truth of such feelings:

> His eyes do drop no tears, his prayers are in jest,
> His words come from his mouth, ours from our breast; (V iii 100–101)

The externalization of grief and the flows of tears that contend with blood along Richard's walk to Golgotha cannot be separated from the excessive, visual representations of Christ's Passion in contemporary iconography.[27] Richard is no longer the hieratic king found in *The Wilton Diptych* or on his official portrait,[28] but a Baroque character who "pray[s] with heart and soul, and all beside" (V iii 103).

The Counter-Reformation displays a dramatization of faith that animates paintings and sculptures, a culture of ex-stasis which bends and tortures bodies. Richard's last speech works out a complete atomization of the body, pursuing the drama of life inside his own brain. "Yet, I'll hammer it out"—which reflects in miniature the great stage of this world. His thoughts, one by one, impersonate all the humors of his world, turning from saintliness to pride, from self-content to despair. He is both king and beggar, but never at peace until he finds complete dissolution. In the theater of his own mind, Richard is everyman, sighing for rest in this valley of tears.

The broken harmony is concomitant with the wish for dissolution. Time is broken for Richard literally and figuratively. But as he cannot call back time, he can only marvel at the man who gives him music, a sign of love "and love to Richard / Is a strange brooch in this all-hating world" (V v 65–66) — unless he has already reached a spiritual stage that allows him to hear the music of the spheres. The ruin of the man is now complete.

---

[27] See the tormented and expressionist style of Christ on the Cross in the Issenheim altarpiece, by Mathias Grünewald, 1512–1515. Musée Unterlinken de Colmar (France).
[28] c. 1390, Westminster Abbey.

The movement is upward at the very moment when Richard reaches the bottom. His next step is sudden death liberating his aspiring soul:

> Mount, mount, my soul; thy seat is up on high,
> Whilst my gross flesh sinks downward, here to die. (V v 111–12)

The spiraling downward of Richard's body is complemented by the rising flight of his soul upward, the consummation to be wished by more than one Baroque character who reaches ecstasy at the moment of death. Ecstasy and true spiritual kingship: for Richard is undoubtedly the king at the end of the play and it is not certain whether a voyage to the Holy Land could wash the blood from Henry's hands. In the *Henry IV* plays, the voyage, ominously, never happens.

Shakespeare's poetry and Richard's wavering thoughts, his qualms and changing postures have given movement to the static and majestic quality of *The Wilton Diptych*. Its many angels are made to fight while the tortured soul of Richard is undergoing its own passion in a performance that is closer to seventeenth century esthetics than to medieval art, closer also perhaps to the Bard's soul, which may explain why *Richard II* stands out as the most poetical as well as the most tragic of his history plays.

RICHARD II CERTAINLY MARKS A TURNING POINT IN SHAKE-speare's production. Here history has truly grown into tragedy of a new kind and Richard's character, by assenting to his own dissolution, by playing with it, eventually forming one body with it, foreshadows Hamlet. In the fluidity of his postures and contortions, he is closer to a Baroque character than to a medieval one. Through history, Shakespeare addressed contemporary politics, risking his life, no less. But like most great artists, he was also heralding as well as paving the way for major artistic changes. The faults, or rifts, perceived in his characters and translated into the structure and the style of his plays, perfectly mirrored the malaise of the time. In England, as in most continental kingdoms, the feeling, intensified by the approaching turn of the century, was one of pessimism and melancholy at the dislocation of past orders and beliefs, but it was also an ideal breeding ground for new esthetics and renewed religious convictions.

At the heart of *Richard II*, at the turning point in the king's fortune (III, iv), the gardeners appear as active commentators on current affairs. The head gardener's metaphorical language brings together state and garden care in a powerful lesson of government to his assistants. The gardeners are not only well-informed, but their wisdom comments on the events that would not have happened, had the king himself been a better gardener. The common sense of the people, which the author never fails to put forward, their understanding of "hierarchical yet collaborative working relationship,"[29] gives a touch of realism to the Edenic vision of England earlier given by John of Gaunt. If Richard's England ever was a paradise, nature alone did not provide the key to good government. Men have to use their intelligence and even sometimes the violence of good trimming, in order to preserve the harmony of the whole. The wisdom of the medieval garden is used as a political metaphor, which Shakespeare will later expand through the use of the pastoral genre, which he would explore throughout his work. He had to find a way toward hope. He must have realized that the only way to avoid a rigid confrontation between opponents, be it political, religious, or private, was the ability to work change. Now the process of metamorphosis could be viewed from different perspectives. Shakespeare inherited literary metamorphoses from Ovid, but his own religious convictions also made it a personal, moral renewal, which could blend nicely with Ovid's ideas, as evidenced by the numerous moralized versions of his work made during the Middle Ages.

Yesterday, just as today, the governing elite might lack the pinch of common sense that allowed any foundation to endure. It may be the reason why they needed some country holiday, a healthy retreat among the natural inhabitants of the earth. Turning to the polymorphous genre of the pastoral, Shakespeare would never cease to bend it to his own purpose. The pastoral is conveniently tied to exile, whose rigor it helps assuage, providing the esthetic form that allows the playwright to link tragedy and comedy, history and fiction. No doubt the Stratford man found in it not only convenient esthetic codes as well as sweet memories of his youthful years, but also a whole philosophy of life that was absent from London and the court. The multiple shapes of the pastoral genre also suited his protean discourse and allowed him, like melancholy Jaques, to rail on the faults and evils of this world under the various guises of foolish clowns or bitter exiles without attracting inordinate attention to himself. Who would have taken seriously those "tales, tempests, and such-like drolleries,"[30] which even Ben Jonson mocked? ♣

[29] Introduction to *Richard II* by Anthony B. Dawson and Paul Yachnin, the Oxford University Press edition of 2011, 31.
[30] Ben Jonson, *Bartholomew Fair*, "The Induction," vol. 2 (London: Dent, 1963).

4. The Mannerism of the Pastoral

*D*EVISED BY THEOCRITUS IN HIS *IDYLLS* AS LONG AGO as the first half of the third century B.C. (c. 270), the pastoral world he describes evokes the Sicilian landscapes of his youth with gossiping herdsmen, straying sheep whom the men have to head back home, or a goatherd quarrelling with a shepherd. However, Theocritus, who then lived at the court of Ptolemy Philadelphus in Alexandria, was neither a shepherd, nor a naïve poet. The pastoral world he created was not, strictly speaking, a genre but its atmosphere and themes could permeate all genres. Like the Golden Age, it was perhaps "less of an adventure than a state of mind,"[1] a literary projection created by city dwellers. Some two hundred years later, Virgil transferred the pastoral vision into the Latin imagination, erasing the few realistic details which Theocritus had kept and replacing them by delicacy of feelings intermingled with landscape in "a sweet and lovely nostalgia."[2] Whereas Theocritus took a paradoxical subject from the world of myth and treated it naturally, Virgil took a subject from real life and treated it romantically, playing down the humor, stressing the pathos and the poetry. He even encouraged the reader to identify him, the poet, with the shepherd. He did more: in his *Fourth Eclogue* he managed to transport the idealistic golden age of the pastoral world from the past to the future, predicting a glorious lifetime for his friend's new baby boy, the consul Ollio's son. Virgil would remain the poet who somehow apprehended the Nativity some forty years beforehand:

> The salute to the babe whose birth would usher in a new order, coming in conjunction with the reappearance of Virgo, would lead pious Christians to identify the goddess Astraea with the Virgin Mary and to read the poem retrospectively as a prefiguration of the nativity of Christ forty years afterward.[3]

In the Middle Ages, the Christian symbolism of the pastor and his flock would conveniently fuse with the Classical vision depicting nature as some kind of Golden Age in which shepherds passed away the time in sweet amorous exchange. Following Virgil, Ovid's *Metamorphoses* turned

---

[1] Harry Levin, *The Myth of the Golden Age in the Renaissance* (Oxford: Oxford University Press, 1969), 26.
[2] Thomas McFarland, *Shakespeare's Pastoral Comedy* (Chapel Hill, NC: The University of North Carolina Press, 1972).
[3] Levin, *The Golden Age*, 18.

Hesiod's myth[4] into a literary *topos* and provided a mine of themes and stories used and imitated by poets and artists up to the twentieth century. In Shakespeare's time, Ovid's *Metamorphoses* was used in schools as a textbook, which all students had mastered by age seven. In the fourteenth century, the tales had duly been reinterpreted by moralists in parallel with the biblical tales. The golden age prefigured the earthly paradise, where man lived free from hunger, thirst, heat, cold, evil, pain, or distraction:

> En ce deliteuz paradis
> Vivoit lors hom a son devis
> Sans faim, sans soif, sans chaut, sans froit,
> Sans mal, sans paine et sans destroit.[5]

Renaissance poets added a Christian sense of purity and renewal to the pastoral, emphasizing the virtuous feelings of peace and concord recovered far from the brawls of city and court life. Nature became the *locus amoenus* where a sense of the initial golden age, which had been lost over the generations, could be recaptured. In nature, the city dwellers found comfort and the inner balance which enabled them to become better beings. Going back to nature was, and still is, the best way to touch base with one's true self.

The pastoral vision disseminated itself into the culture of Europe, in Italy first, in France, and in Spain. When it reached England in the sixteenth century, it had been "powerfully enhanced" as McFarland puts it, by Petrarch, Sannazaro (*Arcadia*, 1504), Ronsard (*Odes*, 1550), Montemayor (*Diana Enamorada*, 1559) published in Valladolid in 1561, Tasso (*Aminta*, 1573) and Guarini (*Il Pastor Fido*, 1585). In England, the subject was exploited by Spenser in his *Shepheardes Calender*, 1579, as well as in *The Faerie Queene*, Book IV, 1576, by Philip Sidney in his *Arcadia*, 1590, and a few other writers such as Greene and Lyly. Shakespeare, therefore, was able to draw on a singularly powerful and vital tradition. As previously noted, the success of the pastoral can be explained partly because its motifs were bound to no specific genre or poetic form. One found side

---

[4] Hesiod was apparently the first to call the first generation of men a golden race, followed by a silver then brazen race, then the race of heroes created by Zeus, which disappeared from subsequent versions of the tale. The last generation (fifth or fourth) is the Iron race, forsaken by their gods, the worst of them all, in which we still are.

[5] Cornelis de Boer, ed., *Ovide moralisé: Poème du Commencement du XIVme siècle* (Amsterdam: J. Müller, 1915), I 809–12. "In this delicious paradise/ lived men in good company/ Without hunger, thirst, heat or cold/ Without evil, pain or destruction" (my translation). Note the similarity between the last two lines expressing negatively the happy frugality of the first men and Shakespeare's concluding line in Jaques' famous speech "The Seven Ages of Man": "Sans teeth, sans eyes, sans taste, sans everything" (*As You Like It*, II vii 166).

by side the pastoral romance (Longus's *Daphnis and Chloe* and Sidney's *Arcadia*), the pastoral eclogue with Virgil and Spenser, the pastoral lyric (England's *Helicon*, a collection of some of the best English poetry) and from Tasso and Guarini, a new tradition of pastoral drama. What they all had in common was a preoccupation with shepherds and shepherdesses in what looked like a highly benign and highly artificial environment. As Drayton explained it to his readers, "Pastorals, as they are a species of Poesie, signifie fained Dialogues, or rather speeches in Verse, fathered upon Heardsmen."[6] Drayton logically concludes that the subject as well as the language of such poetry ought to be "poor, silly, and of the coursest Woofe in appearance. Nevertheless, the most High, and most Noble Matters of the World may be shadowed in them." Shakespeare would explore the subject in all its potentialities, playing with delight on the many literary, esthetic and philosophical shades of the pastoral. The very flexibility of the pastoral genre suited his own hidden spiritual agenda.

For a long time, however, Shakespeare is not even mentioned in critical works on the pastoral. The tradition, like Italian mannerist esthetics at large, reached England rather late and the European influence could be critically summed up by those lines of W. W. Greg: "The pastoral tradition . . . finally reached this country in three main streams, the eclogue borrowed by Spenser from Marot, the romance suggested to Sidney by Montemayor, and the drama imitated by Daniel from Tasso and Guarini."[7] Daniel was a University poet well-known at court, who wrote an adaptation of Guarini's *Pastor Fido* for the queen in 1606, but Shakespeare, who was two years younger, had included the pastoral in his plays long before that time. Contrary to Daniel, he never tried to produce a pastoral per se, a genre which, like the masque, was probably too sophisticated for the public theaters, but always adapted his borrowings to his own purpose. He was nine when *Aminta* was first performed at Ferrara. Tasso's play was translated in French as early as 1584, and by 1591, it was known and imitated in all Europe, printed in Italian in London by John Wolfe,[8] and translated into English by Abraham Fraunce.[9] Italy and the pastoral both became fashionable in a country suddenly eager to make up for lost time,

---

[6] Michael Drayton, *Pastorals, Contayning Eclogues With the Man in the Moone*, in Michael Drayton, *Poems* (Menston, England: The Scolar Press Limited, 1969).

[7] W. W. Greg, *Pastoral Poetry and Pastoral Drama* (London: Bullen, 1906), 215, quoted by Richard Cody, *The Landscape of the Mind* (Oxford: Clarendon, 1969), 81.

[8] Christine Sukic, "Samuel Daniel et les traductions anglaises du *Pastor Fido* au XVIIe siècle en Angleterre: du voyage d'Italie à la naturalization," *Epistémè* 4 (Autumn, 2003), 19–20. *Aminta Favola Boschereccia* "del divinissimo Sig. Torquato Tasso" is published in London after Guarini's *Pastor Fido*, on June 19, 1591.

[9] Abraham Fraunce, *Amyntas Pastorall, The First Part of The Countess of Pembrokes Yvychurch* (1591).

and it would have been very strange if Shakespeare, who was attracted by Italy for so many reasons and always displays a wonderful mastery of literary genres and conventions as well as of the subtleties of language, had been ignorant of a text which all of Europe knew by heart. He must have known about Guarini's *Pastor Fido* as well as Tasso's *Aminta*. The artificiality of the Italian pastoral comedy provided many devices that could be successfully used on stage. One is surprised to discover a great community of spirit between some of Shakespeare's comedies and Tasso's *Aminta,* not only concerning their use of neo-Platonism, but also in the playful irony that permeates their language and the dramatic liveliness of their characters. Numerous avatars may be found in *Love's Labour's Lost,* in *As You Like It,* or in *The Merchant of Venice* and the pastoral is of course at the heart of the last plays.

THE TWO GENTLEMEN OF VERONA

In *The Two Gentlemen of Verona,* the character of Proteus, which works in a minor key along the same principles as Richard III, seems to find its origins in Tasso's *Aminta,*[10] which also provided Shakespeare with some of the best tricks of mannerist drama. It probably was Shakespeare's first dramatic attempt in the genre, which may account for some of the plot's inconsistencies. All the ingredients of his later plays can be found in it, yet they somehow fail to provide the harmonious whole that we are led to expect. There are the contrasted pairs of leading characters, who may be too radically contrary for the sake of harmony, the comic parody of the second roles, with the very memorable duet of devoted Lance and his dog Crab (always a very hilarious moment on stage), there is the opposition of town versus country—but ill-defined and only taking shape at the very end of the play—we have the girl disguised as a boy in order to chase her lover, and the pastoral with its exiles in the forest, but its potentialities are hardly explored and the timing is wrong. It comes too late in the play, which appears at moments to be torn between different goals, as if the author was trying to fit contrary designs together. A close reading reveals an unquestionable textual density in a play whose structure lacks perfection. There are early sketches of *Romeo and Juliet* , of *A Midsummer Night's Dream,* and of *As You Like It* in the plot, while a cast of clownish secondary characters offers a somewhat farcical parody of the main plot. *The Two Gentlemen of Verona* looks somewhat like a laboratory experiment, whose varied themes and situations are explored more deeply in subsequent plays. This does not prevent it from being a joyful experience on stage, however.

---

[10] Torquato Tasso, *Aminta,* edited and translated by Charles Jernigan and Irene Marchegiani Jones (New York: Italica Press, 2000).

Much depends on the agility and wit of the actor playing Proteus, and of the willingness of the dog to undertake Crab's role!

The comedy stages a double faithlessness, one engendered by sexual desire, which Proteus's wit tries with subtle casuistry to justify rationally, the other by an extravagant, absolute conception of friendship or love, which leads Valentine, as well as Julia (and Lance) to self-sacrifice. As in religion, there are the deft ratiocinators and the innocent, devoted believers. The god of comedy being Love, it fits well enough the pastoral tradition, which, as in Tasso's *Aminta*, celebrates love while mocking the romantic illusions it provokes. But it sometimes looks as if Shakespeare had another faith in mind and the play does not quite manage to harmonize the allegorical and the literal level. We meet our gentlemen as Valentine is about to leave Verona "to see the wonders of the world abroad" (I i 6), chiding his friend Proteus for staying at home, being a fool in love, wearing out his "youth with shapeless idleness" (I i 8). Young men ought to discover the world, seeking an education and preferment — a word with religious connotation — as later advised by Proteus's uncle "in the cloister" (I iii 2). The journey, for both of them, is meant to lead them away from the vagaries of love, for "experience is by industry achieved" (I iii 22). Both gentlemen are being generously offered what Orlando craves for at the beginning of *As You Like It*.[11] Yet, the choice of Milan, which is to be reached by embarking on a ship, a surprising journey from Verona unless you knew about Italian waterways, carried an ominous subtext in England. It may explain why Proteus is apprehensive and promises to pray for his friend, who is about to *embark* on a perilous voyage: "I will be thy beadsman, Valentine" (I i 18), adding "Upon some book I love I'll pray for thee" (I i 20), which is a rather ambiguous reply to Valentine's question. Double entendre equally qualifies the subject of the book: "That's a deep story of a deeper love" (I i 23–24). Is Proteus being witty or deliberately provocative?[12] Upon which book does one normally pray? After all, Campion and his missionaries, who loved Christ, had, not so long ago, arrived from Milan to Warwickshire, handing out Cardinal Carlo Boromeo's "Spiritual Testament," one copy of which was found to bear the name of Shakespeare's own father.

---

[11] A journey Shakespeare himself had probably long been dreaming about.

[12] "After Henry VIII's break with Rome, the rosary became suspect as a 'Popish practice.' In particular, the prayers of the rosary were problematic because they invoke a saint, the Virgin Mary. Article 22 of the Thirty-Nine Articles (which define the Church of England) describes the invocation of saints as 'a fond thing vainly invented and grounded upon no warranty of Scripture, but rather repugnant to the word of God. . . .' In 1571, the year after Queen Elizabeth was formally excommunicated by the Pope, a statute was passed declaring rosaries and other Roman Catholic accessories illegal." Chris Laning, Paternosters, Sunday, Dec 12, 2004 (https://paternosters.blogspot.com/2004/12/).

Does it mean that these characters are English young men about to go on a continental journey to Italy? If so, the fact that they all stop at the emperor's court, which was one of the routes to Milan and Rome for English exiles, is not so much indicative of carelessness, as it is of Shakespeare's deep preoccupations. For the emperor's court (repeated six times in the space of seventy lines) can only be that of Habsburg Rudolf II of Bohemia, King Philip's nephew, with its capital at Prague. Rudolf II was a great and influential patron of the arts as well as a religiously tolerant monarch, who certainly attracted Shakespeare's interest, since he would return to Bohemia as a *locus amoenus* in *The Winter's Tale*. Prague attracted many great minds at the time and Edmund Campion, who had spent there a few fruitful years teaching philosophy, had founded the School of Rhetoric at the Clementinum, the Jesuit Academy in Prague, in 1574. Rudolf, who was a rather self-centered, reserved monarch, preferring his occult studies and his books to the government of his land, may also have inspired Prospero's character in *The Tempest,* where he is Duke of Milan. That Rudolf did not actually rule over Milan, still in the hands of his grandfather Charles V Habsburg, was incidental. The least we can say is that Shakespeare insists heavily on the imperial destination of his gentlemen, a journey that had famously been made by such people as Philip Sidney and Arthur Throckmorton, "whose diary recorded the opportunities that drove so many Midlanders to seek a haven on the metaphorical coast of Bohemia."[13] Had Shakespeare, with the Bassano brothers, taken that route too, we wonder? On his religious uncle's advice, Proteus will accompany "Don Alfonso," a Spanish gentleman, on his way "to salute the Emperor," and is furnished "with commendation from great potentates" (II iv 77). Even if we allow for the lack of historical reality of a comic landscape, the names that crop up seem like the emerging layers of a mental palimpsest.

Was the dramatist distracted by too personal ideas when he conceived the play? Was he thinking of some of his friends who had embarked on the dangerous continental journey? Was he thinking of Anthony Munday, his colleague and a notorious mole, who travelled with a Catholic friend via Milan to Rome, where he stayed at the English College only to betray those he befriended? One thing is certain, Verona has been quite forgotten in the process.

---

[13] Richard Wilson, *Secret Shakespeare: Studies in theatre, religion and resistance* (Manchester: Manchester University Press, 2004), 74. "In 1577 Campion had written from Prague to Robert Arden, a Jesuit, later Canon of Toledo, operating in Warwickshire and possibly related to Shakespeare's mother, that his 'abundant harvest' of recruits should be told of the hospitality awaiting them if the storms of persecution swept them towards 'the pleasant and blessed shore' of Bohemia."

Hardly have our gentlemen reached their destination when it disappears in its turn, not to be mentioned again. "The Counter-Reformation wind that blows toward Bohemia remains unexploited."[14] Meanwhile, our young men dive into the woods of a very English pastoral, with Robin Hood presiding over the adventure. Valentine has been betrayed by his bosom friend, whom he had praised as a paragon of the age to the Duke,[15] who himself has fallen under Proteus's charm. Cynical Proteus, who was madly in love at the beginning of the play, does not hesitate to give Silvia's father notice of Valentine's plan to run away with her. He delineates his crafty plot to the audience in a long soliloquy full of the cheek and twisted syllogisms of a Richard III, betraying his own love for Julia, making an enemy of his best friend in order to appropriate the woman he desires, vowing to get rid of another pretender, Thurio, chosen by the Duke himself, and last but not least, lying to the Duke who favors him. This is certainly a volte-face in the shape of a contrapposto. Proteus suddenly appears to be the exact reverse of what he was, and the reversal may be a little too violent for comedy.

Tasso's dancing Proteus, who does not exist in Fraunce's translation, may naturally have inspired Shakespeare's creation of a youth, who swears his faith to Julia, whereas he falls in love with Silvia, whom he swears to obtain by force even though he will betray his best friend in the process. He is both the bashful lover who gives up his studies and the honors of the world for his mistress — "Thou, Julia, thou hast metamorphosed me" (I i 66) — and the satyr pursuing the object of his own desire.[16] In *Aminta*, the threat comes from the Satyr and it is interesting to note that after Cupid's prologue where, as the master of the revels, he prepares to wound with his arrow the cruel nymph for scorning Aminta, Proteus himself is introduced to point out his influence on the changing colors of love, just before the entrance of the Satyr. In Tasso's play, Proteus presides over the link between love and the wild force of desire — the mythic reconciliation of Bacchus and Apollo — whereas Satyr (the wild force of desire) is the only character whose humor is shifting and who, like Shakespeare's Proteus, goes from moaning and flowers to resentment and violence.[17] In

---

[14] Wilson, *Secret Shakespeare*, 75.

[15] Nothing indicates that Silvia's father, the Duke, is the same character as the Emperor, even though he tells of Proteus, whom Valentine has just praised: "He is as worthy for an empress' love / As meet to be an emperor's counsellor. / Well, sir, this gentleman is come to me" (II iv 74–75).

[16] The common name of the young preys may simply be due to the silvan origin of the Pastoral.

[17] One is tempted to think that *Aminta*'s Interlude was a source for Shakespeare, even if we have no evidence for it. Interludes, generally intervals devoted to music and dancing, were rarely ever published with the text of the play. They do not appear

The Two Gentlemen, as in *Aminta,* there is the same enraptured language in the presence of sacred love. Yet when Proteus decides to steal his friend's beloved, he forgets his principles and turns into a true satyr. His protean nature is also love's nature, as Julia describes him:

> Fie, fie; how wayward is this foolish love
> That like a testy babe will scratch the nurse
> And presently, all humbled, kiss the rod! (I ii 57–59)

Julia appears to be as fickle as her beloved and through them, it is capricious Cupid that Shakespeare seems to impersonate. However, because of the hints of the general background, Shakespeare's Proteus, who appears rather sinister in his "imperial" intervention, is the epitome of the changing lover, as well as that of the traitor. In Act II, scene vi, his character is closer to the informer Anthony Munday[18] than to a Shakespearian lover. Exiled Valentine finds refuge in the forest, where he makes friends with the outlaws who waylay him. They happen to need "a linguist" and ask him to be their general. The word "linguist" evidently corroborates the idea that the outlaws, all banished men "endowed with worthy qualities," (V iv 150–51) are foreigners in Italy.[19] Shakespeare is evidently writing his comedy on a palimpsest.

His forsaken mistress decides to follow him, pretending "holy confession" at Friar Patrick's cell, a trick also used by Juliet, but possibly here another muffled echo of Edmund Campion, who had chosen Friar Patrick as an alias at Lough Derg in Ireland, where Saint Patrick was said to have discovered the mouth of purgatory. She apparently skips confession,[20] which surely her purity and holiness made less urgent than escaping the spies she believes follow her. And truly, here they come — the Duke, her

---

in Fraunce or Wolfe. In many court divertimenti, they did not even have a thematic link with the plot. For the first time, it seems that the symbolism of the Interlude is integrated to the play. Jerniga and Marchegiani Jones have equally chosen to keep them as part of the whole. Shakespeare may have seen a representation of *Aminta* with its mythological interludes, which he seems to integrate within the body of his plays, as play-within-the-play, in *Love's Labour's Lost* and *A Midsummer Night's Dream,* where mythological characters are part of the casting. In *The Tempest,* it is a masque of goddesses which blesses Ferdinand and Miranda's love, while *The Winter's Tale* offers the more hieratic chorus of Chronos. There too it seems that Shakespeare innovates and plays on genre.

[18] Anthony Munday, *The English Roman Life* (1582), ed. Philip J. Ayres (Oxford: Clarendon Press, 1980).

[19] The reference to "a linguist," the earliest quotation for the word given in OED, is interesting as it reminds us of Mowbray's despair when he is sentenced to lifelong exile by the king: "The language I have learnt these forty years, / My native English, now I must forgo, / And now my tongue's use is to me no more / Than an unstrung viol or a harp" (*Richard II,* I iii 159–62).

[20] If we believe the words of Friar Lawrence, who will materialize in *Romeo and Juliet.*

own father, Proteus, and Thurio with Julia, who has decided to run after her lover, dressed as a pageboy.

Should we believe, with Richard Wilson, that the fact that the lovers never meet "at Friar Patrick's ominous cell" and their flight in the forest among outlaws, all "banished men" "endowed with worthy qualities" is one instance of Shakespeare's efforts to change "confession for performance and a clerical black for player's plumes, as he groped for a way out of his liaison with those real Jesuit outlaws who followed 'Friar Patrick' from Milan"?[21] Or should we rather see (literally "changeable") Proteus's betrayal of Julia for Silvia as symbolizing England's betrayal of the old faith in favor of the new, as does Clare Asquith? Both scholars may be bending the elements of the play a little too far out of shape. At Friar Patrick's cell, Silvia does meet Sir Eglamour, her self-appointed guardian angel, in order to pursue her Valentine to Mantua. They immediately run away "out at the postern by the abbey wall" (V i 9) because Silvia fears she is attended "by some spies." Eglamour comforts her: "Fear not. The forest is not three leagues off. / If we recover that, we are sure enough" (V i 11–12). Curiously, the dangerous ways she feared treading alone happen to be safer than the spies running after her. The story Shakespeare has in mind seems to dissolve into the pastoral design, where the wild animals and highwaymen are not those we expect. In Elizabethan England, spies and informers were more dangerous than petty robbers. Exile in the forest will bring rebirth eventually. Forgiveness and mercy will restore harmony and truth at the end of the play, even if it happens like a new theater turn. After all, the author was writing a comedy, whose end was to entertain and arouse wonder.

Silvia is at all times fair and pure, holy and wise; to Valentine she is "a heavenly saint," whereas Proteus calls her "celestial," she "excels each mortal thing"(IV ii 50) and Julia shows "but a swarthy Ethiope" (II vi 26) in comparison. She herself praises Silvia as virtuous, mild and beautiful. These details make it difficult to believe in an allegory of the old and new faith, Silvia's indulgence and generosity more certainly evoking the Virgin Mary. That she does admonish Proteus for his perjury and lack of faith does not make it any less significant of Shakespeare's deep meaning:

> Thou hast no faith left now, unless thou'dst two,
> And that's far worse than none. Better have none
> Than plural faith, which is too much by one,
> Thou counterfeit to thy true friend. (V iv 50–53)

A man could not swear allegiance to two masters without being perfidious. Proteus suddenly discovers that constancy offers as many benefits. Those

---

[21] Wilson, Secret Shakespeare, 79.

Shakespeare had in mind, however, may rather have been the queen's government and the way they forced each Catholic to "descend into perjury" in order to show allegiance to their queen.[22] The religious subtext that haunted him keeps cropping up at times in names, locations, and dates, as well as in themes that invariably reappear in his plays. Exile, for instance, remains a constant, which is gradually fused with the rustic ideal of the pastoral in order to further self-knowledge and rebirth. Accordingly, Valentine offers an early sketch of exiled Duke Senior's philosophy[23] by praising "unfrequented woods" over "flourishing peopled towns" (V iv 23).

When all is said and done, Valentine's amazing forgiveness of his friend Proteus, whose sudden shame and guilt, as he is caught red-handed, hardly sounds convincing to a modern audience; it sounds as far-fetched as any fairytale ending. As a token of his love, Valentine asserts, "All that was mine in Silvia I give thee," (V iv 83) which sounds like a ludicrous reversal of values making the very plot of the play a thing of nothing. Yet, if we keep in mind the *amicorum communia omnia* ("everything should be in common among friends")[24] of the Golden Age, Valentine's gift is wholly symbolic of a pastoral that ends well, and of course, it perfectly agrees with the absolute faith of a true Christian. After all, it could be a parody of John 15:13: "Greater love hath no man than this, that a man lay down his life [or wife!] for his friends." Besides, it is certainly possible to interpret it as a touch of the self-derisive spirit of the playwright himself as he stages his own too generous infatuation. After all, the situation is not so different from the love triangle of the *Sonnets*. To recover his male friend is as precious for the betrayed poet as to keep his female lover.

TASSO AND SHAKESPEARE: ITALIAN SOPHISTICATION

We have of course no absolute evidence that Shakespeare read Italian, or that he traveled in Italy,[25] but it seems undoubtable that he knew Tasso's *Aminta* well. Even if the evidence of linguistic borrowings is not easily found, it is obvious that many dramatic situations have inspired him, not to mention the mythological language used to express the mysteries of a neo-Platonic poetic theology which, according to Richard Cody, probably

---

[22] Those who refused to attend Church of England services were called recusants. Many Catholics, however, were "church papists"— Catholics who outwardly conformed to the established church while maintaining their Catholic faith in secret.

[23] *As You Like It*, II i 1–17.

[24] A sentence from Aristotle which became a proverb, turned into Latin by Cicero and quoted as an epigraph by Erasmus in his *Adages*.

[25] See Francesco da Mosco's BBC film, *Shakespeare in Italy*, in which he "reveals the debt Shakespeare owes to Italian theater and explores how Italy acted as a cloak for Shakespeare's most dangerous observations about Elizabethan England." BBC Worldwide Ltd., 2012.

is the clearest link between *Aminta* and Shakespeare's first comedies. He argues that *The Two Gentlemen of Verona* forms a pastoral medallion with *Love's Labour's Lost*, with the reconciliation by Cupid of pleasure and virtue on one side and Hercules choosing between the two on the other side.[26] These founding themes of the pastoral, such as they are found in Tasso's work, people many Renaissance paintings and were at the heart of a contemporary debate at the court of the Virgin Queen.

If, as the story goes, Elizabeth I envied the House of Este their reputation for enlightened patronage, one is entitled to think that with *Love's Labour's Lost* Shakespeare rivalled with Tasso to offer a sophisticated court performance suited to the nature of his sovereign. This exquisite pastoral play seems indeed to mock itself by frustrating the heroes, the King of Navarre and his attendant lords, from all expected resolutions. Their scholarly attempt at a philosophical retreat is thwarted at the outset by the arrival of the Princess of France and her courtly ladies, forcing the men to forswear their promise and gradually reveal their bad faith and immaturity. There is neither feigned death, nor sudden fainting as preludes to a final resurrection of love, as Shakespeare chooses to pit their wit against true death instead, whose intrusion in the pastoral answered the laws of the genre: "Et in Arcadia ego," translated by Erwin Panofsky as "Even in Arcady there am I."[27] The pedantry and superfluity of wit is brutally deflated. The king's death postpones reconciliation for the talkative lovers who have merely debated on the language of love without really feeling the passion. They can only hope to be victorious over the ordeals finally imposed on them as a moral lesson so that they may eventually discover the nature of true love. Everyone remembers Rosaline's punishment of mocking Berowne:

> *Rosaline*: And your task shall be
> With all the fierce endeavour of your wit
> To enforce the pained impotent to smile.
>
> *Berowne*: To move wilde laughter in the throat of death?
> It cannot be, it is impossible.
> Mirth cannot move a soul in agony. (*Love's Labour's Lost*, V ii 818–23)

Berowne's reply, underlying the oxymoronic contradiction of the condemnation, also points to the "impossible" style that the author himself is trying to achieve, bringing mirth and pain, as well as pleasure and moral

---

[26] Cody, *The Landscape of the Mind*: "These two comedies in fact form a pastoral medal, rather like Raphael's companion paintings *The Dream of Scipio* and *The Three Graces*. Back to back with Cupid's reconciliation of virtue and pleasure is set the choice of Hercules between the two" (105).

[27] Erwin Panofsky, *Meaning in the Visual Arts* (New York: Doubleday, 1955), 340–67, 353.

together. He thereby directs a critical glance toward the scholarly productions of some of his contemporaries, mocking the sophisticated courtly
compliments of euphuism, like Berowne's "replete with mocks, / Full of
comparisons and wounding flouts," (V ii 825–26) in which the manner
far surpasses the matter and the pastoral is furnished with everything
except a body.

Shakespeare shares with his Italian predecessor a kind of skepticism
allowing him to keep a delicate balance between tragic temptation and
saucy comedy (the *serio ludere* oxymoron of the traditional pastoral). We
find in both Tasso and Shakespeare echoes, scenic tricks, and a common
inspiration, which the Elizabethan poet gradually turned into his own.
Now let's briefly compare the original text of *Aminta*,[28] with the very
fanciful, sometimes extravagant, translation of Abraham Fraunce. Such
taste and sobriety is clearly not Fraunce's quality; faithful to the technique
of *amplificatio* fashionable in his time, he never says anything unless he
says it three times; his hexameters and weak rhymes often seem "dull,
feeble, and incompetent" to use C. S. Lewis's words.[29] They are full of
alliterations, anaphora, and clumsy pleonasms with bombastic or wholly
ridiculous effects:

> Once on a day (ô day, ô dismalist day of a thousand)
> Once on a sommers day (ô sommer worse than winter)
> Under a beech (ô beech of Amyntas woe the beginning)
> Phillis sate her downe, and down sate Cassiopoea,
> And I betweene them both.

Speaking of Cupid, the Satyr uses the same language as the forsaken lover:

> Yet this least least Love, when he smiteth, maketh a great wound,
> Great great mortall wound, great cureles wound in a lover....
> If that I fetch her flowrs, fresh fragrant flowrs fro the forrest,
> My fresh fragrant flows, ô spite, with a scorne shee rejecteth
> For cause her faire cheekes with fairer flowrs be adorned.

His bombastic rhetorical style at times makes such unpronounceable
twaddle that it can only be used as a parody on the stage. Shakespeare
perfectly perceived this and uses it as such in *Pyramus and Thisbe*, the inept
play put on by the Athenian mechanics in *A Midsummer Night's Dream*:

---

[28] Torquato Tasso, *Aminta*. Charles Jernigan and Irene Marchegiani Jones have chosen to preserve Tasso's poetical form by turning his hendecasyllabic blank verse with
variations of seven- or eight-syllable lines into English iambic pentameters, with
trimeters and tetrameters when needed, and by keeping rhymes wherever the original
requires them.

[29] C. S. Lewis, *English Literature in The Sixteenth Century* (Oxford: Oxford University
Press, 1954), 1.

O grim-look'd night! O night with hue so black!
O night which ever art when day is not;
O night, O night, alack, alack, alack,
I fear my Thisbe's promise is forgot!
And thou, O wall, O sweet, O lovely wall,
Thou stand'st between her father's ground and mine,
Thou wall, O wall, O sweet and lovely wall,
Show me thy chink, to blink through with mine eyne.
(*Midsummer Night's Dream*, V i 168–75)

The text reflects the incompetence of the players, who have taken great care to underline the artificiality of their art, thus ruining all possibility of dramatic illusion. However, the "distance" thus effected clearly reveals the poet's will to move away from the stereotypes of the traditional pastoral. He is no doubt also mocking Abraham Fraunce's translation, thus revealing through the pastiche of the English version, an implicit knowledge of the original. The Italian text of *Aminta* is not only simple and flowing, it is also very often ironical and the Italian language certainly needs no emphasis in order to create a dramatic effect. One is therefore tempted to believe E. K. Chambers when he asserts that the death alluded to among the list of pastimes offered for Theseus and Hippolyta's marriage is no less than Tasso's death:

Lysander (reads): "The thrice three Muses mourning for the death
Of learning, late deceased in beggary."
Theseus: That is some satire, keen and critical,
Not sorting with a nuptial ceremony. (*Midsummer Night's Dream*,
V i 52–55)

And this is also recorded by Thomas Churchyard in a note: "Torquato Tasso an Italian knight and poet laureat ... departed from oblivion to immortalitie this last Aprill 1595, whose memorie shall never vanish."[30] Refusing what is called the "old device" of Orpheus's death and the muses mourning for the death of learning, Theseus chooses the "very tragical mirth" of *Pyramus and Thisbe*, thus approving of the pastoral and its *discordia concors* as a play-within-the-play of the lovers' folly. This *divertimento* in the manner of Fraunce becomes a parody of *Aminta* as well as of Shakespeare's own play, where it acts like a distorting, yet reflecting mirror. The question it puts to the capricious lovers is perhaps that of their love's inner landscape, of their ability to overcome obstacles and wild beasts, to engage themselves body and soul in a journey which always necessarily ends in death. It is marriage's conundrum playfully staged. Where a bush miraculously saves

---

[30] E. K. Chambers, *William Shakespeare* (Oxford: Oxford University Press, 1930), 1:360; Thomas Churchyard, *A Musicall Consort of Heavenly Harmonie (compounded out of Manie Parts of Musicke) Called Churchyards Charities* (1595), 42.

Aminta from death, Pyramus kills himself with extravagance after ordering the moon to disappear from the night: "Moon, take thy flight. / Now die, die, die, die, die" (V i 299–300) and Thisbe shortly follows him. Death is rendered ludicrous by the jerking rhythm of irregular tetrameters, which turn the characters into disarticulated puppets. It is from such farcical premises that Shakespeare will learn to play on the pastoral, drawing from it its promise of wonder as well as its potential for tragedy.

Shakespeare always has an eye for the lively linguistic detail that will impress itself on the listener's mind, such as the image of the spaniel, which is found in Fraunce's translation as well as in *The Two Gentlemen of Verona* in Proteus's mouth, and in Helena's in *A Midsummer Night's Dream*. However, other passages from Tasso's comedy, omitted by Fraunce, found their way into Shakespeare's work. Thus, Fraunce shortens the quarrel between Daphne and Silvia about Amyntas to eight lines from twenty-one, and gives Silvia the very English name of "Phillis." The original version is much more powerful and to the saucy stubbornness of Silvia (Phillis) Dafne retorts: "Oh, see your ways! / See how dispiteous a girl she is!"[31] very much like Hermia and Helena's tearing each other's hair out in the forest of Athens.

In *A Midsummer Night's Dream* Shakespeare reaches the mastery of his mannerist pastoral style, with a serious and playful celebration of the powers of love and poetry for Theseus and Hippolyta's wedding. Refining his previous attempts, he widens his range of characters from the simple English mechanics to Greek mythology and the Fairy Queen. He mingles farce and the pastoral, the reality of courtly life with mythology, and preciosity and plain style. He juxtaposes the cosmic quarrels of ancient gods with the petty jealousies of young people who pursue each other wildly in the forest led by an improvised and facetious conductor, Puck. The miracle is the harmony that emerges from all this tumult—"I never heard / So musical a discord, such sweet thunder" (IV i 116–17).

Among the most stereotyped scenes of the time, there is in Tasso as well as in Shakespeare the melancholy lover pinning or carving poems on the trees of the forest, turning them into a paper forest, an anthology of his passion. The literary theme allegedly goes back to Aristophanes, and was used by Virgil and Ariosto. Closer to Shakespeare, the incident is to be found in Thomas Lodge's *Rosalynde* (an important source for *As You Like It*)[32] and in Greene's *Orlando Furioso* (1591–94), where it becomes a trap to make Orlando mad.

---

[31] Dafne: "Or guata modi! / guata che dispettosa giovinetta!" (I i 100–121).

[32] "One day among the rest, finding a fit opportunitie and place convenient, desirous to discover his woes to the woodes, hee engraved with his knife on the barke of a Myrtle tree, this pretie estimate of his Mistres perfection." Thomas Lodge, *Rosalynde* (1590), Bullough, *Narrative and Dramatic Sources of Shakespeare*, 2:199.

> Now don't you know
> what Tirsi wrote about when full of love
> he wandered like a madman through the woods,
> so that the gracious nymphs and shepherds there
> were moved to pity and to laugh at once?
> And although he wrote nothing laughable,
> The things he did were truly laughable.
> He wrote it on a thousand trees, that verse
> And tree would grow as one (I i 220–29)[33]

Of particular interest is the fact that in *Aminta*, the passage is framed by a succession of narrators fitting into each other, a technique of "encasing," which Shakespeare more than likely used in his comic representation of the literary pastorals in *As You Like It*.

AS YOU LIKE IT, OR FAY CE QUE VOUDRAS

As You Like It is a gem in which the Bard explores all the thematic and structural limits of the pastoral as literary and dramatic genre. The play is built like a Chinese nesting box, each box representing a level of the pastoral world, itself enclosed within the real, violent world of the court. Ironically, this violent world is introduced by a parody of the Fall, not out of the innocent and happy life of the Garden of Eden, but out of Oliver's Orchard, which rather resembles a garden of evil. Orlando, Oliver's younger brother, rebels against the ungentlemanly life, "this servitude," that he has been made to live by his elder brother since their father's death: "He keeps me rustically at home . . . for call you that keeping for a gentleman of my birth, that differs not from the stalling of an ox?" (I i 5–7) The two brothers are intent on competing with each other. Even fratricide is contemplated by Oliver as a solution to the problem. Finding no justice, even after he defeats the Duke's wrestler, Orlando is eventually compelled to run away in exile accompanied by his faithful servant Adam. The name has been intentionally chosen by Shakespeare to give the scene a more symbolic meaning.[34] Adam is a kind and generous old man despised by his master Oliver, who calls him "old dog." He

---

[33] Or tu non sai
ciò che Tirsi ne scrisse, allor ch'ardendo
forsennato egli errò per le foreste,
sì ch'insieme movea pietate e riso
ne le vezzose ninfe e ne'pastori?
Né già cose scrivea degne di riso,
Se ben cose facea degne di riso.
Lo scrisse in mille piante, e con le piante
crebbero i versi; (I 220–29).

[34] In Lodge's romance, Orlando's servant is more prosaically called Adam Spencer.

will help Orlando turn his fall from grace into a redeeming experience.

The figure of Adam appears several times in Shakespeare's plays, where he is traditionally regarded as a gardener, and as the gravedigger implies in *Hamlet*, at the time gardeners were the only gentlemen: "There is no ancient gentlemen but gardeners, ditchers and gravemakers; they hold up Adam's profession" (V i 29–30). The garden was historically a metaphor for social order and, as already mentioned, the famous garden scene in *Richard II* shows the gardeners, humble people, criticizing the court and its great men in language and ideas drawn from their rural discipline (III iv 24ff.). Peter Ure asserts that it is "the device of pastoral, the contrast between the good and the bad shepherd (here, gardeners) which allowed Renaissance pastoral much latitude for satirical comment on the great, put into the mouth of the humble and detached shepherd who looked at the court with innocent but perceptive eyes."[35] In *Richard II* the gardener's man wonders why they should keep their garden in order while the whole land is full of weeds for want of care. The gardener explains the necessity of cutting off the heads of too fast growing sprays to preserve the trees (III iv 34). In Oliver's garden, the irony lies in the fact that what is "unkept" is Oliver's brother, not his trees. Thus Cain's crime, not Adam's disobedience, becomes the original sin, "the primal eldest curse," as Claudius calls it in *Hamlet* (III iii 37). It is a pervasive theme of Shakespeare's tragedies, and here, as in *The Comedy of Errors*, tragedy is hovering over the first two acts of the play, which are full of discord, sound, and fury.

The world of the pastoral is introduced into *As You Like It* by the most unlikely of all commentators, the duke's wrestler. Charles, contrary to Lodge's fierce Norman giant, is a tender-hearted brute who conjures up for the audience the delicate picture of a cradle and of Celia and Rosalind's sisterly love (I i 103). His unsophisticated intellect has not gone beyond the bedtime stories of his childhood and that the exiled Old Duke should have survived in the forest surrounded by his faithful lords gives his life the legendary hue of old tales (I i 109–13). For Charles, he has become a new Robin Hood, a righter of wrongs in the greenwood[36] with courtly manners and natural philosophy. A good many people among Shakespeare's audience, who had no doubt seen the Robin Hood plays at the Rose

---

[35] Peter Ure, Introduction to *Richard II* (London: The Arden Shakespeare, Methuen, 1956), lv.

[36] The Greenwood Lore identified the forest with outlaw life. The greenwood refers to the protection of nature and of hunting, i.e., to medieval laws protecting the king's deer or the venison and the vert or greenwerd. The law protecting the king's game being hard and unfair, Robin was a poacher. The many tales of Robin Hood don't agree on his lineage, but from the sixteenth century onward, the chroniclers accepted the tradition of the noble outlaw who surrounds himself with disinherited noblemen.

Theatre in 1598,[37] would have been able to visualize the English pastoral of their popular hero (which was only just sketched in *The Two Gentlemen of Verona*). As a good pedagogue, Shakespeare knew that any reference to Theocritus or even Sidney's *Arcadia* wouldn't have hit the mark so well. Naturally, Charles's description of Duke Senior's court in exile as a renewed golden world, added to the eviction of Adam and Orlando from what may rightly be called a garden of evil, throws some light on Shakespeare's own philosophy. It seems evident that the possibility of primeval halcyon days does not even occur to him. If a golden age is possible, it is transposed into the future, to an age of Christian moral regeneration. Shakespeare was not afraid of reinterpreting the Bible occasionally. The original sin of mankind is, he proposes, Cain's crime, born of envy, rather than Adam's temptation, which is parodied later in the play when "a wretched, ragged man, o'ergrown with hair," who might be old Adam but turns out to be Oliver, is threatened by "a green and gilded snake," under an old oak, Jove's tree in the golden world. Orlando saves his brother and characteristically, Adam's temptation becomes the cause of the brothers' reconciliation and the beginning of a new love story.

The other pastoral worlds are subtly grafted on this one and all of them played against each other. In the Forest of Arden, where exiled Duke Senior is playing Robin Hood, live authentic Warwickshire shepherds, whose life is not always a holiday, even though Celia and Rosalind, also on the run, have a mind to spend some time with them, turning their banishment into a holiday. Corin the shepherd tells them that his master "little recks to find the way to heaven / By doing deeds of hospitality" (II iv 80–81). This single sentence is enough to reveal the shepherd's background and religious inclination[38] as well as his doubts as to Silvius's ability to buy himself a cottage. For Silvius and Phoebe could come straight out of *Aminta*, a couple of traditional pastoral lovers, who would not soil their hands at true rustic labors. He keeps bemoaning the scorn and coldness of his shepherdess who, like Tasso's Silvia, remains aloof and shows him an executioner's hard heart. Between reality and the literary pastoral, there is the heroic quest and the courtly pastoral of Orlando, who, sword drawn, first stumbles on the Greenwood Lore of Duke Senior in the forest before turning into the sophisticated melancholy lover, who speaks sonnets and

---

[37] *The Downfall of Robert, Earl of Huntington* (Quarto, 1598, Munday and Chettle; acted 1598; altered for court, Nov. 18, 1598) and *The Death of Robert, Earl of Huntington* (Quarto, 1601, Munday and Chettle) are two different plays.
[38] Shakespeare must have known many such men around Stratford who, no matter what, still went on with the old faith that had been transmitted to them by their fathers. The new idea that good works were not necessary to be saved by God must have sounded like city foolishness to them.

does transform the forest trees into books with paper for leaves and poems for fruit, a playful stage translation of the Duke's earlier conclusion: "And this our life, exempt from public haunt, / Finds tongues in trees, books in the running brooks, / Sermons in stones, and good in everything" (II i 15–17). However, and this is where Shakespeare complicates the game exceedingly, the young woman Orlando loves is now disguised as a boy, Ganymede, who decides to play his own girl self to test Orlando's love, whereas his boyish charms throw a spell on the foolish shepherdess Phoebe, who now pursues him ardently, adopting, like Helena, the Satyr's role, each pursuing her own Proteus in the forest. Unlike Tasso, Shakespeare's dramatic genius, tied to the necessity of satisfying not simply a courtly audience, but all levels of society, required a greater variety of characters and tone, no doubt. The kaleidoscopic world of Arden is characterized by considerable imaginative freedom, with a polyphonic structure which could have made Tasso envious indeed. Shakespeare knew how to extract from *Aminta* all the irony and the bewildering comic situations, without discarding the profound moral meaning which had been woven into the design of his plays since the beginning.

Like Tasso, but with even more spirit, he mocks the passionate pledges of green lovers who claim they want to die for love. When *Aminta*'s chorus claims with vigor: "we don't need death at all: for heart to heart to bind,"[39] Rosalind alias Ganymede saucily retorts to Orlando's wish to die: "Men have died from time to time, and worms have eaten them, but not for love" (IV i 97–98). She had already debunked mythical Leander's own death: the foolish youth was merely taken with a cramp while bathing on a hot summer night in the Hellespont.[40] But Shakespeare's subtlety also expands love to all its meanings, making Jaques, who loves to play the part of the Duke's own Fool, choose religious retreat in the midst of hymen's celebrations at the end of the play.

The typical pastoral plot, faithful to the *Memento Mori* tradition, does come very close to death, but the chorus in *Aminta* maintains a kind of reasonable frame to the representation of love's excesses by commenting doubtfully upon them. When Tirsi loses track of Aminta, he has a dark foreboding since Aminta, rejected by Silvia, only dreams of putting an end to his life. The chorus, however, is more skeptical: "It is usual / for one who loves to darkly threaten death; / infrequently the act will follow

---

[39] "Non bisogna la morte, / ch'a stringer nobil core / prima basta la fede, e poi l'amore" (III ii 147–49).
[40] The reference to the mythical lovers is naturally coupled with a bow to the dead poet Marlowe (1593), who had himself launched a famous debate on the pastoral with *The Passionate Shepherd to his Love*, answered by Sir Walter Raleigh's *The Nymph's Reply to the Shepherd*.

words"[41] (*Aminta*, III i 131–33). The fact that the action is always told by a witness allows for the possibility of playing on the various levels of credibility of the story. The passionate lovers often react to a mere glimpse, which confuses them and leads them astray, often triggering a series of mistaken encounters which the expert playwright has to orchestrate toward an ebullient conclusion. Thus, when Silvia is reported dead, Aminta rushes over the cliff—in spite of the fact that he has no evidence of her death— only to be rescued by a bush. A little later, his cry, "Oh, veil! oh, blood! Oh Silvia, you're dead!"[42] (*Aminta*, III ii 89–90) not only inspired the mock-pastoral of Pyramus and Thisbe in *A Midsummer Night's Dream*,[43] but perhaps, too, the incident with the bloody handkerchief which reveals Ganymede's femininity in *As You Like It* (IV iii 93–183).

In *Aminta*, the final meeting of the lovers, like their supposed deaths, remains offstage and Elpino and the chorus are the only characters left to draw conjectures on the possibilities of happiness of the reconciled lovers:

> I'd rather win my nymph
> with brief entreaties and with service brief.
> And may the condiment
> of our contentment be
> not serious torment,
> but games of gentle scorn
> and sweet refusals, and
> affray and quarrels, which cease
> and yield to hearts rejoiced in truce and peace. (*Aminta*, V i 150–58)[44]

Fraunce must have found this a very disappointing ending because he adds a scene of badinage between Aminta and his Phillis, who pretends she needs coaxing and will be possessed "when tyme is appointed" only.

It seems that in writing *As You Like It*, probably the most harmonious of all his pastoral plays, Shakespeare, better than Tasso, took the heart's wisdom into account in creating his characters. Passionate excesses are

---

[41] "E uso ed arte / di ciascun ch'ama minacciarsi morte: / ma rade volte poi segue l'effètto" (*Aminta*, III i 131–133).
[42] "Oh velo, oh sangue, / oh Silvia, tu se' morta!" (III ii 89–90).
[43] Fraunce's translation is truly grotesque at this point.
[44] "me la mia ninfa accoglia
dopo brevi preghiere e servir breve:
e siano i condimenti
de le nostre dolcezze
non sì gravi tormenti,
ma soavi disdegni
e soavi ripulse,
risse e guerre a cui segua,
Reintegrando i cori, o pace o tregua" (*Aminta*, V i 150–58).

quickly defused by laughter or courtesy. As for the love chase, it is mastered by Rosalind's impersonation as Ganymede, which allows her the verbal excesses denied to a young woman in love under pain of losing her man. Would Orlando, whose initial rebellion is clearly not against the feudal values of his world, but rather against the perversion of those values, be ready to worship his lady in the tradition of courtly love if he knew the truth and discovered what a saucy girl Rosalind can be? Probably not. The very courtly gentleness of the young man, who should certainly be played as a some-what old-fashioned, idealistic hero, also prevents Rosalind-Ganymede from falling into an excess of insolence and violence. *Coincidentia oppositorum.* For beside *Venus Urania*, there is indeed *Venus Pandemones*, representing carnal love without which a human cannot be complete. Orlando knows it, and ends up admitting: "I can live no longer by thinking" (V ii 48).

Both Shakespeare and Tasso are conscious of the paradoxical nature of the word honor: "vain abstraction, empty word" for Chorus,[45] "air" for Falstaff to whom the author gives a wonderful speech very close to that of *Aminta*'s Chorus in its tonality.[46] Honor seems to represent a diptych, with woman's honor on the one hand and man's honor on the other. In both cases, the word suffers from the same evil. When it is no longer tied to a firm spiritual ideal, when *logos* is no longer linked to the spirituality that founds it, it becomes a tool for derision and a lie. Honor and chastity are mocked for being tyrants, the idols through which society enslaves souls and bodies alike. According to Chorus, honor is responsible for the end of the Golden Age, "O bell'eta de l'oro,"(I ii 319) imposing lie and pretense instead of nature's motto: "do what pleases you": "S'ei piace, ei lice" (I ii 344).

This sentiment also reverberates like a refrain in Shakespeare's comedies, "Now kiss, embrace, contend, do what you will" (*Two Gentlemen of Verona*, I ii 130), and the very titles stating the nature of the plays: *Twelfth Night: or, What You Will*, and *As You Like It*. It is strange that these unlikely titles have often been misinterpreted as mere invitations to give the plays whatever titles you please. It grants Shakespeare too little spirit indeed. Among the sources of *As You Like It*, one finds *Orlando Furioso*, translated by Sir John Harrington, the queen's godson, who also found his inspiration in Rabelais, whom he loved and annotated. Shakespeare must have known Rabelais too, who is particularly interesting for his fanciful utopia, the Abbey of *Thélème* (in Greek θέλημα: free will) with its motto written over the entrance: *Fay ce que vouldras*, which is nothing else but the exact translation of "Do what thou wilt," or in other words, *as you like it*. The Abbey welcomes men and

---

[45] *Aminta*, I ii 332–33, 358–82.
[46] *1 Henry IV*, V i 129–40. "What is honour? A word. What is that word honour? What is that honour? Air" (V ii 134–35).

women whose ideal is the pastoral world, a new Golden Age in which residents freely seek wisdom — very much the world of Arden in fact. There are no walls round the Abbey, for "where there are walls, all around, there are plenty of murmurs, envy and mutual conspiracy."[47] This world of envy and reciprocal violence naturally recalls the courtly world of Duke Frederick. When the residents of the Abbey finally go back to the world, it is in order to change it, to breathe into it the *concordia discors* they have discovered. Shakespeare here appears much closer to Rabelais than to Tasso, perhaps because *Aminta* was a bubbly, lightly satirical tragicomedy performed at court by courtiers, which prevented them from returning to the world since their world *was* the pastoral itself. The praise of Alphonso II by Tirsi makes him a Duke Senior with a good knowledge of neo-Platonic philosophy. The opposition of city to country tends to disappear behind the praise of an aristocracy that has precisely discovered the harmony of physical, intellectual, and moral life. Such is not the case in Shakespeare's plays, which never waste an occasion to underline the difference between court and country. As his pastoral evolves toward greater innocence and purity of heart, the ability to change, evoked by his protean characters, is turned to more profoundly moral purposes. Young Perdita will neglect "streaked gillyvors" because, she says, "There is an art which, in their pied-ness, shares / With great creating nature" (*The Winter's Tale*, IV iv 87–88). Her devotion to nature does not tolerate any tampering with it:

> I'll not put
> The dibble in earth to set one slip of them;
> No more than, were I painted, I would wish
> This youth should say 'twere well, and only therefore
> Desire to breed by me. (IV iv 99–103)

Polixenes tries to convince her of the advantages of grafting:

> Yet nature is made better by no mean
> But nature makes that mean: so over that art,
> Which you say adds to nature, is an art
> That nature makes. You see sweet maid, we marry
> A gentler scion to the wildest stock,
> And make conceive a bark of baser kind
> By bud of nobler race. This is an art
> Which does mend nature — change it rather — but
> The art itself is nature. (IV iv 89–97)

---

[47] My translation. "[. . .] où mur y a, et davant, et derriere, y a force murmur, envie, et conspiration mutue." François Rabelais, *Oeuvres* (Paris: Jean de Bonnot, 1973), vol. 1, chap. 52. The story of the Abbey runs from chapter 52 to 58.

But innocent Perdita is faithful to God's nature, "natura naturans," and won't have a slip of those flowers whose variable color she compares to makeup. The irony, of course, lies in the fact that Perdita is ignorant of her true "mixed" nature which, once revealed, renders all this debate useless insofar as the resolution of the plot is concerned. She and Florizel won't marry beneath their station. Yet the risk has been evoked, and with it the inconsistency of Polixenes' philosophy, which agrees to better the race by grafting for plants but refuses it for men. Just as there may be death in Arcadia (*Et in Arcadia ego*), man's protean nature, his ability to go beyond or to contradict himself, to exert the "I-know-not-what,"[48] which against all expectations changes the course of destiny, is capable of the best and the worst. After all, wasn't this aptitude for metamorphosis what made man's dignity according to Giovanni Pico della Mirandola?[49] Nothing is ever predestined, therefore man's nature can change and improve, provided it is well guided.

It is such moral consciousness that is aroused by the pastoral in the audience, who, besides learning about contemporary controversies, are taught to put things in perspective. The expected purpose, if one accepts the underlying existence of a Platonic mythology of Love, is that the lovers, when they are united at last, emerge the wiser for the ordeal they have gone through, and that everyone else may join them in this revelation of cosmic harmony. If one sides with Tasso's Chorus however, it may simply be an initiation to doubt and tolerance. Artificial as the denouements may be, they reveal all the better the need to suspend one's judgment. There's no dupe; everyone comes out better armed to face the world.

During the Renaissance, the Golden Age had disappeared and nature itself, now in the Iron Age, could be dark and dangerous, barren and inhospitable, with forests harboring wild beasts. It still retained its redemptive power, but its lessons were harsher, based on the Christian ideals of work and humility. From the courtly spirit which permeates *Aminta* and which seems to be reflected in *Love's Labour's Lost*, where the verbal game is predominant and landscape mostly symbolic, Shakespeare

---

[48] Vladimir Jankélévitch, *Le Je-ne-sais-quoi et le Presque-rien* (Paris: le Seuil, 1980).
[49] "Quis hunc nostrum chamaeleonta non admiretur? aut omnino quis aliud quicquam admiretur magis? Quem non immerito Asclepius Atheniensis versipellis huius et se ipsam transformantis naturae argumento per Proteum in mysteriis significari dixit. Hinc illae apud Habraeos et Pythagoricos metamorphoses celebratae" (8–9). "Who would not admire our chameleon? Or who would have for anything else more admiration? Asclepios of Athens was not wrong when he said that in the Mysteries, because of his changing nature, because of his ability to transform himself, man is called Proteus. Hence the metamorphoses celebrated by the Hebrews and the Pythagoreans" (my translation). Giovanni Pico della Mirandola, *De Hominis Dignitate*, trans. Yves Hersant (Combas, France: Editions de l'éclat, 1993).

evolved toward a more religious vision of the pastoral in which exile and hardship provide the freedom necessary for rebirth. From the Italian model, Shakespeare gradually transformed, modulated, and metamorphosed images and themes in keeping with the moral questions that haunted him. On the barren and cold heath, old Lear will discover the true nature of man, "a poor, bare, forked animal," (III iv 90–91) and Imogen and Posthumus, the true nature of love. Whereas *Cymbeline* offers an arid and hostile landscape where survival depends on courage and physical fitness, *The Tempest* transforms the whole pastoral into a utopia where the exiled sovereign, thanks to his "art," himself creates the meteorological accidents of redemption. Obeying a similar design, Pericles and Marina, Hermione and Perdita are banished from their own life and status, to wander like strangers to themselves or to the world, until time, patience, and pardon allow them to be reborn. From Tasso, Shakespeare's pastoral evolved toward a true Christian pastoral without ever shedding the multicolored garments of its origins. ♣

5. The Mannerism of Metamorphosis

*T*HERE ARE WORDS THAT CHARM OR CAST A SPELL, words that give free rein to the imagination. Metamorphosis is such a word, its music and the languorous transformations it implies are the very essence of life, no less. This diamond word reveals an infinity of facets, whose ever changing colors never ceased to fascinate. Metamorphosis was also the quintessence of Shakespeare's endeavor: to represent life, to mend, to change men for the better, and to work on their minds and souls to save them from the gloomy prospects of the day. The very essence of the pastoral is based on metamorphosis and movement. The idea that life—or art for that matter—could be pigeonholed might be reassuring but it was a lie, a dead vision which could not be accommodated in Shakespeare's kinetic imagination.

The most celebrated of metamorphoses on the Elizabethan stage is without doubt Bottom's sudden transformation into an ass in the heart of fairyland, a grotesque, potentially obscene encounter, which Shakespeare manages to make so delicate and tender that one is left speechless. It might seem that, when he wrote such a delightful comedy, Shakespeare had overcome his youthful anger and it is true that the joy and exhilaration provided by his comedies probably healed some of his initial grief, as they do ours. However the attempt to understand human nature was there as vibrant as ever, Shakespeare's mind always alert to the variable meanings of life.

BOTTOM'S BANQUET OF SENSE

Nobody would deny the marvelous syncretism and metamorphic quality of *A Midsummer Night's Dream*. Shakespeare always knew how to imitate, adapt, or transmute elements to his own ends. This was what invention was like at the time, and he was indisputably a master at it. It is therefore a mistake to turn *A Midsummer Night's Dream* into a sort of neo-Platonic treatise or mythological allegory.[1] It is neither, even though it freely uses neo-Platonic and mythological elements and symbols. *A Midsummer Night's*

---

[1] For neo-Platonic interpretations of *A Midsummer Night's Dream*, see Richard Cody, "A Midsummer Night's Dream: Bottom Translated," *The Landscape of the Mind: Pastoralism and Platonic Theory in Tasso's "Aminta" and Shakespeare's Early Comedies* (Oxford: Clarendon Press, 1968), 127–50. Also see Jane K. Brown, "Discordia Concors: On the Order of *A Midsummer Night's Dream*," *Modern Language Quarterly* 48 (1987) and Maurice Hunt "The Countess of Pembroke's *Arcadia*, Shakespeare's *A Midsummer Night's Dream*, and The School of Night: An Intertextual Nexus," *Essays in Literature* 23.1 (1996): 3–20.

Dream is first and foremost a play, and is full of allusions to contemporary persons and events. One of those events may have been the publication in 1595 of a poem by Chapman, *Ovids Banquet of Sense*,[2] generally considered "the most difficult poem in the language."[3] This deliberately obscure piece of verse has long been taken to be the evidence of a neo-Platonic philosophy meant to puzzle or shock the "profane" reader. However, we may think that Shakespeare knew better, and was not fooled by the moralizing irony of this "Banquet of bestial love" dressed up "to look like a true *convivium*."[4] Bottom's own banquet of sense in Titania's bower may even have been a parody of Chapman's intent.

Love and marriage are the playwright's subjects in *A Midsummer Night's Dream*, the play being most likely performed on January 26, 1595, for the very aristocratic marriage of William Cecil's grand daughter, Elizabeth de Vere, to William Stanley, sixth Earl of Derby, in the presence of the queen herself. William Stanley's older brother, who held the title, Fernandino, Lord Strange, had died in very doubtful circumstances a few months earlier. As the lawful heirs to the throne of England through Mary Tudor, sister of Henry VIII, the Stanleys were known for their Roman Catholic sympathies, and were certainly kept under close watch by Lord Burghley's men. More than ever, Shakespeare had to reach the harmony of contraries — *coincidentia oppositorum* — and manage the impossible feat of remaining undetectable.

The action takes place in the four days separating the mythical couple, Theseus and Hippolyta, from their "nuptial hour," a time devoted to the preparation of revels and festivities. The play is presided over by the Moon, triple goddess of chastity, fecundity, and witchcraft, whose changing mood heralds the confusion of the night. The ritual of purification and rebirth which generally precedes the ceremonies of Hymen is left to the whim of Oberon and Titania, the Fairy Queen and King, who are themselves engaged in a lover's quarrel fed by jealousy and mimetic desire. The fickle moon appears to be linked from the very first lines to Theseus's own lingering desire which it hinders, setting the pattern of oppositions that will rule the long midsummer night until the silver bow of the new moon encompasses in its symbol both the Amazon Hippolyta and the queen of the night, Titania. That Oberon and Titania may be the "night doubles" of the protagonists — they were very probably played by the same actors in Shakespeare's time — only intensifies the violence of desire which is at the heart of the play.

---

[2] George Chapman, *Ovid's Banquet of Sense* (Menston, England: The Scolar Press, 1970).
[3] Gerald Snare, *The Mystification of George Chapman* (Durham, NC: Duke University Press, 1989), 3. See chap. IV, 111–38 for a proof to the contrary.
[4] Frank Kermode, quoted in Snare, 118.

The Amazon, whom Theseus wooed with his phallic sword, keeps him at bay, protracting the musical discord of the hunt, whereas frustrated Oberon asks, "Am not I thy lord?" (II i 63) when he meets his scornful queen in the night. The music is likely to be harsh and grating before it can actually rise to harmony.

The key is given, immediately followed by variations. The first scene informs us of Hermia and Lysander's vexed love, of Demetrius's frustrated attempt, and of Helena's vain doting. It may be interesting at this point to quote Pico della Mirandola:

> Love is not betwixt things unlike; Repugnance of two opposite natures is natural hate. Hate is a repugnance with knowledge. Hence it followeth that the nature of the desired is in some manner in the desirer; otherwise, there would be no similitude betwixt them: yet imperfectly; else it were vain for it to seek what it entirely possesseth. (Book II, iii[5])

> Likes seek likes, yet, as desire generally follows knowledge, so several knowing are annexed to several desiring Powers. We distinguish the knowing into three degrees: Sense, Reason, Intellect. (Book II, iv)

The whole problem is therefore to differentiate, or find out, which kind of knowledge ties the different lovers. Appetite, Pico tells us, will denote brutes, Reason, men, and Intellect, angels intent on "Contemplation of Spiritual Conceptions." Shakespeare obviously plays with the whole gamut of possibilities, turning them upside down and taking them across boundaries of genres and matter.

Oberon's will to punish his queen by making her fall in love with a monster seems a direct answer to neo-Platonic theories: she, the Fairy Queen, belonging to a Middle World, immortal and invisible, cannot possibly love a rude mechanic, what's more, one turned into an ass. This strange conjunction, at the heart of the play, not only draws wonder, but moreover seems to be the riddle that has to be solved before the nuptial ceremony may come to pass. In order to understand the full import of the scene, it may therefore be necessary to go back over the neo-Platonic idea of love at the end of the sixteenth century. It will shed light on Shakespeare's own interpretation of the tradition and on the importance of Bottom's metamorphosis and his dream.

The idea developed by Pico della Mirandola in his discourse on Platonic love states that the desire of beauty *is* love, which arises from one knowing

---

[5] Giovanni Pico della Mirandola, *A Platonick Discourse upon Love*, ed. E. G. Gardner (Boston: Merrymount Press, 1914).

faculty, the sight. He even refers to Plotinus who, in his *Enneads*, derived Love, ἔρως, from ὅρασις, sight. To the Platonic objection that such love of visible things cannot be applied to ideas, he answers that sight is twofold, corporeal and spiritual, which corresponded to the neo-Platonic attempt to find the resolution of discord and uniting opposites. Beauty and love, which is aroused by the sight of beauty, became mediators between the world of the senses and the celestial world. They helped the soul to apprehend its superior condition. Beauty itself was defined by Pico as "arising from contrariety, without which is no composition; it being the union of contraries, a friendly enmity, a disagreeing concord" (Book II v). The example he gives, taken from the fiction of poets, is the love of Mars and Venus. The beauty of Venus would not be so complete if it were deprived of the destructive influence of Mars. Needless to say, this definition was particularly well understood by Shakespeare who never ceased to pursue such perfection.[6] But, Pico goes on, since sight is twofold, beauty and love are equally both vulgar and celestial as shown by Plato's two Venuses. Much has been made of Oberon's "Venus of the Sky" (III ii 107) whom he wishes on Demetrius in the shape of Helena. But Demetrius is hardly the kind of character likely to want a celestial love; like the Proteus of *The Two Gentlemen of Verona*, he appears to be a philanderer and of all the youth, he is the least articulate. That the Celestial Venus should herald peace and harmony among the young couples is unlikely, and the author, and perhaps even Oberon, are being tongue-in-cheek.

It is easy to see how these ideas fit the subject of the play and how Shakespeare, always an adept of Erasmus's *wise fool*, uses the Renaissance philosophical scheme of the *coincidentia oppositorum* to his own end. Just as he uses Apuleius's *Golden Ass* in a parody of Lucius's metamorphosis,[7] he adapts the ideas of neo-Platonism to his own deep sense of the human. The vogue had reached England with Sir Thomas Hoby's translation of *Il Cortegiano* in 1561. Ficino and Pico's mystical creed of love and beauty found its most "rapturous expression" on the lips of Bembo in the closing pages of what had become the most influential book of manners for the English gentleman, with no less than three different editions between 1561 and 1603:

> What mortal tongue then, O most holy love, can worthily praise thee?... Vouchsafe, Lord, to hearken to our prayers. Infuse Thyself into our hearts, and, with the splendour of Thy most holy fire, illumine our darkness, and, like a trusted guide in this blind labyrinth, show us the true way. Do Thou correct the falseness of

---

[6] The perfect achievement of *Antony and Cleopatra* may be said to obey Pico's rules.
[7] See my own article on the subject: "La métamorphose de Bottom et *l'Ane d'Or*," *Etudes Anglaises* 34 (1981), 1.

the senses, and, after long wandering in vanity, grant unto us the true and sound joy. Make us to smell those spiritual odours that vivify the virtues of the understanding, and to hear the heavenly harmony with such ineffable melody, that no discord of passion may any more have place within us. Do Thou inebriate us at that inexhaustible fountain of contentation that always doth delight and never doth satiate, and that giveth a taste of true beatitude to all that drink of its living and limpid waters. With the rays of Thy light, purge Thou our eyes from misty ignorance, that they may no more prize mere mortal beauty, and that they may know that the things that, at the first, they thought themselves to see, are not, and those that they saw not, are in very sooth.... And may we, alienated from ourselves, be transformed like true lovers into the beloved; and, being uplifted from the earth, may we be admitted to the banquet of the Angels, where, fed with ambrosia and immortal nectar, we may at last die a most blissful and life-giving death. (Book IV, 362–63)[8]

This prayer might be that of most characters in the play which, from the discord of its beginning, takes them through the blind maze of confused passion and mimetic violence, until the juice of the flower of love, idly squeezed by Robin, the mercurial messenger of Oberon, can at last restore them to their original true vision. Robin's mistake, due to his master's lack of precision, "Thou shalt know the man / By the Athenian garments he hath on" (II i 263–64), may stand for fate, which rules the creatures of appetite, whereas rational creatures desire by election of reason, and celestial creatures have will. But Robin, the "Hobgoblin," the "knavish sprite," may also be the principle of confusion induced by mimetic desire. Athenian garments can hardly be deemed sufficient proof of identity, and Oberon's description looks more like a case of "indifferentiation,"[9] in a world already turned upside down by the Fairy King and Queen's dissension. Demetrius loves Hermia, daughter of Egeus who loves him too, but Hermia sees in Lysander as worthy a gentleman. What strikes us is the reason given by Hermia for disobeying her father: the man she loves is as good as the man chosen by her father. Hermia is intent on asserting her own will, and she wishes that her father looked with her eyes, those eyes which reveal beauty which in turn, arouses love. However, the similarity between Lysander and Demetrius puzzles our judgment and does not make Hermia's plea very convincing. Another Shakespearean heroine, Desdemona, when accused of being bewitched by her lover, knows better

---

[8] Baldassare Castiglione, *The Book of the Courtier*, trans. George Bull (London: Penguin Books, 1967).
[9] René Girard's word.

how to express her love and to convince her judges. She, in a very neo-Platonic fashion, "saw Othello's visage in his mind" (I iii 250). For her, Othello's worth is not interchangeable.

The confusion grows worse when Demetrius decides to pursue the lovers into the wood, himself pursued by Helena. The language of the lovers is the first vehicle of metamorphosis. If love purges the lover's eyes of their misty ignorance, the lovers' erroneous perceptions of their beloveds seem to establish the power of the moon and the inconstant nature of their love. The structure of the play provides a pattern to this mirror effect and after having both men running after Hermia, the movement is inverted and now they chase Helena, who, desperate, turns against Hermia. Their greater love seems so perfect that it reflects poorly on the men's faith:

> So we grew together,
> Like to a double cherry: seeming parted,
> But yet an union in partition (III ii 208–10)

Here is the perfection of Platonic love, if "the nature of the desired is in some manner in the desirer," what better situation than that of the double, who loves himself when he loves the other. "Two seeming bodies but one heart," the girls are interchangeable, so close to each other that one can be the other, their similarity shedding light on the easily shifting love object of both males.

The fact that all this confusion is staged by Oberon, simply stresses the transient quality of love. How easily the hateful fantasies of love can turn a dove into a bear, or a vixen into a goddess, especially when an uncertain identity prevents the characters from knowing themselves well: "Am not I Hermia? Are not you Lysander?" (III ii 273). Their bewilderment manifests the superficial quality of their beings, intent on imitating others more than on being truly what they are. Ficino insisted on the necessity for the soul, "animus," to penetrate matter in order to give it shape and meaning, before emerging out of matter to be reborn. Oberon may release their "charmed eyes" "from monster's view," but they themselves have to cope with their fears and desires.

Like Psyche,[10] Hermia is unconsciously marrying death. Actually, when she pushes Lysander away — a distance which convinces Robin of their coldness — she has a somewhat Freudian dream in which a snake attacks and stifles her. The sexual connotation is unmistakable. Like Psyche, young Hermia finds herself in the night, unable to see her lover, confident in the closeness of their bodies, but apprehensive of more. As has been pointed out, she is as yet hardly differentiated from her bosom friend and it is

---

[10] Erich Neumann, *Amor and Psyche, The Psychic Development of the Feminine* (Princeton, NJ: Princeton University Press, 1956).

possible that she loves Lysander simply because Helena loved Demetrius. She needs to discover herself, so that she may be fully conscious of her own individual self as part of the encounter between feminine and masculine. This is what the story of Amor and Psyche[11] has come to mean, even though Shakespeare only borrows elements of it. On the grassy bank, there will be no sensual banquet, and the audacity of the lovers extends no further than parental opposition.

In another corner of the wood, "rude mechanicals" are rehearsing the play they will offer on the wedding night. Meanwhile, Oberon is planning his own revenge on the Fairy Queen who has denied him a changeling. Titania will also share Psyche's fate and is condemned to dote on whatever monster she lays her eyes on:

> The next thing then she waking looks upon —
> Be it on lion, bear, or wolf, or bull,
> On meddling monkey, or on busy ape —
> She shall pursue it with the soul of love. (II i 179–82)

So close is this passage to Ovid's description of Proteus in *The Art of Love*,[12] where the old dissembler is introduced as an example for the wise man who wants to be successful in love, that we are tempted to say that Proteus, as much as the moon, presides over this initiatory love night: "Hearts have as many fashions as the world has shapes; the wise man will suit himself to countless fashions, and like Proteus will now resolve himself into light waves, and now will be a lion, now a tree, now a shaggy boar." (Book I 760–62)

Now, is not Bottom the character who has the greatest desire of multiplicity in the play? When he learns that his part will be that of "A lover, that kills himself most gallant for love" (I ii 21), the mere idea of moving the audience with Pyramus, makes him wish he could also play the other parts of *Pyramus and Thisbe*, as if impelled by a strange curiosity to try on other shapes:

> Yet my chief humour is for a tyrant. (I ii 24)

> And I may hide my face, let me play Thisbe too. (I ii 47)

> Let me play the lion too. (I ii 66)

> But I will aggravate my voice so that I will roar you as gently as any sucking dove. I will roar you an' twere any nightingale. (I ii 76–78)

---

[11] Apuleius, *The Golden Ass*, trans. W. Adlington (Cambridge, MA: Loeb Classical Library, Harvard University Press, 1971). The story of Amor and Psyche runs from Bk. IV, chap. 28 (185) to Bk. VI, chap. 24 (285).

[12] Ovid, *The Art of Love, and Other Poems*, trans. J. H. Mozley, Vol. II (Cambridge, MA: Loeb Classical Library, Harvard University Press, 1969).

To disguise his voice, to hide his face, to become a lion who can in turn pass for a dove or a nightingale, aren't these the first steps toward the ass-head and the monstrous Cupid's part that our bold weaver will be led to assume? Does not this protean ability predispose him to the ultimate metamorphosis, that of the perfect lover, in the shape of an ass? Continuously dreaming of change, Bottom, like Lucius in *The Golden Ass*, ends up being trapped in his own desires. His love of the theater carries him, unaware, beyond the appearances, which remain for him the essence of the theatrical game, toward deeper change and magic.

As the rehearsals in the forest demonstrate, for Bottom a role is little more than a set of stereotyped rules. In the craftsmen's play, there is truly little difference between Pyramus's part and the moonlight. A few external details seem sufficient to fill the part well, and if the role runs a risk of being too persuasive, let it be explained rationally that the character is not really what he seems to be, but a true craftsman! Bottom remains imperturbably "himself." At no point in his actor's life, have his dreams of metamorphoses ever threatened his "identity." In fact, he does not even see the link there could be between himself and any role he might play: "tell them that I, Pyramus, am not Pyramus, but Bottom the weaver" (III i 15). For this rather domineering craftsman, drama is a game that cannot be related to life. This dichotomy is of course the cause for Bottom's fundamental inability to play a part. The entrance of Puck at the moment when Bottom is leaving the stage still adds to this incapacity. Puck's nature is worlds removed from Bottom's: essentially moving and elusive, it has as many shapes as names. Like Proteus, Puck can transform himself into anything he likes, he is the epitome of the actor and the most characteristic example of Oberon's evanescent kingdom. Puck represents freedom, especially compared to Bottom's massive bulk,[13] one of those vegetative natures more akin to plants or beasts than to Pico's divine man.[14] Bottom can only be Bottom, and things are for him as he sees them. Their identity is warranted by a name which somehow solidifies them. A name is also a guarantee of identity for the individual, who can only be what he is: "'I am a man, as other men are'—and there, indeed, let him name his name, and tell them plainly he is Snug the joiner." (III i 32–33)

---

[13] It corresponds rather well with Sartre's être-en-soi, without self-consciousness, without an inner side that would be opposed to an outer side, a being which is what he is, without a secret. Jean-Paul Sartre, *L'être et le néant* (Paris: NRF Gallimard, 1943), 33–34.
[14] *De Hominis Dignitate*, trans. Yves Hersant (Combas, France: Editions de l'éclat, 1993); Giovanni Pico della Mirandola, *Oration on the Dignity of Man*, in *The Renaissance Philosophy of Man*, ed. E. Cassirer, P. O. Kristeller and J. H. Randall (Chicago: University of Chicago Press, 1948), 233–54, 225.

Shakespeare who, as it happens, is the sorcerer or the magus of the play, obviously enjoys showing Bottom, with Puck's help, that drama is much more than this, that its spirit, the spirit of its art, penetrates much more deeply into man's nature, revealing its truth even if he is not completely conscious of its process. The temptation and the incongruity of throwing such an oaf among elves and of giving him the most ethereal mistress of all must have been irresistible. Therefore, Bottom, with "an ass's nole" (III ii 17) on his head, becomes the monster with whom Titania falls in love.

Paradoxically, it is precisely when his opinionated spirit refuses to be taken in that he perfectly impersonates the new part that has been thrown upon him. Both characters are completely unconscious of Robin's manipulation, hence the innocence and the perfect enjoyment of the scene. Unlike Apuleius's Lucius, whose consciousness renders the physical change he has undergone odious to him and makes him regard his metamorphosis as a kind of punishment, Bottom can enjoy being a tender ass without remorse. Shakespeare emphasizes the essential gratuity of the metamorphosis. Bottom is neither punished nor rewarded: he *is*. Shakespeare does not seek to perfect a nature that would in itself be despicable, he prefers to show such nature in its true and complex reality.

In the amazing conjunction of Titania and Bottom, Shakespeare is not only truly Ovidian,[15] he also uses Ovid to correct a few excesses of the neo-Platonic philosophy that was so fashionable in his time. The audience is invited to believe the unbelievable, to encompass the whole human being with his celestial temptation and his sensual attraction. The extraordinary union of Bottom and Titania is meant to show us that there can indeed be concord in discord, even though fleetingly, that this is what beauty is about, and the success of the play over the centuries seems to corroborate this. Shakespeare plays with the neo-Platonic creed: Bottom's translation happens to be what every adept of neo-Platonism dreams of. He will reach celestial bliss, thanks to the love Titania bears him: "And I will purge thy mortal grossness so / That thou shalt like an airy spirit go" (III i 151–52). Without the least effort, he is taken into the Fairy Queen's bower where he is offered all kinds of pleasures, all those pleasures that Ovid is striving to reach in Chapman's poem — hearing, smell, sight, taste, and the most prized of all, touch, which Ovid himself is refused in spite of his prayers:

Then sacred Madam, since my other sences
Have in your grace tasted such content,
Let wealth not to be spent, fear no expences,

---

[15] For a detailed and perceptive analysis of the influence of Ovid in Shakespeare's plays, see Jonathan Bate, *Shakespeare and Ovid* (Oxford: Clarendon Press, 1994).

But give thy bountie true eternizement:....
This sayd, hee layde his hand upon her side,
Which made her start like sparckles from a fire.[16]

The lady does not let him approach. Like Hermia, she is proud and defeats the poet's intent. Bottom has more luck. Titania is most bounteous, she refuses him nothing, music, conversation, scratching, eating dainty food, entertainment, and kisses:

Sleep thou, and I will wind thee in my arms.
Fairies, be gone, and be all ways away.
So doth the woodbine the sweet honeysuckle
Gently entwist; the female ivy so
Enring the barky fingers of the elm.
O how I love thee, how I dote on thee! (IV i 39–44)

Like a man who has eaten well, sated Bottom feels like having a nap. It may be that Oberon will come in time to prevent any slip of Titania's honor, but the truth is that when given excess of pleasure, Bottom, who is a natural, not corrupted by the fashions of the court, takes only what is necessary, and far from Orsino's surfeit, his appetite is not sickened. Of amorous exploits, there are of course none, even though some critics did not hesitate to interpret the scene as sexual debauchery.[17] It is interesting to note that when he could have been most saucy, in the middle of an epithalamion not lacking in frivolous allusions, a play where love's violence is ever present, Shakespeare chooses to erase all sexual reference. The moral might be that man, for all his dreams, can only take so much, or that Bottom gains everything precisely because he wants nothing. While the rest of the cast is either fleeing unwelcome love or pursuing unattainable love, Bottom the ass haphazardly finds himself in the Fairy kingdom and receives, without sword or violence, the love of his queen. What irony! What a lesson!

Bottom is so placid, so unlikely to be other than himself, that he is not susceptible to mimetic desire. He enjoys his pleasure without any intellectual preconception and when he is at last made aware of his experience, he does not know what to make of it. His senses have been filled and his poetic satisfaction is expressed in a pre-Baudelairean harmony: "The eye of man hath not heard, the ear of man hath not seen, man's hand is not able to taste, his tongue to conceive, nor his heart to report what my

---

[16] George Chapman, *Ovid's Banquet of Sense*, 1595, E2.
[17] Jan Kott even goes as far as to speak of the "rapture and disgust, terror and abhorrence" the love scenes between Titania and the ass must have provoked. "Titania and the Ass's Head," *Shakespeare Our Contemporary* (New York: Doubleday and Co., 1964), 159.

dream was" (IV i 207–10). He does garble the biblical text from Saint Paul, but in his very confusion he perfectly agrees with Paul's teaching a few verses before the passage referred to: "But God hath chosen the foolish things of the world to confound the wise" (1 Cor 1:27).[18] Bottom's vision may be that of the Fool, but the Fool was often wiser than the king in Renaissance philosophy. The ass in him does not prevent him from understanding intuitively the mystery he has just lived, an ineffable mystery because it is at the heart of things. Only faith can explain this union which, through its strange alchemy, transcends its grotesque nature. Those who are looking for moral or psychological causes are wasting their time. There is no cause, unless it is Oberon's capricious jealousy. The domain of imagination, which is also the domain of love and myth, is poles apart from the domain of the intellect and reason. The winner is life itself, with all its profusion and generosity, which cannot be content with a mere dichotomy between good and evil.

Contrary to Chapman's Ovid who revels in the erotic pleasure of his own artistic inventiveness, Bottom stumbles on words and is unlikely to write *The Art of Love*. The true esthetic *jouissance* is left to the audience who has witnessed the concord of this discord and filled their eyes and ears with this unlikely tableau.

Theatrical illusion, reality of life, where does the one begin and the other end? Who knows? Rather than a moral lesson that would deny the nature of individuals to turn them into disincarnated beings, the dramatist chooses a more beautiful, slightly bittersweet conclusion, which, while asserting the magic of love, does not blind itself to its fragility and its complexity. Can its rare essence even be captured by the more tangible link of marriage? Shakespeare seems to say "yes," leaving us, like Bottom, perplexed in the presence of "a most rare vision."

If Shakespeare was celebrating "the union between the Cecil family and the earldom of Derby, which had passed to William Stanley after the murder of his brother, Fernandino, Lord Strange,"[19] he certainly had to

---

[18] It may be interesting to note that Bottom's dream contradicts Bembo's apology for beauty in the very same words: "And as a mann heareth not with his mouth, nor smelleth with hys eares: no more can he also in anye maner wise enjoye beawtye, nor satisfye the desire that shee stirrith up in oure myndes, with feelynges, but with the sense, unto whom beawtye is the verye butt to level at: namelye, the virtue of seeing. Let him laye aside therefore the blinde judgemente of the sense, and enjoye wyth his eyes the bryghtnesse . . . of beawtye; especially with hearing the sweetnesse of her voice . . . and so shall he with most deintie food feede the soule through the meanes of these two senses, which have little bodelye substance in them, and be the ministers of reason," *The Courtier*, Bk iv, 353. It seems that the whole play is a refutation of Bembo's philosophy.
[19] Asquith, *Shadowplay*, 106.

be very cautious about the message he wanted to convey. A profusion of complex literary references was a good way to mislead those who must have been looking for some proof of Shakespeare's true allegiance. Thus Theseus's view of the poet imaginatively bodying forth "the forms of things unknown" (V i 15) seems indeed to agree with the assumption shared by many religious reformers of the time that art is fictive, feigning, illusory, and therefore a thing of nothing.[20] However his point of view is immediately contradicted by Hippolyta's beautiful plea:

> But all the story of the night told over,
> And all their minds transfigured so together,
> More witnesseth than fancy's images,
> And grows to something of great constancy;
> But howsoever, strange and admirable (V i 23–27)

implying not only the existence of a solid core behind these frivolous appearances, but equally the existence of a truth hidden behind the lies of poetry. ♣

---

[20] Among them, Stephen Gosson, *The School of Abuse*, which was, as the title indicates, *a pleasant invective against Poets, Pipers, Players, Jesters &c* (Brookline, MA: Elibron Classics Series, Adamant Media Corporation, 2005).

6. Shakespeare's Manner:
THE ART OF BUILDING A PLAY

*B*Y THE TURN OF THE CENTURY SHAKESPEARE HAD achieved the mastery of his medium. He was an expert at indirections and plays within plays just as he was an expert at words, puns and irony. He had also, as Stephen Greenblatt points out, "perfected the means to represent inwardness." As already suggested, the pastoral was a landscape he kept exploring for its many shades of meaning and contradictions, as well as its philosophy of life, which had been rehabilitated over the centuries to accommodate Christian morality. With *As You Like It*, the author could refine still another aspect of the pastoral: music, originally included in intermezzi, that is, between the scenes. Shakespeare's goal was to make music part of the whole design and to compose his plays as Monteverdi would have an opera.

AS YOU LIKE IT: A FANTASY FOR BROKEN CONSORT

As You like It is generally regarded as Shakespeare's most joyful comedy and even critical Doctor Johnson enjoyed its mild extravagance. It is not surprising therefore that it should also be the most musical of his plays with the greatest number of songs, unfortunately cut from some modern productions, even though they have a dramatic as well as a thematic function in a pastoral play celebrating love and concord. As mentioned already, Shakespeare was close to the Bassano family, who had come to England, recommended to Henry VIII by Venetian ambassador, Edmund Harvel. Five of the six brothers were given permanent employment as musicians at court, while the oldest one, Jacopo, made instruments for Henry. The youngest brother, Baptista, would become Emilia's father.

Songs were a very popular entertainment in Elizabeth's reign, which saw the blooming of vocal music, in particular the air accompanied by a lute. When the play was listed in the Stationers' Register, John Dowland and Thomas Morley had each published a book of Airs, *Songs and Ayres* (1597) and *First Book of Ayres* (1600). They were remarkable for the simplicity of their melodies whose natural rhythm closely followed the texts. This was a particularly rich time for composers encouraged by a well-read queen, who loved playing the lute or the virginal for her courtiers. A good musician, she always supported musical creation and interpretation at court and in the public and private theaters.[1] And perhaps she thought, like Lorenzo, that only a man that had music in himself could be trusted, since, as stated on page 33, she kept two staunch Catholics as her chapel masters: Thomas Tallis and William Byrd. Thomas Weelkes, Orlando Gibbons, Tobias Hume, and John Dowland all lent their talents as polyphonists to fantasies for voice and instruments. These were played by consorts of instruments belonging to the same family (whole consorts) or to different families with the possible addition of voices (broken consorts). Thomas Morley, Bachelor of Musicke and Gentleman of Her Majesty's Royal Chapel, one of Byrd's disciples, published the first English madrigals, whose harmonies, unlike Italian madrigals, were stripped of ornaments and closer to popular songs for inspiration. He was also the author of a handbook of musical instruction, *A Plaine and Easie Introduction to Practicall Musicke* (1597). The musical wealth of the time was equal to its literary and dramatic wealth and it is not surprising to note a fruitful collaboration between the greatest artists of the period. If a number of poems set to music remain anonymous, others were written by Lyly, Sidney, Donne, Ben Jonson, and Shakespeare. It is therefore very frustrating to note that amidst such abundance, Shakespeare's musicians have left so few traces. Apart from two airs for Ariel in *The Tempest*, which we know to have been set to music by Robert Johnson (father or son, we don't know), the music of Shakespeare's plays mostly remains a matter of conjecture. Out of the six songs of *As You Like It*, one only, *It was a Lover and His Lass,* has kept its contemporary harmonization. Yet that Shakespeare knew music well is evident in his many accurate references to it throughout his plays and the fact, already mentioned, that he often seemed to compose his plays like a musician, alternating themes and tempi rather than cutting them into acts and scenes. We have to suppose a close connection between his musician friends and himself.

Naturally, the notion of copyrights did not have then the meaning that we give it now. Borrowings were frequent and numerous among artists. In the history of Renaissance music, which is inseparable from the history of dance, England distinguishes itself by the mingling of rustic genres and more formal ones. Emphasis was placed more in the skillful use of forms and in the clever variations upon them than in the invention of new, unknown forms, although the manner would eventually modify the content. The spectators took great pleasure in recognizing their favorite air clad in new garments, or words they knew by heart dressed in a new musical fashion.

---

[1] The importance of music in the education of the gentleman was emphasized by Sir Thomas Elyot in *The Governor* (1531) and Henry VIII had taken care to give a humanistic education to all his children.

It is not by chance that the two plays, whose titles imply freedom as well as a bow to the public taste, *As You Like It* and *Twelfth Night: or, What You Will*, are also the ones which contain the most songs. Shakespeare found his inspiration in the many vocal forms at hand: the ballad, the air accompanied by the lute or by a consort, the canon, the drinking song, the rondo, and the song with a chorus asking for a choir. [2] In 1599, the arrival in the company of the musician-actor Robert Armin gave Shakespeare the opportunity to develop what Sternfeld calls "adult songs,"[3] namely songs whose function was to characterize rather than simply enchant, as boys' choirs used to do. As the Lord Chamberlain's Men were acquiring the Globe Theatre, Armin succeeded William Kemp in the clown's parts. He created Touchstone, then Feste in *Twelfth Night*, the Fool in *King Lear*, and Autolycus in *The Winter's Tale*, all plays in which the number of songs is important. There was keen competition with the children's choirs at Blackfriars, where their angels' voices conquered the public,[4] but Shakespeare did not scorn this other genre of which *It Was a Lover and His Lass* may be one instance, and which Ariel employs extensively in the enchanted atmosphere of *The Tempest*.

Having at hand a number of well-known composers, talented musicians, and the collaboration of a musical fellow actor, Shakespeare could avail himself of the masque tradition at the court of Elizabeth. Such entertainment, whose origins go back to pagan celebrations of the seasons, brought a banquet of the senses on the stage: "the dance is made to speak, the comedy to sing, the eye, the ear and the understanding are equally satisfied."[5] This definition of the absolute performance, addressing the eye as much as the ear, the body as much as the mind, reminds us of Bottom's wonder and his confusion of senses. As Shearman reminds us, one aim of mannerism was "to excite wonder,"[6] to create *meraviglie* that would confuse the senses. The fact is that the strict separation usually perceived by today's critics and scholars between the plastic and the performing arts did not exist in the Renaissance. The use of analogy already characterized Leonardo's creative principle and the great painter, we learn, also composed

---

[2] "The refrain of a medieval carol, for instance, is known as a 'burden.' In modern times, a refrain is often synonymous with 'chorus,' because it is usually sung by a group as opposed to a soloist." *The Oxford Companion to Music*, 1040.
[3] F. W. Sternfeld, *Music in Shakespearean Tragedy* (London: Routledge and Kegan Paul, 1963), 98–118.
[4] In 1576, Richard Farrant, master of the royal chapel, found in the former convent of Blackfriars, which had been enfranchised from the lord mayor's jurisdiction, a place propitious to the children's choirs he directed. After various events, the theater was used again in 1600 by the boys of Henry Evans who succeeded Farrant. It only became the property of Shakespeare's company in 1608. See Michel Grivelet, *Shakespeare de A à Z* (Paris: Aubier, 1988).
[5] Enid Welsford, *The Court Masque* (New York: Russell and Russell, 1962), 164.
[6] Shearman, *Mannerism*, 112.

music for the theater as well as costumes and stage scenery, and may have been the first inventor of opera, long before Monteverdi.[7] According to Michel Foucault, until the end of the sixteenth century, analogy played a major role in the building of knowledge in the Christian world. It was instrumental in the exegesis and the interpretation of texts, and through the symbols it created, made possible the knowledge of visible and invisible things, and guided the art of portraying them.[8]

Until recently Opera could still give us an idea of what those masque performances must have been like, mingling ballet, songs, allegory, and myth with the most sumptuous costumes and settings.[9] The Elizabethan public theater could not fail to benefit from the popularity of the genre, and Shakespeare, like Ben Jonson, knew how to use its symbolic nature: "The masque, both as Jonson created it and as he received it from its Elizabethan predecessors, is always about the resolution of discord; antitheses, paradoxes, and the movement from disorder to order are central to its nature."[10]

From disorder to order, from chaos to harmony, isn't it also the design of the pastoral and therefore of *As You Like It,* where the apparition of Hymen concludes the four marriages of the play with a nuptial song and dancing? Where, by its nature, the "wooden O"[11] imposed severe limits on set design, music by its suggestive power appealed to the imagination of the audience. Today, the Cartesian mind that cannot understand the symbolic nature of the whole has probably also lost the music of the soul which enabled it to correspond with the universe. Shakespeare perfectly explained such correspondences in *The Merchant of Venice,* a few years before *As You Like It:*

---

[7] Lexa, *Léonard de Vinci: L'invention de l'opéra.*

[8] "Jusqu'à la fin du XVIè siècle, la ressemblance a joué un rôle bâtisseur dans le savoir de la culture occidentale. C'est elle qui a conduit pour une grande part l'exégèse et l'interprétation des textes; c'est elle qui a organisé le jeu des symboles, permis la connaissance des choses visibles et invisibles, guidé l'art de les représenter. Le monde s'enroulait sur lui-même: la terre répétant le ciel, les visages se mirant dans les étoiles, et l'herbe enveloppant dans ses tiges les secrets qui servaient à l'homme. La peinture imitait l'espace. Et la représentation — qu'elle fût fête ou savoir — se donnait comme répétition: théâtre de la vie ou miroir du monde, c'était là le titre de tout langage, sa manière de s'annoncer et de formuler son droit à parler." Michel Foucault, *Les mots et les choses* (Paris: 'Tel' Gallimard, 1966), 32.

[9] It is unfortunately less and less true and the often-drab contemporary performances reveal the lack of sufficient financing as much as the loss of a certain sense of beauty in our world.

[10] Stephen Orgel, ed. *Ben Jonson: Selected Masques* (New Haven: Yale University Press, 1970), 3.

[11] See *Henry V,* Prologue: "...can this cockpit hold / The vasty fields of France? or may we cram / Within this wooden O the very casques / That did affright the air at Agincourt? / O, pardon! since a crooked figure may / Attest in little place a million; / And let us, ciphers to this great accompt, / On your imaginary forces work.... Piece out our imperfections with your thoughts."

How sweet the moonlight sleeps upon this bank!
Here will we sit, and let the sounds of music
Creep in our ears. Soft stillness and the night
Become the touches of sweet harmony.
Sit, Jessica.
Look how the floor of heaven
Is thick inlaid with patens of bright gold.
There's not the smallest orb which thou behold'st
But in his motion like an angel sings,
Still choiring to the young-eyed cherubins
Such harmony is in immortal souls,
But whilst this muddy vesture of decay
Doth grossly close it in, we cannot hear it.

(The Merchant of Venice, V i 54–65)

Lorenzo does not say anything in those lines that would not have been familiar to most educated Elizabethans. The Pythagorean doctrine of the harmony of the spheres provided an apt backdrop tying music, moonlight, love, and serenity together. The heavenly concord resounds in the amorous hearts of Lorenzo and Jessica who, for a brief moment, manage to transcend the vagaries of the flesh to reach the everlasting serenity of immortal souls. Such a vision — a perfect, geocentric world, a projection of God spilling himself through the many levels of the universe, the planets and the elements, from the sphere of the seraphim down to man — found a zealous interpretation in Robert Fludd's book published as late as 1617,[12] at the very time when Galileo was confirming the existence of a heliocentric system. The ancient vision could certainly be viewed ironically but it was nonetheless much more satisfying to the poetic minds, and to those who harked back to the old faith. According to Fludd, musical intervals and scales were the link between man and God. Is there any true musician nowadays who would contradict him?

It is therefore in 1600, in a veritable musical crucible, that *As You Like It* was born and, echoing Lorenzo, Duke Senior does not fail to remind his followers that "If [Jaques], compact of jars, grow musical / We shall have shortly discord in the spheres" (II vii 5–6). Indeed, sparing no one with his jarring commentaries, the melancholy Jaques is paradoxically the first to ask with passion for more songs after Amiens's first performance:

Jaques: More, more, I prithee, more.
Amiens: It will make you melancholy, Monsieur Jaques.
Jaques: I thank it. More, I prithee, more. I can suck melancholy out
of a song as a weasel sucks eggs. More, I prithee, more. (II v 11–13)

---

[12] R. Fludd, *Utriusque Cosmi Historia* (Oppenheim, 1617). See Kathi Meyer-Baer, *Music of The Spheres and the Dance of Death* (Princeton, NJ: Princeton University Press, 1970), chap. IX, 188ff.

Duke Senior—who knows Jaques well and does not hesitate to reproach him for the hypocrisy of chiding other people's sins while forgetting his own—suspects some affectation in this sudden love of music. Isn't Amiens's song simply the occasion for him to dash off his own satirical couplet? In the *Anatomy of Melancholy*, Robert Burton devotes a whole chapter to music as a remedy against melancholy, "it is a sovereign remedy against despair and melancholy, and will drive away the devil himself."[13] What are we then to think of Jaques's declaration in the last act, "I am for other than for dancing measures" (V iv 188) and when Duke Senior tries to retain him, "Stay, Jaques, stay," he gets away with these words, "To see no pastime, I" (V iv 189–90). What are we to make of Jaques's paradoxical nature, which provokes many discordant judgments?

The truth is that the melancholy Jaques must be faithful to his role as *burden* in the present fantasy. Celia provides the definition of the word: "I would sing my song without a burden; thou bringest me out of tune" (III ii 239–40), perfectly suggesting the intrusion of a refrain, generally at the bass, an undersong destabilizing her melody.[14] In his famous soliloquy on the seven ages of man (II vii 139–66), Jaques surpasses himself in his dark and wintry vision of humanity full of discord and harsh sounds: the mewling babe, the whining schoolboy, the lover sighing like furnace, the quarrelling and swearing soldier, the preaching justice, who is bound nonetheless to see his "manly voice" turn again to "childish treble," piping and whistling in his sound, until total oblivion leaves him "sans teeth, sans eyes, sans taste, sans everything." Orlando's irruption with his "venerable burden" happily alleviates the tonality of Jaques's interpretation. Burdens were not necessarily disruptive after all. Musically speaking, the burden also acted like a resounding altar of repose, underlying the musical structure. It was the constant bass on which the musical discourse came to rest, as well as the foil out of which harmony was created. Both were intimately tied together though, the burden providing the breeding ground, the reassuring primal sound out of which the melody surged. Jaques's own burden eventually leads him toward spirituality, whereas Adam's salvation points to the possible rebirth of fallen humanity.

The forest of Arden, far from being a paradise, is a place of hardship devoid of flattery. Before hearing the harmony of the spheres, the ear has to endure a lot of dissonance. Far from concluding that music appears in *As You Like It* only to be untuned and disturbed, it is important to

---

[13] Robert Burton, *The Anatomy of Melancholy* (London: J. M. Dent and Sons Ltd, 1932), Pt. 2, Sec. 2, Mem. 6, Subs. 3, "Music a Remedy."
[14] A burden, from the Middle English "bourdon" (from the French, literally "drone") is a bass part underlying a melody.

understand that harmony can only be born of the opposition of contraries.

Thus, when Amiens begins to sing in the second part of Act II, the play's emphasis has mostly been on discord rather than harmony. Contrary to *Twelfth Night* which starts with the melancholy lover Duke Orsino, whose desire is to surfeit himself with music to cure his unrequited love, [15] *As You Like It* first plunges the audience into the cacophony of family quarrels. Mimetic violence takes hold of the stage with a first conflict between Orlando and his elder brother Oliver, then a second conflict, confirmed by Charles the wrestler, between the Duke and his elder brother, whose position he has usurped after banishing him. These violent deeds are given reality in a fight pitting Orlando against Charles, whose mission is to do away with him. The wrestling, to which the ladies are invited, aptly mirroring the violent and corrupted atmosphere of the court, triggers Rosalind's first ironical remark about music: "But is there any else longs to see this *broken music* in his sides? Is there yet another dotes upon rib-breaking?" (I ii 127–29) If the reference to *broken consort* suggests the then popular ensemble of instruments belonging to different families, the play on words and the mention of rib-breaking also imply broken instruments and the musical disaster it entails, in agreement with the general discordant atmosphere of the play.

In such a world, the shared love of Rosalind and Celia assuredly looks like a strange exotic plant. And since they decide to play at falling in love to pass the time, will not violence erupt between them? Indeed, since victorious Orlando entered the love triangle, how could they both love him and stay friends? Celia's father tries hard to arouse his daughter's jealousy by telling her that she will show more bright and virtuous once witty Rosalind is banished. If Celia applies the amorous logic of her friend—"The Duke my father loved his father dearly" (I iii 21)), which is also her father's: "Thou art thy father's daughter—there's enough" (l. 49)—she must therefore deny Rosalind. However, loyal Celia refuses to obey this kind of fatalism. [16]

After an opening full of sound and fury, where the only real music is the flourish introducing the usurper and his retinue, Celia breaks with the spiral of mimetic violence, which could turn the play into a tragedy, by refusing to inherit her father's revenge. Even though Shakespeare gives her the name of Thomas Lodge's Aliena, symbolizing her exiled destitute condition, she chooses to see the freedom of their banishment rather

---

[15] Duke Orsino: "If music be the food of love, play on, / Give me excess of it that, surfeiting, / The appetite may sicken and so die" (I i 1–3).

[16] It is the same fatality which condemns Romeo and Juliet's love, and which draws Hamlet against his will into a revenge which he cannot possibly escape alive. Very sensibly, free-minded Celia questions the false syllogism of her cousin: "Doth it therefore ensue that you should love his son dearly? By this kind of chase I should hate him, for my father hated his father dearly; yet I hate not Orlando" (I iii 30–31).

than its loss. Both cousins run away together far from the Duke's threats, putting on new roles to ward off the assaults of men.

As for Orlando, he learns from Old Adam that Oliver's vengeance is more menacing than ever since he threatens to burn him alive in his house. It is enough to send Orlando and Adam running away on the harsh road of exile, the third flight in what must be called the *exposition* of the play, which thus recalls, literally and metaphorically, a *fugue*. Derived in the sixteenth and at the beginning of the seventeenth century from instrumental forms such as the fantasy, the fugue, from the Latin *fuga*, flight, is characterized by the successive entry of three or four voices, each of which introduces the theme(s). The exposition is followed by a series of rather free divertimenti and by the development of the contrapuntal themes of each voice until the final *coda*. This form, very strict in its principle, actually left a lot of freedom to the imagination and there are many varieties of fugue which were perhaps best exemplified by Johann Sebastian Bach. If the fact that Shakespeare deliberately used the structure of the musical work to build his play cannot be proved, it is nonetheless evident that *As You Like It* is by far the most musical of his plays due to its structure, its polyphonic design, and its almost total absence of plot.

Toward the middle of Act II, all the "good" characters have fled willy-nilly and are bound to meet in the forest of Arden. The "bad," nonetheless redeemable, characters are left behind in the corrupted world of reality. With the exception of a short scene (III i) recalling the fury of Duke Frederick who drives Oliver out for not finding his brother—recalling the first theme (sibling hatred, revenge, banishment), for which it is also a coda. This action incidentally introduces the voice which was missing in the second theme (freedom, love, and concord), namely that of a lover for Celia. Nothing now prevents the characters from enjoying the delights of the pastoral world far from the treachery of the court. Plot development per se stops here.[17] We have to reach the end of the play to learn that Duke Frederick himself, triggered by the attractive power of the exiled court, has decided that he, too, should hunt his own brother in the forest, where a fortuitous meeting with a religious man converts him from his heinous and worldly life. The play is in all senses of the word a fugue out of this harsh wrestling world to a reformed life of love and prayers.

As Harold Jenkins points out, "The course of true love has not run smooth. But most of its obstacles have really disappeared before the main

---

[17] Violence, death threats, social, and parental prohibition are kept away from the world of the pastoral where the only serious obstacle to the realization of love is, in this case, the evident pleasure of the heroine impersonating Ganymede and making herself the master of the game. See the excellent article "As You Like It" by Harold Jenkins in *Shakespeare Survey* 8 (Cambridge: Cambridge University Press, 1955), 40–51.

comedy begins." From this moment on, characters are jousting verbally and wittily in contrasted duets of differentiated voices, from the jarring tunes of Jaques and Orlando to the unison of the young pages who sing *It was a lover and his lass* "both in a tune, like two gipsies on a horse" (V iii 13). In order to ensure the freedom of his melodic design Shakespeare has chosen the forest of Arden. Its very name implies that everyone knows it and many critics have looked for it on geographic maps. Historically, it points to the real forest of Ardennes, where so many British exiled Catholics and "convertites" found refuge. A psychoanalyst might enjoy linking it to Shakespeare's mother, Mary Arden, and the loving paradise of the womb. Its paradoxical nature, however, makes it clear that this is, just like Rabelais's Abbey of Thélème, an imaginary place where Sherwood oaks stand side by side with palm and olive trees, where stags languish shedding "big round tears" in the swift brook (according to Jaques who has turned ecological), and where lionesses feed on lost travelers. This is a space out of time too — "There's no clock in the forest," (III ii 291–92)[18] sensible Orlando reminds us. The spring of love succeeds the winter of exile and music conveniently stresses the allegory of the seasons, which is as spiritual as it is material.

Thus the first two songs, for which we only have Thomas Arne's 1740 musical adaptation, celebrate the joys of pastoral life, simple and natural, where winter's icy winds are infinitely more tolerable than human ingratitude. If we believe Jaques and those lines by Thomas Morley, their music must have been melancholy:

> It follows to show you how to dispose your music according to the nature of the words which you are therein to express, as whatsoever matter it be which you have in mind such a kind of music must you frame to it. You must therefore, if you have a grave matter, apply a grave kind of music to it; if a merry subject you must make your music also merry, for it will be a great absurdity to use a sad harmony to a merry matter or a merry harmony to a sad, lamentable, or tragical ditty.
>
> You must then when you would express any word signifying hardness, cruelty, bitterness, and other such like make the harmony like unto it, that is, somewhat harsh and hard, but yet so that it offend not. Likewise when any of your words shall express complaint, sorrow, repentance, sighs, tears, and such like let your harmony be sad and doleful.... If the subject be light you must cause your music to go in rhythms which carry with them a quickness of time; if it be lamentable the notes must go

---

18 There's no clock either in Thélème, Gargantua judging that it is a waste of time to count the hours. (Bk. I, chap. LII)

in slow and heavy rhythms; and of all this you shall find examples
everywhere in the works of the good musicians.[19]

Morley, who may have been the original composer for those songs,
continues to insist on the necessity to suit the notes to the syllables of the
words. His remarks show how composers adapted their music to the spoken
imagery of the poems. The first two songs, meant literally to pass the time
between the various developments, also underlie the melancholy atmosphere of exile while setting the stage for a sweeter pastoral life. The ironical
couplet added by Jaques to *Under the Greenwood Tree* somewhat modulates
Duke Senior's idyllic philosophy of the first scene, reminding us that only
a fool would pretend to find happiness apart from a wealthy comfortable
life. A moment before, the quick financial transaction between Corin, the
shepherd, and the two runaway young women has proved that gold was
not to be scorned in the pastoral world and that Jaques was not wrong:

> *Corin*: Assuredly the thing is to be sold.
> Go with me. If you like upon report,
> The soil, the profit, and this kind of life,
> I will your very faithful feeder be,
> And buy it with your gold right suddenly. (II iv 95–99)

Jaques is paradoxically the only character who does not go back to court at
the end of the play, not because he is obstinately antagonistic, but because
he chooses to accompany Duke Frederick into religious life. Whether
he will choose conversion or keep his part as an observer is left to our
imaginations. Auden interprets his gesture in a rather interesting manner:

> ... Jaques is the only character who chooses to leave his wealth and
> ease — it is the critic of the pastoral sentiment who remains in the
> cave. But he does not do this his stubborn will to please, for the
> hint is given that he will go further and embrace the religious life.
> In neoplatonic terms he is the most musical of them all for he is
> the only one whom the carnal music of this world cannot satisfy,
> because he desires to hear the unheard music of the spheres.[20]

Whether Jaques's words really allow us to conclude anything of the kind is
debatable of course. He may simply be searching for new facets of human

---

[19] Thomas Morley, *A Plain and Easy Introduction to Practical Music*, ed. Alec Harman
(New York: W.W. Norton, 1973), "Rules to be observed in dittying," 290. If Morley
participated in the composition of *It was a lover and his lass*, there is no evidence that his
contribution was unique. One thing is certain, the music of Thomas Arne, written one
century and a half later, is not in total agreement with the tone of the piece.

[20] Wystan H. Auden, "Music in Shakespeare, Its Dramatic Use in His Plays," *Encounter*
(1957), 31–44. Quoted by Peter J. Seng, *The Vocal Songs in the Plays of Shakespeare*
(Cambridge, MA: Harvard University Press, 1967), 72.

nature to feed new railings,[21] even though he has in several instances criticized the hypocrisy of the cast's position in the forest as usurpers of the natural world.

For the time being, his part as burden in the overall polyphony means that he will not hear a song without adding his own personal refrain. All three parts of the song thus catch up on the first theme of the play, exile, with the implied oppositions between nature and culture, country life and city life. If exile is, according to Celia, more freedom than banishment, such freedom is made of modesty and "low content," according to Orlando.

Throughout the play, such relativity of judgments is maintained, with the oppositions caught up by the various characters in a counterpoint where no voice is ever preponderant, the only esthetic purpose being the final harmony. Thus when Orlando bursts in on the Duke's retinue, turned into a threatening lunatic by the harshness of his life —"The thorny point / Of bare distress hath ta'en from me the show / Of smooth civility," (II vii 94–96) — he is welcomed by Duke Senior who tells him to "sit down and feed." Orlando then is made to reconsider the scene: "I thought that all things had been savage here," (II vii 107) as he understands that his host, far from being a woodman, is the perfect example of humanistic gentleness, a man who loves music and even asks for a second song, which is even more melancholy than the first. Fortunately, the dramatic action presently contradicts the misanthropic words of the song, "Most friendship is feigning, most loving, mere folly," (II vii 192) as Orlando, full of the Duke's generosity, comes back carrying Adam, "his venerable burden," on his back, creating a new musical and dramatic contrast.

The second theme of the play, which has until now merely been suggested, is love, which will be modulated in all tonalities from Act III to the end of the play. The freedom and lack of censure of the forest of Arden allow the playwright all kinds of juxtapositions of his voices. The romantic lovers meet with the conventional pastoral lovers who, through the artifice of their feelings, provide a wholly human perspective to the love of Rosalind and Orlando, whereas the country lovers, Touchstone and Audrey, remind one that the sexual dimension of desire is not to be dismissed. The ambiguity of the whole is still emphasized by the double play of Rosalind on registers which, for all their differences, are nonetheless strangely similar, as if the soprano sang the countertenor part and vice versa. As Ganymede offers to cure Orlando of his love sickness, Rosalind catches his mind, forcing him

---

[21] Alexander Leggatt thinks that behind the posture, there exists in Jaques a real interest in human nature. "He collects people, prizing Touchstone in particular as a rare item." He may want "to add Frederick to his collection of interesting people," *Shakespeare's Comedy of Love* (London: Methuen, 1974), 201, 216.

to call Ganymede Rosalind, thus turning the lie into truth while enjoying the freedom provided by her disguise.

> *Orlando*: I would not be cured, youth.
> *Rosalind*: I would cure you if you would but call me Rosalind and come every day to my cot, and woo me. (III ii 404–5)

But Orlando, like the male quartet of Navarre's academe, prefers indulging himself in his whimsical love humor. Pitted against his refusal, Ganymede's insistence, his "but call me Rosalind" and "woo me" betray a passion in the young woman that is certainly not purely Platonic.

The *chassé-croisé* of the lovers is doubled by suggestive hunting images which make up the gist of the following songs. Those airs, the first two sung by Touchstone (*O, sweet Oliver* and *Wind away*) and the next one required by Jaques (*What shall he have that killed the deer?*), come within the development of the second theme, to modulate the idyllic image of pastoral love, just as the first two songs of the play offered a minor tonality of country life.

Whereas Orlando is carving on every tree the "huntress' name that my full life doth sway," (III ii 4) Celia notes that "he was furnished like a hunter" (206) and Rosalind concludes "O, ominous — he comes to kill my heart," (207) while under Ganymede's mask it is she who goes hunting. The theme of the hunted hunter is taken up by the pastoral shepherds Silvius and Phoebe, when he accuses his love of being his executioner and she replies by taking up to the letter the metonymy of the killing eye:

> *Phoebe*: Now I do frown on thee with all my heart,
> And if mine eyes can wound, now let them kill thee. (III v 15–16)

An image that Orlando takes up again a little later, "I would not have my right Rosalind of this mind, for I protest her frown might kill me" (IV i 99–101). And while they are at it, they may as well go on:

> *Rosalind*: O, my dear Orlando, how it grieves me to see thee wear thy heart in a scarf.
> *Orlando*: It is my arm.
> *Rosalind*: I thought thy heart had been wounded with the claws of a lion.
> *Orlando*: Wounded it is, but with the eyes of a lady. (V ii 19–24)

This playful mannerist exchange diverts attention from the unexpected love at first sight of Celia and Oliver, whose meeting is compared to a ram struggle, then one of Caesar's victories. There is nothing musical in all those images and Shakespeare enjoys creating dissonances and multiplying contrasts. The final harmony will appear all the more magical. Love and hunting imagery are transposed to a bawdier register with the fourth couple of lovers,

Touchstone, called a "material fool" by Jaques, and the peasant girl Audrey, whom he steals from William, and marries for the immediate satisfaction of his desires. Touchstone wittily develops the reasons which make being a cuckolded husband a better state than being a lonesome bachelor:

> A man may, if he were of a fearful heart, stagger in this attempt; for here we have no temple but the wood, no assembly but horn-beasts. But what though? Courage. As horns are odious, they are necessary. It is said many a man knows no end of his goods. Right: many a man has good horns, and knows no end of them. Well, that is the dowry of his wife, 'tis none of his own getting. Horns? Even so. Poor men alone? No, no; the noblest deer hath them as huge as the rascal. Is the single man therefore blessed? No. As a walled town is more worthier than a village, so is the forehead of a married man more honourable than the bare brow of a bachelor. And by how much defence is better than no skill, by so much is a horn more precious than to want. (III iii 43–57)

His declaration is followed by a tentative pastoral wedding discouraged by Jaques, who compares such union to faulty wainscoting: "This fellow will but join you together as they join wainscot; then one of you will prove a shrunk panel and, like green timber, warp, warp" (III iii 78–80).

The words of the two following ballads have been lost but they were sung on the tune of *Hunt's Up* or *Peascod Time*, which perfectly agrees with the theme at hand and the next song, *What shall he have that killed the deer?*

The lovers' comings and goings in the forest have put the Duke and his retinue in the background. As Orlando prepares to join them for dinner, he asks Ganymede to wait for him some two hours. The exiles must be brought back on stage and to pass the time, what better and more appropriate *intermezzo* than a return from hunting? The words play beautifully on the ambiguity of *horns*, the hunting trophy offered to the winner, but also, as Touchstone explained, the inevitable trophy of the married man. Before the four marriages of the play's ending, this is the last bachelor's games or "stag party" as well as a skillful transition between winter and spring. The time is not yet ripe for harmony and therefore, according to Jaques: "Tis no matter how it be in tune, so it make noise enough" (IV ii 7–8).

The music has evolved from the expression of melancholy, through "the musical confusion"[22] of hounds and hunting horns, to the perfect chords of love. Whereas the first four songs offered a satirical counterpoint to the pastoral romance, the music now truly expresses the joy of love with *It was a lover and his lass*, even though Touchstone enjoys being a spoilsport.

---

[22] *A Midsummer Night's Dream*, IV i 106.

Has Jaques thrown some doubt in him? Contrary to R. Noble who judges the scene useless,[23] this air, probably composed by Thomas Morley, marks the perfect climax of a scene which looks as if it had been conceived for a musical comedy. The lovers reply, probably together in perfect unison, to Silvius's exposition, while Rosalind strikes up a contrary burden:

> *Phoebe*: Good shepherd, tell this youth what 'tis to love.
> *Silvius*: It is to be all made of sighs and tears,
> And so am I for Phoebe.
> *Phoebe*: And I for Ganymede.
> *Orlando*: And I for Rosalind.
> *Rosalind*: And I for no woman.
> *Silvius*: It is to be all made of faith and service,
> And so am I for Phoebe.
> *Phoebe*: And I for Ganymede.
> *Orlando*: And I for Rosalind.
> *Rosalind*: And I for no woman.
> *Silvius*: It is to be all made of fantasy,
> All made of passion, and all made of wishes,
> All adoration, duty, and observance,
> All humbleness, all patience and impatience,
> All purity, all trial and obedience,
> And so am I for Phoebe.
> *Phoebe*: And so am I for Ganymede.
> *Orlando*: And so am I for Rosalind.
> *Rosalind*: And so am I for no woman.
> *Phoebe* (to Rosalind): If this be so, why blame you me to love you?
> *Silvius* (to Phoebe): If this be so, why blame you me to love you?
> *Orlando*: If this be so, why blame you me to love you?
> *Rosalind*: Why do you speak too, "Why blame you me to love you?"
> *Orlando*: To her that is not here nor doth not hear.
> *Rosalind*: Pray you, no more of this, 'tis like the howling of Irish
> wolves against the moon.... (V ii 78–105)

This half-religious, half-burlesque mock wedding, lasts twenty-five lines until Rosalind-Ganymede, beside herself, orders them to stop their invocations, and promises help and satisfaction to each one of them. Tomorrow, the longed-for harmony, impossible now because of Rosalind's double game, will be realized. She only has to give up her Ganymede persona. The interest of this scene, which is worth any opera quartet, is that it reaches

---

[23] "It has nothing to do with the evolution of the action; it is a waste of time and is a diversion and nothing more." Seng, *The Vocal Songs in the Plays of Shakespeare*, 88. Referencing R. Noble, *Shakespeare's Use of Song with the Text of the Principal Songs* (London: Oxford University Press, 1923), 76.

harmony through its melodic structure even before it can actually occur in deeds. Hence the perfect timing of the song *It was a lover and his lass*, to herald spring and the coming wedding festivities, celebrating love in another register, less conventional, more epicurean, in agreement with Touchstone's sensual philosophy. Inspired by Horace and Virgil, the Renaissance found in *Carpe Diem* a profoundly human attitude to life, nature, and love. A sentence like "How that a life was but a flower" (V iii 29) echoes numerous others on the passing of time and the brevity of love, and was nothing new in those days, which is probably what Touchstone means with his "no great matter in the ditty." To argue about the originality of the words, whether they were written by Shakespeare or Morley, or maybe the two of them together, or neither of them, seems indeed a fruitless exercise. Similarly, the order of the stanzas is indifferent to the general meaning. The Oxford edition places "And therefore take the present time" last, turning it into a philosophical conclusion, but its second position in the Folio has its arguments: you who are in love, take the present time, go lie between the acres of the rye for life is but a flower! The harmony between the words and Morley's joyful music gave this song its popular appeal and made it one of the best known in Shakespeare's work. It reminds us that spiritual harmony is often born of the harmony of the senses and that to deny the latter is often to destroy the former.

The miracle can now happen with the entrance of Hymen and Rosalind and Celia returning as themselves. A "Still music" gives the nuptial ceremony solemnity and magic, with Hymen dedicating and expanding the newly realized harmony to cosmic dimensions:

> Then is there mirth in heaven
> When earthly things made even
> Atone together. (V iv 103–5)

Those lines were later set to music by Thomas Arne, even though they are not italicized like the other songs in the Folio. Seng also points out that the still music could be required to conceal the noise of the machinery which brought Hymen down from the heavens.[24] It is very likely that music continued as a background throughout the scene with the song *Wedding is Great Juno's Crown* wittily celebrating Hymen's divinity, the god who peoples cities!

This sketch of a masque then brought all actors and spectators together in its courtly dances and entertainments:

---

[24] The fashion of the masque was greatly enhanced by the invention of stage machinery which made for spectacular effects. In 1605, Ben Jonson started to work with Inigo Jones, the famous architect who found in Italy the inspiration for a great number of sumptuous decors and new theatrical machines. They would be mostly used in Blackfriars, the stage of the public outdoor theatres making them difficult to use.

> Play, music, and you brides and bridegrooms all,
> With measure heaped in joy to th' measures fall. (V iv 173–74)

Shakespeare artfully adapted the symbolical meaning of the masque to his comedy and would incorporate such episodes every time the action justified it in his plays. The magic elicited by Hermione's resurrection in *The Winter's Tale*, the nuptial benediction of Juno and Ceres in *The Tempest* are among many such examples of Shakespeare's adapting the stage artifices of the masque to his own mannerist ends. With the triumph of sexual and spiritual love, the characters reach harmonious relationships at last. Aren't they compared to musical instruments by the heroine herself when she chides Silvius: "Wilt thou love such a woman? What, to make thee an instrument, and play false strains upon thee? — not to be endured" (IV iii 68–70). Like the instruments of an orchestra, the characters have to play in tune and should not play tricks on each other lest discord ensue.[25]

In *As You Like It*, music supports the atmosphere and the moods, and also creates the scenery. As in most of Shakespeare's plays, it is used as metaphor, as a symbol of human harmony or disharmony, while being a popular entertainment which acted as a curtain in the course of the drama. It seems however that in *As You Like It*, more than in any other play, music is used deliberately as an exercise of style in imitation of the musical compositions of the time. The very structure of the play, whose action is essentially verbal, seems to imitate the musical genres of the time, whether an instrumental fantasy, or a madrigal for four or five voices. The first part of the play, by its structure and theme, evokes *the fugue,* and the songs that give rhythm to life in the forest of Arden, obey the structural necessities of the themes developed and their counter-themes. They are integrated like the divertimenti of the fugue which follow the exposition and the development of a theme. To claim that they are useless is not to understand the general design of the whole. One can easily imagine Shakespeare winking at a colleague musician, just as Rosalind winks at the audience when she reveals the boy who played her part in the epilogue. For lack of any commentary on the performances before 1740, we can only make conjectures. In the space of a century and a half, the spirit of the

---

[25] Hamlet uses the image in a well-known scene where he unmasks Rosencrantz and Guildenstern, asking the latter if he can play the recorder. When Guildenstern replies that he lacks the skill, Hamlet retorts: "Why, look you now, how unworthy a thing you make of me! You would play upon me, you would seem to know my stops, you would pluck out the heart of my mystery, you would sound me from the lowest note to the top of my compass; and there is much music, excellent voice in this little organ, yet cannot you make it speak. 'Sblood, do you think that I am easier to be played on than a pipe? Call me what instrument you will, though you can fret me, you cannot play upon me" (III ii 346–54).

time had changed a lot and music, now at the climax of classicism, had lost part of the cosmic correspondences which made it an integral part of the humanistic vision of the comedians at the Globe.

Now the coda, because we need a coda, concerns the only character who does not go along with the final harmony of the weddings: Jaques. He refuses to join in the dance and prefers to share the religious retreat of a convertite. He is also the character who enjoins Touchstone to marry properly with a good priest. Throughout the pastoral he plays the part of the burden, the voice that comments, disrupts, scolds, mocks, and moralizes. As a companion of the exiled Duke in the forest, he helps maintain the balance between idealistic reveries and the blunt satisfaction of personal desires. His encounter with Touchstone's common sense is a delightful experience, which leads him to wish for himself the freedom of speech that has always been granted to the motley fool. Jaques's ambition is to play the social doctor, cleansing the world of its sins for the good of everyone, even explaining why he cannot be accused of any personal denunciation since he does not aim at nor name anyone in particular. Yet the license of the fool would protect him from higher sanctions. Shakespeare may indeed have winked at Ben Jonson by painting such a satirist, but Jaques could just as well, and more secretly, play Shakespeare himself, who, play after play, keeps coming back to the ills and follies of men, exercising the license of the fool in a world where speaking one's mind was ever more dangerous and censure ever more active. Have we here a dramatist who fancies himself a doctor and, even while writing his most joyful master-piece, wishes that he could join his exiled friends in Douai on a religious retreat? The theme of healing runs throughout his work, and Jaques's aloofness resembles Shakespeare's own apparent detachment from the bubbling underground life of the London theater world. Behind the happy comedy, there was a serious purpose: to mend broken consorts and bring harmony back to the realm. It remained Shakespeare's relentless objective.

While he was working on the pastoral and exile in *As you Like It*, Shake-speare also returned to themes adumbrated in *The Comedy of Errors*, namely: twins, shipwreck, loss, and recovery in *Twelfth Night*, another gem of a comedy. Just as art students of the day employed mirror-anamorphoses and other illusionistic tricks in order to master perspective, the characters in *Twelfth Night* have to puzzle out illusory images of themselves before they can gain true perspective on who they are.

MIMETICISM AND MIRROR GAMES IN *TWELFTH NIGHT*

In *Twelfth Night*, the usual comedic obstacles to the fulfilment of the lovers' desire seem to have been eliminated from the start: there are no grumbling fathers to oppose the marriage of the lovers, no royal power to denounce it. Orsino and Olivia are both independent young people with full executive control over their own lives, they are both handsome and noble, and according to Elizabethan social codes they each provide the ideal match for the other; only Olivia's grief seems to postpone their expected union. In Illyria, conflicts belong to the past and the Duke's most aggressive opponent has the good-natured appearance of Antonio, the pirate, who has just rescued Sebastian and is now risking his life in Illyria for love of him:

> His life I gave him, and did thereto add
> My love without retention or restraint,
> All his in dedication (V i 74–76)

Antonio is a secondary character but his clandestine presence in the play is not gratuitous; he comes as a discreet counterpoint to the main plot and a foil to the main characters. He is a man of action and a man of his word, contrary to Orsino, whose moods make him assert one thing and then another. Antonio, like his namesake in *The Merchant of Venice*, gives the sole example of truly disinterested love in the play, and the only one which paradoxically brings forth life. It evokes the manly, fatherly tenderness of the *Sonnets*. His discretion is rewarded in the way the others' zeal is not, by the revelation of the true identity of the loved one to whom he dedicates his life most generously, since he never asks for anything in return. Yet, his loyalty and trust will eventually be pitted against the violence and confusion generated by mimetic rivalry.

For the laws of mimesis rule most of the play's characters. Shakespeare multiplies illusions and misunderstandings, lies and deceit through a play of masks and disguises. As Feste, the most lucid of commentators, notices: "Nothing that is so, is so" (IV i 8). Nobody really is what he thinks he is, and it is in rivalry that resemblance is most obvious. As René Girard puts it, "Growing equality does not give birth to harmony but to more and more intense competition,"[26] since according to the laws of mimetic desire, men, having denied or lost the single idol they had in God, or a godlike king, copy each other, rousing each other's rival desires. Now what do we see in Illyria? First the competition of the nobles, who converse through ambassadors only. Duke Orsino, who rules the country, is put in a difficult situation by Olivia's rejection, her household being a sort of mirror of his

---

[26] "The increasing equality—the approach of the mediator in our terms—does not give rise to harmony but to an even keener rivalry"; René Girard, *Deceit, Desire and the Novel* (Baltimore: The John Hopkins University Press, 1965), 136–37. "L'égalité croissante n'engendre pas l'harmonie mais une concurrence toujours plus aiguë"; René Girard, *Mensonge Romantique et Vérité Romanesque* (Paris: Grasset, 1961), 160.

own. He even shares her fool, Feste, who lends his talent to one or the other, depending on his humor. Thus by going through the looking glass, Feste knows better than most what illusion they live in, which justifies the title he gives himself: a *corrupter of words*. Words, like men, and like cheverel gloves, can be turned inside out. As Feste very rightly concludes, "words are very rascals since bonds disgraced them," (III i 15–16) i.e., since a man's word cannot be trusted unless it is duly written and sealed.

Orsino is not Olivia's only suitor, he has a rival in Sir Andrew, introduced by his friend Sir Toby as "as tall a man as any's in Illyria" (I iii 16). Sir Toby's systematic refusal to obey the rules of propriety and respect he owes his own niece only goes one step further toward confusion. Yet he also bluntly reminds Malvolio of his social position: "Art any more than a steward?" (II iii 106). The comic spirit seems always on the verge of disorder and chaos. Shakespeare was particularly conscious of the problem, which he had Ulysses define in *Troilus and Cressida*:

> O when degree is shaked,
> Which is the ladder to all high designs,
> The enterprise is sick. How could communities,
> Degrees in schools, and brotherhoods in cities,
> Peaceful commerce from dividable shores,
> The primogeniture and due of birth,
> Prerogative of age, crowns, sceptres, laurels,
> But by degree stand in authentic place?
> Take but degree away, untune that string,
> And hark what discord follows. Each thing meets
> In mere oppugnancy. (*Troilus and Cressida*, I iii 100–110)

This speech, all too often interpreted as a purple patch of reactionary patriarchal politics, merely unveils the mechanism of mimetic desire leading to confusion and violence. According to Girard, murderous rivalry is not occasioned by distinctions but by their loss.[27] If such chaos is propitious to comedy, it is only in so far as rivalries are kept at a play stage and everyone will resume his position in the end. Elizabethan society was built on rigid hierarchies, which were dangerous to overlook. The temptation and the threat, however, was always there, intensified by Shakespeare's choice of twins and mirror situations. Only a few conventions separate comedy from tragedy, the aim of both being, for Shakespeare in particular, the representation of life.

Girard asserts that in many primitive societies, twins inspired a tremendous fear on account of their lack of differentiation. Their birth was a bad

---

[27] Girard, *La Violence et le Sacré*, 77.

omen that anticipated violence. Confusion developed between biological twins and sociological twins, who started proliferating.[28] Shakespeare, who obviously had not read Girard but had a remarkably similar intuition about the mechanism of human cultural and social order, built this plot on the parallelism between the sociological twins Orsino and Olivia, and the biological twins Viola and Sebastian, thus intensifying the risks of confusion brought about by mimetic desire. Suppress the biological twins, and it is not difficult to imagine a future of conflicts between the two rival leaders of Illyria, recalling Oberon and Titania's discords in *A Midsummer Night's Dream.*

The effects of mimesis don't stop at that since Viola, whose fate is parallel to that of Olivia (both mourn the loss of a brother), is instinctively attracted by her—"O, that I served that lady," (I ii 38)—paradoxically turning this wish into "I'll serve this duke" (I ii 52) as she learns that Olivia is courted by a handsome bachelor, whom she refuses to see. Olivia becomes the mediator of Viola's almost instantaneous love for the Duke. She decides to become the brother she has lost and to put on a boy's garment: "Thou shalt present me as an eunuch to him" (I ii 53), she tells the captain who saved her. The trick immediately triggers violence *de facto* since she is not what she appears and thus actually deceives both Olivia and Orsino about her identity.

To understand the part played by Viola toward Olivia, it is necessary to go back to the relationship of the leading couple at the beginning of the play. Since in Illyria, apparently, everything seems to concur to a happy marriage of the protagonists, why is Orsino, "A noble duke, in nature / As in name" (I ii 22–23) unsuccessful in his courtship of the beautiful Olivia? They both seem made for each other, yet Olivia vehemently rejects the duke's messengers and even refuses to be seen. Like a mysterious goddess, she seems to reign over the mortals that surround her. The resemblance that should bring them together divides them. Why? If the tears she sheds over her dead brother are not the true cause of her scorn—she quickly forgets him when she meets with Cesario!—what is the real cause of the indifference she shows toward Orsino and his household? And why does Orsino keep wanting to conquer the only woman who does not want him?

For Orsino, Olivia's beauty represents purity: "O, when mine eyes did see Olivia first / Methought she purged the air of pestilence" (I i 18–19). Her purity is what arouses his desire, yet has he not just declared in a disillusioned mood that the spirit of love lost its sharpness and passion, were it as vast as the sea, the very minute it was translated into act?

[28] Ibid., 87.

> O spirit of love, how quick and fresh art thou
> That, notwithstanding thy capacity
> Receiveth as the sea, nought enters there,
> Of what validity and pitch so e'er,
> But falls into abatement and low price
> Even in a minute! (I i 9–14)

Orsino seems to contradict himself, on the one hand asserting the fanciful quality of desire, which cannot survive the pleasure of satisfaction, on the other hand feeling the most romantic[29] desire for Olivia. Will Olivia's purity lose its value once he has possessed her? In a second soliloquy, Orsino uses the image of the sea again to show, by contrast, the voracity of his own love which this time can digest all that made him sick before. The surfeit that was his he now assigns to the woman, whom he judges inconstant and superficial, unable to bear a love such as his:

> Alas, their love may be called appetite,
> No motion of the liver, but the palate,
> That suffers surfeit, cloyment, and revolt.
> But mine is all as hungry as the sea,
> And can digest as much. (II iv 96–100)

It would be wrong to judge Orsino's first speech as a mere mood, without perceiving the reflection it entertains with the next soliloquy, where he transfers the surfeit and the boredom he feels when he has at last possessed the object of his desire, the woman's love, which can only be changing and superficial. This time he says he wants Olivia voraciously. But isn't it precisely speaking *before* the possession that would spoil his appetite? Olivia appears pure and constant only in so far as she resists him. If she relented, she would immediately become ordinary and he would become bored.

Can it be that Orsino is consumed by desire only inasmuch as it is never satisfied, but suffers surfeit as soon as he possesses his object? It is as if Olivia, by refusing Orsino's pleas, attracts him more. The more she locks herself up in haughty isolation, the more he desires her. It is her inaccessibility which makes her desirable, Orsino's desire imitating in this Olivia's own narcissistic desire. Intuitively, he knows that Olivia is like him, is his feminine double. He perceives that she maintains with her suitors the same kind of relationship he maintains with women: she does not like men who are conquered too easily and is bound to be attracted by those who offer resistance. As Girard again puts it, "if she gave up the type of

---

[29] I take romantic to mean the *illusion* of a unique and personal passion, which is in reality the imitation of another's desire, according to Girard in his book *Mensonge romantique et vérité Romanesque* (*Deceit, Desire and the Novel*).

142 ~ SHAKESPEARE, THE MAGICIAN AND THE HEALER

superiority they both crave in their relations with the other sex, he would immediately cease to love her."[30] The evidence is in the fact that Olivia forgets her mourning and her pride the minute she meets Viola disguised as the Duke's servant Cesario, "that same peevish messenger" (I v 290). She even loves "his" scorn: "O, what a deal of scorn looks beautiful / In the contempt and anger of his lip!" (III i 143–44), and goes as far as conceding that it is better to fall before the lion than the wolf (III i 127).

Orsino and Olivia, whose names echo each other, are separated by their resemblance. They both are proud and in the midst of the court with which they surround themselves, it is the cruel object which refuses to be theirs, the dissonant voice, which arouses their desire. Viola's disdain is by Olivia taken for superior self-love, which teases her vanity. For "indifference is never totally neutral. It is never a pure absence of desire. It always appears to the observer like the outward face of self-love. And it is this supposed desire that calls for imitation."[31]

Mimetic desire spreads itself all the more easily as the characters lose their distinctions. When Viola-Cesario reveals her aristocratic birth, it stirs up Olivia's desire and she throws herself, body and soul, against her most unsurmountable obstacle. As for disguised Viola, she manages to maintain the distinction between herself and her role, until Olivia's desire arouses another suitor's jealousy and Sir Andrew challenges Cesario to a duel. In the face of this violent threat, Viola cannot feign the physical strength and warlike fury she does not possess.

A petty noble, Sir Andrew is among the despised suitors for Olivia's hand. In another example of mimetic rivalry, Sir Andrew conspires with Sir Toby and Maria to arouse the desire of a third would-be lover, Malvolio, in order to punish his vanity. A letter supposedly from Olivia, whose handwriting has been imitated by Maria, convinces Malvolio of Olivia's love for him, who had already seen himself as master of the house. His ambition is eventually derided by the merry accomplices who have been secretly watching Malvolio's enraptured metamorphosis.

In his turn Sir Andrew is being played upon by his fellow jokers, who goad him into challenging Cesario-Viola to a fight, since Olivia has shown the latter more favor. Envy is once again the fuel that leads the characters to action. Sir Toby, who believes Cesario is not very dangerous, has no compunction about taunting him even though, or perhaps because, he knows what a reluctant combatant he is. He and Sir Andrew get their come-uppance, when they encounter Sebastian — whom they take for Cesario — an entirely more daunting adversary.

---

[30] René Girard, *A Theater of Envy* (South Bend, IN: St. Augustine's Press, 2002), 115.
[31] Girard René, *Mensonge*, 127 (my translation).

Rival desires multiply, giving birth to misunderstandings and violence. In this theater where each player seems to be the double of someone else, Malvolio does appear to be the epitome of vanity and mimetic desire, and his misadventure, like all plays-within-the-play, reflects upon the characters of the main plot. Thus, Olivia's judgment: "O, you are sick of self-love, Malvolio, and taste with a distempered appetite" (I v 85–86), can apply to Orsino's first monologue as well as to Malvolio, and it actually reflects on her as well. The "sportful malice" that turns Malvolio into a lovesick fool also reverberates on the Countess's lack of reason when she ridiculously courts a woman without knowing it. When she asks Cesario, "I prithee tell me what thou think'st of me" (III i 136), Malvolio's smug dream of being his mistress's beloved cannot eschew our thought: "I have heard herself come thus near, that should she fancy it should be one of my complexion" (II v 22–24). After all, the day draws near when the abolition of privileges will enable the house butler to marry the lady of the manor without ridicule!

Even in a comedy, though, Shakespeare does not completely forget social order, and when the time of discovery and reconciliation comes, vain Malvolio is made a scapegoat, while Sir Toby and Sir Andrew receive a serious thrashing. Peace can come back only if the community is purged of its evil; Malvolio's arrogance and the vanity that makes him believe he can pretend to his mistress's love make him the perfect scapegoat. However, the final reunion of the lovers is conditioned by his return since he seems to be the only one who knows the location of the captain who has Viola's womanly clothes. Do Orsino and Olivia realize that he is but a magnifying glass of their own weaknesses? The truth is, Malvolio is, like all the others, a victim of mimetic desire, which is perfectly impersonated by the sudden arrival of Viola's twin, Sebastian.

The appearance of Sebastian really throws Illyria into confusion. Even subtle Feste is deceived and despite all his wit has difficulty managing the boy he takes for Cesario. Sir Andrew and Sir Toby have just started sensing the difference between the two. Sebastian, of course, cannot guess that he is the double of a sister who pretends to imitate him in everything ("For him I imitate," III iv 374) and who, he is persuaded, died at sea. He both unties the knots of impossible desires and falls victim to those same desires. When Olivia, whom Cesario's constant rebuff has exasperated, mistakenly begs Sebastian to give in to her prayer, he becomes a kind of hostage to the strength of her desire to which he abandons himself, amazed but delighted. Suspecting some error that Olivia is unconscious of, he seizes the day, forgetting Antonio's devotion and his own promise to him. Antonio, in turn, is not recognized by Cesario. This is *The Comedy of Errors* all over again, and in the midst of such imbroglio, true violence erupts with Orsino's threat to sacrifice, if not the woman he loves, at least the boy who has become his own rival:

> Since you to non-regardance cast my faith,
> And that I partly know the instrument
> That screws me from my true place in your favour,
> Live you the marble-breasted tyrant still.
> But this your minion, whom I know you love,
> And whom, by heaven I swear, I tender dearly,
> Him will I tear out of that cruel eye
> Where he sits crownèd in his master's spite.
> Come, boy, with me. My thoughts are ripe in mischief.
> I'll sacrifice the lamb that I do love
> To spite a raven's heart within a dove. (V i 117–28)

Jealousy and spite have led noble Orsino to reciprocal violence and the situation is not far from becoming a tragedy. Fortunately, a lovesick Cesario ready to die for his master keeps the comedy alive, even if it does not put an end to the rivals' war. Olivia deals the next blow, calling for the priest's testimony. Orsino's vexation suddenly makes him clairvoyant: "O thou dissembling cub!" (V i 160), seeing the truth which until now escaped him. When Sebastian, Viola's double, enters Orsino declares:

> One face, one voice, one habit, and two persons!
> A natural perspective, that is and is not. (V i 209–10)

Orsino perfectly sums up the problem of lack of distinctions. "The disappearance of natural differences can truly evoke the dissolution of categories within which human beings are distributed, in a word, this is the sacrificial crisis."[32] Even the categories of understanding are being destroyed since it becomes impossible to distinguish truth from falsehood, reality from illusion. In the field of art, this is also what one calls a *trompe l'oeil*, the perfect illusion of perspective which makes a painting a convincing imitation of nature. For a moment, nothing is what it is, but fortunately, all's well that ends well. Olivia finally gains the strong and beautiful man she saw in Cesario and Orsino finds the wife who has succeeded in seducing him without ever revealing herself or giving up her own nature. Yet, the insistence with which he wants to see Viola in women's garments before marrying her reveals the confusion that the twins' likeness has planted in his mind. Will the costume, which was a mere theatrical convention, be assurance that such confusion cannot occur anymore? This is not certain at all.

---

[32] Girard, *La Violence et le Sacré*, 86.

Feste's song comes as a coda to the play, recalling the audience to lucidity. With a common sense full of melancholy, he announces the return to reality with the comedians bowing to the public. Would their laughter be tinged with a slight anxiety when the boy actor playing Viola came back as himself beside Duke Orsino? Could Shakespeare offer a more troubling image of mimetic confusion than that of a theater reflecting the world in which a boy played the part of a woman disguised as a boy who is mistaken for yet another boy?

SPY-WORK AND ANAMORPHOSES IN *HAMLET*

Play-within-the-play, drama within drama, the structure of Shakespeare's theatricals keeps toying with a multitude of changing shapes and reflections which are likely to appear like chaos and confusion to more rigid minds. With astonishing independence, Shakespeare makes light of the hallowed Aristotelian rules in order to invent a theater of life, joyfully mixing tragedy and comedy, nobles and clowns, poetry, music and ballet. Whatever we may say, he remains still closer to Italian mannerism than to the rather uncouth drama tradition of England. The structure of *Hamlet* evokes the illusionism of Mantegna's *Camera picta,* later called *Camera degli Sposi,* with characters peeping from every corner, hiding behind draperies, and spying in a court which was, no doubt, as stifling and dangerous as Elizabeth's at Whitehall. The poet, who has all too often been judged ignorant, reveals in fact a subtle appreciation of the arts and esthetic creations of his time. Whether in the visual arts or in music, he always knows the apt reference to emphasize his own art or his words, without ever being caught preaching. His knowledge is always subdued, his brilliance humble; Shakespeare was not a name-dropper, which certainly makes his evocation of Giulio Romano unique, an occurrence rare enough not to be overlooked. Such bewildering mastery of his art allowed him, no doubt, to intersperse, without too many risks, allusions and references that only well-informed people could perceive and decode. The character Hamlet in particular could well be representing Shakespeare himself outwitting his enemies and censors. It is the only play where he spends some time explaining his dramatic requirements for actors, insisting on the play's esthetics and the seriousness of its purpose, which is to hold "the mirror up to nature" and to show "the very age and body of the time his form and pressure." And it is surely an understatement to assert that "the very age and body of the time" was all askew! Thus, the play which may be the most famous tragedy of all time is entirely built on structural obliquities and perspectives which are very close to the art of anamorphoses.

By its Latin etymology, the word perspective means "to see clearly"; it presupposes not only the primacy of the human eye, but also the truth of its vision, or at any rate the assurance that what it sees translates some truth. Now *Hamlet*, from the very first lines, precisely questions the reliability of eyesight concerning a vision that passes human understanding and troubles the peace of the soul:

> Horatio says 'tis but our fantasy,
> And will not let belief take hold of him
> Touching this dreaded sight twice seen of us. (I i 23–25)

Later Horatio calls, "Stay, illusion" and insists: "A mote it is to trouble the mind's eye" (Q2 I i 112).[33]

Introducing an apparition which is the very image of Hamlet's father, the late king, the first act of the play stages a complex game of reflections and likenesses, which puzzles the minds of the witnesses. The terrifying vision, whose martial appearance is emphasized by the soldiers, evokes the spirit of the time — the spirit of revenge? — which "doth make the night joint-labourer with the day," (78) Denmark being at the time engaged in impressive war preparations. On the stage, it has often been very tempting to turn the apparition into the tormented spirit of an innocent victim, but the attentive reader learns that the old king has himself triggered the chaos that has invaded his land by taking up Fortinbras's challenge to personal combat. The line "pricked on by a most emulate pride," (I i 83) with which Horatio qualifies Fortinbras, necessarily reverberates on both men.[34] Studying the text very closely, it even becomes evident that this is the likeness of the dead king which frightens the guards more than the apparition as such:

> *Barnardo*: In *the same figure like the King* that's dead. (41)

> *Barnardo*: *Looks it not like the King?* — Mark it, Horatio.
> *Horatio*: *Most like.* It harrows me with fear and wonder. (I i 43–44)

> *Marcellus*: *Is it not like the King?*
> *Horatio*: As thou art to thyself. (I i 58–59)

> *Barnardo*: "this portentous figure / Comes armed through our watch so like he King / That was and is the question of these wars." (Q2 I i 109–11)

---

[33] This passage (I i 108–25), like others quoted in this analysis, has been omitted from G. R. Hibbard's edition and collected in Appendix A (Oxford University Press, 1987). These passages, taken from the second quarto, nonetheless offer very interesting points regarding this study's purpose. The relevant quotations are preceded by Q2.
[34] This line, between brackets in the Folio, is truly paradoxical since it applies to Hamlet's father as well as to Fortinbras. Such lack of differentiation seems to have been deliberately intended by Shakespeare who thereby emphasizes the mimetic rivalry between both men.

Note that the word "ghost" is not even pronounced in this first scene. The study of language, the proliferation of "like," evidently translates Shakespeare's desire to make the nocturnal vision of Elsinore not so much a ghost as such, but rather a double, an imitation of reality which troubles reality, and therefore already a *mise en abyme* of the theatrical play. This likeness to the late king creates a disturbing reflection likely to trouble the eyes and mind of the prince. The prince has enough on his mind as it is, having just been evicted from the throne by his mother's lover, now his step-father as well as his father's brother, and therefore a double.[35] When Claudius asks Hamlet to regard him as his father (I ii 107–8), then to "be as ourself in Denmark" (I ii 122), denying him his own identity through this loss of differentiation, he intensifies by as many deceiving mirrors, the confusion which leads both men to violent rivalry, reinforced by the echoes of the king's earthly thunder in heaven.[36]

Since his father's identity cannot, for Hamlet, bear reproduction — "A was a man. Take him for all in all. / I shall not look upon his like again," (I ii 186–87) — his metaphorical effort to stress the differences between both brothers breaks upon the incomprehensible passage of his mother from the one to the other:

> So excellent a king, that was to this
> Hyperion to a Satyr, so loving to my mother
> That he might not beteem the winds of heaven
> Visit her face too roughly! (I ii 139–42)

In this scene, just as in the queen's closet, Hamlet's outrageous language, which in any case, qualifies the moral more than the physical appearance of both men, does not manage to conceal the surprising parallelism existing between them and which comes through in the speech's structure:

> Look here upon *this* picture, and on *this*,...
> This *was* your husband. Look you now what follows.
> Here *is* your husband ... and what judgment
> Would step *from this to this*? (III iv 54–72)

The most perplexing is that he is calling for the queen's judgment while repeatedly invoking her eyes: "Have you eyes?" (III iv 66, 68), whereas he himself is unable to grant any credit to appearances. Who is being befuddled? The queen or Hamlet?

---

[35] There would be much sense in a production staging Claudius and the apparition as similar characters, thereby emphasizing the mimetic rivalry at work in the play.
[36] "No jocund health that Denmark drinks today
But the great cannon to the clouds shall tell,
And the King's rouse the heavens shall bruit again,
Re-speaking earthly thunder" (I ii 125–28).

On greeting Horatio earlier in the play, his substituting "I think it was to see my mother's wedding" for Horatio's "My Lord, I came to see your father's funeral," (I ii 176–78) looks like a conjuring trick, an optical illusion such as what was to be seen in so-called "perspective cabinets" so fashionable with art students at the time.[37] Not only men, but space and time have lost their reference point. Searching for an essence, a spiritual reality, Hamlet is confounded by the play of appearances: the ambiguity of the word "like," "his like," is evident in the theater where physical likeness can stand for both moral likeness and mask. For having used it in his comedies, Shakespeare knew how disquieting and fascinating the mirroring of the same could be: "this marvel" (I ii 195), "this troubles me" (I ii 225), the echoing answers of Marcellus and Barnardo to Hamlet's questions seem to put the finishing touches to the *trompe-l'oeil*.

Old King Hamlet looks not very different from Fortinbras, while he is the armed double of his brother Claudius, who inherits his crown, his wife, and his war. Even the ghost's words somehow testify to the "wit" and "gifts" of Claudius, who seems to have conquered Gertrude exactly as Othello conquered Desdemona, by the grace of his wit:[38]

> Ay, that incestuous, that adulterate beast,
> With witchcraft of his wit, with traitorous gifts —
> O wicked wit and gifts, that have the power
> So to seduce! — (I v 42–45)

After all, no character in the play seems to contest the new order of things except Hamlet, who is drawn — in spite of himself, and ironically, by his uncle who asks him to be as himself in Denmark and by a ghost whose reality is necessarily elusive — into a spiral of reciprocal violence. What indeed is the talion law if not the mimetic repetition of the primal murder? Caught in such a double bind, how can Hamlet be himself and accomplish his duty without looking like all the others?

Between the call for revenge which his father's spirit imposes on him and the absurdity of revenge when opponents have become so interchangeable that they send forth the same reflection, Hamlet seems paralyzed. He has no allies in Denmark unless it is the foolish multitude who, according to Claudius, only judge what they see. Now, do they see the deceiving drama of

---

[37] Leeman, *Hidden Images*, plates 76–78, 79–81, 93–95. In the two Dutch Cabinets presented, one can see the interiors of a Protestant church and of a Catholic church. The joinings of the flagstones draw the eye into the distance, whereas if one looks at the pictures without using the peephole, the two side walls create a sharp angle. The fact that the basis of these cabinets is triangular is interesting in relation to René Girard's mimetic triangle of desire.

[38] "She'd come again, and with a greedy ear / Devour up my discourse . . . / This only is the witchcraft I have used," *Othello*, I iii 149–50, 169.

the court which is, as it appears, peopled with excellent actors who haven't protested the power change? Only Hamlet has difficulty impersonating his new role, which, admittedly, is ill-defined. Must he weep at the funeral or applaud at the wedding? Must he be son or nephew, should he be prince, heir apparent, or king? In order to reach a true perspective in the midst of so many illusions and deformed realities, he only has one solution: to use illusion itself as a tool of enlightenment and control.

Obliquity for Hamlet begins as soon as he meets with his friends. He cannot say what he has heard without provoking a coup. The only safe part for him is to play the fool: "As I perchance hereafter shall think meet / To put an antic disposition on" (I v 178–79). Far from being a mental disorder, it is a political weapon, a mask behind which Hamlet keeps a free hand, the dream of Jaques in *As You Like It,* and no doubt a kind of game Shakespeare used to his own advantage. The fool, whose freedom was deemed innocuous, was traditionally granted license to speak and act as he pleased. In Shakespeare's plays, the Fool is very often the character who, in the midst of flatterers, brings the king back to reason. It is probably significant that Yorick has never been replaced at the court of Denmark, where a fool now seems necessary to cleanse the air, which is totally infected. There is no sharp wit to question appearances, which for Hamlet are all lies. It is now time for him to don the buffoon's livery.

If his answer to his mother is to be believed, it is his obsessional disgust for an act which would only be the representation of itself which drives him to play the fool—"'Seems,' Madam? Nay, it *is*. I know not 'seems'. . . . These indeed 'seem,' / For they are actions that a man might play;" (I ii 76, 83–84)—Hamlet cannot abide the loss of the spirit behind the letter. His aim is to feign appearances in order to debunk them. Throughout the play, Hamlet is haunted by the idea of a balance, of harmony between form and content, passion and judgment. He requires of the actors that they:

> Suit the action to the word, the word to the action, with this special observance: that you o'erstep not the modesty of nature. For anything so overdone is from the purpose of playing, whose end, both at the first and now, was and is to hold as 'twere the mirror up to nature, to show virtue her own feature, scorn her own image, and the very age and body of the time his form and pressure. (III ii 16–23)

It is in this search for the right perspective that the true action of the play is to be found. Hamlet has to find the truth that will enable him to join without disproportion the two senses of the verb: to act, as in "to do" (action) with to act, as in "to portray" (to seem), since he cannot do otherwise. Since the kingdom is being invaded by chaos, which prevents any clear vision of things, one has to have recourse to stratagems and indirections to reach the truth.[39]

The whole play *Hamlet* is thus built on successive indirect strategies of spying scenes and cunning speeches, indirectly confirmed by Polonius when he laboriously explains to Reynaldo the best means to discover the truth about his son, Laertes:

> Your bait of falsehood takes this carp of truth;
> And thus do we of wisdom and of reach
> With windlasses and with assays of bias
> By indirections find directions out. (II i 62–65)

Hamlet uses folly as an indirect means to reach the truth, whereas his own metamorphosis, "Hamlet's transformation" (II ii 5), triggers against him the same indirect strategies as those he uses. Polonius sends Reynaldo spying on Laertes and similarly manipulates Ophelia in order to discover Hamlet's game. Claudius employs Rosencrantz and Guildenstern, then Gertrude, as informers to corner Hamlet into unveiling his own plans. The audience themselves always have an indirect vision of the action since they, too, are in the position of a character hidden behind a wall or a tapestry spying on, commenting on, and interpreting the proceedings. This "Russian dolls" structure turns the spectators into actors. They realize that they are being spied upon by the author, who is himself probably observed by some cunning agent or royal spy, himself in the pay of Robert Cecil, and so on and so forth until we reach God's eye.

The problem is of course that these indirections supposedly leading to truth never stop colliding with the adverse party's indirections so that truth is lost in this game of mirrors and obliquities. Hamlet's sarcasms against Polonius show that he knows himself to be watched and the old man is not so senile that he cannot perceive Hamlet's more complex game: "Though this be madness, yet there is method in't" (II ii 204). Similarly Hamlet tells Rosencrantz and Guildenstern that he keeps an eye on them and that his folly depends on the wind, which unfortunately they will be unable to assess on the vessel taking them to England: "I am but mad north-north-west; when the wind is southerly, I know a hawk from a handsaw" (II ii 373–74). Rosencrantz and Guildenstern, who, for generations, have represented the epitome of servility and sycophancy, just like Ophelia, who agrees to play the bait without measuring the importance of her betrayal, are merely pawns in the war game of the great.

---

[39] Leeman, *Hidden Images*, 16; see note 17, p. 74 above.

The arrival of the actors constitutes the absolute paradigm of this play of illusions, with Hamlet's supreme trick, to catch the conscience of the king and the truth that is still eluding him. "The Mousetrap" becomes the mirror revealing, under the pretense of entertainment, the canker at the heart of Denmark. For one moment Hamlet appears as the arch manipulator, yet he still has to pass from metaphor to reality. He may have caught the conscience of the king, but Claudius remains the master of reality. Ironically his conscience drives him to seek God's forgiveness at the very moment when Hamlet could at last finish the job of revenge. This seems to indicate that a superior mind is now outdoing everybody's tricks. Hamlet becomes the spectator of an action which eludes him.

When he finally leaps upon a shape behind the arras in his mother's bedroom, he only grasps at the king's shadow, meddling Polonius, who was careless enough to stand in for his king in the queen's apartments. Although a failure, this new stratagem indirectly advances the action by bringing Laertes back to Denmark, while it is also the passionate outburst that openly turns Hamlet into the dangerous rival of Claudius: "O, 'tis most sweet / When in one line two crafts directly meet" (Q2 III iv 209–10).[40] All the indirect stratagems set up by the king and Polonius to discover Hamlet's purpose lead to this vast diversion to England, where the prince should be executed. Once again, Hamlet manages to outsmart his adversaries' plans by having Rosencrantz and Guildenstern sent to the gallows in his place and himself coming back to Denmark by even more diverted routes, since he becomes the hostage of a crew of pirates.

Although the return of the prince, emerging from the water on the coast of Denmark, looks like a Christian rebirth for Hamlet, who is now resigned to his fate and willing to forgive, his actions demonstrate that he is also now unmistakably playing the revenger. All great Neptune's ocean could not wash from his hands the blood that he has shed. Now

---

[40] Hamlet's reflection: "For 'tis the sport to have the engineer / Hoist with his own petard" (Q2 III iv 206–7) is an echo to Claudius's own: "But the great cannon to the clouds shall tell, / And the King's rouse the heavens shall bruit again, / Re-speaking earthly thunder" (I ii 126–28), the boomerang effect being again highlighted when Claudius explains to Laertes why he could not act directly against Hamlet: "so that my arrows, / Too slightly timbered for so loud a wind, / Would have reverted to my bow again, / And not where I had aimed them" (IV vii 21–24). Needless to say, this mirror effect which recurs throughout the play is essential to understand the indirect strategy of the characters. Like Hamlet, Claudius does not merely attempt to find the truth about his adversary, he is also very conscious of the danger he would be running if he acted directly. René Girard again sheds light on this mechanism: "Thanks to the notion of strategy, men can indefinitely postpone their revenge without ever giving it up (my translation)," "Grâce à la notion de stratégie, les hommes peuvent repousser indéfiniment leur vengeance sans jamais y renoncer." Girard, Shakespeare. Les feux de l'envie, 347.

that he has discovered Claudius's desire to kill him, Hamlet has no reason to hesitate. The words that he uses to warn Horatio look very much like those the ghost used to warn him, as if both were now one and the same: "I have words to speak in thine ear will make thee dumb" (IV vi 23) seems indeed to be the echo of, "I could a tale unfold whose lightest word / Would harrow up thy soul" (I v 15–16). However, Ophelia's death and Laertes's grief lead him once more away from his purpose and to a new scene of folly. What truly happens is that Laertes's passion produces at last on him the mimetic attraction that no one until then had managed to rouse in him. In Laertes, Hamlet sees at last the very image of himself and it is this "most emulate pride" (I i 83) which, like his father, drives him toward violence and, indirectly, the accomplishment of his revenge.

I have emphasized earlier the fact that likenesses and mirroring structures underlined the mimetic attraction which is at work in the play. As early as the first scene, the apparition of a figure *like* the king but which *is not* the king was emblematic of the loss of distinction which traditionally triggers reciprocal violence in all revenge tragedies. As René Girard puts it, "If the victim's victim is already a killer and if the revenge seeker reflects a little too much on the circularity of revenge, his faith in vengeance must collapse.... Claudius and Old Hamlet are not first blood brothers and then enemies; they are brothers in murder and revenge."[41] In a world where everyone mimics everyone else, revenge, or the law of reciprocal violence, fuels politics. But before this, there is another rivalry born of envy. If we follow Girard's definition of triangular desire, for each desire there must be a mediator, a character admired and envied precisely because he possesses what the other does not have. The closer the mediator, the surer obstacle he is to the accomplishment of the other's desire, and the greater the risk of violence. Hamlet effectively points to the way hierarchy has disappeared in the kingdom: "The age is grown so picked that the toe of the peasant comes so near the heel of the courtier he galls his kibe" (V i 132–34). Claudius suggests that Gertrude was the object of his desire—"She's so conjunctive to my life and soul / That, as the star moves not but in his sphere, / I could not but by her" (IV vii 14–16)—and very likely the cause of rivalry between both brothers. As for Gertrude, he asserts, she only lives for Hamlet—"The Queen his mother / Lives almost by his looks" (IV vii 11–12)—who thus becomes another rival for

---

[41] Girard, *A Theater of Envy*, 273. *Les Feux de l'envie*, 333–34. "Si la première victime est un premier tueur, celui qui cherche à la venger risque de repérer la circularité de la vengeance; il ne peut que cesser de croire aux vertus de cette dernière.... Claudius et le vieil Hamlet ne sont pas d'abord frères de sang et ensuite ennemis; ils sont frères par le crime et la vengeance."

him. However, in the scene where Hamlet faces his mother, mimeticism occurs in the identity of the reproaches they have for each other, as if to confirm the deep resemblance between the two men (Old Hamlet and Claudius) who make the third side of the triangle:

> *Getrude*: Hamlet, thou hast thy father much offended.
> *Hamlet*: Mother, you have my father much offended.
> *Getrude*: Come, come, you answer with an idle tongue.
> *Hamlet*: Go, go, you question with a wicked tongue. (III iv 10–13)

As for Polonius, he recognizes that his jealousy made him discredit Hamlet in Ophelia's eyes — "I feared he did but trifle / And meant to wreck thee. But beshrew my jealousy!" (II i 113–14) — as if he feared lest Hamlet dispossess him of his daughter. This second desire triangle places him on the king's side and intensifies Hamlet's isolation, Laertes being away and having equally warned Ophelia against the prince. Hamlet has evidently become the arch mediator, the man everybody envies and fears at the same time.

Only Horatio, a stranger to the court with remarkable equanimity and judgment, can provide Hamlet with an alter ego. Yet having no passion, he cannot really help his friend in his revenge. Hamlet knows he has to act quickly, but somehow remains disengaged. No one has managed to arouse in him the passion necessary for action, be it theatrical: neither the actor who feigns Hecuba's despair, nor valiant Fortinbras who finds quarrel in a straw.

Why can't Hamlet be aroused to passion? What keeps him from acting? The answer comes with Laertes: Hamlet lacks a mirror, a model arousing his envy, a mediator. Incidentally we learn that Hamlet admires Laertes's talents to the point of jealousy. There is the tragic flaw which seemed to be absent from him:

> *Claudius* (to Laertes): Your sum of parts
> Did not together pluck such *envy* from him,
> As did that one. (Q2 IV vii 72–74)
>
> Sir, this report of his
> Did Hamlet so envenom with his *envy*
> That he could nothing do but wish and beg
> Your sudden coming o'er to play with him. (IV vii 101–4)[42]

Hamlet himself confides, "For by the image of my cause I see / The portraiture of his" (V ii 78–79), the inverted sentence revealing once more the trouble caused by this mirror effect. If indeed the only "semblable" of

---

[42] This passage is found in *The New Shakespeare* edition (Cambridge: Cambridge University Press, 1969). The italics are mine.

Laertes is his reflection in his mirror,[43] Hamlet, by the alchemy of envy, has now become this very reflection. He competes with him for "the bravery of his grief" (V ii 79) and now finds himself facing him in a last stratagem which is also a remarkable staging of mimetic rivalry: a duel in which Hamlet and Laertes both "play" the act of revenge in front of all the court. It is meet that this show put on by Claudius to get rid of his adversary should fall back on his head. It was dangerous to arouse the mimetic rivalry of two revengers who eventually make friends on the back of the third.

At the end of the play, the ghost seems to have been forgotten and the subject matter focuses on the confrontation with the same, the mirror which awakens Hamlet's passion and drives him to accomplish his fate, a little haphazardly, indirectly, as if in spite of himself. Polonius was perhaps not such an old fool after all and as often in Shakespeare, precious information is often to be gotten from unlikely characters:

> So, oft it chances in particular men
> That, for some vicious mole of nature in them —
> As in their birth, wherein they are not guilty,
> Since nature cannot choose his origin,
> . . . that these men,
> Carrying, I say, the stamp of one defect,
> Being nature's livery or fortune's star,
> His virtues else be they as pure as grace,
> As infinite as man may undergo,
> Shall in the general censure take corruption
> From that particular fault. (Q2 I iv 23–36)

Hasn't the word "mole" been used already to qualify the frightening vision on the battlements? Is it too daring to suggest that this "vicious mole" in the nature of men is indeed the mimetic violence which pushes them to revenge, an act so little in Hamlet's nature that he spends the play resisting it? Ironically the process of revenge comes full circle with the arrival of Fortinbras on the throne of Denmark. Who knows if, indirectly, by his death and the unexpected support it gives to his enemy, Hamlet does not finally break the spiral of reciprocal revenge? ♣

---

[43] "I take him to be a soul of great article, and his infusion of such dearth and rareness as, to make true diction of him, his semblable is his mirror" (Q2 V ii 110–11).

7. Shakespeare's Healers

*H*AMLET'S ATTEMPT AT PURGING DENMARK OF ITS rottenness, his playing the Fool in order to discover the truth of the matter, is not so far from Jaques's role as a social doctor. Shakespeare's moral conscience as an artist would not be satisfied by the mere fun of mirroring human nature. So much disease in the realm and in the history of England certainly required fools and satirists as well as appropriate healers and comforters. Shakespeare realized very early that the only way to avoid a rigid confrontation between opponents, be they political, religious, or private, was to work change, through metamorphosis. Now the process of metamorphosis could be viewed from different perspectives: the Bard inherited literary metamorphoses from Ovid, but his own religious convictions also made it a matter of personal, moral renewal, which could blend nicely with Ovid's ideas, as evidenced by the numerous moralized versions of his work produced during the Middle Ages. Shakespeare's reverence for monks and friars, whose art and benevolence only stopped short of the miraculous in some of his plays, would gradually lead him to include physicians and healers among those characters who sustained the welfare of others. The physician John Hall, who became his son-in-law in 1607, probably had some influence on his interest, all the more so as that era was rife with threats of plague and typhus, and death and illness were constant shadows of life. Over the years Shakespeare, in his admiration for the art of healing, created a few beautiful, and sometimes surprising physician characters. Unlike Molière for instance, Shakespeare always displays a deep respect for doctors, probably because he linked them with the healing power once dispensed in monasteries. His desire to cure the world and improve his fellow men can be traced in all his plays, and as Leo Salingar suggests,[1] this *art* that could mend nature gradually became more and more important to him, a kind of trope for what he was trying to do in the theater.

FROM THE PRIORY HERB GARDEN TO THE KING'S SURGEON

Shakespeare may have been taught firsthand the mysteries of the herb garden. One can even imagine that the young "Romeo" bursting in at

---

[1] Leo Salingar, *Dramatic Form in Shakespeare and the Jacobeans* (Cambridge: Cambridge University Press, 1986), 16–18. Art, in Shakespeare's use of the word, "comes nearer to Francis Bacon's view of scientific endeavour than to the notion of art in critics like Vasari. Possibly modern aesthetic preconceptions interfere with our understanding of this side of Shakespeare." Art, for the Bard, was primarily the ability to work magic and metamorphoses, essentially moral metamorphoses.

dawn on Friar Lawrence's early task might — some years earlier — have been called William. *Romeo and Juliet* displays a deep wisdom in Friar Lawrence's praise of nature's bounty which our postmodern world is only now rediscovering:

> Now, ere the sun advance his burning eye
> The day to cheer and night's dank dew to dry,
> I must up-fill this osier cage of ours
> With baleful weeds and precious-juicèd flowers.
> The earth, that's nature's mother, is her tomb.
> What is her burying grave, that is her womb,
> And from her womb children of divers kind
> We sucking on her natural bosom find,
> Many for many virtues excellent,
> None but for some, and yet all different.
> O mickle is the powerful grace that lies
> In plants, herbs, stones, and their true qualities,
> For naught so vile that on the earth doth live
> But to the earth some special good doth give;
> Nor aught so good but, strained for that fair use,
> Revolts from true birth, stumbling on abuse.
> Virtue itself turns vice being misapplied,
> And vice sometime's by action dignified. (*Romeo and Juliet*, II ii 5–22)

Shakespeare's love of nature is evident in this ode to garden wisdom, which he also applied metaphorically to men. Good Friar Lawrence does not err in his knowledge, whose beneficial effect depends on the faith of the "patient." Hence his advice to desperate Juliet who should, by feigning death, escape death:

> If, rather than to marry County Paris,
> Thou hast the strength of will to slay thyself,
> Then is it likely thou wilt undertake
> A thing like death to chide away this shame,
> That cop'st with death himself to scape from it;
> And, if thou dar'st, I'll give thee remedy. (IV i 71–76)

Friar Lawrence is ready to advocate death as a masterful mannerist peace broker and miracle worker. Juliet's reply looks like some grisly drawing out of Dante's *Inferno*, or some mural of the Last Judgment. Nothing is spared, the charnel house, "O'ercovered quite with dead men's rattling bones, / With reeky shanks and yellow chapless skulls," was no doubt a sight the Elizabethan public's eyes and noses knew all too well. There is something of a deliberately Baroque posture in Juliet's will to hide "with a dead man in his tomb," rather than damn her soul by marrying the man her father imposes on her. We are far from the sobriety of the Reformed church and much closer to Saint Ignatius's advice "to see in imagination the length, breadth, and depth of hell" using one's five senses and meditate on points of such desolation in order to conquer oneself (Fifth Exercise). Friar Lawrence takes great care to depict for Juliet all the shades of anaesthesia her body will undergo to reassure her and boost her motivation.

> Take thou this vial, being then in bed,
> And this distilling liquor drink thou off,
> When presently through all thy veins shall run
> A cold and drowsy humour; for no pulse
> Shall keep his native progress, but surcease.
> No warmth, no breath shall testify thou livest.
> The roses in thy lips and cheeks shall fade
> To wanny ashes, thy eyes' windows fall
> Like death when he shuts up the day of life.
> Each part, deprived of supple government,
> Shall, stiff and stark and cold, appear like death. (IV i 93–103)

The whole scene is like a freeze frame mentally preparing Juliet and the audience for the deadly metamorphosis. And no doubt, were Juliet to wake up again under the loving gazes of Romeo and the friar, it would be a wonderful rebirth and a great relief for the stunned audience. However, unlike *Much Ado About Nothing*, where Friar Francis uses a similar stratagem with more success, *Romeo and Juliet* is a tragedy and Romeo's youthful haste will turn this beautiful, mannerist plan into failure. Unless of course the audience really believes that death is life and that the two lovers will, by their untimely death, gain eternal love.

A resolution in the shape of a resurrection seems to have been one of Shakespeare's theatrical and moral aims as early as *The Comedy of Errors*, where the wonder aroused by the reappearance of someone thought dead had proved its dramatic effectiveness. "After so long grief, such nativity"[2] (V i 408) concluded the Abbess, who was part and parcel of this happy resolution.

In *Much Ado About Nothing*, Shakespeare had Friar Francis give the full meaning of the active wonder he meant to create on stage. It is first to be noticed that in this verbose play, where people jump to hasty conclusions from hearsay and blurry perceptions of shadowy figures at night, where

---

[2] Emended to "festivity" in the Oxford edition, although a note recognizes it may not be warranted, since nativity, or rebirth, is the theme of the Abbess's speech: "Thirty-three years have I but gone in travail / Of you, my sons, and till this present hour / My heavy burden ne'er deliverèd" (V i 402–4).

the propagation of rumors and gossip is the most effective cause for action, Friar Francis, amidst the general agitation, has remained silent, observing the victim's reactions, which he translates in a very emotional, mannerist portrait. His quiet discernment is remarkable, even though nobody seems to take him very seriously, so that he has to insist:

> Call me a fool,
> Trust not my reading nor my observations,
> Which with experimental seal doth warrant
> The tenor of my book. Trust not my age,
> My reverence, calling, nor divinity,
> If this sweet lady lie not guiltless here
> Under some biting error. (*Much Ado About Nothing,* IV i 161–67)

This was of course a very subtle way for the author to draw attention to a character he seems to play down, all the while insisting on his reverence, calling, and divinity—a wise old man who is all too often portrayed as the usual foolish monk on stage. This is the man, therefore, who explains in detail the reason why it is advisable to maintain the pretense that Hero is truly dead. He expounds the plan to be carried out in very rational successive points, and it is not surprising that he follows the method of Saint Ignatius's *Spiritual Exercises*. His aim is not only to "change slander to remorse," but to work a spiritual rebirth of Claudio's character.

> For it so falls out
> That what we have, we prize not to the worth
> Whiles we enjoy it, but, being lacked and lost,
> Why then we rack the value, then we find
> The virtue that possession would not show us
> Whiles it was ours. So will it fare with Claudio. (IV i 217–22)

There is more to it than a stage trick. This is a forty-three-line homily explaining the psychological workings of wonder on a human soul. Friar Francis is not a Jesuit, but is somehow given a Jesuit mind, strongly believing that human will can activate God's grace. This, of course, should not be ascribed to Shakespeare's ignorance, as some have sometimes tried to do, but to his knowledge and perfect mastery of indirections. He had already toyed with the death trick in *Romeo and Juliet,* but there, Friar Lawrence was acting from expediency, attempting to counteract fate and save the secret marriage he had performed. There was a moral end to be reached, which was "To turn your households' rancour to pure love" (II ii 92), yet the time of tragedy prevented him from expanding on the usefulness of feigning death, an illusory game that would be thwarted by Romeo's "distemp'rature." Wonder could not be the end of tragedy. Slowly and wisely,

Shakespeare would invent his own special dramatic genre which would combine both tragedy and comedy in *The Winter's Tale*, which stages his most astonishing resurrection.

A CHARACTER STRANGELY REMINISCENT OF JOAN OF ARC

In *All's Well That Ends Well*, Helen appears like a chaste warrior in a world of mocking, sexually arrogant men. She is not the best loved of Shakespeare's heroines, not even — and surprisingly so — the best known, but she is undoubtedly the most daring and boldest young woman he created in a comedy: Helen decides to put on the garments of her own father, a famous physician who has just passed away, and to offer the king of France, whom his own physicians judge a lost cause, the cure she has inherited from her father. The agreement is that she will save the king and obtain as a reward the husband she dreams of, or else she will die with him.

In this venture for love — and of course the word also points to *The Merchant of Venice* — Helen, like Joan of Arc, is ready to give all:

> Tax of impudence,
> A strumpet's boldness, a divulged shame;
> Traduced by odious ballads, my maiden's name
> Seared otherwise, nay — worse of worst — extended
> With vilest torture, let my life be ended. (II i 168–72)

That she, or Shakespeare, had the clearest vision of how she would be judged by posterity has in many ways proved true. Just as in the case of Joan, to have a girl, even the most beautiful and chaste, assume the part of a man toward her King first, and then, throughout the play, pretend that she has gone on a pilgrimage to Santiago in Spain, although she is actually hunting down her new husband in Italy, was a little too much. Many critics however, would have had nothing to say if Helen had been called Bertram, and Bertram Helen.

The words are not lacking that proclaim her cure a miracle and she herself a wonder. Helen, like Joan, is trusted by her King who lets himself be convinced by her arguments. It was for her a rather dangerous way to win a husband, but like most of Shakespeare's heroines she is fearless and adventurous. Midwives were all too often suspected of witchcraft at the time, so a young woman surgeon — how bold! And to dare this for love, imagine the folly of it! Needless to say that at the time, for a King to have a woman doctor was most improbable. When faculties of medicine were founded during the thirteenth century, women were excluded from advanced medical education. Yet, there had been women doctors or surgeons in the past[3] and many a noble lady of the Middle Ages, some of whom became prioresses, could boast healing talents. Nevertheless, Helen's stance has something which sounds entirely postmodern and even in our time of women's liberation, few girls would dare engage in such a risky deal. The confidence she reveals is simply astounding.

Now is a stratagem enough to win somebody's heart? Can one force someone to love? Certainly not. However, in Elizabethan England, where most aristocratic marriages were arranged, the idea was probably more acceptable than today. Conversely, love today has been generally so debased that the idea of a young woman counting on faithfulness and loyalty, together with patience and will, to convince the man she loves of her value seems completely outlandish. Yet Shakespeare tells us that honesty and faithfulness, will and patience, can create miracles, and this is the agenda that will emerge his in most of his last plays. And if illusion can help, so be it! Helen's stratagem looks more like the ordeal the loving medieval knight had to undergo in order to win his lady than a shady trick. Having successfully healed the king and fulfilled her part of the bargain, Helen obtains the right to choose the man who will be her husband. The official engagement follows suit in spite of the young man's resistance. The reversal of usual roles is not without flavor and no doubt the play must have been very popular among ladies, who generally had to submit themselves to the choice of their fathers. Let us not forget either that a young man close to Shakespeare's heart, Henry Wriothesley, had been obstinately resisting his guardian's choice of a wife for him, consistently refusing to marry Lord Burleigh's granddaughter Lady Vere (daughter of Anne Cecil and Edward de Vere, 17th Earl of Oxford), for which he would be fined the huge sum of £5000. This "breach of promise" would durably impact his finances.

Shakespeare's young Lord Bertram, for all his beauty, sounds like a perfectly immature male adolescent, whose harsh sexual experiences hopefully eventually gain for him an understanding of the truth of marital life.

---

[3] "Women as well as men practiced medicine and surgery; as with their predecessors in the Roman empire, women's practice was limited neither to obstetrical cases nor to female patients. For example, the names of twenty-four women described as surgeons in Naples between 1273 and 1410 are known, and references have been found to fifteen women practitioners, most of them Jewish and none described as midwives, in Frankfurt between 1387 and 1497.... Even in the twelfth century, however, the accomplishments of Trota and Abbess Hildegard were highly unusual. Once university faculties of medicine were established during the thirteenth century, women were excluded from advanced medical education and, as a consequence, from the most prestigious and potentially lucrative variety of practice." Nancy G. Siraisi, *Medieval & Early Renaissance Medicine: An Introduction to Knowledge and Practice* (Chicago: The University of Chicago Press, 1990), 27.

Was Shakespeare reflecting on the days of his own ingenuousness and lack of experience when he was tricked into marrying Anne Hathaway?[4] This is a recurrent theme in his plays, where girls are generally infinitely more determined and audacious than their male counterparts. Helen's action broadly obeys Jesuit teaching concerning what was permissible and what was not. The famous issue of equivocation, taken up in *Macbeth*, is clearly suggested in her definition of intention (her plot), namely: with a disloyal husband, mischief can lead to good result. By indirection, find direction out. In other words, one is allowed to lie for the preservation of the truth. Going to Santiago is a case in point, all the more intriguing as it is Shakespeare's own addition to his borrowed story, deniable in so far as she never actually goes there, yet overtly propounded as a pilgrimage to obtain the miraculous return of her love. The suggestion of a miracle and of the purification intended is there, blatant by its very absence in contemporary England, where no spiritual means was left for the Christian to alleviate his grief or his remorse. So Helen can lie for a good cause, feign a pilgrimage to Santiago while heading for Tuscany where she does not hesitate to enroll Diana in her seduction plan, meanwhile giving free rein to the rumor of her death. The undercover stratagems of the Friar-Duke Vincentio of *Measure for Measure* naturally come to mind, just as does Paulina's subterfuge toward Leontes's moral and psychological recovery in *The Winter's Tale*. But in fact Shakespeare had nurtured the idea for a long time. As early as *The Comedy of Errors* he had tested what kind of wonder can be aroused from such an unexpected return to life.

In *All's Well*, Friar Francis's wisdom is taken over by the King who, having himself undergone a rebirth, makes a point of finding the truth about Bertram's deeds and Helen's death:

> Our rash faults
> Make trivial price of serious things we have,
> Not knowing them until we know their grave.
> Oft our displeasures, to ourselves unjust,
> Destroy our friends and after weep their dust. (V iii 60–64)

He certainly means to teach Bertram a lesson and the last scene of the play

---

[4] In that case it would perhaps show that, unlike most assumptions that his marriage was a failed one and that he nourished resentment and sour anger toward his wife, the "slight in his will to his wife" was perhaps the result of a deep mature agreement between husband and wife to favour the daughter most likely to bring an issue and take care of her aging mother, eight years older than William. Curiously this detail often pointed out concerning his marriage is never mentioned in connection with his death. One can imagine an intelligent, sensible woman who did not think it fit for her to inherit houses and lands which in turn she would soon be forced to bequeath and would in any case not be able to manage for long.

looks very much like a judgment scene, recalling in many ways the end of *The Merchant of Venice*. It would have been too easy for Bertram to be given Lafeu's daughter, without any justice done. It would have been too easy for him to see his wife revived, without any moral settling of scores. Bertram thought he slept with Diana, therefore is engaged to her. This has to be disentangled before anything else happens. For an Elizabethan public, Bertram was engaged, just as were Claudio and Angelo in *Measure for Measure*. The ring business is here the evidence upon which the case is founded and is certainly better integrated into the whole than in *The Merchant of Venice*, even though the judgment, for various reasons, fails to appear momentous. It is often staged rather jokingly as a piece of comic business; in our world of sexual promiscuity, a man's youthful indiscretions are still looked upon with fondness (at least until recently). After all, the audience know that Helen is not dead and that she has herself concocted part of the trick—whereas we don't know until the end whether Shylock will relent. And of course, Bertram is a rather naïve young aristocrat, a tiny bit vain and easily fooled by appearances.

The truth is, the playwright has not yet found the means to create absolute wonder and the spectator, who is made to share all the facts, becomes a little lost in the entanglement of events. He is even led to think that Helen's plot will fail, since hardly has her death been announced when all her supporters turn toward her supposed successor. Revelations follow each other quickly as in a thriller, depriving the play of the element of sacredness, the suspension of disbelief that would make the end awe-inspiring.

The genius of *The Winter's Tale* would be to use an intercessor, instead of exposing the main character and having her develop her own tricks, and to fuse all this into a brilliant last scene meant to arouse the spectators' as well as the characters' wonder. The true stage mannerism was to have everybody believe Hermione was dead. The other major scenic trick was Time, the chorus. After sixteen years of prayers and penance over the tomb of the woman he believed dead, it is reasonable to think that Leontes has had time to change and to learn the lesson. But in *All's Well*, when to reappearing Helen, who claims that she is but "the shadow of a wife" with "the name and not the thing," Bertram abruptly replies "Both, both, O, pardon!" (V iii 308), the reversal is too sudden and unexpected. It is easier to believe that, seeing her still alive, he is only trying to save his skin, than to attribute to him a love suddenly turned sincere and repentant. Of course, in *Much Ado About Nothing*, Claudio's readiness to swap women after he mistakenly killed the one he was to marry has already demonstrated that women really seemed interchangeable to men, as implied by the bed trick conveniently used in a few comedies by the dramatist.

Shakespeare's variations on the theme of rebirth reveal the improvements of his scenology. He was aspiring to sacred art, no less, and trying, in Michelangelo's words "to move mortals to tears and devotion." Before Michelangelo, Dante had already expressed those thoughts, that would be emulated by many Counter-Reformation artists: "What master were he of brush or of graver, who drew the shades and the lineaments, which there would make every subtle wit stare?"[5]

The healing talents revealed by some of Shakespeare's women characters, their infinite patience together with their subtle analyses (which are also to be found in tragedy, even if they are prevented from asserting those virtues), all of these make for a very fine appreciation of the "fair sex" and a very subtle analysis of the reasons why men and women can sometimes fail to connect. Unlike the solidarity of women, the rivalry that exists between men often leads them to their defeat. Helen is one of Shakespeare's benevolent characters who try their best to mend those failures, with the help of a host of monks, friars, and priests. These helpers listen, advise, marry in secret, and further invent stratagems in order to save a desperate situation. Yet in *Much Ado About Nothing* as in *All's Well*, the timing does not provide enough space for a complete and satisfactory denouement. Once again, we see a young man ready to swap a lost love for another without much ado — no remorse, no self-questioning. These were the tricks of comedy, but Shakespeare was looking further to a true representation of life and the possibilities of redemption. And we have to accept the evidence that much of his inspiration in that sense came from the Catholic education he had received. The old faith is there in his work like a palimpsest, and even when he seems to be denying it, Shakespeare manages to work on one's imagination so that one is constantly reminded of the forbidden world, the spiritual support, the comfort, the trust and protection once found with the local priest or a friar from a nearby convent, or best of all, the peace found in confiding in the Holy Virgin, the greatest woman intercessor, and in praying to the saints and angels which filled the churches. The method, unsurprisingly, was that advocated by Ignatius in his *Spiritual Exercises,* which, one feels, Shakespeare must at all times have kept handy on his bedside table: how to work on men's imaginations and senses in order to make them visualize, to be carried away body and soul by the beauty and desire of Christ's love. The old faith not only offered solace and redemption, it provided beauty, color, and stimulated the imagination. As Professor Greenblatt very rightly concludes, Shakespeare "had infused his theatrical vision with the vital remnants of that faith" for

---

[5] "Qual di pennel fu maestro o di stile, / che ritraesse l'ombre e i tratti, ch'ivi / mirar farieno ogn'ingegno sottile?" *Purgatorio*, Canto XII.

which he never found a replacement. "Being lacked and lost," it is prized all the dearer. In comparison, the new faith, essentially Calvinistic at the time, appeared like a mere political contrivance without spiritual grandeur, effectively depriving the people of comfort and of a sense of forgiveness.

The fact that Shakespeare chose a young maid sharing the faith, the will, and courage of Joan of Arc for his first physician is surely not haphazard. She was an apt interface between the wisdom of the monastery and the medical art. Shakespeare's physicians always seem to be good psychologists, aware of the limits of their earthly power. In *Macbeth*,[6] the doctor cannot cure Lady Macbeth's delirium, neither can he provide a miracle to Macbeth's fear of damnation, yet he is given a respect no one else receives from the tyrant. In *King Lear*, the doctor, whose part is so small that it is most of the time cut out, nevertheless provides an interesting light on the old man's deterioration. He alone seems to understand that rest is the exhausted old man's greatest need, that he will recover his mind after a good sleeping cure against a background of sweet music. This is very New Age. The doctor further recommends not to remind him of events his memory has buried deep until he has recovered peace and quiet. This man, who is a good psychologist and has Cordelia's respect, understands old Lear better than most critics, who reduce him to a madman in spite of the fact that until the end there is much method in his madness.

Gradually, the doctor evolves into a sort of magus, the art of healing bodies, which can pass for a miracle, being incomplete without the ability to heal the minds. The author has gradually chiseled new figures for the wisdom and healing virtues of the now long-gone monasteries. In his last plays, he does reach this delicate balance between the medicine of the body and that of the mind. In *Pericles, Prince of Tyre* Lord Cerimon launches into an explanation of his art which would look good, even now, over the door of our Medical schools:

> I held it ever
> Virtue and cunning were endowments greater
> Than nobleness and riches. Careless heirs
> May the two latter darken and dispend,
> But immortality attends the former,
> Making a man a god. 'Tis known I ever
> Have studied physic, through which secret art,
> Turning o'er authorities, I have,
> Together with my practice, made familiar
> To me and to my aid the blest infusions
> That dwells in vegetives, in metals, stones,

---

[6] See below, Chapter 8: "Macbeth's Angels and Babes."

And so can speak of the disturbances
That nature works, and of her cures, which doth give me
A more content and cause of true delight
Than to be thirsty after tott'ring honour,
Or tie my pleasure up in silken bags
To glad the fool and death. (III ii 23–41, Sc. 12)

Cerimon, this hieratic, sensitive, scholarly character, who, thanks to his knowledge, manages to revive Pericles's dead queen, appears to all like a divine agent. As Pericles says:

Reverend sir,
The gods can have no mortal officer
More like a god than you. (V iii 83–85, Sc. 22)

Cerimon, who may have been an early study for Prospero's character, has no equivalent in *Cymbeline*, where the doctor, although he saves Imogen's life, remains a minor character. For some reason, which may be a bow to Lady Magdalen Montague, who had just died in 1608, the character who presides over the resurrection of Hermione and the restoration of family ties in *The Winter's Tale* is a woman, Paulina. She no doubt represents the feminine descendent of the Abbess, a bold, virtuous, obstinate character who, having lost her lord, has nothing to fear, and like Lady Magdalen, who was bold enough to assert her faith and support her household in theirs throughout her life without being unduly troubled by Cecil's henchmen, she could call on faith and resist measures against herself "with complete equanimity, a pleasing countenance; and a protestation of loyalty to [the] King."[7]

HEALING THE STATE: *MEASURE FOR MEASURE*

Among the many variations on the subject, *Measure for Measure* holds a pivotal role, with Shakespeare fusing together the parts of the monk and the ruler. Duke Vincentio, a precursor of Prospero, is facing a problem: his rule has been too soft with regards to the law, which has not been strictly applied these past fourteen years. His benevolence, like that of a "fond father," has engendered too much slackness and self-indulgence in his subjects, who are no longer afraid of the law and are now mocking his authority. How can he change things without seeming a tyrant? He chooses to disappear, leaving the dirty job to his deputy Angelo, "a man of stricture and firm abstinence," (I iii 12) who will, in all likelihood, be inflexible. Thus the law will be restored without the Duke losing his popularity. It could in itself be the straightforward plot of a Machiavellian play

---

[7] Michael C. Questier, *Catholicism and Early Community in Early Modern England* (Cambridge: Cambridge University Press, 2006), 230.

about government, yet unlike Richard III, for instance, Vincentio does not affect any hypocritical posturing, nor does he feign devotion in order to deceive his people about his moral superiority.

The Duke's plan, of course, may sound a little devious, but he makes it clear that he has more in mind. His plot cleverly investigates a second problem, which relates to the moral quality of the ruler himself, a quest which no doubt has been his for some time already, as Escalus later corroborates, describing the Duke as "One that, above all other strifes, contended especially to know himself" (III i 488–89). The Duke's decision to put on the habit of a true friar in order to keep an eye on Angelo while visiting his people *incognito* is part of such an apprenticeship. That the play, performed at court during the Christmas season 1604, may sound like a veiled, indirect political lesson to the new monarch, James I, is not altogether far-fetched, all the more as the Duke shares a few common features with the new king. This may also be one of the instances when Shakespeare may have been inspired by Rudolf II and his somewhat detached and lenient way of governing his people. The mannerist dramaturgy ensured a perfect cover for the dramatist, who did not hesitate to deal almost openly with religious and moral aspects of power.

The title *Measure for Measure*, while apparently dealing with aspects of retributive justice, which are indeed central to the plot, is also a mirror play ultimately revealing to each character a true reflection of himself. Whereas the Law (as repeatedly expressed in the Torah)[8] measures out the punishment each criminal deserves, the Gospels enjoin men to examine themselves before condemning their neighbor, for fear they should be judged by the same measure.[9] The crux of government is precisely in the art of finding the harmony of such contradictions, between the rule of the Law and the teachings of religion. "Judge not, that ye be not judged," says the Gospel of Luke, implying the equality of all men in the eyes of God. This hardly condones the arrogance and privileges of hierarchy. The play uses this to reveal the substitutive character of each man. "For with the same measure that ye mete withal it shall be measured to you again" (Luke 6:38). Not only is one man as good as the other, but he can be made to play the other's part if necessary. The judge can become the criminal just as the bawd can become the executioner.

Within the frame of a morality play, which Shakespeare implements using the methods of Thomas Aquinas's *Summa*,[10] he manages to question

---

[8] Ex 21:23–25, Lev 24:19–20, Deut 19:21.
[9] Mt 7: 1–5; Lk 6: 37–42.
[10] "the taxonomy of vice in the play can be found in the *Secunda Pars* of Aquinas's *Summa Theologica*, specifically under the virtue of temperance (1981, 2a2ae 146–58),"

the traditional antitheses of desire versus order, grace versus temptation, the flesh versus the spirit, light versus darkness, and God versus the devil, playing with them and their many paradoxes, turning them upside down, so that virtue is caught by vice, purity engenders lust, justice is mocked by the judge, and promiscuity appears to be the easiest cure for desire. Angelo is a devilish angel and Lucio wields a doubtful light, playing the part of the medieval Vice in the comedy. As Beauregard specifies, "the precision of Isabella's phrase about 'concupiscible intemperate lust' (V i 99) and the tight cluster of virtues and vices described by Aquinas (2a2ae 146–58) and exhibited in the play (abstinence, fasting, sobriety, drunkenness, virginity, sexual intemperance, fornication, seduction, sacrilegious lust, clemency, severity, and anger), can hardly be coincidental."[11] It was essential to give the play an emphatic moral grounding so that the substitutions set up by the Duke clearly contribute to blurring all the differences. If Angelo can replace the Duke, if Mariana can replace Isabella, then the dead body of Ragozine can surely pass for Claudio and the bawd can be an apt executioner. Angelo has committed the same crime as Claudio, and the Duke concludes the play by offering Isabella exactly what was abhorrent to her: the loss of her chastity.[12] In this play of mirrors, the moral categories have dissolved as well, so that if one thing is certain at the end of the play, it is that one does not govern by excluding one side of life. The whole tapestry is much more complex and truth infinitely more varied. The comic plot also confirms the confusion of morality as well as language. We never learn the nature of the crime committed by Elbow's "two notorious benefactors" and the parody of a trial ends with this unexpected sentence: "Thou art to continue now, thou varlet, thou art to continue" (II i 182). Shakespeare appears to be laughing at the attempt of temporal powers to regulate men's moral behavior, just as he is showing the abuses and excesses of too strict chastity.

The Puritans had long railed against the theater and its loose morals and the arrival of James I on the throne of England did not curb their sanctimoniousness, nor did it bring the Catholics the toleration they had expected. Both sides rather vied with each other for extremes of purity. As already pointed out, Shakespeare's deep nature seems to have loathed extremes, which not only failed in the essential Christian lesson of meekness and benevolence, but were also antithetic to his esthetic beliefs. Besides, could such high moral standards be maintained by ordinary men?

David Beauregard, "Shakespeare on Monastic Life: Nuns and Friars in *Measure for Measure*," *Shakespeare and the Culture of Christianity in Early Modern England*, ed. Dennis Taylor and David Beauregard (New York: Fordham University Press, 2003), 311–35.

[11] Beauregard, *Shakespeare and the Culture of Christianity*, 315.

[12] It can be argued of course that marriage is not exactly the same as forced sex, yet in the play, it appears more like a way to legalize sex than a sacred door toward it.

Will Angelo turn out to be as precise and puritanical as he pretends to be? That's the question, expressed very clearly to Friar Thomas. The Duke has left his government to a substitute with the intent to spy on him from the wings. It is even clear very early that the play is mostly concerned about this second aspect of the Duke's plot. Interestingly, his disguise as a friar will give him the freedom to walk among his people and collect their innermost thoughts without arousing suspicion.[13] Moreover, his religious aura will give more power to the advice he feels entitled to give. In a very subtle way, Shakespeare is granting his Duke the spiritual powers of God's anointed kings, unveiling, albeit comically, the essential weakness of the modern ruler, divested from the sacred status that empowered him. The Law should not be deprived of the spirit of the Law. Rigor should not exist without mercy, which itself requires strong authority in order to be effective.

Lucio's slander, throughout the play, is another aspect of the corrosive atmosphere that has invaded the city. Vienna is a world of denunciation, calumny, and easily ruined reputation, probably reflecting London at the time. The Duke has a lot on his hands and his disguise is evidently the best way to ascertain the situation. He can even be tempted to usurp God's part, especially in the denouement, where, like Jupiter in *Cymbeline*, he could say: "Whom best I love, I cross, to make my gift, / The more delayed, delighted" (*Cymbeline*, V iii 195–96). The character of the Duke has been variously interpreted, "as an emblem of divine providence, as an ideal ruler, as a cold-hearted manipulator, and as a ridiculous old busybody,"[14] but just as in real life, one may appear to be different things to different people. None of these aspects is exclusive of the others, which is precisely what blurs any attempt at fitting the character into any preconceived category and gives a wider scope to the play.

The city's institutions and the government's justice therefore are used as covers to put on trial the private and moral religious inclinations of the characters. Interestingly, the tone is discreetly and indirectly set in a conversation between Lucio and two gentlemen about the private arrangements of a "sanctimonious pirate" with his own conscience and the Ten Commandments. Can soldiers departing for war say grace and pray for peace? Yes, says the second gentleman, before Lucio retorts that he surely never was "where grace was said" (I ii 19). Surreptitiously, the talk has slid toward the idea that "Grace is grace, despite of all controversy," that is to say "in any religion," as the first gentleman has just

---

[13] This "trick" had already been experimented with by King Henry V to know his men's feelings before Agincourt.

[14] N. W. Bowcutt, ed., *Measure for Measure* (Oxford: Oxford University Press, 1991), "Introduction," 53.

asserted. [15] Lucio, who in many ways plays the part of the Vice, ceaselessly provoking the Duke with his taunting remarks, is the one who expresses here the heart of the matter. Is there grace in Angelo? This is what the play is about to reveal.

Meanwhile, the play, like most of Shakespeare's tragicomedies, begins with tragedy: Claudio is condemned to death for making pregnant the woman he loves and is engaged to. Angelo shows no empathy and makes no use of casuistry. He insists on the strict application of the law and in a very puritanical style, he favors public shaming, having charged the Provost to expose Claudio to the world on his way to prison. This is poles apart from the Roman Catholic Sacrament of Penance, with its very private confession, which the Duke in Franciscan habit hears from Claudio, Juliet, and later Mariana. [16] Angelo shows himself exacting toward others but, as we can readily witness, not regarding his own comportment during the length of the proceedings, which he finds boring:

> This will last out a night in Russia
> When nights are longest there. I'll take my leave,
> And leave you to the hearing of the cause,
> Hoping you'll find good cause to whip them all. (II i 128–31)

Thus, there are two sets of rules right from the very first intervention. The man immediately appears to be a sanctimonious prig, imbued with his own superiority, discreetly disapproved of by Escalus, [17] whose wisdom would no doubt have better fitted him for the job. In the preceding scene, Lucio has encouraged Isabella to go to Angelo and beg his forgiveness for her brother Claudio. The first part of the play is therefore devoted to the confrontation of both characters, each embodying an extreme position on the religious spectrum of the day, the Puritan versus the Nun — two absolute purists. The encounter, which remains one of the most famous moments in Shakespeare's work, gives body and soul to the opposition of contraries, which pervaded England's religious life at the time and which sustains Shakespeare's artistic manner. This opposition should naturally be visible on the stage. The young virgin, shy and innocent, impressed by

---

[15] If we admit that Shakespeare, as a Catholic, knew the *Summa*, he would have found there too an essential definition of grace, a moot point in the religious division of the time, which he very cautiously puts in the mouth of secondary characters.

[16] Now, some take this to prove that the Bard is mocking the Church by having a false monk usurp the priesthood. If it were so, the very essence of the theater would be condemned, as it was by arch puritans like William Prynne.

[17] When Angelo insists on Claudio's execution "by tomorrow morning," Escalus replies "Well, heaven forgive him, and forgive us all! / Some rise by sin, and some by virtue fall" (II i 37–38), pointing out the lack of measure and lack of judgement of so-called justice.

the austere appearance and reputation of this newly promoted ruler, has to be goaded on by Lucio, whereas the strict deputy, entrenched in his binary vision of life, swiftly confirms Claudio's condemnation. Isabella has to move him, to use the rhetoric of the preacher, appealing to the Bible from Genesis and the Fall of Adam and Eve to the coming and death of Christ in order to redeem men's sins and save the world. But Angelo holds to the law as to a lifeline; without the law, which he uses to sustain his authority, he finds himself naked, ignorant of his own "glassy essence." At this point the confrontation becomes formidable and reaches the climax of a tragedy. Angelo has gradually been divested of his words while Isabella seems to be carried away. She voices the matter very eloquently:

> But man, proud man,
> Dressed in a little brief authority,
> Most ignorant of what he's most assured,
> His glassy essence, like an angry ape
> Plays such fantastic tricks before high heaven
> As makes the angels weep, who, with our spleens,
> Would all themselves laugh mortal. (II ii 119–25)

Her description applies to Angelo, whom it accuses of arrogance and hypocrisy, as well as, ironically, to the Duke, who is looking for his own essence by means of fantastic tricks indeed. Isabella, like Portia in *The Merchant of Venice*, appeals to the ruler's understanding and mercy in the name of the Highest Judge:

> How would you be
> If He which is the top of judgement, should
> But judge you as you are? O, think on that,
> And mercy then will breathe within your lips,
> Like man new made. (II ii 75–79)

Sadly, Angelo shows little self-consciousness and no moderation in his response to individual vice, unlike Isabella, who first advocates marriage when she learns of her brother's fault. If as Portia describes,

> The quality of mercy is not strained.
> It droppeth as the gentle rain from heaven
> Upon the place beneath. It is twice blest:
> It blesseth him that gives, and him that takes.
> 'Tis mightiest in the mightiest. (*Merchant of Venice*, IV i 181–85)

Angelo's ensuing bargaining with Isabella surely makes him twice damned. He is damned for making her beg again and again for her brother's life all the while refusing to grant mercy, and damned again for measuring

Claudio's life by a few minutes of personal gratification. He uses his power to tempt the girl and plays with her like a cat with a mouse, which Isabella's honesty perceives soon enough:

> Ignominy in ransom and free pardon
> Are of two houses; lawful mercy
> Is nothing kin to foul redemption. (II iv 112–14)

There is neither compassion nor generosity in the man. If he eventually agrees to save Claudio, it is to satisfy his foul desire, and even this bargain he will betray eventually. The climax of the play is one of corruption and ignominy. Angelo very adroitly uses his authority to force the young woman, whose voice has no power against him. The play has reached a crux. How can this lie be revealed, and distorted reality be restored to fairer proportions? A tragedy cannot accomplish it without deaths. Claudio is to die whatever Isabella's decision and in a sane world Angelo would be dismissed and condemned to death by the returning Duke. Can this be avoided? Is there any other way to solve the situation?

Measure for Measure is fundamentally ambivalent in its dramatic treatment of characters and plot, precisely to avoid these tragic consequences. How can the hidden Duke alter the predetermined course of tragedy and turn it into a benevolent ending for all? That's the question. The play is Shakespeare's first literal experiment in the new mannerist genre of the tragicomedy. From now on, he will use and misuse this ambivalent genre, which had been previously termed "tragical-comical-historical-pastoral,"[18] by Polonius, who, even though he was mocked by Hamlet, gave a rather apt definition of what the playwright was trying to achieve in order to enlighten and deepen his representation of life. This was not new to Shakespeare, of course, but these twists and reflections, which he had used "within" a comedy, or "within" a tragedy, are now structurally applied to the genre of the play itself. The minute the Friar-Duke decides to intervene, whether it be like God's providence or like a busy stage manager, *Measure for Measure* loses its tragic quality. Mirror plays and debates alternate with mischievous substitution tricks, and truth is hopelessly entangled with illusion and lies, unsettling the characters as well as the audience and rendering any act of judgment almost impossible.

Differentiation is insidiously abolished by the substitutions that fuel the plot. Like a chess player, the Friar-Duke, who has left his own part to Angelo, hopes that by a few skillful moves, by substituting one character for another, having another disappear *en passant*, he can win the game, correct the extreme zeal of his deputy and turn evil into good. Mariana

---

[18] *Hamlet*, II ii 393.

will take Isabella's part, thus saving both women's honor and Claudio's life. That is, only if Angelo is true to his word, which unfortunately he isn't. Another move has to be improvised quickly. Enter Barnardine. There is surely no other scene in Shakespeare laden with so much meaningful absurdity, than this drunken Barnardine refusing to be executed. The good Friar-Duke can only comply with this sudden farcical obstacle to his project. But it means he is newly in check. The head of Ragozine, a pirate who died of fever, comes on cue to be served as an evidence for Angelo. The perspectives and tricks, which reveal a jocund indeterminacy of genre as far as the play is concerned, do not, however, preclude the existence of a firm moral standpoint, which goes against the anti-Catholic conventions of English Protestant drama, where friars and nuns were regularly mocked and satirized.[19] Here, the settings of the Franciscan monastery and convent duly represent the contemplative life away from the bustling, corrupted world of the city, mostly revealed through its government and prison. They represent a *locus amoenus* in this urban play. If Vienna harbors vices and corruption, the nuns and friars are not part of it. We cannot doubt the sincerity of the Duke when he confides to Friar Thomas:

> My holy sir, none better knows than you
> How I have ever loved the life removed,
> And held in idle price to haunt assemblies
> Where youth and cost a witless bravery keeps. (I iii 7–10)

The monastery must have been his peaceful retreat a good many times before, and the friar habit and manner he decides to put on reveal his true character more than they conceal it.[20] As his words to Escalus indicate, they are the outcome of a ruler's meditation on himself and power. Unlike Angelo, who merely applies the letter of the law, without any interest in its human consequences, the Duke wishes his justice to improve individuals rather than annihilate them. The fact that he does not hesitate to entrust Friar Thomas with his secret plan confirms his familiarity with the monastery and its spiritual support.

In this play, Franciscan cloistered life is once again shown as a refuge (rather than a place of transgression), where men and women humbly reflect on their humanity and the necessity to show compassion and

---

[19] "With the advent of Reformed theology, however, the essential elements of the religious life itself came under literary attack, and such things as vows, the cloistered life, celibacy, and the priesthood were pilloried. In early Reformation drama, the conventional figure of the Vice was often portrayed as a Roman Catholic priest-player," Beauregard, *Shakespeare and the Culture of Christianity*, chap. 12.

[20] I have the feeling that William Shakespeare must occasionally have been such a visitor, when he himself had enough of the London hubbub and its political and religious conspiracies.

mercy to their brothers and sisters. Not surprisingly, mercy had been duly
mentioned by the Duke as part of Angelo's commission:

> In our remove be thou at full ourself:
> Mortality and mercy in Vienna
> Live in thy tongue and heart. (I i 44–46)

However, to be a lover of virtue is one thing, to impose virtue on others
is an entirely different matter. Once the main question has been put of
how to govern with justice and how to apply the law or soften its rigors,
Shakespeare gives it a life and a complexity that surge every time the law
has to be applied to a human situation. To implement the law as a strict
application of the severest punishments in order to deter others from
sinning might soon become a bloody carnage likely to unpeople the city,
all the more inacceptable as it is unfair, since, as Angelo admits, justice
randomly seizes only what is made visible to its authority. The cynicism
and hypocrisy he seems to encourage are made obvious here.

Conversely, the attitude of the Duke, throughout the play, is one of
patience and tolerance, which contrasts with Angelo's impatience at the
stupidity and sluggishness of Elbow the constable and his "two notorious
benefactors," Pompey and Froth. Flesh and blood matters are always more
complex than law decrees, which are obstructed by the slow, meandering
rhetoric of Pompey, who revels in useless details that slow down and
confuse the cross-examination. Matter always impedes the spirit. Those
subtle oppositions of characters are meant to multiply perspectives, and
keep the audience on tenterhooks, the comic scenes counterbalancing the
tragic ones, laughter counterbalancing tears, fear and anguish counterbalancing boldness and insensibility. In the philosophy lesson the Duke gives
Claudio there appears a Christian stoic advising the young man to use
his own effort and reflection to reach a state of moral equanimity in the
face of death. No mention is made of an afterlife, rather life is belittled in
order to make death less frightening. Claudio, however, readily translates
these words into the official Christian oxymoron:

> To sue to live, I find I seek to die,
> And seeking death, find life. Let it come on. (III i 42–43)

But as the next scene reveals, these are words, which his own quick flesh
does not recognize:

> Ay, but to die, and go we know not where;
> To lie in cold obstruction, and to rot;
> This sensible warm motion to become
> A kneaded clod, and the delighted spirit

> To bathe in fiery floods, or to reside
> In thrilling region of thick-ribbèd ice;
> To be imprisoned in the viewless winds,
> And blown with restless violence round about
> The pendent world; or to be worse than worst
> Of those that lawless and incertain thought
> Imagine howling — 'tis too horrible!
> The weariest and most loathed worldly life
> That age, ache, penury, and imprisonment
> Can lay on nature is a paradise
> To what we fear of death. (III i 121–35)

Surely "the most loathed worldly" Barnardine knows it intuitively, even if he does not possess the poetical imagination of Claudio. The inexorable perspective of death, which fills Claudio with fear and anguish, is turned upside down by Barnardine's drunken insensibility and his utter imperviousness to his fate and execution is used like equipoise to Claudio's moving painting of the world of death, thus restoring a certain relativism into human affairs.

Claudio's vision of "the undiscovered country from whose bourn / No traveller returns"[21] finds inspiration in Dante's *Inferno*, whose Second Circle contains the souls of carnal sinners. Claudio evidently considers himself such a one and visualizes himself endlessly whirled around the world by fierce winds in total darkness. It is all the more moving as it is not a poet's reverie but the fear of a man condemned to die on the morrow. The frightening vision he delineates for his sister suddenly impels him to beg for life, which in turn makes Isabella's violent reaction "O you beast, / O faithless coward, O dishonest wretch," (III i 139–40) seem cruel and insensible. The contrast is extreme. Suddenly the pure young nun, who appeared as the victim of a sanctimonious prig, becomes Angelo's alter ego: "I'll pray a thousand prayers for thy death, / No word to save thee" (III i 149–50). In the preceding scene, she had already concluded against stooping "to such abhorred pollution," hoping for her brother's agreement:

> Then Isabel live chaste, and brother die:
> More than our brother is our chastity. (II iv 185–86)

Was it merciful to mention Angelo's request to her brother, to give him the slightest hope only to crush it vehemently, when he begins to beg for his life? Here, pitiless Isabella sounds more like a rigid *dueña* than like a

---

[21] *Hamlet*, III i 80–81. Hamlet and Claudio's preoccupation with death at this particular time probably also reflects Shakespeare's own, following the loss of his father, the sudden death of the Earl of Essex in 1601, and the unexpected grace granted by the Queen to the Earl of Southampton.

loving sister. She appears to be as sanctimonious and arrogant as Angelo. The Duke's ensuing compliment may therefore sound a little strange, unless it is understood theologically. Beauty can last only as long as it comes from the soul, whose virtue lives by grace, a disposition to live and act in keeping with God's call.[22] The Duke has just heard the exchange between brother and sister; unless he has already fallen under Isabella's charm, her lack of *caritas*[23] cannot have escaped him, while her own defense of her chastity cannot displease him. His address can be taken as wishful thinking, a kind of encouragement to Isabella not to spoil the grace she has received and her ability to lead others to God. He knows too, since he has been playing the confessor, that God is infinitely merciful, and sanctifying grace can always be restored to the penitent heart, through the Sacrament of Penance.

Isabella is therefore reminded of her divine essence by the Friar-Duke, who questions her on her way to solve her dilemma: How will she save her brother and satisfy Angelo in the bargain? Her reply is curiously slightly different from what she told her brother. She no longer invokes her dear chastity, but the child she might get out of wedlock. From excessive prudishness and an extreme desire for purity, she is now speaking of law and honor, which incidentally prepares the audience for the possibility of her accepting the Duke's proposal at the end. After all, most girls entering a convent did so only because they could not afford the right party, and it would seem that Isabella and Claudio did not own the estate that might have bailed them out of their present fate. It is true that we are not given any inkling of what motivated her in the first place. Her excess may be attributed to her youth and inexperience. Both Angelo and Isabella are novices in life matters and like all beginners, they tend to be a little too absolute.

What the Friar-Duke had not quite figured out in this experiment is the resistance of matter, of base human nature for a start, as he discovers that, whatever his good intentions, "back-wounding calumny / The whitest virtue strikes" (III i 444–45). Through Lucio's "slanderous tongue," he acquires an image of himself quite different from the benefactor that he means to be. At the end of Act III, he had taken the role of Chorus, explaining in rhyming couplets that he must apply craft against vice to catch Angelo at his own game. The following scene reveals how unrealistic his confident

---

[22] According to a commonly accepted categorization, made by St Thomas Aquinas in his *Summa Theologiae*, grace can be given either to make the person receiving it pleasing to God (*gratia gratum faciens*) — so that the person is sanctified and justified — or else to help the receiver lead someone else to God (*gratia gratis data*).

[23] According to Thomas Aquinas, it was "the most excellent of virtues," which was a spiritual love extended from God to man and then reflected by man, who is made in the image of God, back to God. God gives man the power to act as God acts (God is love), man then reflects God's power in his own human actions toward others.

optimism sounds even to his Provost, who has a keener eye than he as to Angelo's true nature, "It is a bitter deputy" (IV ii 78). The pardon the Duke is expecting from Angelo, following Mariana's bed-trick, thus turns out to be a renewed execution order for both Claudio and Barnardine, whose case had been doubtful these nine years. The Friar-Duke now truly fits Lucio's vision of "the old fantastical Duke of dark corners," (IV iii 154–55) his strategy gradually shaken by unlikely obstacles, necessity increasingly limiting his free choice. Ragozine's death looks like a stroke of luck to save the endangered plot. There is but one solution left for Vincentio: to resume his own power and to come back as the Duke for the final revelation.

The play has moved from potential tragedy to something between farce and thriller. As in *All's Well*, the long last act of *Measure for Measure* is a judgment scene, busily clarifying the situation and giving each character his due. The Duke suddenly decides to return for a great show of authority, at first pretending to support his substitute's decision so that the latter is gradually caught in his own lies. Playing the disingenuous discoverer, the Duke manages to confuse most characters, so that even loyal Escalus gets things wrong and Lucio's babble loses all precautions. For a moment, the absent Friar becomes a convenient scapegoat, until he is daringly revealed by Lucio. With the sudden realization that the Duke has been spying on him all along, Angelo can no longer lie. He himself asks for death, which is not immediately answered, however. The Duke enjoys prolonging Angelo's agony and keeps extending the threat of death as long as he possibly can, postponing Angelo's condemnation until he has married him to the woman he cravenly forsook, and letting Isabella believe that her brother has truly died. He wants to test the characters' truthfulness, particularly Isabella's, whose grace looks tainted after she angrily wished for her brother's death. After all, she could now refuse, as the Duke forcefully suggests, to plead with Mariana for Angelo's forgiveness. That she accepts proves that she has heard the Friar's words in the prison and probably repented for her harshness. Yet does that mean that she is now ready to accept the Duke's proposal?

The indecisiveness of the ending as to Isabella's destiny is of course part of the whole questioning of preconceived categories. Over the centuries, the interpretations of Isabella, just like those of the Duke, oscillated between extremes, from "a sense of steadily ripening intimacy between her and the Duke,"[24] which brought their final union as no surprise, to the 1987 production, where Isabella stared at the Duke "in what appeared to be incredulous distaste at the sheer crassness of his timing."[25] From the

---

[24] Bowcutt, *Measure for Measure*, Introduction, 40.
[25] Ibid., 40.

outraged nun jealous of her chastity to the relieved young woman who is offered a match beyond all her expectations, the author did not choose. Stage directors can indulge their own whims. The Duke himself seems to stumble upon this proposal, which he had not once contemplated. His spontaneous reply to Lucio's charges against the absent Duke, who, according to him, "had some feeling of the sport" (III ii 113), sounds honest. He says of himself: "I never heard the absent Duke much detected for women. He was not inclined that way" (III i 383–84).

The Duke's proposal, right out of the blue, which he himself concedes to be out of time, may be taken as a sign of sudden relief, and the final shift from tragedy to comedy. The mood is one of general forgiveness and restored order. Whatever answer Isabella will give the Duke is for our own mind's eye. Having restored law and order, the Duke can afford to be merciful. The greater the fear, the more effective the act of mercy. One cannot exist without the other. Unrelenting severity and the death penalty merely instill fear and despair into the heart of the people, who are led to extreme action rather than moderate self-reflection. If Isabella has understood the Duke's lesson, she may contemplate marrying the man for his goodness and patient efforts to do good. In any case, her status as a novice is never blamed or belittled. On the contrary, whoever can make such self-sacrifice for God will necessarily possess great virtues that a husband will appreciate. As Theseus expressed it in *A Midsummer Night's Dream*:

> Thrice blessed they that master so their blood
> To undergo such maiden pilgrimage;
> But earthlier happy is the rose distilled
> Than that which, withering on the virgin thorn,
> Grows, lives, and dies in single blessedness. (I i 74–78)

Had she refused to forgive Angelo, he would have died, Mariana would have been left without a husband, and one may believe that Vincentio would never have made such a proposal. Until the end, then, the Duke's efforts could have met with impediments and the play would have remained dark and bitter. The Duke's action in disguise mimics Shakespeare's own action, casting the characters, effecting substitutions, and modifying the plot when necessary. The aim, like that of the ruler, is to teach and delight for the better moral satisfaction of everyone. Showing every character his own reflection in the eyes of others, *Measure for Measure* reveals that all men share the same humanity. Before we judge others we must know and judge ourselves. ♣

8. Damnation, Salvation: A DIPTYCH

*T*HE FIRST YEARS OF THE SEVENTEENTH CENTURY INItiated a dark period of intense religious and philosophical meditation for William Shakespeare. It is as if he needed to probe evil and explore hell before he could hope to recover the path to light and faith again.

In *Hamlet*, the title role is so important, Hamlet throws himself into such a breath-taking plot that we sometimes tend to forget the vital part played by the couple of Claudius and Gertrude in this thriller. They, in many ways, foreshadow the demonic couple of Macbeth and his wife, with the passion that unites them as well as the bad conscience that torments the usurper king when he realizes what he has done. It is never completely clear whether Gertrude was part of the plot against Old Hamlet or not. Hamlet's doubts somehow save her from being characterized as a fellow-conspirator. Who knows what distortion would be wrought in her soul, if she lost this beautiful son of hers? For some reason, Shakespeare stages fiercely passionate, possessive mothers, all of them strong women, sometimes torn apart by their sons' cruelty, sometimes defeated by sheer misunderstanding of this unknown part of themselves, sometimes hardened by the loss of their child. Such a mother may have been Lady Macbeth.

THE ANGELS AND BABES OF *MACBETH*

In the oppressive night which Macbeth's conscience has become for him, the owl's scream and the cricket's cry suddenly acquire a vivid intensity, piercing the silence of the night like the last vestiges of fleeing life, the sonorous images of the terror that has taken hold of his soul, the tiny witnesses of the felony he will never manage to cast off, any more than he will succeed in washing his hands clean of the blood of the trustful man, his king and father, who was a guest in his own house. "Had he not resembled / My father as he slept, I had done't" (II ii 13–14), says Lady Macbeth as an apology for not doing the job herself. And we discover that this seemingly cold and murderous lady had a father and a heart after all. She could not have killed her own father, so she sent her husband instead. Yet she fears lest he should not be up to the deed either. She knows all too well the humanity and the great heart of her man, whom she keeps scolding and pestering. She begs him not to think of it, knowing full well that the mere thought of their monstrous deed will make them mad. The flaw of the characters is not their unnaturalness but their weak humanity, their ability to be moved, which Shakespeare unveils to us by tiny touches — a sentence, a detail, clues with which the actor builds up his character. The terror-stricken confrontation of husband and wife quaking at the least noise, Macbeth's tortured soul and his wife's inflexible will, the destruction of Macbeth's peace of mind, Lady Macbeth's fear of having done all this for nothing if they relent now, the very intensity of this moment of panic, which conjugates *never more* with *too late*, leaves the audience flabbergasted, with racing hearts and moist hands. For, contrary to Roman Polanski's interpretation, Shakespeare knew that terror and pity are not only aroused by gory sights, but most surely by the shadow of evil as it slowly possesses the soul of the murdering couple. Madness is human and the most ordinary of men can be seized with murderous madness, whenever the love of power invades him, the boundless dream of some divine power, this delirium of pride called *hubris* by the Greeks.

What is fascinating and enduringly troubling is the brilliant intuition with which Shakespeare has desire and omen meet each other, reality and imagination colliding, with Macbeth suddenly investing himself in the three witches' prediction to such a degree that it seems to emanate from his own subconscious self. The encounter of desire with chance? A particular form of serendipity, this art of finding, haphazardly, something that you are not looking for but which a favorable state of mind suddenly renders very plausible? There is sometimes so little difference between what one would like to see happening and what truly happens. And if it is not yet, how easy it is, then, to provoke the event which destiny places so conveniently at hand. And how does Macbeth's reaction compare with Banquo's, whose ambition is also awakened? What mean for him the seeds of time? The innocence of Banquo's soul, though, preserves him from the bondage of destiny. Both friends already are, unconsciously, prisoners of the mimetic desire that will ruin their friendship. If Macbeth becomes king and Banquo's sons succeed him, the missing link necessarily means something disloyal, suspicious has happened. The seed of evil is planted.

As he has just been promoted Thane of Cawdor, Macbeth, whose dreams run faster than the reality of the predictions that have been made to him, turns toward Banquo and asks if now he does not believe that his children will be kings. That he omits a stage in the prediction is revealing of the unspeakable thing that has taken hold of his heart, the crown, a dream which is now at hand, and the ruin of which is already threatened by the foretelling made to Banquo. The latter has felt the danger almost instantly and warns his friend of the grievous consequences of such temptation:

> But 'tis strange,
> And oftentimes to win us to our harm,
> The instruments of darkness tell us truths,
> Win us with honest trifles to betray's
> In deepest consequence. (I iii 124–28)

His friend's imagination, however, is already riding loose on the wings of the augury, building kingdoms where nothing exists but the force of his own desire. He is in such a hurry that he has already sent a letter to his wife, even before he has had time to talk the matter over with Banquo as he suggested: "Think upon what hath chanced, and at more time, / The interim having weighed it, let us speak / Our free hearts each to other" (I iii 154–57). This conversation, which might have saved the king, will never happen. The letter has gone faster. If it is evidence of the intimacy and trust of the couple, this gesture is also fatal, for Macbeth is now preceded by his dream, taken over by his wife, who wrests control of the situation even before his arrival: "Only look up clear. . . . Leave all the rest to me" (I v 70–72). Whatever way he now chooses to interpret the witches' prophecy, he is now pushed by one more convinced than himself. Thus it sometimes happens that we bind ourselves hand and foot by entrusting our neighbor or lover with our own dreams. From this fatal impulse the tragedy is unleashed and both husband and wife soon become haunted characters obsessed by hallucinations that no doctor can cure. A few lines are enough to reveal the strength and weaknesses of each character, in particular the fatal flaw of the instigator wife, who would willingly have done the deed *if* the king had not resembled her father in his sleep — *if*, this little word, the "almost nothing," which from the beginning undermines the deed and condemns Lady Macbeth to sleepwalking in her guilt and madness.

As for Macbeth, face to face with the consequence of his desire, he is mortified. Even before the deed is done, Macbeth's imagination pictures angels and babes riding the tumultuous elements and blowing the dire news to the world at large:

> Besides, this Duncan
> Hath borne his faculties so meek, hath been
> So clear in his great office, that his virtues
> Will plead like angels, trumpet-tongued against
> The deep damnation of his taking-off,
> And pity, like a naked new-born babe,
> Striding the blast, or heaven's cherubin, horsed
> Upon the sightless couriers of the air,
> Shall blow the horrid deed in every eye
> That tears shall drown the wind. (I vii 16–25)

It is a strange, very mannerist vision of animated heaven, where tears compete with the fury of the wind to express the horror of Macbeth's deed. The passage is sufficiently striking for it to have a specific meaning in an obviously Counter-Reformation style. Duncan is pictured like a Christ figure[1] in his meekness and benevolence, reflecting on Macbeth as a Judas, whose betrayal can only arouse cosmic grief and protest. In an England where church walls had been whitewashed, Macbeth's vision here evokes a not too distant past, where Christians where surrounded by hosts of angels and allegorical figures sharing their joys and sorrows, their faith and fears on the walls and ceilings of parish churches.

One might get the feeling that Shakespeare was inspired by some particular painting, evoking Tintoretto's moving heavens perhaps, where babes and angels, sometimes ghostlike, seem indeed to be "horsed / Upon the sightless couriers of the air."[2] Unlikely as it may be, there is a strange similarity of vision between both artists, who share a tremendous sense of drama and a similar kinetic conception of art. Even their lives and the legend of their making have common points. Heaven and earth are one with the actors of the drama. In Tintoretto's paintings, the viewers are made to share the action represented, sometimes even to the point of becoming actors in it, just as Shakespeare manages to manipulate his spectators' imaginations in order to make them part of his plays. Tintoretto's paintings seem almost to burst their frames, just as Shakespeare's plots are made to invade the spectator's inner life.[3]

As if Shakespeare had here refined on the idea of play-within-the-play, or invented a new kind of ekphrasis, he opens a kind of spiritual vista within the scene itself, *a trompe-l'oeil* recreating the perspective within which Macbeth's act is to be visualized. All the believers in the audience, and more particularly the Catholics, would have immediately understood the core of the tragedy. It is not primarily a political play, Macbeth does not simply usurp power, he loses his soul in the process, and he does it in full knowledge of the consequences. By denying his king and betraying his pledge, Macbeth has transgressed his Christian code of values; he knows he has sold his soul to the devil and renounced his faith and all possibility of redemption. Whoever Shakespeare had in mind is a matter of conjecture of course, but one has to be both blind and obdurate not to

---

[1] This will become unmistakeable a little later.

[2] See Tintoretto, the transparent horses running in the background of *Moses Drawing Water from the Rock*, or the angels contemplating *The Baptism of Christ*.

[3] Daniel Huguenin, Erich Lessing, *La Gloire de Venise*, "Un enfant de Venise: Tintoret" (Paris: Ed Terrail, 2001), 119. "So much vigour, so much power can only be born of immeasurable torment; they can only be expressed through the exuberant movement of shapes and colours" (my translation).

feel the appalling tableau of a land that has lost its soul as well as its crown.

Moreover, Macbeth does not picture the God of Wrath storming down upon him as a scourge, but with pity represented like a new-born babe, which calls to mind the infant Jesus born to save and redeem. The image may also have been inspired by Robert Southwell's poem *The Burning Babe*,[4] where the burning babe's tears are quenching the flames which nourish their flood.[5] A similar apocalyptic vision is devastating Macbeth's own conscience. Not surprisingly Macbeth's hallucinated description of dead Duncan a little later recalls Christ's Descent from the Cross:

> His silver skin laced with his golden blood,
> And his gashed stabs looked like a breach in nature
> For ruin's wasteful entrance. (II iii 114–16)

Is he trying to move Macduff and Donalbain with the horror of the scene, or to convince himself of the reality of what he has done? Macduff has been first to take it all in:

> Most sacrilegious murder hath broke ope
> The Lord's anointed temple and stole thence
> The life o' th' building. (II iii 69–71)

The metaphor clearly "has overtones of the destruction of the old religion, in particular the removal of the Real Presence from the centre of English spiritual life."[6] Shakespeare had used similar metaphors of the body as a church or abbey, deprived of its soul or life by a sacrilegious rape, in *Edward III*.[7]

That a few lines later, Lady Macbeth, in a strange counter-Nativity image, should feel ready to dash the brains out of her own new-born babe, turning the tenderness of maternity into a murder scene, only intensifies

---

[4] "And lifting upp a fearfull eye to vewe what fire was nere / A pretty babe all burninge bright did in the ayre appeare / Who scorched with excessive heate such floodes of teares did shed / As though his floodes should quench his flames, which with his teares were fedd," Robert Southwell, "The Burning Babe," *Collected Poems*, ed. Peter Davidson and Anne Sweeney (Manchester: Carcanet Press, 2007).

[5] Christopher Devlin, *The Life of Robert Southwell: Poet and Martyr* (London: Longmans, Green and Co, 1956), contains a chapter "Master W. S." discussing the probability of Shakespeare being the dedicatee meant by Southwell's encouragement to "show how well verse and virtue suit together" (261). This might explain the change of theme from *Venus and Adonis* to *The Rape of Lucrece*. Whether or not Shakespeare and Southwell were connected, there is no doubt that verse and virtue went hand in hand in Shakespeare's overall project.

[6] Asquith, *Shadowplay*, 221.

[7] "As easy may my intellectual soul / Be lent away, and yet my body live, / As lend my body, palace to my soul, / Away from her, and yet retain my soul. / My body is her bower, her court, her abbey, / And she an angel pure, divine unspotted: / If I should lend her house, my lord, to thee, / I kill my poor soul, and my poor soul me" *King Edward III* (II i 236–43).

the image and the reality of a desolate, Christ-killing world, in which innocence and faith are being sacrificed to satisfy lust and ambition. In no other play is there such an absence of gentleness, of feminine grace, of light. In order to turn her husband into a killer, Lady Macbeth has to be harsh and callous. Her denial of her sex, her absence of grace and compassion, are the elements which condemn Macbeth to hell. In no other play by Shakespeare is the "hero" so utterly denied the intercession of women. *Othello*, as a play, may share with *Macbeth* "the uniqueness and intensity of their tragic plots,"[8] but Othello is made to realize what a manipulated fool he has been before dying "upon a kiss." Desdemona's purity, although denied by him, still has power to work upon his heart. Lady Macbeth, on the contrary, is the hellhound who goads her husband to murder. Unlike most other women characters in Shakespeare's plays, she never softens, never relents over their common murder. She has sent him on a bloody trip from which there is no return.

Shakespeare renders palpable Macbeth's descent into hell. He does it with a vocabulary borrowed from the miracle plays about Christ's death, the gate of hell, and the Last Judgment. The whole play is a striking vision of an apocalyptic world, in which good and evil fight to the death, in which defenseless women and children are murdered in their own homes, while good men suspect each other of being traitors. A world of lie and equivocation, where the best becomes the worst, where "false face must hide what the false heart doth know" (I vii 83). Unlike Othello, Macbeth never repents. Macduff, the man who was not of woman born, and insistently knocks on hell's gate like Christ before him, at last appears as the savior of Scotland at the end of the play, and relentlessly pursues Macbeth as a monstrous figure of evil that has to be eradicated.

There is however a scene which is very quickly dismissed in many productions but reveals much of the character's entrapment and Shakespeare's own wisdom. Indeed, despite the diabolical aspect of his endeavor, as he prepares to fight his enemies gathering around Dunsinane, and no longer trusts anyone around him, Macbeth is shown anxiously inquiring after his wife's health:

> Canst thou not minister to a mind diseased,
> Pluck from the memory a rooted sorrow,
> Raze out the written troubles of the brain,
> And with some sweet oblivious antidote
> Cleanse the fraught bosom of that perilous stuff
> Which weighs upon the heart? (V iii 39–44)

---

[8] Peter Milward, S. J., *Shakespeare the Papist* (Ave Maria, FL: Sapientia Press, 2005), 200.

The doctor, who recognizes in an aside at the end of the scene that he would much rather be far from Dunsinane at such a time, dares reply very honestly and straightforwardly to the tyrant Macbeth has become, that he cannot do much, that Lady Macbeth is not sick, but "troubled with thick-coming fancies." "Therein the patient / Must minister to himself" (IV iii 45). Macbeth's reaction is, not surprisingly, violent: "Throw physic to the dogs; I'll none of it." (46) What is surprising however is the measure of respect and leniency he shows the doctor. Few people have been close to him in the last acts without incurring death. Here we have a physician disappointing his hopes and showing himself powerless, who not only escapes whipping but is temporarily used as a confessor by his king, who confides that he has lost the support of his thanes and wishes the doctor could miraculously cure his realm:

> If thou couldst, doctor, cast
> The water of my land, find her disease,
> And purge it to a sound and pristine health,
> I would applaud thee to the very echo,
> That should applaud again. . . .
> What rhubarb, cyme, or what purgative drug
> Would scour these English hence? Hear'st thou of them? (V iii 49–55)

There we have a despot capable of killing his best friend, suddenly briefly leaning on the shoulder of the man of science, a healer, asking to be saved from the impending tragedy in which he finds himself trapped. A Macbeth who has denied his God and, not unlike modern man, now turns to his doctor and the power of science, with the hope of being healed and redeemed. An almost moving Macbeth, so distraught, so helpless in the face of illness and death, that he is not ashamed to admit his ignorance and powerlessness in front of the physician, who happens to be the only man treated decently in the play. Such respect toward the men of the art was not common among playwrights. However, not only does Shakespeare rarely ever mock physicians, who generally have a talent for diagnosis even when they are only given a few lines, as in *King Lear*, but he very intuitively delineates their field of competence in a new world where men tend to expect from them the role formerly played by monks and friars. But they are neither and do not have the power to heal sick souls.

Macbeth has cut himself from his God by murdering a Christ-like father-figure, his king. He has emptied the world around himself, lost all supports and his wife is incurable. He stands alone, with no intercessor on earth or in heaven, no spiritual life.[9] Macbeth can only pray to the one

---

[9] This scene may hint at the frightening solitude of the sinner in the Reformed religion

who seems to have the power to cure, but he knows that the doctor cannot cure his soul, nor can he cure his wife's guilty dreams. He is a despairing man trying to deceive himself a little longer with the witches' predictions, but knowing from the very beginning that his deed is unredeemable.

SUCH A LITTLE PIECE OF CLOTH

Evil in *Macbeth* surges from the title character's inner self and a temptation of power induced by the witches' omens, a heresy of occultism and magic so to speak, revealing not only a flaw in his nature, but also an uncertain faith in his own good conscience. In *Othello* evil takes a very concrete shape in Iago who, like a diabolical engineer, methodically untunes the beautiful harmony of the lovers' paradise. Iago has no convincing reasons whatsoever to justify his hatred, unless it is a devilish satisfaction in doing ill. Next to Iago, Othello appears to be a paragon of virtue, or a big ninny, depending on the value one places on trust. Iago himself insists on his honesty, his "free and open nature," his trustful, guileless mind that believes what he is told and what he sees. Othello is a good Christian too, testifying to his faith by his courage and warlike engagement. Around the "divine Desdemona," who is hailed by Cassio as if she were the Virgin Mary—"Hail to thee, lady, and the grace of heaven / Before, behind thee, and on every hand / Enwheel thee round!" (II i 85–87)—it is a world of beauty, of reverence and trust that unfolds. It is a prime setting for the jocund sport of the arch-liar! Milward speaks of a "morality play of salvation" as compared to Macbeth's "morality play of damnation;"[10] if his point is valid, the difference is in the women. Macbeth is led forward into crime by his own wife who asks the "spirits" to unsex her:

> Come, you spirits
> That tend on mortal thoughts, unsex me here,
> And fill me from the crown to the toe top-full
> Of direst cruelty. (I v 39–42)

Desdemona remains the most admired and discreet of fellow warriors to Othello, his best support and companion. She is his "fair warrior," his wonder. Even Iago has to recognize it: "She is so free, so kind, so apt, so blessed a disposition, she holds it a vice in her goodness not to do more than she is requested" (II iii 307–9). In our strange and stained world, critics have sometimes found her a little insipid, too good to be true. But of course, the garrison in Cyprus is a world of warlike men, a woman to them is like an angel — or a whore, if like Joan of Arc, she starts to be doubted.

---

where God's intercessors have been banished.
[10] Milward, *Shakespeare the Papist*, 201.

When at the end of the play, she appears at last in a very homely scene with Emilia, singing the *Willow Song,* her innocence and fondness contrasting with Emilia's sharp tongue, we wish she were a little less innocent. We wish, like Shakespeare perhaps, she and Othello had known how to dissemble a little, how not to wear their hearts on their sleeves for daws to peck at.

Still, Shakespeare leaves us one indication of how different things could have been, a very mannerist little piece of cloth which soon becomes like a *Leitmotiv*: the handkerchief. This little piece of cloth seems so out of place in a garrison, and yet reveals so much of what haunts men, charms and irritates them, deceives and comforts, that it probably is the most powerful element of the tragedy. It is impossible to understand Othello's tragedy unless one has deciphered the meaning of this little prop, so banal that it becomes invisible, but without which the play loses its deep meaning.

Shakespeare understood the almost magical quality that we impart to the things that surround us. Objects are not just accessories revealing a meaning of the plot, they are permeated by a spirit that animates them. This little nothing, whose disappearance focuses attention at the heart of the play, carries all the intuition, all the love which Othello is lacking. That he himself tells us the story of the handkerchief and its true meaning is naturally very ironical and sheds light on an aspect of the play which is generally ignored. We learn that the handkerchief was passed on from one generation to the next by women, starting with the Sibyl which bequeathed it to the Egyptian magician who gave it to Othello's mother who gave it to him for his wife. There is a charm in its very texture, says the Moor; the handkerchief symbolizes sexuality through the worms that made the silk and chastity through the color extracted from the mummified hearts of young virgins. The handkerchief is not merely a piece of woman's coquettish adornment, it encloses the gift of life possessed and transmitted by women. By receiving it, Desdemona, the young Venetian aristocrat brought up in a patriarchal world, inherits a long tradition of women's practical knowledge, and, which is not the least of paradoxes, it comes to her from a line of African women. Like the Sibyl and the magician, Desdemona is also visited by prophetic dreams: the *Willow Song,* which "will not go from [her] mind," was sung by her mother's maid, upon her death, after she had been forsaken by her lover. Her name, Barbary, bespeaks her North African origins. Unsurprisingly, Desdemona feels her destiny linked to that of Barbary.

When he asks Desdemona for the handkerchief Othello reinterprets its meaning, turning it into a mere trifle, something vouching for Desdemona's loyalty to *him.* In a revealing lie, he even pretends that it was given to his mother by his father (V ii 214). Perverting its meaning, he refuses his own position as a link in his mother's inheritance, and chooses to appropriate the handkerchief as a selfish, personal symbol. This is his failure. Once doubted, the vital force contained by the handkerchief lessens and disappears, soon replaced by a desire for possession and death.

Desdemona, who has a foreboding of her impending death, refuses to deny her faith in the man she loves. How then could anyone see in her death a claim by Shakespeare of masculine power? Isn't it evident that Othello has turned mad when he failed to recognize the magical feminine value of the handkerchief which he later transforms into a pretext for revenge? When he started to doubt Desdemona's love and his own faith in her? Just as she perceived Othello's visage in his mind, Desdemona knows what spirit inhabits the things of everyday life. When the handkerchief disappears, she immediately senses danger. This piece of cloth embroidered with strawberries gives a body and a soul to the vital feminine intuition at the heart of the play, which becomes a tragedy precisely because the action nullifies it. And for those who might not be sensitive to the symbolism of the handkerchief, Shakespeare offers yet another lighting in Emilia's racy defense of women's freedom:

> But I do think it is their husbands' faults
> If wives do fall. Say that they slack their duties,
> And pour our treasures into foreign laps,
> Or else break out in peevish jealousies,
> Throwing restraint upon us; or say they strike us,
> Or scant our former having in despite;
> Why, we have galls; and though we have some grace,
> Yet have we some revenge. Let husbands know
> Their wives have sense like them. They see, and smell,
> And have their palates both for sweet and sour,
> As husbands have. What is it that they do
> When they change us for others? Is it sport?
> I think it is. And doth affection breed it?
> I think it doth. Is' t frailty that thus errs?
> It is so, too. And have not we affections,
> Desires for sport, and frailty, as men have?
> Then let them use us well, else let them know
> The ills we do, their ills instruct us so. (IV iii 81–98)

This is a pithy reply to her mistress's moral questioning. Emilia does not like to see young and innocent Desdemona so lovingly devoted to a man who treats her badly. Obedience in marriage is a virtue, but as spirited Kate had so well understood, there is an implicit and reciprocal condition that the husband's will be honest and his care and protection warranted in the bargain.[11] Desdemona, of course, is meant to be a more spiritual character, hailed in the play as full of grace, and with such a blessed condition that she is employed as an intercessor, by Cassio as well as Iago, like the Virgin Mary. Her reply to Emilia is, not surprisingly, Christ-like: "God me such uses send / Not to pick bad from bad, but by bad mend!" (IV iii 99–100). So, she dies a martyr in spite of the healthy warning of Emilia, who also dies for supporting her.

It is men's frailty then which, according to Emilia, sows the seed of discord and evil among people. Men's frailty seems to come from their arrogance and the confidence they have in their own strength, as if strength could ever compensate for lack of intuition and gentleness. Strangely, but coherently, throughout Shakespeare's work, whenever men refuse to listen to women, when they disparage and mock them, when they ignore their grace and ability, they end up losing the best part of themselves. Conversely, when women forget their own gift and play at imitating men, they lose the blessing which is theirs and end up transformed into monsters.[12]

KING LEAR AND STULTITIA

King Lear is another case in point, tying together in one tapestry the threads of kingship, fatherhood, and folly, and the poet's third woman warrior, Cordelia, whose love and loyalty bring her back from France to fight for her father's endangered kingdom. From France, but daughter to the king, she is a more suitable character than Joan of Arc, whose courage and frankness she shares. Like Joan, she is betrayed and her pure intent will not save her. Fifteen years after creating the character of Joan, the Bard was still obsessed by the same themes of evil, human folly, and the legitimacy of kingship. *King Lear*, surely, marks the culminations of Shakespeare's vision of man and power. He had now implemented his vision esthetically and philosophically. And in Cordelia we have the seed of rebirth and the hopeful vision of the last plays. What a generation could not do, the next one, given the time and opportunity for it, would perhaps accomplish.

When reading *King Lear* it is difficult to forget the Apostle Paul's Christian paradox: "But God hath chosen the foolish things of the world to confound the wise; and God hath chosen the weak things of the world to confound the things which are mighty" (1 Cor 1:27). Indeed, the foolish of the world represent no other than Christ handed over to his persecutors. They become the guardians of divine wisdom. There is in *King Lear* the same conviction that the weak, the honest, the idiots of this world are

---

[11] *The Taming of the Shrew*, V ii 147–48, 158.
[12] Could it be a prophetic lesson for our time?

those who are delivered to their persecutors without any other justice than the law of the strongest and the most deceitful. Cordelia's untimely death brings the finishing touch to the cruel vision of a mad world on which only the love and loyalty of a handful confer some sort of redemption.

The play paints the fatal breaking up of family relationship as the introductory symbol of a kingdom gone mad. Lear, in a dangerous and senile attempt to assert his authority chooses to dissociate the two bodies of the king, his own natural body and his politic body, bequeathing the latter to his daughters with the intent to share it with them. In the Elizabethan context, the very act was in itself sacrilegious and Lear, having given over his political body, the spiritual part of his power, very quickly finds himself reduced to his own natural and mortal human body.[13] When moreover he disowns the only daughter who refuses to flatter him, he himself performs a monstrous reversal of the father role that should be his, thus poetically calling upon himself the unnatural treatment he will receive at the hands of his two deceitful daughters. Having most foolishly given up his titles as king and father, how could he still claim the benefit of their privileges?

Such lack of judgment, such folly, which Erasmus playfully denounced in the voice of *Stultitia* as a tribute to his dear friend Thomas More, was one of the favorite themes of the Renaissance. His *Praise of Folly* had been circulating in English for a few decades[14] when Shakespeare began to write. Most of his plays are so deeply permeated with its spirit that it is difficult to ignore. Lear does not act differently from those pontiffs mocked by Folly: "As it is now, what labor turns up to be done they hand over to Peter and Paul, who have leisure for it. But the splendor and pleasure they take care of personally."[15] Following the example of Erasmus, Shakespeare develops the Christian paradox which says that the simple-minded are beloved of God, who opens wide the gates of heaven to these innocent natures. In *King Lear*, the Fool partakes of this strange and venerable identity. He represents without a doubt a kind of grotesque double of the king, being both his political counter-truth as well as a merciless alter ego. At no point does this tender buffoon allow his master any moral self-indulgence. The old king will not know any rest until he has acknowledged his total responsibility in the disaster which is his. Maurice Lever thus defines the particular status of the court buffoon whose foolishness often partakes of clairvoyance:

---

[13] See note 10, page 71, above.

[14] It had been translated by Sir Thomas Chaloner in 1549 but Shakespeare had probably read it in Latin.

[15] Erasmus, *The Praise of Folly*, trans. Hoyt Hopewell Hudson (Princeton, NJ: Princeton University Press, 1941), 99.

He inspires both fear and veneration: he fascinates and frightens at the same time. Nobody would think of locking him up or attempting to cure him: he belongs to the sacred. It is thought that his extraordinary abilities come from the fact that his soul is partly disconnected from his body, directly communicating with the powers above. Thus does he share with the dying the gift of prophecy.[16]

The oxymoronic concept of the wise fool was elaborated from the Pauline paradoxes by such men as Thomas à Kempis in his *The Imitation of Christ* and Nicholas of Cusa in his *De Docta ignorantia* in 1440. "The *holy simplicity* of Kempis, the *learned ignorance* of Cusanus, and the *wise fool* of Erasmus are all ideologically derived (at least in part) from the Philosophy of Christ taught at Deventer,"[17] a school they all attended. Paul does not hesitate to introduce himself as God's fool in his epistle to the Corinthians and even goes so far as attributing his share of folly to God himself when he condemns the wisdom of the world:

> For it is written, I will destroy the wisdom of the wise, and will bring to nothing the understanding of the prudent. Where is the wise? Where is the scribe? Where is the disputer of this world? Hath not God made foolish the wisdom of this world? (1 Cor 1:19-20)

Thomas à Kempis's *holy simplicity* and Nicholas of Cusa's *learned ignorance* had paved the way for Erasmus's *wise folly* which was to become the bestseller of the century. The paradoxical concept of Erasmus was wittily defined as follows:

> Erasmus places both folly and wisdom on a whirligig where they keep changing position until they are linked to one another. The *Praise of Folly* evidently has the structure of Moebius strip (The *Möbius strip*, also called the twisted cylinder, is a one-sided nonorientable surface), and it cannot be oriented: the obverse and the reverse are one. Folly has no contrary.[18]

---

[16] Maurice Lever, *Le sceptre et la marotte* (Paris: Fayard, 1983), 26. "Il inspire un mélange de crainte et de vénération: il fascine et il fait peur. On ne songe certes pas à l'enfermer et moins encore à le guérir: il appartient à l'ordre sacré. Ses facultés extraordinaires sont dues, pense-t-on, à ce que son âme, en partie déliée de son allégeance au corps, communique sans médiation avec les énergies qui nous gouvernent. Aussi partage-t-il avec les agonisants le privilège de parler en prophète" (my translation).

[17] Walter Kaiser, *Praisers of Folly* (Cambridge, MA: Harvard University Press, 1963), 9.

[18] Jean Birnbaum, "Entretien avec Jacques-Alain Miller, Psychanalyste. Erasme: une révolution culturelle en douceur," *Le Monde*, June 20, 2008. "Erasme installe folie et sagesse sur un tourniquet unique où elles échangent incessamment leurs places jusqu'à se nouer l'une à l'autre. L'Eloge a évidemment la structure de la bande de Moebius

The way Shakespeare stages folly in his plays and the part he gives to the Fool, which finds no equivalent among his fellow dramatists, testify to his knowledge of *Moriae Encomium*. All senses of the word are to be found in *King Lear*, the characters reflecting in turn on the meanings of folly and its connotations, in a structure once again closer to the musical variations on a theme,[19] than to any classical model. The search for contrasts, the opposition of rhythms and sound levels, the play with repetition and fugue, these dramatic structures all reflected in music as well as in Shakespeare's theater the existence of a conflict between antagonistic forces, which nonetheless appeared interchangeable. The use by Shakespeare of the wise fool in his comedies as well as in his tragedies goes beyond the mere ludic presence of a comic interlude to reach the deeply complex and human creation of a character like Falstaff, the most faithful descendent of *Stultitia,* according to Walter Kaiser.

Lear's Fool belongs to the same order, even if his appearance seems closer to his medieval ancestors. Noble households often kept a good number of fools, of whom some were truly handicapped. Their physical deformities and their intellectual shortcomings were precisely what made people laugh:

> It was impossible to find a single monarch in Europe who did not maintain a collection of dwarfs and idiots in his Cabinet of Curiosities: they competed as to who would possess the puniest specimen or the most retarded simpleton; they could even be lent or sold again.[20]

Their head being full of wind, like the bellows which etymologically gave birth to the word (Latin: *Follis*), these simpletons had freedom to wander here and there since they were not thought dangerous. They used to be pampered, were sometimes even awarded titles, which obviously could foster envy and inspire imitators. The most cunning would start playing the fool, a good way to win support and to acquire freedom of speech. The fool, thanks to his innocence, was allowed to speak and act irreverently without risking the chastisement anyone else would have incurred in similar circumstances. His insolence would soon be adopted by the professional fools:

(bande tordue a un seul bord), et on ne peut l'orienter: l'envers et l'endroit ne font qu'un. La folie n'a pas de contraire" (my translation).

[19] *La Folia* was to become the maddest "hit" of the sixteenth century.

[20] Lever, *Le sceptre et la marotte*, 104. "Il n'y avait pas de souverain en Europe qui ne collectionnât les nains et les détraqués pour son cabinet de curiosités: c'était à qui posséderait l'avorton le plus menu ou le jocrisse le plus arriéré; il arrivait même qu'on se les prête, qu'on se les échange ou qu'on se les revende" (my translation).

> Thus the license of the natural fool was appropriated for the arti-
> ficial fool; his nonconformity was turned into iconoclasm, his
> naturalism into anarchy, and his frankness into satire.[21]

Whereas everyone was supposed to know and obey the rules of a society whose first task was to limit the expression of passions and individual free-dom, the fool, free to transgress those rules, was to become the spokesman for all rebellious desires and frustrations.

Not even evading the origin of the word, *King Lear* is structured around the ambiguity of the word folly and its paradoxical link to wisdom. The word folly is also supplemented by this other, more sinister word, madness, which literally translates a state of mental alienation, dementia, which can also figuratively represent any state of excessive anger or violence. There are sweet and furious kinds of folly. Not all fools enter the kingdom of heaven, but in *King Lear*, assuredly, there are few characters who escape folly. However, the Fool is the only one of these fools who knows that he is a fool; hence his keen conscience and his astonishing verbal skill. Like Feste in *Twelfth Night*, he is "a corrupter of words," which he turns upside down to extract new original meanings.

Lear's Fool does not simply mark the apotheosis of the court and stage fool, he is also the symbol of the fall of a king who puts on his motley coat. The gist of the play lies in this metamorphosis, the transfer through increasingly greater sufferings, of the wisdom and clairvoyance of the Fool to the fallen and declining monarch, whose folly is visible long before the Fool actually appears. As suggested earlier, the opening scene of the tragedy with the king in full majesty dividing his kingdom between those of his heirs who flatter him most was probably much more shocking to Elizabethans than to twentieth century audiences. If the absolute authority of the monarch could not be questioned, his mad decision assumed the appearance of inexorable fate. However, since this is not a Greek tragedy, fate is here arbitrated by men who carry the full responsibility for their acts. Kent, the loyal friend, is the first who dares venture "between the dragon and his wrath" to criticize the brutal and inhuman decision of his king:

> Be Kent unmannerly
> When Lear is mad. What wouldst thou do, old man?
> Think'st thou that duty shall have dread to speak
> When power to flattery bows? To plainness honour's bound
> When majesty falls to folly. (I i 136–140, Sc. 1)

Like a stubborn physician, Kent tries desperately to cure the debilitating sickness of his master to whom he gives a familiar "thou" warranted by the

---

[21] Kaiser, *Praisers of Folly,* 7.

king's own lack of respect for his position. What he gets in return is his own banishment, as if old Lear had suddenly decided to banish from his kingdom all those who dared speak their mind openly and resist him. A little later, once Lear has enacted his own version of the parable of the cockle and the wheat,[22] the two favored daughters coldly reflect on their father's behavior:

> *Goneril*: You see how full of changes his age is.... He always loved our sister most, and with what poor judgement he hath now cast her off appears too grossly.
> *Regan*: 'Tis the infirmity of his age; yet he hath ever but slenderly known himself. (I i 278–283, Sc. 1)

Goneril ascribes his "unruly waywardness" to age and a choleric humor that keeps increasing with the years. At this stage, and notwithstanding both sisters' hypocritical love pledges to their father, the audience can only agree with their verdict. The old man has just played an abominable farce and looks exactly like the power-crazed man, ignorant of himself and playing the "angry ape" condemned by Isabella in *Measure for Measure*:

> But man, proud man,
> Dressed in a little brief authority,
> Most ignorant of what he's most assured,
> His glassy essence, like an angry ape
> Plays such fantastic tricks before high heaven
> As makes the angels weep, who, with our spleens,
> Would all themselves laugh mortal. (II ii 119–25)

There is therefore no doubt about who the Fool is mocking when he appears. Lear's folly is still merely moral and political arrogance, but it may be the worst kind of folly since, as *Stultitia* tells us:

> like a fatal comet he may bring destruction in his train. The vices of other men are not so deeply felt or so widely communicated. A prince is in such a position that if he lapses ever so slightly from honesty, straightway a dangerous and vital infection spreads to many people.[23]

From Tarquin and Titus the theme has never abated and once again it seems that Shakespeare is questioning the legitimacy and rationality of giving one man the power of wreaking havoc on a whole kingdom. Kent has immediately tied folly and madness together revealing the subtle

---

[22] The word *cockle*, used by Shakespeare in *Love's Labour's Lost* (IV iii 354) is the word used in the English translation of the New Testament from the Latin Vulgate by the English College at Rheims (1582), unlike chafes, or tares (used by the Geneva Bible 1560), which testifies to Shakespeare's use of the Catholic Version.

[23] Erasmus, *Praise of Folly*, "The king's trappings," 94.

gradation between the two. The old man is morally to be condemned and his kingship becomes ridiculous. He plays the fool, but his power renders his folly dangerous. Lear's reckless decisions will have disastrous consequences for his kingdom and family.

Thus reason has just been banished from Lear's kingdom where symbolically fools are now welcome: banished Kent comes back, disguised as a manservant to serve his old master. He is engaged right away. True it is that Kent's new tone somewhat partakes of the elementary, therefore insolent wisdom of the Fool. No bowing and scraping for this new witty servant who speaks riddles:

> *Lear*: How now! What art thou?
> *Kent*: A man, sir.
> *Lear*: What dost thou profess? What wouldst thou with us?
> *Kent*: I do profess to be no less than I seem, to serve him truly that will put me in trust, to love him that is honest, to converse with him that is wise and says little, to fear judgment, to fight when I cannot choose, and to eat no fish. (I iv 8–15, Sc. 4)

Lear immediately associates him with his Fool: "Where's my knave, my fool? Go you and call my fool hither" (I iv 40–41, Sc. 4). The question, frenetically repeated, says a lot about the privileges of the character and the peculiar position he holds in the old man's heart. Has not the king struck one of Goneril's gentlemen because he dared chide the Fool? A few lines were sufficient to delineate the perversion of affections and of the hierarchy in the kingdom. Lear's leniency toward his Fool contrasts sharply with the harshness and rigidity of the monarch toward his youngest daughter who refused to flatter him. It is as if the Fool arrived to replace Cordelia who later reappears only when the Fool's presence by the king has become redundant.

The Fool immediately appears like a philosopher — a "foolosopher"[24] — constantly moralizing upon the circumstances that led his master to barren nothingness. Were it not for his grief, he could well be thought some kind of devil purposely harassing the king to make him mad. He keeps hammering his refrains and exasperating jokes into the old man's conscience like nails, relentlessly, mercilessly:

> I had rather be any kind o'thing than a fool; and yet I would not be thee nuncle; thou hast pared thy wit o'both sides and left nothing i'th'middle; (I iv 176–79, Sc. 4)

> Now thou art an O without a figure. I am better than thou art, now. I am a fool; thou art nothing. (I iv 184–85, Sc. 4)

---

[24] Erasmus, *Praise of Folly*, 10.

The image naturally evokes the etymological bellows. Very few twists will be needed for this empty O of the crown — this thing that even the Fool would not want to be — to become the Fool. Thus from nothing Lear, by becoming a fool, becomes something. Existence springs from emptiness.

The Fool appears to be the mirror and the conscience of the king, who is gradually led to acknowledge the lack of wisdom he showed when he turned his world upside down, making his daughters his mothers, and his blindness for choosing flattering empty words over Cordelia's true affection. Cordelia's truth has been perverted by the exaggerated accolades of her sisters, who explained at length why it was impossible for them to find the right words to express their love. Cordelia does not say anything different, but where can she now find the words to say it? Between her conciseness which looks like coldness, and her sisters' flattery, where does honesty lie? For lack of a sensitive knowledge of human nature, which Lear only reaches at the end of the play after the terrible ordeals that we know, only the deeds are able to confirm the words.

Unable to capture the truth in Cordelia's words, Lear is now bombarded by the Fool with sometimes foolish, sometimes witty, always wise questions, which the king gradually learns to answer to the point, slowly absorbing the Fool's spirit which he ends up impersonating. When he manages to reply promptly that the Pleiades' seven stars are seven because they are not eight, Lear seems to have recovered the logical mind he had been missing up to that point. The Fool is delighted: "Yes indeed. Thou wouldst make a good fool" (I v 35, Sc. 5).

The Fool cannot lie — Lear even threatens him with whipping if he does — and painful as the truth may be he hammers it into the king's mind. He has no name because he personifies the king's folly, his conscience too, which scolds and pierces him until he realizes his own irrationality. Therefore, it is not surprising to see the old man slowly declining toward madness; the painful birth of his conscience is all the more tragic as his new perceptiveness makes him fully aware of his responsibility in the disaster:

> O, Let me not be mad, not mad, sweet heaven!
> Keep me in temper; I would not be mad! (I v 42–43, Sc. 5)

This prayer to stormy heavens, which seem to have been forsaken by God, becomes his *Leitmotiv*. The denial of his daughters who, one after the other, are becoming bolder and hardening their position against him, overwhelms him with grief. In his turn he does not find the words to express his feelings and his vengeful threats stumble through the excess of tears convulsing him:

No, you unnatural hags,
I will have such revenges on you both
That all the world shall — I will do such things —
What they are, yet I know not but they shall be
The terrors of the earth. You think I'll weep.
No, I'll not weep.
I have full cause of weeping, but this heart
Shall break into a hundred thousand flaws
Or ere I'll weep. O Fool, I shall go mad! (II ii 434–444, Sc. 7)

Meanwhile, the wise Fool sticks to his master even though he knows the folly of such loyalty, but better be a true fool than a knave. Awakening Lear's heart, he is Lear's wisdom. The old king loses his mind only to find a true Christian heart bent on forgiveness and love. But does he truly lose his mind?

The storm marks the climax of the play with Edgar grimed as a Bedlam beggar, zealous Kent, Lear on the verge of madness, and the court Fool all gathered on the wintry heath. The storm is pictured as a mad crisis of pitiless nature which frightens even animals. But Lear stands tall like a magus "contending with the fretful elements" (III i 3, Sc. 8) commanding them, like the Old Testament God, to erase the ungrateful humans from the earth. He keeps measuring his rage against nature's fury, refusing to seek shelter: "But where the greater malady is fixed, / The lesser is scarce felt" (III iv 8–9, Sc. 11).

He is haunted by his daughters' ingratitude and the tempest blowing in his mind overshadows all other disturbances. He is now worried by the poor beggar's wretchedness whereas not long ago he refused to remove a single man from his train to comply with his daughters' desire. His folly reaches a head with the sudden revelation of naked Edgar out on the heath. Lear is suddenly impressed by the true nature of man: "Thou art the thing itself; unaccommodated man is no more but such a poor, bare, forked animal as thou art" (III iv 96–97, Sc. 11). He has been obsessed by this nagging question which was born in his mind when his hard-hearted daughters refused him his most elementary need, a servant. Lear had begun to sense the insidious sliding toward bestial nature which happens in a man as soon as he is denied the superfluous of art and style in civilization: "Allow not nature more than nature needs, / Man's life is cheap as beast's" (II iv 261–62, Sc. 7).

Out on the heath, however, deprived of all comfort, his judgment corrects this opinion when he discovers that vile things can become precious if necessity renders them so. The descent into hell resembles a long spiral of wrongs always put into perspective by others' sharper pains. Edgar, whose madness is feigned, also understands the comparative degree of his own sorrow.

> But then the mind much sufferance doth o'erskip,
> When grief hath mates, and bearing fellowship.
> How light and portable my pain seems now,
> When that which makes me bend, makes the king bow.
> He childed as I father'd. (III vi 99–103, Sc. 13)

Brought to feel the wretchedness of beggars, Lear, mending the mistakes of his reign, suddenly perceives the necessity of fairer justice. He immediately identifies with Edgar whom he believes to be like him the father of degenerate daughters. There is obviously a great irony in the meeting of this son disavowed by his father with that father rejected by his daughters at the heart of the tempest. In this *coincidentia oppositorum*, there is still however the idea of some sort of harmony, a wisdom springing up from all this folly. A spiritual bond can sometimes be more loyal than any blood filiation, be it legitimate. Lear wants to take off his clothes and share Edgar's nakedness, get rid of everything that is not himself. This scene where symbolism is mixed with the crudest reality reveals his own folly to the king. When the Fool asks him if a madman is a gentleman or a yeoman, Lear immediately replies, "A king, a king." (III vi 11, Sc. 13). Having lost everything, his kingdom, his daughters, and his roof, plumbing the depth of misery, he is now literally alienated, without any personal interest to defend or any selfish desire to satisfy, and the truth is now seen springing from his mouth just like the folly he seems to have absorbed.

The judgment scene ends this transvaluation of values[25] with the Fool sitting as *sapiens vir* beside Edgar in the imaginary trial of Goneril and Regan, whom Lear wants to dissect to discover what makes her heart so hard. Thereupon, the Fool disappears on a verbal pirouette as if he had accomplished his duty. His long absences lamented by the king at the beginning of the play—"But where's my Fool? I have not seen him these two days" (I iv 66–67, Sc. 1)—have prepared us for his final disappearance, which has now become poetic necessity. Since the king has put on the role, the Fool is no longer needed.

The old king is met again through Cordelia's eyes and her description seems to corroborate the dementia diagnosis:

> Alack, 'tis he! Why, he was met even now,
> As mad as the vexed sea, singing aloud,
> Crowned with rank fumiter and furrow-weeds,
> With hardocks, hemlocks, nettles, cuckoo-flowers,
> Darnel, and all the idle weeds that grow
> In our sustaining corn. (IV iii 1–6, Sc. 18)

---

[25] This is a Nietzschean expression meaning the inversion or the reevaluation of values.

There is nothing here but a very traditional image of folly. Absent Cordelia, unaware of her father's tragedy, is bound to think of him as of a demented old man. The doctor, though, corrects this impression and merely recommends rest. Lear's language, full of somewhat incoherent fantasy, has yet a sharper and sharper satirical edge. His newly acquired prophetic status turns him into a scathing critic of his kingdom and of men's blindness. To Gloucester who protests that he sees nothing, Lear throws out "look with thine ears" (IV v 146, Sc. 20). Still obsessed by his daughters, he denounces flatterers together with royal power, justice, adulterous women, the rascal beadle, the usurer, the "scurvy politician," and more liars and hypocrites at large in a society founded on the power of money. Like Erasmus's *Stultitia* Lear considers pell-mell "this great stage of fools" where tears seem to be the most democratic inheritance. "Reason in madness" claims Edgar, as if folly was finally the wisest and most reasonable condition in a world where a man's mind can be so split open by sorrow.

His recognition of Cordelia suddenly brings a balm to Lear who describes himself as "old and foolish." Certainly mad with a tenderness that he expresses afterward in one of the most beautiful love duets ever, the father is born again with the return of his beloved daughter. Both of them, locked in prison, renew a relationship far from the vagaries of court life:

> Come, let's away to prison.
> We two alone will sing like birds i'th' cage.
> When thou dost ask me blessing, I'll kneel down
> And ask of thee forgiveness; so we'll live,
> And pray, and sing, and tell old tales, and laugh
> At gilded butterflies, and hear poor rogues
> Talk of court news, and we'll talk with them too —
> Who loses and who wins, who's in, who's out,
> And take upon's the mystery of things
> As if we were God's spies; and we'll wear out
> In a walled prison packs and sects of great ones
> That ebb and flow by th' moon. (V iii 8–19, Sc. 24)

There is neither folly nor madness in those words. Lear has never been more to the point, intensely clear and true. Just like Shakespeare himself who seizes the occasion once again to inveigh against courtly hypocrisy as opposed to the saintliness of those who are daily sacrificed in the kingdom's gaols: "Upon such sacrifices, my Cordelia, / The gods themselves throw incense" (V iii 20–21, Sc. 24).

It is a loving, intellectual, spiritual relationship as few fathers may boast having with their daughter, a link that redeems all the wrong committed by Lear against this beloved child. These words, belated but laden with meaning, probably enable us to understand retrospectively the two other sisters' jealousy and hatred for this father who visibly preferred the younger sister to them. Shakespeare does not excuse their bloody madness, but he reveals how emotional frustration inexorably drives them toward hatred and all the excess it contains. Goneril even goes so far as hating her too good husband, Albany, whom she places among the tender-hearted fools who have nothing to afford her: "My fool usurps my body"(IV ii 29, Sc. 16).

When Lear later reappears howling, carrying the inanimate body of Cordelia—"And my poor fool is hanged"(V iii 300, Sc. 24)—the spiritual knot linking the king, his Fool, and his daughter, whose banishment had initially plunged the Fool into a great sadness, is at last tied. The community of spirit between the two of them suddenly appears luminous. They were the only characters in the play daring to speak the truth and defy the king whom they loyally supported.

As *Stultitia* had specified, there are indeed two kinds of folly, one good, the other bad:

> For certainly all madness is not calamitous.... The fact is that "madness" is a genus comprising two species: one the revenging furies send secretly from hell whenever, with their snaky locks unbound, they put into the hearts of mortal men lust for war, or insatiable thirst for wealth, shameful and illicit love, parricide, incest, sacrilege, or any other bane of the sort; or when they hound the guilty and stricken soul with fiends or with torch-bearing goblins. The other kind is far different from this. It comes, you see, from me; and of all things is most to be desired. It is present whenever an amiable dotage of the mind at once frees the spirit from carking cares and anoints it with a complex delight.[26] (51–52)

The description covers all aspects of the play. Whereas evil characters are diabolical fools destroying one another by sheer ambition, jealousy, and lust, the good fools are destroyed by their weakness, which is to love their neighbor. Love is nothing but softness and weakness for the minions of evil, but it remains a balm for Lear, whose final moment of distraction allows him to die with the blessed assurance of Cordelia's life: "Do you see this? Look on her. Look, her lips. / Look there, look there" (V iii 285–86).

If *King Lear* is a tragedy caused by the recklessness and irresponsibility of one man of power, it is not the absolute inhuman void that some would like to see in it. On the contrary, it is in the middle of the raging storm, in a state of complete loss and degeneration, that human warmth

---

[26] Erasmus, *Praise of Folly*, 51–52.

is strongest. One is entitled to feel desperate in the face of such absolute barbarity, but one has to recognize that it is when he is confronted by such barbarity that man truly reaches greatness. Are not Kent and Edgar the true witnesses and heirs of this humanity whose folly they have just lived through to its climax?

To this day, there is no means to prove the superior wisdom of love, unless it is faith, Christian faith, which alone can lead a man to opt for gentleness and loyalty over selfishness and the satisfaction of personal desires. The greater fool is of course the king who divests himself of his role, turning himself into his daughters' child by handing his prerogatives over to them, but the Fool is also the man who offers his services to a fallen and destitute master. If folly is the reverse of wisdom, it is foolish in this world to set out on an enterprise that will lead you to the scaffold, but in the world of the spirit, is not the Fool saved and therefore wiser than the man who knows the world but is nothing but a knave?

Those who choose goodness are Christ's fools indeed, and so are the Fool and Kent, who supports the King even when he knows that he has bungled his authority. The Fool himself hires him and gives him his coxcomb "for taking one's part that's out of favour," (I iv 82, Sc. 1) thus welcoming him among the brotherhood of fools. So is Edgar too, Gloucester's betrayed son whose "foolish honesty" (I ii 141) makes him an easy prey for cunning Edmund. And is not Gloucester himself like Lear a blind fool, who begins to see only after he has lost his eyes?

Finally the Fool has no name because he is everyman in this mad world where fools guide the blind. If, as Gloucester puts it in a moment of despair, the gods play at killing their creatures like wanton boys kill flies, those gods cannot be the merciful God that presides over Lear and Cordelia's reconciliation. Furthermore, the play makes a point of showing that men do not need the help of gods to revel in atrocity. Bastard Edmund ironically shows, against the backdrop of his father's blindness, the total responsibility of men in their misery:

> This is the excellent foppery of the world, that, when we are sick in fortune, often the surfeits of our own behaviour, we make guilty of our disasters the sun, the moon, and stars; as if we were villains on necessity, fools on heavenly compulsion, knaves, thieves, and treachers by spherical predominance, drunkards, liars, and adulterers by an enforc'd obedience of planetary influence; and all that we are evil in, by a divine thrusting on. An admirable evasion of whoremaster man, to lay his goatish disposition to the charge of a star! (I ii 96–103)

The Christian God is never clearly mentioned in the play,[27] but as for men's responsibility, it is whole and cannot be dismissed, whether the responsibility be that of diabolical fools, or that of God's fools who have chosen to believe in love and compassion regardless of the consequences. Man's dignity remains that envisaged by Pico della Mirandola, i.e., the freedom to choose between good and evil. In that light, *King Lear* is a profoundly Christian play since it insists on the faith that enables the few who have courage enough, to fight against barbarity with goodness and love instead. Is not faith always man's wager on the existence of God? ♣

---

[27] Except in Lear's words to Cordelia where *God's* is a possessive case (V iii 17), which is notably the only such instance in Shakespeare's work.

9. The Transformations of the Roman Hero

*I*N HAMLET WE HAD A BRILLIANT ACTOR, A PRINCE WHO never shied from playing parts in order to discover the truth. Coriolanus might be his reverse or counterpart, a man who has absolutely no taste for acting, a man who, like Bottom, is what he is, incapable of understanding the subtleties of politicians—the antihero of his own tragedy.

"BISSON CONSPECTUITIES"

The expression in itself is oxymoronic and wholly Baroque. It could beautifully apply to the press today and much social networking. Blind clairvoyance, blinded certainties. Shakespeare knew how deceiving images and perspectives could be, and the tragedy of Coriolanus is a case in point. Even though everyone has a very determined opinion of the character, nobody actually manages to know him. But the words apply to him as well and to his blinded appraisal of the social, political situation in which he is involved.

In *Coriolanus*, the conflict between being and seeming acquires disconcerting dimensions. At the beginning of the play, Coriolanus's nature, with its many discordant aspects, has escaped the "bisson conspectuities" of most people. Indeed, Menenius's oxymoron truly puts the key question about Coriolanus's character, for who can pretend—through suppositions and hypotheses, hasty conclusions based on rumor, or extrapolation and conjecture—to know the true nature of a man?

From the beginning of Act I, Martius, who is not yet Coriolanus, already appears as the cynosure of all eyes, everyone's preoccupation. He is being assessed, judged by the patricians and the rabble, the tribunes of the people, his personal enemy Aufidius, and his own mother. Everyone pretends to know him and expects or fears a specific reaction from him. According to Joyce Van Dyke, "People are always impinging upon Coriolanus, literally and figuratively, and he is always pushing them away."[1]

The play starts with Martius's paradoxical character being debated upon by the citizens of Rome: his pride and utter contempt for the people arouse the hatred of some even though he has done service for the country (I i 29–30). Even these warlike acts of bravery are contested by some who think that he simply tried to satisfy his own pride and to please his

---

[1] Joyce Van Dyke, "Making a Scene: Language and Gesture in *Coriolanus*," *Shakespeare Survey* 30, 139.

mother. Menenius arrives in time to suppress the uprising by a very politic speech on the running of the State, "a pretty tale" (I i 87), which puzzles the citizens: "How apply you this?" (I i 144). Their reaction shows that they are not deceived by the speciousness of Menenius's allegory. They are about to praise his affability and skill when he suddenly calls the first citizen "the great toe of this assembly," which he later likens to the rats of Rome. Has Martius's appearance provoked this change of lexicon, or is Menenius merely a sophist despising the people he pretends to defend?

With such a vision of Rome's skewed ideals as a backdrop, Martius enters the scene thanking Menenius for his "Hail, noble Martius!" and turning straight onto the crowd, shouting abuse at them:

> What's the matter, you dissentious rogues,
> That, rubbing the poor itch of your opinion,
> Make yourselves scabs? (I i 161–63)

The citizen previously reviled by Menenius opposes a good amount of humor to Martius's heavy artillery: "We have ever your good word," (163) which does not prevent the latter from launching into a long speech against the capricious mind of the people who like neither war nor peace and have no reliable opinion. This is no new evidence in Shakespeare's world but Martius's tone is excessively incriminating, each word being a guilty verdict against the mob whom he later calls Hydra. (III i 95) One feels stunned when, after twenty-two railing lines, he finally turns toward Menenius to ask what should have been his first question: "What's their seeking?" (I i 185), as if noble Martius had indeed absolutely no mastery of his atrabilious humor, which he freely disgorges upon all occasions.

The least we can say is that Martius hasn't got the "manner"; he uses words not to argue or implement his judgment, but like weapons, bullets he shoots on sight. True, he is a soldier who could say, like Othello, "Rude am I in my speech / And little blessed with the soft phrase of peace" (I iii 82–83), except that he does not seem to share the latter's ability to examine himself, nor does he have the Moor's exotic grace. The image he projects is that of a hard, scornful man and one has to wait until Cominius's praise (II ii 80–120) to appreciate the portrait of the perfect classical hero, manly and brave, loyal and disinterested, tireless and fearless. How can these contradictory images be reconciled, especially when, in the meantime, the man has also revealed his own dissatisfaction with himself in the admiration he vowed for his enemy Aufidius?

> I sin in envying his nobility,
> And were I anything but what I am,
> I would wish me only he. (I i 228–30)

Is the mimetic rivalry between both men, which is born of envy, the flaw in the hero's nature? How can one account for the contradictions and tensions which seem to tear Coriolanus apart?

When stubborn Coriolanus has made a mess of the show, ruining the hero's glory by excessive violence, it is Menenius, the great mender — "This must be patched / With cloth of any color" (III i 253–54) — who faces the tribunes:

> Consider this: he has been bred i'th' wars
> Since he could draw a sword, and is ill-schooled
> In bolted language. Meat and bran together
> He throws without distinction. (III i 323–26)

Obviously Coriolanus does not mean to apologize or say anything but what is on his mind. No doubt at this stage, the audience begins to share the tribunes' feelings. Coriolanus seems far too quick-tempered to occupy the supreme role. Why is this remarkable man unable to project an image of himself other than that of a ruthless boor? Is the Senate's granting of five tribunes to the people, a number which he finds excessive, the cause of his anger? Why, coming back a victor from war, does he refuse to submit to the tradition that would make him a consul? Is it because he cannot bear being ruled? Menenius, who often at the most untimely moments, brings forth enlightening details about the man, tells us, "What he bids be done is finished with his bidding. He wants nothing of a god but eternity and a heaven to throne in" (V iv 22–24). The divine metaphor is recurring: Coriolanus, the hero who acts like Hercules on the battlefield is every inch a god, accepting orders or constraints from no one and receiving homage without ever begging for it. Like God, he is what he is, being *per se*, possessed of some invisible essence which nobody should doubt. The character has a surprising rigidity, a frightening impenetrability. Even Volumnia tells him, not without irony since she encouraged this in the first place: "You are too absolute" (III ii 41). His fits of anger, like God's, are unpredictable and nobody seems capable of containing the flood of abuse pouring out of his throat.

In this respect, the Forum scene is enlightening. Coriolanus has to submit himself to the approval of the people by revealing the wounds which made him the chosen candidate for consulship. He immediately associates this ceremony with a big theatrical farce. He first protests like an uncouth peasant little accustomed to social graces: "yet oft / When blows have made me stay I fled from words" (II ii 70). In Othello's mouth, those words would be quickly contradicted by some story of wonders. Coriolanus, however, lacks the imagination and the flexibility of mind, unless it is a hatred of words instilled in him by the dubious polysemic language of his politic friends. They try hard to convince him to make an effort not to ruin his victory. After the eulogy of Cominius, a man who loves him more than he loves himself, Coriolanus protests on moral grounds, his scrupulous conscience unwilling to pretend that he fought only for the votes of the people:

> To brag unto them "Thus I did, and thus,"
> Show them th'unaching scars, which I should hide,
> As if I had received them for the hire
> Of their breath only! (II ii 146–49)

He looks like an inept and frightened actor entering the stage beseeching, "What must I say?" yet the next lines also evoke the spoiled brat who wants to say neither please, nor thank you:

> What must I say?
> "I pray, sir"? Plague upon't, I cannot bring
> My tongue to such a pace. (II iii 47–49)

And now we have him parodying himself:

> "Look, sir, my wounds.
> I got them in my country's service, when
> Some certain of your brethren roared and ran
> From th' noise of our own drums"? (II iii 49–52)

Coriolanus will never bow to the people whom he despises. As Sicinius perceived very clearly, "his surly nature ... endures not article / Tying him to aught" (II iii 191–93). He is not shy, neither is he deprived of words, far from it. He vomits them with sickly easiness. But the mere idea of "playing a part" is obnoxious to him, especially when urged to play for a mob whose values are poles apart from his.

Let us not forget that for him Rome's destiny and ideals are one with himself, whereas Sicinius strives to convince the people that *they* are the city (III i 201), hence the conflict. How can two opposite extremes represent the same entity? There is an impassable chasm between Coriolanus, brought up by his mother to embody Roman values, and the changing people and their tribunes who are ready for any compromise in order to keep an ounce of power. Coriolanus cannot recognize himself in the image of Rome that his friends and mother now want him to embrace. His bravery has given proof of his nobility and honor; he does not understand why he should now justify himself to anyone, let alone to people whom he considers cowardly and inferior. Compared to an ideal which is objectively superior, the opinion of the majority — whose values and happiness are founded on the lowest common denominator, in a word, their daily bread ration—seems pathetic to the hero and outrageous when they presume to judge his merits. These are conflicting values in a Rome torn between the ancient ideals of a city hierarchically governed by those who know the truth and can distinguish between good and bad, and the birth of a Republic which makes the opinion of the majority the basic rule of life. There is equally conflict between the values of the soldier and those of the politician his friends want to make of him. The bravery and strategies of war are not, contrary to Volumnia's beliefs, applicable in the field of politics in Republican Rome, where the people must be persuaded, not commanded. Dissimulation and bad-faith compromise are obviously more efficient tools, which seems to shock Coriolanus deeply.

One thing is certain: he can play but one part, his own, and refuses any attempt to the contrary. Thus the beggar's part he has to feign in order to be elected is a lie for him: "Would you have me / False to my nature? Rather say I play / The man I am" (III ii 14–16). He keeps protesting, "You have put me now to such a part which never / I shall discharge to th' life" (III ii 107–8), which pushes his friends to offer to prompt him—a scene which surely did not go without laughter: "Come, come, we'll prompt you" (108).

The theatrical metaphor, far from being ridiculous, openly questions Coriolanus's nature. After briefly agreeing, he pictures himself in the successive parts of a prostitute, a eunuch, a soft-spoken young virgin or a valet, a school-boy or a beggar, a sample of characters and emotions which are antithetical to him and only confirm his determination not to play. He perceives a threat to his virility, a heroic vision of man planted in him by his own mother, "the honoured mould / wherein this trunk was framed" (V iii 22–23) and which has gradually become, no longer a part to play, but his own deep nature. Like Hotspur, Coriolanus makes no compromise in matters of honor.

Coriolanus's inability to be an actor reminds us of those Athenian crafts-men in *A Midsummer Night's Dream*, who, for fear of being misunderstood in their role, decide that the solution when appearing on stage is to tell their name and trade, revealing their identity under the mask and thereby destroying all form of theatrical illusion: "tell them that I, Pyramus, am not Pyramus, but Bottom the weaver. This will put them out of fear" (III i 18–20), even though Bottom's great desire is to play the tyrant: "Yet my chief humour is for a tyrant. I could play 'erc'les rarely, or a part to tear a cat in, to make all split" (I ii 24–25). It is certainly funny to see Coriolanus, specially trained by his mother to play Hercules's part, sharing the same fear as Bottom of being taken for other than what he truly is. When changing dress, after his beggar's part, he loudly expresses his relief—"knowing myself again"—as if the toga had threatened his own identity.

But what is Coriolanus's identity?

Far from wanting to avoid frightening the ladies, he fears not arousing sufficient dread in the people, as if he had turned his soldier role into a breastplate, against what suffering, what humiliation? Psychoanalysis certainly provides answers, but let us here simply turn to the words. As is very appropriately perceived by one of the officers preparing the scene before the arrival of the officials at the beginning of Act II, Coriolanus is not simply ignoring the people he despises,

> He seeks their hate with greater devotion than they can render it him, and leaves nothing undone that may fully discover him their opposite. Now to seem to affect the malice and displeasure of the people is as bad as that which he dislikes, to flatter them for their love. (II ii 17–22)

His linguistic determination to throw a few home truths in their face as often as possible, to gnaw obstinately the bone of contention, looks more like the obsession of one who insists on being right, clinging to his own vision of the world, even when he sees it crumble as a consequence of his own behavior. The more people try to calm him, the more he sets his will against them, as if contradiction, sheer opposition were his fuel. Menenius never stops staving off the worst, repeating, "be calm, be calm," and "Let's be calm." When nonetheless Coriolanus insists on harping on the taboo subject "Tell me of corn? / This was my speech and I will speak't again," Menenius begs him, "Not now, not now," then "Well, no more," and "Well, well, no more of that," and "Enough with over-measure," to no avail. The barriers having burst, the raging sea of his anger, swollen by his own reproaches, insults, and grievances, destroys everything in its fury. Each one of his appearances adds to the tribunes' conviction that Coriolanus is a choleric character easily ignited, "that's as easy / As to set dogs on sheep" (II i 252–53). This is a long way from the image of an immutable god!

It is as if Coriolanus, suddenly persuaded that he has been deceived, used all his energy to destroy the superhuman character crafted by his mother, who even denies him today. The whole of Act III, scene ii, reveals the wounded astonishment of the hero confronted by his mother's reproaches. She reminds him that his brains should rule his anger to his own advantage:

> I muse my mother
> Does not approve me further, who was wont
> To call them woollen vassals, things created
> To buy and sell with groats, to show bare heads
> In congregations, to yawn, be still, and wonder,
> When one but of my ordinance stood up
> To speak of peace and war. (III ii 7–13)

And since she does not seem to listen to him, he insists:

> Would you have me
> *False to my nature? Rather say I play*
> *The man I am.* (III ii 14–16, emphasis added)

A dutiful and obedient child, Coriolanus? Or is Aufidius, his doppelganger, right when he thinks him not so subtle and easy to vanquish? He was his mother's sun, the man she envisioned, her own god. She nourished him with precepts and exhortations aimed at making him a superman. Volumnia never hides her pride and the harshness with which she brought up her son, preferring his death over dishonor. She scorns the anxious fears of Virgilia, the hero's quiet wife, who insists on keeping a faithful watch for her husband at home — "You would be another Penelope," mocks Valeria — staunchly refusing to accompany the matrons on social calls. Should we not see in this a probable reflection, a mirror of Coriolanus's own refusal to bend to the patricians' and the people's desires?

Volumnia's strong character does not leave much space for the couple and she even replies in her daughter-in-law's place when the latter is questioned about her own son. Volumnia's authority is stifling and it is probable that neither Coriolanus nor Virgilia could ever speak freely. Thus do we have a character who, for lack of loving attention, only learnt to express himself through opposition and provocation. Upon his triumphant return to Rome, does he not ask rather bitingly to his wife if she would have laughed to see him come back "coffined home" since she weeps to see him triumph? The audience naturally remembers Volumnia's words a little earlier: "had I a dozen sons ... I had rather had eleven die nobly for their country than one voluptuously surfeit out of action" (I iii 22–25). Who knows the deep wound of the man who will have been loved by his mother only in as much as he satisfies her glorious ambition? When he returns from Corioles, she turns his scars to market value. She invested in him and never mentions him but as "my boy" (II i 97), "my son" (131). He is her creature, she made him:

> *Volumnia*: I have lived
> To see inherited *my very wishes,*
> *And the buildings of my fancy. Only*
> There's one thing wanting, which I doubt not but
> Our Rome will cast upon thee.
> *Coriolanus*: Know, good mother,
> I had rather be their servant *in my way*
> Than sway with them in theirs. (II i 194–200)[2]

---

[2] The emphasis and italics are mine.

In these few lines there appears, insidiously but clearly, the struggle of two wills trying to assert themselves, each against the other. Maternal desire, imperious and never assuaged, still expects more from this son. The relief given to "only" clearly shows the ferocity of such desire, like a gaping maw threatening to swallow Coriolanus. In the shadow of Volumnia's authority, the *in my way* of her son seems a very discreet prayer indeed, which he will only manage to put in practice by turning violently against his own world. Facing such a mother, and against her, the man who fascinates him is a forbidden father and rival: Aufidius, the abhorred enemy whose resistance makes him all the more attractive. He is the mirror-image, the model to emulate and the objective image of the demon his mother has raised in him. Both men had a shared past of mutual respect, yet the siege of Corioles, carried out by a single man, overstepped the mark. As early as Act I, we learn that Aufidius does not intend to fight honorably anymore. Honor has turned into resentment and the will to revenge.

In Rome, constrained by all, Coriolanus refuses to play a part he does not feel. As he suggests with infinite respect, he has been playing for ever the part his mother taught him to play: "I play the man I am," the only role likely to ensure her love and admiration. But facing the reversal of opinion of the plebeians and what he foresees as the betrayal of the tribunes (he is finally rather clairvoyant in political matters!)[3] he lets his anger burst against the latter and the patricians who gave them so much power. Let us remember his answer to Menenius: "What is granted them?" "Five tribunes to defend their vulgar wisdoms, / *Of their own choice*" (I i 211–13). It seems that their freedom of choice, even more than the number of tribunes, is what scandalizes Martius, as if those louts were being granted something that he himself desires but has not. A little later, he feels necessary to point out that what brought him before them was "mine own desert"..."*Ay, but not mine own desire*" (II iii 62–64).

Forced to go back in order to apologize after being called into question by the tribunes, his laconic replies to his mother show his bewilderment: "Let's go" (III ii 18), "Let them hang" (23), "Tush, Tush!" (47), until he is completely flabbergasted: *"Why force you this?"* (53) He has been betrayed by the woman who made him what he is. From now on his world topples into chaos. The end of the scene has already veered into ridicule when

---

[3] When Sicinus rebuffs the mob and asks them to cancel their "ignorant election" (II iii 215), isn't he saying precisely what Coriolanus has been repeating since the beginning: that these ignorant and incapable men have no right to speak? And we could naturally expand on his reinterpretation of the history of the body of state which turns those vindicating plebeians into the never surfeited belly of the nation, whereas the patricians and Coriolanus in particular sacrifice their own lives in order to ensure the good working of the State.

his old friends teach him like a schoolboy: "Arm yourself / To answer *mildly*" (III ii 140–41), a word he repeats three times with what is easily imagined as concealed fury and misunderstanding. His own mother, for mildness, had sent him to war at the age of sixteen. Two sets of rules. It is not his notion of equality: when he is his own master, among his men, he refuses all kinds of favor concerning the spoils of war.

The man who aspired to be god and the master of his own destiny becomes, in spite of himself, an actor cast against type, manipulated by Volumnia again and again until the end. The irony is that he finds himself, like the plebeians, scolded, contradicted, and treated like a child. His great desire to act as he wants is put into practice only at the end of the play, after the insincere part he played for his mother who had trained him to be hard and indomitable.

> I'll never
> Be such a gosling to obey instinct, but *stand*
> *As if a man were author of himself*
> *And knew no other kin* (V iii 34–37)

> Like a dull actor now
> I have forgot my part, and I am out
> Even to a full disgrace. (V iii 40–42)

Having given up, he does not grant his family and friends the pleasure of his submission and even hands what could be interpreted as a verbal slap in the face to the mother who defeated him: "I shall be loved when I am lacked" (IV i 16).

Exiled from Rome by the tribunes under the passive gaze of his supporters, Coriolanus, in all logic, can now only offer his services to the man he esteems. He can even disguise himself as a beggar having become a beggar in Rome to comply with his mother's will. This gesture, or posture, signifies the absurd reversal engineered by his own mother. Coriolanus willfully humiliates himself to be revenged on her. He will do for Aufidius exactly what he refused to do in Rome, extravagantly playing his solitary hero part until the end.

What lies at the heart of the play may very likely be what Max Scheler[4] calls resentment, resentment of the people and the tribunes toward a

---

[4] Max Scheler, *Ressentiment* (Milwaukee, WI: Marquette University Press, 1994), chap. 1 in particular, "On the Phenomenology and Sociology of *Ressentiment*." This passage seems to me particularly suited to Coriolanus's character: "When the repression is complete, the result is a general negativism — a sudden, violent, seemingly unsystematic and unfounded rejection of things, situations, or natural objects whose loose connection with the original cause of the hatred can only be discovered by a complicated analysis" (51).

man who is too successful, who seems to be gifted with a courage and a strength which all men envy and for lack of which they have to circumvent or annihilate him. Coriolanus harbors resentment against his mother who never ceased to dominate his life. His only outlet for his resentment is the people and their tribunes, that pack of liars and profiteers for whom he has been risking his life. And there is some resentment left over for the patricians who have handed the people the means to overcome them. The political scene is a conjuncture of ruptures and chaos. As Coriolanus perfectly senses it, there is no head to the body of the State and the two opposing powers can only breed rivalry and dissension.

The relation between Coriolanus and the people looks like a vicious circle, each party, for lack of love and respect, denying the very existence of the other. The Romans are indeed ready to give him an ovation "if he would incline to the people there was never a worthier man" (II iii 35–37). They are rather easily persuaded, and all the political shrewdness of the tribunes is needed to convince them of Coriolanus's scorn and irony. On his side Coriolanus does not want to feign a respect he does not feel for qualities he despises: the people are unreliable and easily manipulated cowards, dolts, and robbers. According to him, they have only one desire, to fill their belly while he, the soldier, fights for them. Even if there were any complementarity between them, Coriolanus refuses to explain himself to the majority, which he does not equate with moral quality. His own supporters need as much energy and persuasion to bend his will as the tribunes do to convince the people. If until this moment the hero had been able to believe that he was acting on his own, with only a few exchanges indicating his irritation toward Volumnia, he can no longer be blind to the fact that he, like the Roman people, has been manipulated. It is the annihilation of all the values he entertained, and which made him the man he is.

His return among the Volsces is therefore an act of revolt against the premeditated role he was made to play, as much as the last attempt of the hero at testing his invincibility. He hopes at last to play a solo, to write his own part, except that the political situation in which he operates won't allow it. Unlike Antony, he cannot avail himself of the exotic territory of Egypt to relax from Rome's tensions. He is at odds with the values of his time and the weight of the past keeps him a prisoner. He appears predetermined, everybody having an opinion about him and predicting his gestures and reactions. As Sicinius aptly remarked, he has been trained like a sheep dog to lead the flock, nothing else is expected from him. Rome's great victor is but a role; as an individual he never had any free space in which he could have inscribed his will, unless it is the silence to which he aspires and which his wife Virgilia offers him. There is evidently a conflict between the private aspirations of the man and what his mother, his education, and his reputation made of him: a man who no longer belongs to himself. Since he no longer wants to play Rome's game, nor his mother's, he deliberately chooses exile. And since he only knows one part, he will now play it to the extreme, because, as Didier Souiller puts it, "the greatness of the challenge resides in the free acceptance of an inevitable defeat in an unavoidable fight" (my translation).[5] Thus is defined the promethean hero.

Whereas Antony is disintegrating and cannot recognize himself, Martius tries a last time to find himself in a pathetic act of vainglory. Boasting of his solitary victory over Corioles, he deliberately provokes Aufidius's anger. The solitude of the hero is now conflicting with the notion of sharing which he is seeking in Corioles. Coriolanus esteems and admires Aufidius whom he judges his equal, but the equality of two solitary heroes quickly arouses rivalry and Aufidius's flouted generosity turns to rebellion. In his mouth, the word "boy," which was affectionate coming from Cominius, becomes an insult. Coriolanus has forged for himself a solitary identity rejecting all parentage and affection. So when the man who is the mirror to his own self calls him "boy of tears," he unwittingly touches the deep wound in Coriolanus: never having been able to assert himself as anything but Volumnia's boy. The armored shell of manhood he built himself is suddenly pierced. He feels as if he is disputing with his mother and an irrepressible fury bursts in him who now calls the man he most admired, like the Romans, a "cur" (V vi 108). His reply, if enlightening, remains pathetic: "Alone I did it. 'Boy'!" (V vi 117).

Here we have a man who ceaselessly strove to go beyond himself for an admiring glance from his mother and lost himself in the endeavor. Even the role of Coriolanus is taken away from him when Aufidius denies him the name. Martius dies alone, murdered, after betraying his motherland as well as its enemies. The cause is neither fate nor providence, but the willful self-destructive rebellion of a character in search of himself. The honor for which he fought is finally, as Falstaff thought, only useful to dead men. Martius therefore becomes a hero again in extremis, yet the image of the classical hero is damaged.

All the dark irony of the play, its grating tragedy, seems to emerge from the fact that Coriolanus, the paradigm of the warrior hero, does not want to play the part anymore. He is tired and his memory fails him: "I am weary, yea, my memory is tired" (I ix 91). He has had enough of praises and rewards. He wants to go back home where he could find peace and

---

[5] "La grandeur du défi réside dans la libre acceptation d'une défaite inévitable pour un combat auquel on ne saurait renoncer." Souiller, *La littérature baroque en Europe*, 83.

quiet, near the only person for whom he feels an obvious tenderness, his wife. He is caught in the middle of epistemological tensions which make him a Baroque hero, prisoner of a classical part which no longer means anything to him. Under the mask of the valiant and honorable soldier, one can guess that there is a man aspiring to the freedom to be, to move, to breathe, or to collapse possibly, without having each one of his words or gestures glossed over. However, this too respectful son is never able to betray the ascetic ideal of his mother. His voluptuousness never goes further than a glass of wine — "Have we no wine here?" (I ix 92) — and as Maurice Charney notices,[6] food feeds discordant images of disgust and annihilation more surely than the sensuous repose of the warrior. The harsh and caustic tone of the play springs from the insufficient attraction of the hero for the part he is to play. The order he is supposed to defend, the values he upholds are all disintegrating. Even the patricians are ready to compromise themselves. Last, his mother, this Juno, stoops to asking him to feign in order to obtain the supreme charge. There is nothing but seeming; ostentation has replaced discretion. The necessity to use indirections to reach one's goal disgusts him, whom we see spewing his scorn on all those characters not one of whom embodies his ideals. A revolted man he is, but his is an abortive revolt devoid of apotheosis. On the contrary the god he was becomes conscious of his mortality and will find peace only in the silence of death, for in this esthetics of contrasts, he cannot be what he represents any longer and what he represents no longer exists. He is a hero without a substance if we accept Souiller's definition:

> The hero is first of all a pretext to develop a general questioning of the traditional order at all levels, religious, political, social or simply family. Thus, the Rebel's function is clearly delineated: he has to incarnate all the darings made possible by the collapse of the old value system. Moreover there is a strange fascination about the character: his dubious charm is to be found in most baroque literature, first of all in the theatre, but also picaresque novels: among its avatars, the most recurring one is the *rebellious son*.[7]

---

[6] Maurice Charney, *Shakespeare's Roman Plays: The Function of Imagery in the Drama* (Cambridge, MA: Harvard University Press, 1961).

[7] "Le héros est avant tout prétexte à laisser se déployer une remise en cause sans limite de l'ordre traditionnel, sur tous les plans: religieux, politique, social ou simplement familiale. La fonction du révolté apparaît ainsi clairement: elle est d'incarner toutes les audaces rendues possibles par l'écroulement de l'ancien système de valeurs. Le personnage, d'ailleurs, laisse transparaître une étrange fascination: son charme trouble se retrouve dans les différentes littératures baroques, essentiellement au théâtre, mais également dans le roman picaresque: de tous ses avatars, celui que l'on rencontre le plus fréquemment se ramène au rôle de *fils rebelle*." Souiller, *La literature baroque en Europe*, 66 (my translation).

Of all the rebellious sons, Coriolanus is probably the most fascinating since he manages so well to hide from his mother — who was herself adhering to the values of her time — the deep revolt inwardly gnawing at him. Here we have a man who revolts nobly without ever showing disrespect toward those who made him what he is. All happens so indirectly, through irony and innuendos, that it is easily overlooked, which probably explains the dislike of so many critics who see in Coriolanus the rigid and arrogant character he shows us. As Una Ellis-Fermor intuitively gathered, the play gradually reveals its truth "by secret impressions."[8] Several readings are needed and a more and more precise analysis in order to determine the complex working of this man whose nature has been diverted from life. On the hinge between two eras, Shakespeare spreads throughout *Coriolanus* conjunctions of two contrary movements between the ideals the title character defends and reality, the rituals to be observed and his desires, the general good and his devotion: correspondences do not exist any longer. Menenius's "pretty tale" is but a tale after all. Coriolanus's tragedy is the tragedy of a hero who has lost his substance and his *raison d'être* — a hero undergoing a metamorphosis. "L'homme de pierre" is slowly begetting "l'homme de vent."[9]

THE MAN OF STONE VERSUS THE MAN OF WIND MAY BE A fit transition to *Antony and Cleopatra,* a play officially performed the year before *Coriolanus,* though naturally, Shakespeare's abundant imagination may have conceived them at the same time. At first sight, it seems to contrast greatly with the atmosphere of *Coriolanus,* yet the Roman World with its monumental rigidity is there and we have in Antony another exploration of the decline of the warrior hero caught between his duty to the harsh principles he has been taught to obey, and the whirligig of the world. The oxymoronic tensions of mannerism are ever so present, contained in the relationship of the eponymous characters as well as in the worlds they inhabit.

METAPHORS AND METAMORPHOSES IN *ANTONY AND CLEOPATRA*

George Puttenham defines metaphor, which he calls "the Figure of transporte" in the following manner: "There is a kinde of wresting of a single word from his owne right signification, to another not so naturall,

---

[8] Una Ellis-Fermor, "Secret Impressions: the Dramatic Definition of *Coriolanus,*" in *Shakespeare: "Coriolanus." A Selection of Critical Essays,* Casebook Series, ed. B. A. Brockman (London: Macmillan, 1977), 129–44.
[9] "The man of stone," "the man of wind": Categories of Jean Rousset's, quoted by Didier Souiller, 80.

but yet of some affinitie or conveniencie with it."[10] One of the examples he gives, banal though it may be, is not foreign to the play's lexicon: "Or to call the top of a tree, or of a hill, the crowne of a tree or of a hill: for in deede *crowne* is the highest ornament of a Princes head, made like a close garland, or els the top of a mans head, where the haire windes about, and because such terme is not applyed naturally to a tree, or to a hill, but / is transported from a mans head to a hill or tree, therefore it is called by *metaphore*, or the figure of *transport*."[11] Now the crown, for Cleopatra, is Antony and the vision provoked by this unusual transport, immediately astonishes us: "O see, my women, / The crown o'th' earth doth melt" (IV xvi 65). There we have Antony, this man among men, turned into the most beautiful ornament of the earth and his death likened to molten gold. As G. R. Hibbard insists, "A pair of words are often brought into a vital and unexpected relationship with each other in such a way that they interinanimate, to use a word of Donne's, each other."[12] The melting crown of the earth creates a paradoxical effect, bringing forth wonder out of reality. Those words encompass the space of Antony's conquest, the earth no less, and dissolution, the desired fusion of the two lovers: in a word, they are the essence and the tragedy of Antony.

If the first aim of metaphor remains, according to Puttenham, to adorn speech, he nonetheless insists on its significant function, which is to alter and affect the mind by altering and intensifying the meaning of words. Puttenham, thus, points to the peculiarity of metaphor, which is not only to transport the literal meaning of a word toward a figurative meaning, but to operate a fusion, a transfiguration of meaning altogether. By bringing together two different semantic fields, the metaphor opens a new perspective and it brings an unexpected depth to the object considered, which is transformed by the surprising lighting suddenly shed on it. The space between both elements then becomes the space of metamorphosis, for in the absence of a comparative term, the first object does become, even if only fleetingly, its metaphorical other.

In Shakespeare's time, this play of correspondences was all the easier as the Elizabethans' representation of the universe was still a closed geocentric world whose different levels, modelled on the musical degrees of the scale, depicted the evolution of elements from the simplest to the most spiritual. Man, situated at mid-course on this scale, had correspondences with the

---

[10] George Puttenham, *The Arte of English Poesie*, ed. G. D. Willcock and A. Walker, (Cambridge: Cambridge University Press, 1970), 178.
[11] Ibid., 178.
[12] G. R. Hibbard, "Feliciter audax, *Antony and Cleopatra*, I, i, 1–24," *Shakespeare's Styles* (Cambridge: Cambridge University Press, 1980), 102.

animal world, just as he could have correspondences with the sphere of the planets and that of angelic spirits. Robert Fludd was still attempting to show the harmony of those correspondences in the very year when Galileo was asserting the existence of a heliocentric system in 1617: the Pythagorean vision was not about to die so soon![13] It certainly provided Shakespeare with an endless source of metaphors and poetical imagery. The wealth of references to the world and the universe undoubtedly gives *Antony and Cleopatra* a cosmic setting and perhaps the stage of the Globe does stand for the world in this play more than in any other.

In *Antony and Cleopatra*, indeed, the poetic imagery, the metaphorical language, which is full of paradoxes and hyperboles, place the protagonists at the center of a universe which is as boundless as the human mind, and as fluctuating as life itself. The "world," which substantially reappears forty-one times according to Bartlett, forty-five times according to Charney,[14] truly is the stage, the playground of the leaders Caesar and Antony, with Lepidus very quickly doomed to a walk-on role. The world is also the challenge, the supreme temptation. "Wilt thou be the lord of the whole world," (II vii 59) Menas asks Pompey, pushing him to seize upon the opportunity to get rid of his rivals. In this great game of chess, the cold and calculating Caesar eventually wins, acknowledging the fact that this vast world could not house Antony and himself together. It shows the inextinguishable hunger of those jaws—"Then, world, thou hast a pair of chaps, no more" (III v 12)—similar to the monstrous hell gate in a medieval manuscript[15] and the huge ambition of those men riding in full view of thousands of people, always exposed, always conscious of playing a role, showing off or staging themselves, ready food for the multitude—which surely was not a handicap for the King's Men. Imagining the future performances of their lives, Cleopatra even creates a tremendous *mise en abyme*, telescoping reality, myth and fiction, with a wink to the audience, which she consciously gratifies with the complex image of an ever-elusive historical truth:

> The quick comedians
> Extemporally will stage us, and present
> Our Alexandrian revels. Antony
> Shall be brought drunken forth, and I shall see
> Some squeaking Cleopatra boy my greatness
> I'th' posture of a whore. (V ii 216–21)

[13] R. Fludd, *Utriusque Cosmi Historia . . .* (Oppenhheim, 1617). See Kathi Meyer-Baer, *Music of the Spheres and the Dance of Death* (Princeton, NJ: Princeton University Press, 1970), chap. IX.
[14] Charney, *Shakespeare's Roman Plays*, chap. IV, 80.
[15] See *The Winchester Psalter*, twelfth century, Bridgeman Art Library.

The staggering poetic reality of the play is indeed made of such a multiplicity of viewpoints that truth, if it exists, can only spring forth from the confrontation, or better still the crystallization of these many particles together.

The first image displayed to the audience already contains all of Antony's tragedy in a nutshell: in a remarkable rhetorical outburst, a roman soldier laments the degeneration of his general, who has become "the fan / To cool a gipsy's lust" (I i 9–10). In the wide world of the Empire, ornamented with the onomastic poetry of the many exotic lands he has conquered, and which Shakespeare enjoys naming here and there, Antony has gone too far. All is already contained in the first lines of Philo, who protests against the excessive infatuation of the man he compares to the god Mars, unaware of the irony contained in the comparison:

> Nay, but this dotage of our General's
> O'erflows the measure. Those his goodly eyes,
> That o'er the files and musters of the war
> Have glowed like plated Mars, now bend, now turn
> The office and devotion of their view
> Upon a tawny front. His captain's heart,
> Which in the scuffles of great fights hath burst
> The buckles on his breast, reneges all temper,
> And is become the bellows and the fan
> To cool a gipsy's lust. (I i 1–10)

Overflowing and lack of measure, which characterize Antony here, offer a semantic field appropriate for the definition of the out-of-the-ordinary love shared by the protagonists. It is the unexplored and boundless country which Antony offers his queen:

> Cleopatra: I'll set a bourn how far to be beloved.
> Antony: Then must thou needs find out new heaven, new earth.
> (I i 16–17)

It is not surprising therefore that he should be willing to exchange Rome and the empire for this immeasurable vastness of Cleopatra's love, even if this inordinate wish, this peak of hubris, is considered by some the tragic flaw of the hero:

> Let Rome in Tiber melt, and the wide arch
> Of the ranged empire fall. *Here is my space*.[16] (I i 35–36)

The violence of the opposition echoes, as it reflects, the radical violence of the metamorphosis undergone by Antony according to Philo:

---

[16] My emphasis.

> The triple pillar of the world transformed
> Into a strumpet's fool. (I i 12–13)

The grandiose architecture of the builders of Rome which is evoked here is contradicted, even threatened, by the undefinable presence of the fool.[17] The bellows (Latin=*folia*), the etymological origin of the fool, referred to the empty head full of wind of the same character. Philo remains constant and logical in his lexical research. The play's contradiction is already to be found in this definition. The majesty and solidity of the column is opposed to the inanity and evanescence of thin air, and already, as a mere suggestion, the theme of dissolution, of metamorphosis, or according to Pythagoras, of the transmigration of the soul. If both characters, like anamorphoses, keep varying depending on the perspectives which reveal them, similarly, the world in which they move does not escape transformations along the fluctuating borders of the empire. The rhythm of the Nile's floods, which becomes a kind of *Leitmotiv* in the play, marks Egypt's breathing, and the very elements of air and water are roused with passion upon the queen's appearance. There is an astonishing number of verbs expressing dissolution, fainting, melting, and annihilation in the play as if the universe of *Antony and Cleopatra* was the constant locus of metamorphosis. That in such an unstable world the giant Atlas should turn into the queen's fool well defines the variable nature of the hero, all the more credible as it is painted for us with a good many censorious hyperboles by a transitory character.

Is not hyperbole, as Puttenham defines it,[18] known by the very implausibility of the comparison it suggests, the best means to obtain adhesion: if Antony is one of the three pillars of the world for one who criticizes him, what will he be for the woman who loves him? And yet, paradoxically, for Cleopatra, Antony is first of all a man, her man, a jewel among men: "the arm / And burgonet of men" (I v 23–24), "My man of men" (I v 72). He is also her healer: "that great medicine," her *elixir d'amour*. So much tenderness and simplicity may surprise if compared with the other characters' hyperboles until one understands that Antony, for Cleopatra, is nothing less than the Renaissance ideal defined by Pico della Mirandola:

---

[17] The added irony suggested by the oxymoronic nature of the Fool for the Renaissance spectator should not be underestimated here. That spectator had perhaps just seen a performance of *King Lear* and may also have read Erasmus, which was part of most school curricula. The Fool, according to Professor Kaiser, who cites the philosopher Taine, was the *personnage régnant* of the sixteenth century and was supposed to possess a wisdom hardly ever possessed by ambitious conquerors. Kaiser, *Praisers of Folly*, 3.

[18] Puttenham, *The Arte of English Poesie*, "Hiperbole, or the Over reacher, otherwise called the loud lyer," "whereof one is when we speake in the superlative and beyond the limites of credit," 191.

his nature contains all the spheres of creation. When he dies, Antony becomes a universe of his own, his voice tuned to the harmony of the spheres, his face enlarged to the size of heaven:

> His face was as the heav'ns, and therein stuck
> A sun and a moon, which kept their course and lighted
> The little O o'th' earth. (V ii 79–81)

> His legs bestrid the ocean; his reared arm
> Crested the world. His voice was propertied
> As all the tunèd spheres. (V ii 82–84)

To mark such excess and multiplicity, Shakespeare liberally borrowed from Ovid's *Metamorphoses*. For most characters, Antony is now a Mars, now a Jupiter: "Your emperor / Continues still a Jove" (IV vi 27–28), praises an anonymous Roman soldier. Antony considers himself related to Hercules and his queen sees Atlas in him, or Ajax whenever he is in a rage. If Antony is a god, Cleopatra belongs to the race of goddesses: Enobarbus turns her into Venus, who fascinates the very air that surrounds her. She triumphantly appears dressed in Isis's garments and on the sea becomes Thetis for Antony. There is no superlative that is not attributed to her. She freely migrates from one end to the other of creation, receiving her share of injurious or animal appellations. Be she named a nightingale or a riband-red nag, the Faerie Queen or a witch, Egypt's strumpet holds everyone under her spell. The metaphor is doubtful here as we never know if the spells she casts really have the power to change creatures for good.

Such a profusion of titles could seem ludicrous were it not modulated by a great variety of praising characters in a succession of scenes that is almost as fluid as the waters of the Nile. Although the structure of the play is not my topic here, it is difficult not to be impressed by the cinematic quality of the work, difficult also to separate one part of the play from another, so great is the unity and the density of this "intrinsicate knot."

An unconventional destiny entails unconventional feelings. Antony's heart does not only burst the buckles on his breast, it overflows with love, generosity, and courage; it is literally cramped in the narrow, stoical world of Caesar. According to Antony, no scale of values can measure his love any more than the crocodile of the Nile can be measured:

> It is shaped, sir, like itself; and it is as broad as it hath breadth.
> It is just so high as it is, and moves with its own organs. It lives
> by that which nourisheth it, and the elements once out of it, it
> transmigrates. (II vii 41–44)

The description could apply to Antony as well, whose character, perceived from many contradictory perspectives, seems to elude all definition.[19] Moreover, aren't we doing wrong to the crocodile, whose tears have become the symbol of dissimulation, just as we wrong Antony by mocking his love? "The tears of it are wet" claims Antony revealing an unexpected emotion in this armored reptile. Like the crocodile, Antony is capable of weeping and devouring. His fierce appetite even becomes, as often in Shakespeare, the metaphor of desire. Antony's passion appears like an excess of gluttony to Pompey, who does not expect him to take up the sword again. Yet, how not to be voracious for love, "this amorous surfeiter," when one has in his arms "a morsel for a monarch," (I v 31) who leaves one perpetually hungry? —"she makes hungry / Where most she satisfies"? (II ii 244–45) When even Enobarbus, the cynic, is drooling, Antony does surely deserve some excuse.

The truth is that the queen herself is gifted with an infinite variety which never tires. It is not surprising, therefore, that such a changing hero should fall in love with this quarrelsome queen,

> Whom everything becomes — to chide, to laugh,
> To weep; whose every passion fully strives
> To make itself, in thee, fair and admired! (I i 51–53)

The universe is Cleopatra's own scenery for a subtle play in which she excels at manipulating the man she loves, playing on paradoxes and his feelings.[20] A capricious seducer, a vamp, she leads Antony by the nose, scolding him for leaving, then immediately accusing him of feigning love if he decides to stay. But this game is only the pathetic weapon of a woman who knows that she will never capture her Roman hero for herself alone. Cleopatra spends most of the play waiting for Antony, and Shakespeare has very cleverly depicted this waiting by interpolating no less than four long scenes of Roman activity between the order given by the queen to Charmian: "Bring me word quickly" (II v 115) and the question "Where is the fellow?" (III iii 1), speaking of the messenger who is at last to give all the information she required. Isn't there a touch of misogyny in translating this as an evidence of Egyptian indolence? Cleopatra is waiting. She

---

[19] In his second *Epistle to the Corinthians* the Apostle Paul says this: "But they measuring themselves by themselves, and comparing themselves among themselves, are not wise," (10:12) but of course he has also said "Hath not God made foolish the wisdom of this world?" (1 Cor 1:20), stressing the inanity of reason and revealing the paradox which binds Anthony.

[20] See where he is, who's with him, what he does.
I did not send you. If you find him sad,
Say I am dancing; if in mirth, report
That I am sudden sick. (I iii 2–5)

knows that her beloved has betrayed her since he married another. In spite of such a betrayal, she continues to love him, she is even more eloquent when her lord is away. As early as the first act, she evokes a love that is as vast as it is eternal:

> Eternity was in our lips and eyes,
> Bliss in our brows' bent; none our parts so poor
> But was a race of heaven. (I iii 35–37)

More than nostalgia, the use of the past tense points to her doubt, the fragility of those moments of wonder, which Antony's position hardly permits to officialize. Cleopatra's heartbreak is expressed by the most striking figure as she turns Antony into the metaphor of oblivion:

> O, my oblivion is a very Antony,
> And I am all forgotten. (I iii 91–92)

Antony's forgetfulness suddenly throws her in a turmoil, she feels forsaken and forgets her words. Forgetting and being forgotten corresponds to her desire for dissolution, which is itself the expression of her love and lack of Antony. Thus in a remarkable way, by becoming Antony, oblivion, this void, which is perhaps the most palpable reality of her life, transforms Antony's absence into presence. The paradox is not lost on the sensitive lover who sums up in three lines the nature of their relationship:

> Our separation so abides and flies
> That thou, residing here, goes yet with me,
> And I hence fleeting, here remain with thee. (I iii 103–5)

For Cleopatra, Antony knows no bourn, lives perpetually beyond, on the fringe, between the world of duty and the world of pleasure, always divided: "He was disposed to mirth, but on the sudden / A Roman thought hath struck him" (I ii 81–82), says Cleopatra, who suspects Antony of loving her only halfway. The fact is that he himself is the quintessence of both Rome's greatness and Egypt's lack of measure, such as it is depicted in the crocodile. For Antony, the opposition of Rome versus Alexandria is not so much spatial as it is temporal. Twice he makes the distinction between what he is and what he was. There was a time when Caesar himself did not scorn the pleasures granted to him by Cleopatra. Antony belongs to such a time, he is "this grizzled head," which he suggests Cleopatra should send to the boy Caesar. Simply, this giant, "the demi-Atlas of this earth," has the ability to encompass opposites. Cleopatra praises the "heavenly mingle," (I v 59) which makes him neither sad nor merry, but "between both," whereas Philo, who is unable to understand such contradictions, concludes that Antony has a dual personality:

> Sir, sometimes when he is not Antony
> He comes too short of that great property
> Which still should go with Antony. (I i 59–61)

The idea that Antony is himself only when he is the armored general, displaying his courage on battlefields, leading his men to victory, and enduring starvation with stoicism, is of course that of the Romans, in particular that of Caesar Augustus, who praises his toughness as a soldier and the harsh life he lived then. In Antony, young Caesar sees the hero he tried to emulate, and like him, a number of critics want to reduce Antony to the part of the military hero, splitting the soldier from the lover always perceived as a weakness, a threat to his virility:

> [Antony] is not more manlike
> Than Cleopatra, nor the queen of Ptolemy
> More womanly than he. (I iv 5–7)

Coming from Caesar, the charge could seem final but it is modulated by a parenthesis: "His composure must be rare indeed / Whom these things cannot blemish" (I iv 22–23), which, even though possibly ironical (can Caesar be ironic?), forces the audience to contemplate the possibility of an exception.

The idea that love was an effeminate pleasure was not new and was not to displease the men of a patriarchal society like that of seventeenth century England. They would certainly have joined Enobarbus in his protest: "For shame / Transform us not to women," (IV ii 35–36) in which tears are the symbol of feminine weakness.

But the situation is far more complex and Enobarbus is not Shakespeare, who has for a long time now questioned the character of the steely hero warrior. The disquieting game of gender change, warranted by the mythical example of Hercules, whom Renaissance artists loved to represent dressed in a robe with Omphale carrying his club and his bear skin,[21] reveals the temptation of a deeper harmony, where each one sees himself in the other and becomes the other. Depending on viewpoints, this gender confusion becomes the hero's humiliation, but isn't it also the happiness of totally belonging to the other, of being interchangeable? Cleopatra remembers with maternal tenderness the moment when she put her drunken Antony to bed: "Then [I] put my tires and mantles on him, whilst / I wore his sword Philippan" (II v 22–23), words that echo Agrippa's own a little earlier as he marvels at the power of this "Royal wench!"

---

[21] On the attraction of the Elizabethan period for cross-gender characters in the theatre as well as in the official iconography, see Stephen Orgel, *Impersonations* (Cambridge: Cambridge University Press, 1996).

> She made great Caesar lay his sword to bed.
> He ploughed her, and she cropped. (II ii 234–35)

In bed the sword has become phallus, but great Caesar, for having given up for a while the soldier's uniform, has not, for all that, lost his virility.

The image of an effeminate Antony may be disquieting, but that of soldier Cleopatra playing the general at the head of her army seems even more dangerous. Enobarbus, again, metaphorically protests against such gender confusion:

> If we should serve with horse and mares together,
> The horse were merely lost; the mares would bear
> A soldier and his horse. (III vii 7–9)

The idea that their captain is led by a woman shocks Antony's soldiers who expect authority from him rather than "a doting mallard" (III x 19). The image of a general, metonymically represented by his heart, towed by his lover's ship, beautifully sums up the reversal of parts that has happened. However, far from deploring it, Antony rather seems to reproach Cleopatra for not playing her man's part to the end:

> Egypt, thou knew'st too well
> My heart was to thy rudder tied by th' strings,
> And thou shouldst tow me after. (III xi 55–57)

Having possibly seen Elizabeth in armor, could the audience of the Globe be shocked by the desire of a queen to lead her men to battle? They most probably understood the subtleties of cross-gender dressing, made compulsory by the fact that women were played by adolescent boys.

It is not so much affection, which weakens Antony's sword, but his inability to separate the public sphere from the private. In Antony and Cleopatra's relationship, they seem indeed inseparable. Antony's very name has become a metaphor, "that magical word of war" (III i 31) and cannot be severed from the glory that comes with it. The partner of the queen of Egypt, she who is described by even the most ironical witness as surpassing Venus's beauty, has to be a man capable of offering her kingdoms, no less. She puts it plainly to Caesar's messenger (V ii 15–18). When, after his defeat at Actium, Antony recovers his courage and decides to go back to war—"I and my sword will earn our chronicle" (III xiii 176)—his queen does not hide her joy at seeing again the man she admires: "That's my brave lord!" (III xiii 177). "Since my lord / Is Antony again, I will be Cleopatra" (III xiii 186–87). This Antony however is not exclusive of the other, her wonderful changing lover. The armor and the sword are recurrent images in the play, tokens of Antony's role as a conqueror as well as his role as a lover, and it is precisely Antony's tragedy, and his greatness, not to be allowed to be the one without the other.

Metaphors and comparisons melt together to make Antony and Cleopatra, despite their diverging opinions and the events that divide them, two mirror lovers, who reflect each other to the point of not being able to exist one without the other. Beside the many hyperboles ascribed to them, the cosmic metaphors which they bandy with each other gradually make each of them the image, and the light of the other. Antony's wonder-filled welcome: "O thou day o'th' world, / Chain mine armed neck" (IV viii 13–14), finds its reflection in "Our lamp is spent" (IV xvi 86), which answers Antony's "since the torch is out" (IV xiv 46). With Antony's death the light of Cleopatra's world is put out and she visualizes it as a cosmic disaster: "O sun, / Burn the great sphere thou mov'st in; darkling stand / The varying shore o' th' world" (IV xvi 9–11), but there again, the evoked image is not exclusively born of excessive love. Not long before, Antony's soldiers had reacted the same way: "the star is fall'n! / And Time is at his period" (IV xv 107), turning Antony into their guiding star, and his death, the end of an era. Even great Caesar regrets the absence of an earthquake when half the world collapses:

> The breaking of so great a thing should make
> A greater crack. The round world
> Should have shook lions into civil streets,
> And citizens to their dens. The death of Antony
> Is not a single doom; in the name lay
> A moiety of the world. (V i 14–19)

Considering the sober nature of this character, those words mark the recognition of Antony's greatness as surely as the hyperbolical notions of Cleopatra, even if "so great a thing" is an astonishing antiphrasis. The ghost of Hamlet comes to mind, Othello's disturbing nature too. Caesar seems to feel some disquiet mixed with a touch of awe at this indefinable *thing* that was Antony.

A particular image is shared by Antony and Cleopatra throughout the play: the serpent — the most indefinable, most fluid of all animals, a bewitching, frightening creature whose ceaselessly moving shapes have the ability to metamorphose themselves. It renews itself, changes its skin, and defies death. Cleopatra thinks tenderly of the nickname given to her by Antony: "Where's my serpent of old Nile?" (I v 25), even though she is caught casting the following spell a little later: "Melt Egypt into Nile, and kindly creatures / Turn all to serpents" (II v 79). Such ambiguity fits Cleopatra perfectly. Supple and varied, the serpent is an emblem of life and death; it represents eternity. It is a phallic symbol, later becoming a concrete scenic image with Cleopatra's death.[22] Since Antony has the nature of a crocodile, it is no wonder that he recognizes his own reptilian aspect in his "serpent of old Nile." Lepidus's assertion sounds like a metaphor of the diabolical couple, both blessed by the sun and prospering in the mud of illicit relationships: "Your serpent of Egypt is bred now of your mud by the operation of your sun: so is your crocodile" (II vii 25–26).

Overflowing Nile, whose mud is fertilized by the sun, becomes the image of their stormy and ever renewed love until the lovers annihilate themselves in its waters. Recurring image of a capricious stream, the Nile gives prosperity or destruction, good and evil, crops and serpent's nests. The reptile has its poison, the elixir capable of granting the dissolution of body and soul the lovers hunger for. "Poison" is applied to love with these words which Cleopatra savors: "Now I feed myself / With most delicious poison"(I v 26–27). "Poison" also describes the wine that flows freely during the many banquets of the play, numbing the senses and blurring the clarity of mind required for political transactions: "And then when poisoned hours had bound me up / From mine own knowledge" (II ii 95–96). Such is the apology made by Antony to Caesar who accuses him of breaking his oath. Such poison, Antony says, steeps senses in soft and delicate Lethe, the other mythological river where dead souls reached oblivion.

The vision of the metamorphoses of the clouds in the sky, culminating in a striking tableau, appears as a climax of this poetry of water and of oblivion. It is the philosophical meditation of an exhausted and literally defeated and dismantled Antony to his young aide-de-camp Eros:

> *Antony*: Sometime we see a cloud that's dragonish,
> A vapour sometime like a bear or a lion,
> A towered citadel, a pendent rock,
> A forkèd mountain, or blue promontory
> With trees upon't that nod unto the world
> And mock our eyes with air. Thou hast seen these signs;
> They are black vesper's pageants.
> *Eros*: Ay, my lord.
> *Antony*: That which is now a horse even with a thought
> The rack dislimns, and makes it indistinct
> As water is in water.

---

[22] Dame Judi Dench, when she played Cleopatra, recalls how Director Peter Hall "wanted the last picture to be of a woman who is lifeless, but the snake is still wriggling in her hand." Judi Dench, *Shakespeare: The Man who Pays the Rent* (Penguin Michael Joseph, 2023), 241.

Eros: It does, my lord.
Antony: My good knave Eros, now thy captain is
Even such a body. Here I am Antony,
Yet cannot hold this visible shape, my knave. (IV xv 2–14)

The passage opens a vista similar to those bluish landscapes in Patinir's paintings, in sharp contrast with the colorful action that has held the stage until then. It is as if Antony suddenly became one of those tiny pilgrims devoted to Saint Jerome, solitarily receding in the heart of the landscape. It is not only the soothing effect of the vista, after the raging of the hero, who thinks himself betrayed by his queen, that creates the emotion, but the expectation of a meaning that remains elusive until the final metaphor: here is your captain, he says, an unsubstantial being whose shape moves with the wind and cannot contain itself any longer. The hero is divesting himself of his armor, naked like a hermit, a beggar to his own boy, Eros. The majesty of the "triple pillar of the world" has been eroded away by the torrents of love. We remember the first image of him that was displayed to us, that of a man whose great heart burst his armor. Feeling himself betrayed, he takes off his armor and is now losing his substance, revealing a now wounded heart unable to sustain life any longer. Antony's raison d'être has now disappeared and by breaking his own form, overflowing his own bourn, his vitality trickling away, the warrior now takes up his last challenge.

He has just wished his queen to vanish—"Vanish, or I shall give thee thy deserving" (IV xiii 32)—after a thousand curses against her. Then, believing her dead, he has not ceased longing for a last apotheosis with her in the kingdom of shadows, where, good actors that they are, they intend to outmatch even Dido and Aeneas for love.

Like Cleopatra, Antony stages himself, and the *distanciation* thus obtained (Brecht's *Verfremdungseffekt*) mingles laughter and tears. In *Antony and Cleopatra*, it seems that all the characters, like Enobarbus and Agrippa, who are mocking Lepidus's efforts to flatter both Caesar and Antony in turn (III ii), have a wonderful capacity to remain lucid at the most intense moments, each hyperbole being undermined by its contrary, thus avoiding surfeit, to the extent that Shakespeare's poetry, like Cleopatra, "makes hungry / Where most she satisfies" (II ii 244–45).

If Cleopatra's death transforms into tragedy what could have been a mere pathetic mistake, she also consecrates the lovers' union by bringing together the images which unite them. Like Antony, whom she raises to the status of husband—the familiar, moral note in the midst of cosmic chaos—Cleopatra disintegrates, she becomes air and fire to join the universe of her beloved. The serpent has become "the pretty worms of

Nilus" and its poison has to satisfy the queen's desire for immortality. The expected dissolution is visualized as a peaceful and happy state, the asp sucking at Cleopatra's breast like a greedy baby putting his nurse to sleep. The metamorphosis of the capricious queen into a Madonna is, of all, the most spectacular, a scenic metaphor that transcends all metaphors. There is no massive monument here, no pompous staging of death but rather a very feminine and tender apotheosis (aesthetically poles apart from the bulky pseudo-Egyptian staging favored over the centuries). The now still beauty of Cleopatra in her assumption manages to restore the collapsed architecture of Antony's world.

The breathtaking beauty of both heroes' last moments, even though separate, has yet a strange harmony, as if Antony's landscape, so expressive of Patinir's northern mannerism, provides an apt backdrop for his queen's Madonna-like apotheosis.[23] Such slanting perspective would not be above Shakespeare's art at this stage, and he may well have been inspired by Patinir's own disproportion between the size of his main characters in the foreground, and the receding walk-on parts, pilgrims, peasants, and soldiers in the background.

THERE ARE THOSE, MANY OF THEM, WHO WILL CHUCKLE and suggest that if at last Antony found the boundless space he needed, he narrowly escaped. It is never totally certain that Cleopatra did not plan to cheat on Antony. Diomedes's assertion about her betrayal "which never shall be found" (IV xv 123) is in keeping with the generally ambiguous tone of the play. As we have seen, Antony and Cleopatra, like all of Shakespeare's theater, is full of macho sexual innuendos probably reflecting the mind of a majority of theater goers (and critics), who choose to remember only half of the arguments. Shakespeare chooses to maintain the ambiguity to the end. Once a prey to Caesar's temptation, Cleopatra could indeed have chosen to flatter the new conqueror and tie him to herself as she did with the others. She seems to be waiting until she is certain of her destiny before deciding to end it all, as if there existed some alternative.

The audience, like Antony, has to pledge its faith: to believe in her faithfulness, or let her die a meaningless death. Until the last minute, Shakespeare maintains suspense and doubt, suggesting a dishonest compromise, while the born actress Cleopatra is satirizing Caesar. Hardly has he left the room when she hurries amorously toward her rendezvous. "It is provided," she says. And the spectator realizes once again that, like

---

23 Patinir's *Rest of the Holy Family* (Prado, Madrid) made me think of such a combination.

Antony, he nearly doubted her love, and that faith is difficult, were it not for this complicated pool of images and metaphors commingling the lovers, making each one the reflection of the other until they reach the final dissolution which makes them indistinct "As water is in water." ♣

10. The Last Plays

CYMBELINE: MANNERIST APOTHEOSIS

If *As You Like It* is a fugue, *Cymbeline* is a symphony. This musical genre, still in its infancy, was obviously wider in scope and was often used as a musical introduction to operas in the early seventeenth century:

> Momentum was maintained less by thematic development than by bustling non-thematic passage-work, and interest was generated by a sharp contrast of thematic ideas and orchestral effects, with prominent use of the string *tremolando*, held wind notes, the implied crescendo, and so on.[1]

Likewise, the play seems to be made of heterogeneous (some will say ill-assorted) contrasted elements, uncertain historical time, and still vaguer dramatic time split over three geographical loci — London, Rome and Wales — articulated together by three powerful scenes whose clashing content is emotionally charged (*tremolando*). *Cymbeline* is a mannerist apotheosis hiding within its infinite variety a daring piece of work. Up to now, all Shakespeare's plays have been one way or another concerned with internecine wars and rivalries, usurpation and exile, and the slippery nature of truth in a world fascinated by appearances, double-meanings, and lies. To translate this into stage language the author has used mirror effects and anamorphoses, music, metamorphoses and masks, fools and folly, and ghosts, too, continuously mingling the tragic and the comic with all shades of the pastoral in an attempt to capture the spirit of life. Samuel Johnson's scathing condemnation of the play in the eighteenth century seems to be a description of mannerist art in the negative:

> To remark the folly of the fiction, the absurdity of the conduct, the confusion of the names and manners of different times, and the impossibility of the events in any system of life were to waste criticism upon unresisting imbecility, upon faults too evident for detection, and too gross for aggravation.

The age of reason would ceaselessly pit science against those "mysteries" which they could not explain and thus translated as men's subjective desires or sheer madness. In the twenty-first century, as we realize the error of such judgment and the extremes of violence and horror such rationalism led to, we may be ripe to rediscover Shakespeare's work for its singular beauty and humanity, unfortunately depending, as always in the theater, on the

---

[1] *The Oxford Companion to Music*, 1238.

understanding of stage directors. After watching a girlish Imogen running about the stage in her panties in front of the Italian foreigner who comes on an embassy to see her, I was exceedingly charmed by Helen Mirren's Imogen in Moshinsky's very beautiful, sensitive, and convincing production of *Cymbeline*. The postmodern all too common choice of generalized trash and ugliness as far as costumes and decor are concerned, the characters who seem unable to say three words without tumbling down and crawling on the stage, these and more that seem today the norm of European theater and opera productions, not only do not bring much enjoyment to the audience, but seem to miss the point entirely. Whether in *Cymbeline*, or in *The Magic Flute*, the contrast, which is woven in the tapestry of the plot and must provoke the aesthetic shock that will bring wonder and ultimately the choice of grace and harmony, cannot be deleted without harm to the objective of the work.

In *Cymbeline*, therefore, we have a contrasted setting of two very different worlds: what looks like a sclerotic, isolated court, where an aging and rather rigid king is manipulated by his ambitious new queen on the one hand, and on the other, the cosmopolitan domain of Rome and the civilized gentlemanliness of Caius Lucius and Filario. This is in itself a surprising inversion of the usual polarities such as those in *Antony and Cleopatra*. Unlike Britain, Rome is now attractive and far from rigid. That Cymbeline ruled Britain at the time of the birth of Christ is not incidental in a play that aims to establish a parallelism between Britain's past with its diplomatic resolution of conflicts and the England of James I with its unending war on Catholics at home and abroad.

The plot begins at home with Cymbeline disapproving of his daughter's choice of a husband, which recalls Brabantio and Desdemona, and a few other Shakespearean fathers, who do not hesitate to threaten their daughters with the nunnery or death. Like most Shakespearean girls, Imogen is bold, with a free and open nature; there's no guile in her and she not surprisingly resists her father in order to marry the man she loves. Unfortunately, the young man, Posthumus, is not socially — or religiously? — compatible and finds himself banished by the angry king who had another candidate in mind. Posthumus then runs away to Rome to one of his father's friends. Of course the play's Rome is that of Augustus Caesar, but the international ambience of Posthumus's first night in the city looks more like Jacobean Rome, where many exiles found refuge on account of their faith. For part of the audience, Rome would naturally have signified the pope and a Catholic haunt. After all, the young man could also have chosen to hide closer to his beloved wife in the wilderness of Wales, where twenty years earlier another arbitrary exile, Belarius, had chosen to go underground.

Rome then is not a fortuitous choice. It even includes the Judas character who seems to befriend only to deceive and spreads false rumors, parts once played by men like Anthony Munday and Charles Sledd, whom Shakespeare probably knew all too well. Here we may remember the two gentlemen of so-called Verona, who once embarked for Milan via the Emperor's court. The underlying references would have been obvious to many, even if Shakespeare takes great pains to intermingle the threads of his plots, so that no fewer than twenty-five revelations are needed at the end to clarify the whole.

If faith is not mentioned, Imogen and Posthumus's marriage and their faith in each other are highlighted. They have been introduced as paragons by a gentleman who claims that his praise of Posthumus is still below the full measure of the character, who even managed to live "in court—Which rare it is to do—most praised, most loved" (I i 46–47).

They, like Antony and Cleopatra, seem to be locked up in a mirror relationship and are to be measured by each other only:

> To his mistress,
> For whom he now is banished, her own price
> Proclaims how she esteemed him and his virtue.
> By her election may be truly read
> What kind of man he is. (I i 50–54)

The marriage and fate of Anne and Roger Line,[2] whom Shakespeare might have known or very likely heard about, have been supposed to be the models for Imogen and Posthumus and it is true that the explanations given in the very first scene of the play could perfectly apply to their case. But Roger Line died in exile and never saw his wife again and naturally could not engage in anything like Posthumus's later behavior in the play. As for Anne, she died a martyr for her faith.[3] However, it seems that Shakespeare, who created a fair share of martyred heroines, now had a different purpose in mind and wanted to turn tragedy into a life-giving genre. Toying as he had been for many years with the idea of resurrection, he was now ready to translate it into new, more daring dramatic elements.

Posthumus and Imogen are introduced as the perfect pair; like the Phoenix and Turtle, "either was the other's mine."[4] He is her "jewel in the world" and he promises to be "the loyal'st husband that did e'er plight

---

[2] Martin Dodwell, *Anne Line: Shakespeare's Tragic Muse* (Brighton: The Book Guild Ltd, 2013). There would of course have been no attempt at reproducing their lives realistically, Shakespeare using them as inspiration in a wider allegorical design.

[3] This perfect couple very probably inspired Shakespeare's most hermetic poem, *The Phoenix and the Turtle*.

[4] *The Phoenix and Turtle*, l. 36.

troth" (I i 97). However, those among the audience who had recently seen a performance of *Antony and Cleopatra* surely remembered what happened when that jewel of hers went back to Rome. Such seeming perfection at the outset certainly had to be tested, and those who had Othello in mind, could only shiver upon hearing Posthumus as he exchanges a bracelet for a ring with Imogen: "It is a manacle of love. I'll place it / Upon the fairest prisoner" (I i 123–24). Like Othello, Posthumus distorts the original and free nature of his gift to turn it into possession. This small crack in his nature is surely liable to be manipulated. It is the flaw upon which much of the play's tragedy ensues. A breach of trust, and chaos is come again. In good time Posthumus will require proofs for Imogen's betrayal, without ever realizing, any more than Othello, that proofs can be forged and manipulated. True faith does not need proofs any more than love does, because it cannot be measured by human standards. It simply happens, belonging to another, spiritual order of life. Whoever has it can give all and grow richer in the process. Shakespeare has been toying with the idea in many of his plays, but until now, those who were trustful and loyal, like Desdemona, like Emilia to her mistress, generally died for it, or suffered like Antonio in *The Merchant of Venice*. This is the great change performed by *Cymbeline*. In this play, the life line is maintained by the faithful, by Imogen first of all, but also by Pisanio, who never falters and dares to do what too few have the courage to do: he refuses to obey a too damnable order, obeying his conscience instead, convinced that there must be false play somewhere. Earlier, noble Filario had warned Posthumus against hasty reactions: "Sir, be patient. / This is not strong enough to be believed / Of one persuaded well of" (II iv 130–32). Strange indeed that Posthumus should more easily *believe* Giacomo's words[5] than *believe in* his own wife's true love.

By 1610, Shakespeare was certainly still troubled by the absence of any resolution to the religious divide in his country, but he had obviously had ample time to meditate on his own religious allegiance. The turmoil of English political and religious life and the lack of spiritual guidance did not prevent him from turning to the Scriptures, which he must have read determined to find another perspective in the perilous task of expressing the possibility of the impossible. After having played for many years with the Pauline paradox and reversal of values which had no doubt shaped his religious schooling, he seems to have turned to the Apostle John for a different definition of faith as a source of absolute life. Better than Paul, who was an ideologist, John, refusing the cleavage of man's divine essence, was a *witness* to unheard-of things; he may have inspired Shakespeare's own

---

[5] Also spelled Iachimo in the First Folio.

sense of wonder, which eventually became the gist of his dramatic manner. As man incarnate, had not Jesus completely assumed human pathos and refused detachment (ataraxy), which others, like the Stoics, considered supreme wisdom? Accordingly, Shakespeare, who had earlier shown some admiration for stoic characters like Horatio, now strongly appeals to the emotions. No one is indifferent. Even Shakespeare's Romans have changed in *Cymbeline,* and Caius Lucius's attitude to Fidele is closer to Christian benevolence than to Roman virtue. Faith is not *to believe,* for then you may be thought credulous and naïve, faith is *to believe in,* to trust oneself and the other as God's own, totally, absolutely. Imogen in that sense is faith incarnate and the play can to a certain extent be seen as an allegory of faith in a world of lies and deceit.

Cymbeline seems more than any other play inspired by Counter-Reformation art, like a large Baroque fresco in which action is broken over different times, places and dimensions, in a profusion of characters, tones, and emotions.[6] Shakespeare had always sought to give shape to his own philosophy on the stage, ceaselessly pushing further the boundaries of his art. In *Cymbeline* he was to push the boundaries of his art further than ever before, risking charges of folly, absurdity, and confusion in pursuit of a more profound representation of human experience unattainable through conventional dramatic form.[7]

He probed the differentiation and oppositions which he found in this world and slowly but steadily turned them into intervals, namely, a space encompassing both extremes within the same movement, the same life. Shakespeare was pursuing here three goals in one: to represent life, in its quintessence, as the *event / advent* it should be for a true Christian, to find the aesthetic tool to this end, and to vindicate the spiritual unity of England as it used to be before the Tudor Reformation.

Giacomo's awed admiration for hallowed Imogen lying in her bedroom like a monument in a chapel — the sudden suspension of time on a close-up shot, with, as a backdrop, Shakespeare's own *Rape of Lucrece* remembered. Its poetry and slow motion are a virtuoso's achievement: having aroused the audience's expectation of a wicked rape, he suddenly thwarts their shivering surmise. Shakespeare leads his play, like a tightrope walker, on the edge between comedy and tragedy: Giacomo's emerging from a trunk in the middle of the night has a taste of merry Falstaff comedy about it, quickly turned into some more threatening pastimes as he recalls Tarquin's

---

[6] Once again, Tintoretto's art and imagination seems to me the closest parallel we could find.

[7] James Shapiro, "Fear no more," Cymbeline *Stagebill,* New York Shakespeare Festival, Delacorte Theater (August, 1998), 4.7.

own deadly attempt on Lucrece. But Giacomo, who is moved by Imogen's beauty as soon as he lays eyes on her, is no stoic Roman, simply an Italian braggadocio with a remnant of conscience in him. He is satisfied by a pretense of rape only, his mercenary pillaging of her intimacy rather recalling the spirit that presided over the dissolution of the monasteries. His rape remains purely verbal, mere boasting, which does not prevent it from having a disastrous effect.

Shakespeare plays with the tenuous, porous border between truth and pretense, appearance and reality, showing their interdependence, revealing here the sinister consequences that fiction can have on reality. As in life, no answer is given beforehand, we go forward with our convictions and our beliefs, cautious or trustful, often mistaken, always uncertain. Giacomo's deceit will for a while untune the couple's harmony, but his ensuing torment and confession seem to point to a working of grace, which may have prevented him from defiling Imogen's body. The "cinque-spotted" mole "like the crimson drops / I' th' bottom of a cowslip" (II ii 39), traditionally suggesting the five wounds of Christ, were proof enough to convince anyone of her chaste innocence. Yet when Posthumus is taunted by returning Giacomo, he is soon shaken by the vision of the bracelet he had given as a token to his wife. The eyes remain more powerful than the soul. Even before Giacomo has mentioned the mole under her breast, Posthumus has already pictured his dear wife a whore, and his masculine pride is wounded for losing the possession that was his (the bracelet). Like Othello, like Leontes, he erupts into violence, unable to control himself anymore. Wise Filario can only be sorry for such an absence of patience. Obviously, perfect Posthumus still needs a little ordeal before he can be trusted with a wife.

As hostilities are confirmed between Britain and Augustus Caesar in spite of Lucius's friendly embassy, Pisanio receives the order to kill his master's supposedly adulterous wife. However, good Pisanio knows when disobedience can be a virtue and decides to ignore his master's command. Meanwhile Imogen, who is made to believe that her husband is waiting for her at Milford Haven, bursts with joy, her enthusiasm contrasting with Posthumus's accusations. She shows Juliet's passionate eagerness on her wedding eve and Rosalind's fiery impatience all in one, wanting to be there right away, unsettling Pisanio and the audience, who'd rather have her choose another course —"Madam, you're best consider" (III ii 77).

This journey to meet a husband is undertaken in the guise of a franklin's housewife, a bow to Chaucer, whose tale of perfect faith and gentlemanliness shows like a watermark in Shakespeare's play. When she learns of her husband's accusation, Imogen reacts like Dorigen, and Lucrece before her, and would rather lose her life than be thought faithless. But, like Dorigen, she finds another gentleman in Pisanio, who refuses to execute his orders. Since she cannot go back to the court with him, he advises her to "forget to be a woman" and to follow her luck abroad, as a reply to her "Hath Britain all the sun that shines?" (III iv 137). Exile is once again contemplated as the only lifeline, an escape toward life from an all too narrow, all too dangerous island.

The metamorphosis of Imogen into Fidele opens the play's pastoral world, which is by no means as civilized as the Forest of Arden, but cultivates the same exiled human kindness far from the deceit and injustice of the court. Belarius duly assumes his role as a father and teacher, using perspective as a wise example to express the relativity of man's own position in nature.[8] Belarius's viewpoint remains moralistic however, stressing the greater nobility of their rural life compared to the costly show of courtly life. The audience surely remembered Touchstone and Corin's debate in *As You Like It*. Here the boys, applying Belarius's teaching, defend their own vision of relativity, questioning the advantage and wisdom of such a quiet and simple life for one who does not know anything else:

> Our cage
> We make a choir, as doth the prisoned bird,
> And sing our bondage freely. (III iii 42–44)

The metaphor was earlier used, *a contrario*, by Lear in his last dream of seclusion with Cordelia. What is presently bondage for the eager ignorant youth was seen as freedom by the exhausted old king. Belarius's reply could be Lear's own when he at last realizes the evil and illusion of court life:

> Then was I as a tree
> Whose boughs did bend with fruit; but in one night
> A storm or robbery, call it what you will,
> Shook down my mellow hangings, nay, my leaves,
> And left me bare to weather. (III iii 60–64)

Shakespeare adroitly hints at the absolute arbitrariness and unfairness of the process, "a storm or robbery," depriving a loyal servant of the king of his rights and property for no particular reason, unless it was the sudden denunciation by "two villains" upon "false oaths," which too many

---

[8] The image of man perceived as a crow from afar recalls Imogen's own advice to Pisanio upon his master's departure a little earlier: "Thou shouldst have made him / As little as a crow, or less, ere left / To after-eye him.... / I would have broke mine eye-strings, cracked them, but / To look upon him till the diminution / Of space had pointed him sharp as my needle; / Nay, followed him till he had melted from / The smallness of a gnat to air..." (I iii 14–21).

Catholic families had experienced in the last thirty years.[9] Accused of confederacy with the Romans, Belarius was similarly banished and robbed of his "demesne." Yet he cannot stand long against the fiery zeal of the two young princes he stole from Cymbeline as a revenge. Their blood belies their rustic breeding and they want to know the world.

Before they do, however, the world will come to them in the shape of a charming, famished sister-boy plundering food from their cave. Disguised as the boy Fidele on the way to Milford Haven, Imogen is now looking for "honourable" and "most holy" Lucius, ready to leave Britain for more hallowed grounds. These adjectives are powerful and revealing of the peculiar "light" of the character.[10] It is surely emblematic that such light is Roman and at this point leaving Britain — probably as shocking as having Joan of Arc represent Astraea's daughter. We cannot but realize the constancy of Shakespeare's obsessions. There is a man who never changed purpose over twenty years and kept endlessly imagining the same situations, reinventing the same themes and images that had shocked him as a youth. As if to blur the reference, the most beautiful, poetical, and nationalistic passages of the play are put in the mouth of the most devious characters in Cymbeline's court, his Queen and her son Cloten. The Queen is particularly eloquent and must have moved many hearts when she exhorts her King to remember:

> The natural bravery of [his] isle, which stands
> As Neptune's park, ribbed and paled in
> With banks unscalable and roaring waters,
> With sands that will not bear your enemies' boats,
> But suck them up to th' topmast. (III i 18–22)

It seems that Old Gaunt's visionary lament is more than ever topical, his lyrical praise of the beauty of "this sceptred isle," "this precious stone set in the silver sea,"[11] which he feared was now "leased out," is more than ever true with Cymbeline's court wallowing in shame. Putting such a praise of his beloved isle in the mouth of the most deceitful character certainly points to rather grim irony and a certain disillusion on the author's part. The audience must have wondered who the good characters were and whom to believe. For like the characters, the audience is ceaselessly made to feel

---

[9] See Alison Flood, "William Shakespeare: father's legal skirmishes shed light on bard's early years. Newly found documents in the National Archives show the playwright's father John was harassed by Crown informers, which may have influenced his attitude to power and class," *The Guardian*, September 13, 2018.

[10] The name Lucius, found several times in Shakespeare's plays and attached as it is to Luke and light, would have had a peculiar connotation for many in the audience. See Clare Asquith's "Glossary," *Shadowplay*, 294.

[11] *Richard II*, II i 40, 46.

disorientated, buffeted about by the various currents of the plot, repeatedly lashed by contrary opinions, each declaration immediately contradicted by an aside, as in a storm preventing them from finding their standing. Destabilized, they are freed from their usual preconceptions and have to accept every wind that blows with an open and questioning heart. This is also the mannerist device to keep a tight rein on the audience's emotion, tilling their hearts for a crop of wonder. Shakespeare, like Jupiter, had understood that by confusing his audience, he could make his gift, "the more delayed, delighted," (V iii 196) and unforgettable. He also knew that only this play on perspectives could eventually provide the questioning and the harmonious middle way that would be best for everyone.

Meanwhile he proceeds to tie up a new thread in the plot, with Cloten disguised as Posthumus tracking Imogen on the road to Milford Haven, which moves the center of the play from London to Wales, whose attractive port seems however to recede in the distance as the characters move forward. The scene is on the road, *moving toward* a perfectly symbolical, almost philosophical, locus, Belarius's cave. The poor, ascetic, hermitic Christian life led by Belarius and his wards in the cave demonstrates more clearly the truth of nature and its light than the courtly life of illusions they have fled, yet the day the young men finally emerge into the world is for them like a rebirth from the motherly womb of the earth, or a resurrection from the tomb. It is significant that Imogen is first perceived as an angel by Belarius, an angel who is described reconciling in himself the *contrapposti* typical of mannerism:

> Nobly he yokes
> A smiling with a sigh, as if the sigh
> Was that it was for not being such a smile;
> The smile mocking the sigh that it would fly
> From so divine a temple to commix
> With winds that sailors rail at. (IV ii 53–58)

Surely, Guarini and Tasso found a rival here who mastered as well as they did "the Mannerist virtues of grace, complexity, variety and difficulty." [12] And we now know that for Shakespeare, this style was not mere "virtuoso-performance," such as it may have appeared to be at times in *Love's Labour's Lost*, but an ever-renewed attempt at capturing the true balance between extremes to ensure the kind of general harmony that had been missing in England for so long. At this holy place, Imogen's, Cloten's, and Lucius's roads will cross each other and there, Providence will sift the wheat and the cockle. In the meantime, Fidele is welcome like a brother and a friend,

---

[12] Shearman, *Mannerism*, 84.

and in an aside wonders at the gentleness and virtuous behavior of these so-called "savage" creatures.

Cloten's angry encounter with Polydore/Guiderius, whom he provokes and abuses, ends up in a fight in which Cloten loses his head. His vindication of his rank made no impression on young Guiderius, who leaves him without a head in his rival's coat. Meanwhile, Fidele/Imogen, who felt sick and has swallowed Pisanio's drug, has fallen unconscious. This is the nadir of the play, a kind of descent into hell for the three yet ignorant siblings. Arviragus and Guiderius find Imogen lifeless after she absorbed Pisanio's cordial — actually the Queen's deadly potion — fortunately rendered innocuous by the doctor's clairvoyance. The drug's variable identity witnesses to the tortuous quality of life and its opacity. Tortuous and opaque, such is indeed the center of the play! Arviragus and Guiderius enact solemn burial rites, in which the body of Imogen (alias Fidele) will symbolically be joined with the headless body of Cloten (alias Posthumus). The inexperienced boys are intent on doing things with all necessary propriety, obeying Belarius's codes and reasons. That the oblique reference to laying "his head to th' east" should be taken to emphasize the pagan world, as is generally thought, is unlikely. It is doubtful whether pagans would have taken the trouble to bury Cloten with their beloved friend. Moreover, if Shakespeare, by exiling Belarius on account of his Roman allegiance, meant to hint secretly at the present situation of England, the latter's "reasons" for burying the dead with their heads to the east must be linked to the old faith.[13] Belarius has evidently initiated the boys to his religious practice without giving them any "reason" for what he does, presumably to protect them. They, not being forced, know how to be gentle and respect their father's reasons. They have done their obsequies and then follow Belarius apart to pray on their knees. A line which might rhyme with "knee," however, is absent, the prayer merely (logically) suggested. Since the Reformed religion considered that purgatory did not exist and that prayers were useless for the dead, the only way to be saved being God's grace and "robust faith in the saving power of Christ's sacrifice,"[14] this ritual with prayers at the heart of the play, was naturally another great mannerist comment hidden under the garment of paganism.

The beauty and serenity of the boys' funeral song, which ought to be chanted as suggested, is immediately followed by a violent emotional and artistic shock as Imogen wakes up from the drug's torpor finding a headless man in Posthumus's garments lying beside her. Imogen *hopes she*

---

[13] The dead were buried with their heads nearest the cross, which was naturally East for Westerners; however, there is no prescribed method for burial in the Bible.
[14] Greenblatt, *Will in the World*, 320.

dreams as she cannot comprehend the illusionistic spectacle before her eyes. The whole scene has been masterfully built like a Baroque painting, with shocking contrasts and the emotionally violent coupling of purity with horror, the two extremes of Catholic life in England at the time. Imogen's ensuing grief recalls Mary's lamentation over Christ's body at the foot of the cross. Imogen cradles the headless body she has been led to believe is her husband's in a paroxysm of anguish. That this is illusion, which the audience knows, certainly satisfies the poetic justice of the plot, but in no way diminishes the emotional impact. For the shock is not solely that of Imogen, it is also that of the audience, taken aback by the visual violence of the scene and moved to pity by the heroine's tears. Esthetically, the image of an innocent woman wailing over the dead body of her beloved finds its roots in the deepest part of human consciousness. No one in the audience would have escaped its tragic intensity. This was precisely the aim of Counter-Reformation Baroque Art, to move and persuade through strong images that provoked wonder and pity. *Cymbeline* probably remains Shakespeare's most audacious attempt, and this scene, the nadir of the play, may also be its zenith, esthetically as well as morally. But the dramatic pace does not allow for meditation. When Lucius in turn happens to pass by, the perspective has changed and he finds a boy sleeping on the headless trunk of someone he calls his master, Richard du Champs.[15] Lucius praises Fidele's faith and offers to father him if he would like. Survival means resilience and Imogen is nothing if not resilient. One illusion hides another with the consequence that the dead body receives new burial rites and "a century of prayers" (IV ii 393).

Meanwhile, the state of the court is perplexity and amazement. Cymbeline finds himself completely alone, his daughter vanished, his wife sick at heart over her son's absence. Pisanio has lost track of his master and mistress and the Roman army is about to invade Britain. But, says the King, "We fear not / What can from Italy annoy us, but / We grieve at chances here"(IV iii 33–35), a statement which may have echoed sadly to part of the audience. Did Cymbeline begin to realize that something had gone terribly wrong in his kingdom? Posthumus, now holding bloody proofs of his wife's death in hand, equally has doubts about the course of destiny

---

[15] With this name, Shakespeare confuses the issue a little further since he may wink at his friend Richard Field (1561–1624), the printer and publisher of his poems, who, with his wife Jacqueline, belonged to the exiled Huguenot community of London, as well as refer to another Richard Field (1554–1606), a mild and prudent man, who studied at Douai, became a Jesuit, and was appointed superior of the Irish Jesuit mission. Since the vision is deceiving and the reality of the dead body belies the grief it provokes, Shakespeare may indeed be hinting at his deep friendship for a man who actually belonged to the opposing party.

and his responsibility in it. Having nothing to lose, he too decides to vindicate his good name and to fight with "the strength o' th' Leonati" (V i 31). Conversely, Giacomo is torn apart by guilt, which prevents him from fighting his best. Meanwhile Belarius fears the risks of being discovered and tortured: "that / Which we have done, whose answer would be death / Drawn on with torture" (IV iv 12–14). But youth is somehow taking over and he can only follow his sons' fiery mood. The public consequences of those private dramas are "a day turned strangely," and a plot turning into the most confused thriller.

Back from Rome, Posthumus decides to disguise himself as a British peasant in order to fight for his country and not against it, witnessing to the amazing bravery of an ancient soldier with "two striplings." The irony is that he tells this wonderful story to a lord who evidently has worked no wonder and is now running away. The loyal ones are not necessarily the noblest ones. Shakespeare loses no opportunity to signify his distaste of a sophisticated court, more and more disconnected from the deep truths of moral life.[16] Had not Posthumus decided earlier to launch a new fashion "less without and more within" (V i 33)? Yet, having won the day and escaped death, he decides to be a Roman again and die for Imogen. His being fettered gives him a new occasion to meditate on life, alleviate his heavy conscience and ask the "great powers" to grant him the freedom of death. The oxymoronic language is of course typical of Baroque sensitivity expressing the tragic cast of a civilization in which death has become an "heureux malheur" (happy misery). If life is death, from death can spring new life. The theme binds Posthumus and Imogen together throughout their ordeal, as if there was some telepathic bond between them. Imprisoned, he speaks to her in silence and dreams of strange redemptions. Baroque literature, permeated by the moving reality of life, would try its best to solve the contradiction: "Unite by the strength of reasoning two extreme opposites, an extreme proof of clever subtlety."[17] God and Death were the natural places (*loci*) of tragedy and mystery. For centuries the divine had been the synthesis of contraries, both mysterious darkness and luminous wisdom. Similarly the contradictory nature of man could best be expressed

---

[16] Many wonder why Shakespeare retired to Stratford at an unexpectedly early age, when he was at the top of a successful career: it may have been for health reasons, or, as Clare Asquith suggests, for being at last brought to silence; it may also have been mere discouragement from seeing that all his exertion had brought no improvement to the political or moral life of his country. Prospero's farewell to the world sounds very much like the disillusion of a man who has tried, in all conscience, to mend the world through an art which he had perfected to the utmost.

[17] "Unir par la force du raisonnement deux contradictoires extrêmes, extrême preuve de subtilité." Gracián, *Agudeza*, VIII, quoted in Souiller, *La literature baroque en Europe*, 203 (my translation).

through oxymorons (living death versus lifeless existence), which became a staple linguistic tool of mystics like Theresa of Avila. Posthumus's argument with the gods reflects the double bind which is his, the "intrinsicate knot of life" that holds him a prisoner against his will:

> Most welcome, bondage, for thou art a way,
> I think, to liberty. Yet I am better
> Than one that's sick o'th' gout, since he had rather
> Groan so in perpetuity than be cured
> By th' sure physician, death, who is the key
> T'unbar these locks. My conscience, thou art fettered
> More than my shanks and wrists.... O Imogen,
> I'll speak to thee in silence! (V iii 97–103, 123)

The masque that ensues, with Jupiter's eagle descending from on high, is a third contrasting, exotic, Baroque moment in the play, embodying spiritual reality. The representation of Jupiter's marble and crystal palace in heaven must have been a remarkable *trompe-l'oeil* in the manner of Giulio Romano, with an opening of "marble pavement" allowing the passage of the god on his eagle. Surely, Shakespeare already had the Giant's room of the Palazzo Te in mind. Posthumus's family are ghosts, and this is a dream, but art somehow makes the episode more vivid to him, and to the audience, than the limbo in which he has been living since Giacomo's trick in Rome. Fiction and life become indistinguishable. The otherworldly visions and Jovian riddle must have been another spectacular moment within the play, providing a dreamy musical interlude to ease the dramatic tension, and arousing wonder at Jupiter in majesty descending on his eagle to chide and comfort like a good father:

> Whom best I love, I cross, to make my gift,
> The more delayed, delighted. (V iii 195–96)

If some had begun to stir in the audience, or found the plot tedious, they now had a riddle to decipher, "such stuff as madmen / Tongue and brain not," (V iii 239–40) which would instantly revive their curiosity and interest. Shakespeare, not forsaking the dullards, also grants them a laugh at the expense of a jailer full of oxymoronic witticism on life and death, thus pursuing the philosophical meditation started with Fidele's funeral elegy. Taking on Hamlet's famous speech in a lower key, the Jailer mocks Posthumus's eagerness to go to "The undiscovered country from whose bourn / No traveller returns,"[18] but unlike questioning Hamlet, Posthumus's parable-like reply is full of assurance: "I tell thee, fellow, there are

---

[18] *Hamlet*, III i 80–81.

none want eyes to direct them the way I am going but such as wink and will not use them" (V iii 278–80). Naturally, only faith can give this ability "to see the way of blindness," which seems to be lost on the jailer, who is unable to understand the paradoxical mind of his prisoner.

The masque is very cunningly diverted into some Counter-Reformation apotheosis. Far from being here the nationalistic, king-centered court entertainment it usually was and is still in disguise, it gently urges men to open their eyes on the strange unknown end of their life's journey rather than closing their eyes to it. Now begin the revelations of this complicated plot, slowly bringing Posthumus back into focus and to a just recognition. Shakespeare has to build up wonder and manages a cascade of amazed *ahs* and *ohs* in his audience first, like Jupiter delaying his rewards so they may feel more delicious afterward. After the knighting of the old man and his two sons, followed by news of the queen's death, the focus is on the ring which is on Giacomo's finger and which symbolically contains much of Imogen's fate. Giacomo describes Posthumus as a "true knight" tricked into a shameful bet for honor's sake, and presently Posthumus accuses himself of being a fool who deserves death since he not only swallowed Giacomo's lies, but did not even have the courage to do justice himself. The best moral vows, however, can be betrayed by character. Suddenly interrupted by Imogen, whom he does not recognize, in spite of the many ripples of recognition and stupefied asides among the onlookers, Posthumus reacts with the same impulsiveness that made him want her dead in the first place, striking her down on the spot, and there making a double fool of himself.

Hovering between tragedy and comedy, the author accelerates the alternating moments of revelation and relief with violent reactions that build up the emotional tension in the characters as well as in the audience. We realize that the worst is still possible (in the First Folio, the play is a tragedy!). After all Posthumus and Imogen have not met since their swift parting at the beginning of the play. Their relationship has relied solely on letters, genuine or fake, transmitted by others. The irony of this mistaken violent gesture must have aroused shouts of disappointment in the theater, soon silenced by "new matter" discovered as the princess comes back to life (for the second time). The plot unfolds like the waves of the sea, rolling on breakers then lulling for a while, giving and killing hope, providing perfect immortal lines in the midst of confusion:

> Hang there like fruit, my soul,
> Till the tree die. (V iv 263–64)

It is as if the whole play had been leading to this ecstasy, blessed a moment later by Cymbeline's own tears: "My tears that fall / Prove holy water on thee" (V iv 269). There is never any superfluous rhetoric in Shakespeare, however, and the end cannot be fulfilling unless all secrets and riddles have been solved. The mind has to be satisfied as much as the heart. Thus Cloten's destiny has to be discovered, which brings a reversal of Guiderius's own fate until Belarius steps forward at last to confess his own peculiar treason. Two dead princes are revived and returned to their courtly destiny, freeing their newly discovered sister from the burden of duty that was hers. She can now live happily with her not-so-aristocratic husband, who nobly forgives his foe and sets an example for the king: "We'll learn our freeness of a son-in-law. / Pardon's the word to all" (V iv 422–23).

There might be the end, except that the international situation has not been settled yet and Posthumus's dream remains a riddle. The soothsayer Philharmonus (an apt musical name) is called for to untangle the latter, which leads happy Cymbeline to turn chaos and war into harmony and peace with his Roman enemy. Very diplomatically Shakespeare grants victory to the Britons and their tribute to the Romans. Whether it was a message to Prince Henry, or to his father King James is a matter of conjecture. The message, however, was not heard and reality happened to be more tragic than the play after all, since the brilliant young Prince died at an early age without fulfilling his promise.

THE PERTINENCE OF GIULIO ROMANO

Mentioned in Act V, scene ii of *The Winter's Tale* by an anonymous gentleman, the Italian artist has long aroused disenchanted or ironical remarks from literary critics who generally interpreted the occurrence as one more evidence of Shakespeare's ignorance. Does he not turn Giulio Romano into a sculptor when everyone knows that he was a painter and Raphael's favorite disciple?

This is obviously forgetting that Hermione's statue, which, we are told, has required "many years in doing ... by that rare Italian master Giulio Romano" (Vii 94–95), is given different names in the play. "The queen's picture" or "her dead likeness" creates a verbal ambiguity which would not have shocked Vasari, who calls Giulio Romano a sculptor, a painter, and an architect.[19] The artist's epitaph might have been enough to inspire Shakespeare, who may well have read Vasari: "Jupiter saw the painted and sculpted bodies / That they breathed and the houses of mortals vying with the heavens / owing to the talent of Giulio Romano: he felt a great wrath and after summoning the Counsel of the Gods, took him away from

---

[19] Giorgio Vasari, *Les vies des meilleurs peintres, sculpteurs et architectes* (Arles: Actes Sud, 2005), 2:189–202.

this world" (my translation).[20] In the second edition of Vasari's *Lives*, the epitaph turns the artist and his three arts into one entity. Calling him a sculptor was by no means surprising at the time and reveals on the contrary Shakespeare's perfect understanding of Giulio Romano's protean character.

Could the greatest English dramatist be ignorant of the man, whom Vasari depicts as "the greatest artist in Italy"? Since it is very unlikely that at this stage of his life Shakespeare did not know what he was doing, it is much more reasonable to think that if he chose to mention this particular artist, rather than Michelangelo or Raphael, in the scene preparing for the final suspense, he had a very clear purpose in mind and probably expected part of his audience to understand him.

The disconcerting manner of the last plays with their mixture of mythological and real characters, the contrast between genres and tones, the use of suspense and emotional devices drawing the spectator more directly into the action, seem directly inspired by *la maniera*.[21] The characters' wonder and amazement excite the spectator's imagination and his desire for more, and the metamorphoses, recreating life in intensely dramatic moments, where the creative power of words conjoins with sudden revelation, lead to a regenerating vision of reality, presenting a perfect interpretation of *poiēsis*.[22]

In *The Winter's Tale*, Shakespeare, at the top of his form, casually breaks the classical rules of structures and genres, which aroused passionate debates around Guarini's *Il Pastor Fido* at the time. He openly questions the contemporary definitions of tragicomedy, never tries to blend or soften in any way the contradictory elements of his play, which is "conspicuously ill-made" according to critic Rosalie L. Colie.[23] It seems probable therefore that his discreet but enlightening reference to the Italian artist is the signature of a style, an indirect, almost anamorphic way for the poet to reveal his strategy, *his manner*. However, if *The Winter's Tale* may be regarded as perhaps its most successful instance, we now know that this manner is

---

[20] "*Jupiter voyait les corps peints et sculptés / respirer et les édifices des mortels égaler le Ciel / grâce au talent de Jules Romain: il se mit en colère / et après avoir convoqué le Conseil des Dieux / l'a enlevé d'ici-bas...*" (202). "*[V]idebat Juppiter corpora sculpta pictaque / spirare, et aedes mortalium aequarier coelo / Julli virtute Romani: tunc iratus / concilio divorum omnium vocato / illum e terris sustulit; quod pati nequiret / vinci aut aequari ab homine terrigena.*" Ibid., 202.

[21] *La Maniera*, or stylish style, has been used to define the production of Vasari's generation and his followers in the 1550s since Shearman's outstanding work on Mannerism.

[22] *Poiēsis* (Ancient Greek: ποίησις) is etymologically derived from the ancient term ποιέω, which means "to make." This word, the root of our modern "poetry," was first a verb, an action that transforms and continues the world. Neither technical production nor creation in the romantic sense, *poiëtic* work reconciles thought with matter and time.

[23] Rosalie L. Colie, *Shakespeare's Living Art* (Princeton, NJ: Princeton University Press, 1974), 266.

far from new for Shakespeare, who has been patiently striving to bring together all the means of art in order to present life's metamorphoses. There are to be found here many elements that were dispersed throughout his plays before. Storms had long been for him sources of disasters and metamorphoses, and mysterious and unexpected returns from the dead are recurrent — suffice it to mention Helen in *All's Well*, Hero in *Much Ado About Nothing*, Claudio in *Measure for Measure*, and of course, Imogen in *Cymbeline*. The mastery of mannerism was already Shakespeare's own when he conceived *Cymbeline* and *Pericles, Prince of Tyre* and his reflections on his own art led him to find the means of improving and formalizing his practice through the inspiration of Giulio Romano.

Needless to say that the success of masques in England at the beginning of the seventeenth century, together with the progress of scenography thanks to Inigo Jones's theater machines, provided a fruitful ground for the development of this new style. Shakespeare was never one to praise the masque, whose rich decorum generally belied its frivolous content, but he obviously never hesitated to make his own its scenic advantages. The success met by the performances of *Pericles, Prince of Tyre* at the time cannot be separated from the technical prowess inherited from the delightful entertainments and waterworks of the Italian courts of Mantua, Ferrara, and Florence. The interest of the production, which is very difficult to imagine let alone recreate nowadays, lay no doubt in the amazing diversity, the sequel of unbelievable discoveries and developments, the staging of jousts, dance, and music, alternating with scenes of shipwreck, and the cocky humor of the sailors and the bawds juxtaposed with the solemn, almost other-worldly, wisdom of the narrator and of the physician. It corresponded perfectly to the purpose of mannerist scenography, which was primarily to meet the difficult challenge that ever-changing reality sets against the stasis of mimetic fiction. It had given birth to the transformable stage, which simulated the passage of time, the diversity of places and seasons, all aiming at a more truthful representation of life. Linked to this purpose was the desire to stimulate the emotional involvement of the spectator.[24]

Surely, Shakespeare must already have had the Italian artist in mind, when he gave these words to Simonides: "In framing artists art hath thus decreed, / To make some good, but others to exceed" (II iii 14–15, Sc. 7). This bow to art and to the happy few like himself whose art exceeds others, which intervenes between a tournament scene and the niceties of a banquet, emphasizes the virtuosity of the creator and confirms the mannerist tone of the play. The theater, ever the privileged meeting ground of the

---

[24] Antonio Pinelli, *La Belle Manière*, trans. Beatrice Arnal (Paris: Le livre de Poche, 1996), 235.

literary and the visual, was the testing place *par excellence* for the theme that founds all the critical theories of the Renaissance: *ut pictura poesis* ("As painting is, so is poetry"). But which imitates which? Those who have heard Enobarbus's description of the sumptuous tableau of Cleopatra on her barge, cannot doubt the ability of the poet to paint reality with words. In the last plays, however, it seems that the debate is no longer to know which of painting or poetry comes first, but to use all the means of art to imitate life. And the playwright was obviously fascinated by Giulio Romano's talent and excellence at precisely this. It is not possible to doubt the pertinence of his choice.

The Italian artist was better known at the time than now, if only for the licentiousness of some of his engravings.[25] His irreverence could not be shocking to the poet, who loved Ovid and found in Giulio's scenes a similar freedom of the mind and a similar ability to recreate life from artifice. And the life created by Giulio Romano was full of strangeness and wonders. At Palazzo Te, in Mantua, nature's creation is repeatedly put side by side with the work of art, the rugged and shapeless juxtaposed to severe classical forms, rough stone to stucco, in a purposely unfinished effect which unsettles the observer and forces him to perfect mentally the harmony of the whole. Gombrich compared the effect produced by Giulio Romano's work, not to painting, but to music, whose specificity, he said, was to create imaginary formal universes destined to be modified in order to produce powerful expressive effects.[26]

As noted previously, the structure of Shakespeare's plays often suggests music and the plot of *Pericles, Prince of Tyre* is built like the polyphony of a madrigal. More generally, when tragedy is suddenly altered by a comic discourse offering another perspective on the event, we have a tonal modulation wholly similar to the architectural contrasts of the Roman artist.

The creation of such expressive tension is undoubtedly one that defines Shakespeare's genius and it was probably more easily adapted to the theater than to stonework. It is the reason why it is in the murals which decorate the rooms of Palazzo Te that Romano's language becomes more openly theatrical. There we have painted architectures superimposed on the walls, refined illusionist paintings opening imaginary windows onto luxurious nature. In the Giants' Room, the Gods of Olympus are seen watching from their boxes in a heavenly dress circle the destruction of the Giant race and of the astonished visitor, who fears for his life in the general chaos. In the

---

[25] Interestingly, the engraver signed his work in Latin, *sculpsit*, as opposed to *pinxit* for the painter.

[26] Ernst Gombrich, "Le Palais du Te: 'le bel éclectisme,'" *Les Annales de l'Art de Franco Maria Ricci* (Milan: Editions Franco Maria Ricci, 2014), 5.3:177.

Horses Room, statues of Jupiter, Juno, and Vulcan seem alive in their niches, while four life-sized horses stand on the cornice surrounding the room, before bucolic landscapes with no pretense of blending in with them, as if they belonged to a world halfway between the real life of the palazzo and the murals on which they appear in relief. Now the sculptures, the niches, and the horses are all in *trompe-l'œil* and Giulio Romano manages to create this double and rather unsettling metamorphosis: he turns painting into sculpture and the latter in turn comes alive.

In this theatrical exuberance, his art of *trompe-l'œil* and illusion, his ability to transgress the rules of classicism to give his characters a dynamism, a breath of life, Giulio Romano reveals a sensitivity which is very close to that of the English poet. It would have been surprising, on the contrary, if Shakespeare had not found inspiration in it. Giulio Romano brought the idea of art as a mirror of life to its climax; it was also the basic philosophy of the theater developed by Shakespeare throughout his life as a dramatist.

In *Pericles, Prince of Tyre*, instability and fluidity appear to be the essence of the plot, supervised by Time, the master of change. The eponymous hero goes from one place to the next, rocked by the waves. The storm which, until now in Shakespeare's plays, preceded the action and generally gave birth to confusion as to names and origins, which the plot attempted to solve, now becomes a metaphor of life and fate. Gower, who could well be some kind of ancient sculpture in *trompe-l'œil*, is the witness and the stage manager. He provides an archaic frame to the action which, in this case, does not depend on the will of the hero. Gower is a kind of ghost with almost divine powers since he is the narrator of a centuries-old story, which he freely stages whenever he wants to appeal to the audience's understanding and judgment, or when he needs to justify his assertions. "What now ensues, to th' judgment of your eye / I give, my cause who best can justify" (I i 41–42, Sc. 1).

For the spectator, the effect is that of a surprising succession of murals, which would go well in Palazzo Te, and which foreshadows the visit that Leontes and his retinue make to Paulina's gallery before being allowed to see the Queen's statue in *The Winter's Tale*. That the characters of the play should go through this museum and be confronted with "many singularities" before reaching Giulio Romano's masterpiece, is by no means a meaningless and banal progress. Following the example of Giulio Romano, Shakespeare seems to be exploring the different manners to create images, as if he were testing the limits of his own art in producing illusion.

The genius of *Pericles, Prince of Tyre* lies partly in the constant shift from narrative to representation, in Gower's ability to turn the poem into performance, including the pantomimes to which he gives his own voice.

Because images, as beautiful as they may be, can be harmful if one does not know how to interpret them, appearances must be deciphered. Language clarifies representation, just as the motto gives its meaning to the coat of arms. That Pericles's chosen shield — "A withered branch that's only green at top," (II ii 47, Sc. 6) — should be so close to Lorenzo de Medici's one, the *Broncone,* featuring a withered laurel branch with green leaves at the top, is probably no accident. Nor is the strange, almost hieratic, scene of presentation of the shields with their many devices. Palazzo Te, as a matter of fact, has a room devoted to Coats of Arms. This was part of the intricacies of meaning appreciated at the time. The analogy could even be pushed further and Pericles's chosen motto could signify the content of the last plays, where the withered heart of a father is given life again by the return of a beloved child whose marriage will ensure his inheritance.

The plot of *Pericles, Prince of Tyre* is based on the paradoxical link between truth and fancy. In Antiochus, Prince Pericles is faced with a painful experience, a theatrical moment which probably already contains the seeds of the idea of the statue, which is the climax of *The Winter's Tale.* It is the dazzling image of a woman who arouses wonder around her, yet she is kept distant and unreachable by her father's will. Pericles wants her for his wife. It is actually the only passage in the play where the prince uses his free will. Unfortunately, Antiochus's daughter is not only untouchable, she is like a statue, whose perfect and sophisticated beauty does not show any trace of true emotion:

> Her face the book of praises, where is read
> Nothing but curious pleasures, as from thence
> Sorrow were ever razed and testy wrath
> Could never be her mild companion. (I i 58–61, Sc. 1)

With a smooth face that has known neither sorrow, nor anger, a mask deceiving the fervent suitor, she is the opposite of Hermione, whose statue, far from affectation, reveals her wrinkles as the signs of the passage of time and the evidence of her sorrow. Antiochus's daughter has no name and no real part in the play. She is merely an idealized artistic representation for which men give up their lives, an emblem to be deciphered, and perhaps a style to be rejected. Pericles solves the riddle and runs away. But he now possesses a dangerous truth whose consequences he anticipates by putting out to sea.

The discovery of the deception and its evil turns him into a melancholy character who doubts all things and is regularly taken in by appearances; like the Apostle Thomas, he needs to touch in order to believe. The jewels found in Thaisa's casket are the only evidence of his wife's identity that he knows; he does not want to recognize her even when Cerimon identifies her for him (V iii 38–39, Sc. 22). Unfortunately, the solid marble of the monument that Dionyza shows him also convinces him of his daughter's death. It is as if minerality, safe from the metamorphoses of time, were a pledge of truth for Pericles, who has become the ball used by waters and winds to play in their tennis court (II i 93–96, Sc. 5). The instability of life hardens his conscience and gradually gives him the rigidity of a corpse. He swears "Never to wash his face, nor cut his hairs" (IV v 28, Sc. 18). "He bears / A tempest which his mortal vessel tears, / And yet he rides it out" (IV v 30–31, Sc. 18). It is as if Pericles had gradually transformed himself into stone.

When Marina is introduced to him, Pericles, consumed with grief, sees her first as the statue of *Patience* "gazing on kings' graves and smiling / Extremity out of act" (V i 127–29, Sc. 21). The debate on art and nature, and the necessity of faith, which become the center of *The Winter's Tale*, is only glanced at here. Shakespeare is gathering the elements of a puzzle which he will assemble later. In *Pericles, Prince of Tyre*, the emphasis is on the importance of speech and images and their respective ability to prove and persuade. For instance, the wonder provoked in *Pericles, Prince of Tyre* by the unexpected return of the lost beloved is the consequence of a long dialectical process engendered by the stubborn doubt of the hero, who has to be convinced first. Marina gradually succeeds in moving him with the story of her life, pursuing her relentless effort until her father suddenly bursts out, "O, come hither / Thou that beget'st him that did thee beget" (V i 183–84, Sc. 21). In this mirror-like effect, Pericles projects upon his daughter his own metamorphosis: the stone man is now being revived.

Similarly, and with what generosity of details, Hermione comes back to life after the true metamorphosis undergone by Leontes during his sixteen years' repentance. It is as if *The Winter's Tale* corrected and completed the attempt sketched in *Pericles, Prince of Tyre*. The structure of the play becomes clearer, better shaped, and the emphasis is put on the intensity of the revelation, which is worn out by repetition in *Pericles, Prince of Tyre*. Moreover, in *Pericles, Prince of Tyre*, the hero is the only character who is mistaken in the eyes of the spectator, who is a witness and a judge. The distance thus created can even produce comic reactions in the audience, who keep shifting from stupefaction to laughter.

What is seen in *Pericles, Prince of Tyre* as a whim of time, is later organized toward an aim that nobody discovers until the last act. Time has become Providence, and the spectator, who is kept ignorant of the secrets of the plot, undergoes the effect of the final revelation with the same emotional force as all the characters, thus experiencing a masterful *trompe-l'oeil* that would have baffled Giulio Romano himself.

The statue appears at the climax of the debate on art and nature launched earlier, not without irony. The pastoral is a piece of the sort of illusionism Shakespeare enjoys, allowing him to demonstrate his mannerist virtuosity. It is a verbal joust between a king who knows he is disguised and a princess who does not, a debate in which nothing is quite what it seems, with characters defending theories which do not fit the social reality they are supposed to represent. Whereas, in *The Winter's Tale*, Perdita refuses the "streaked gillyvors" as nature's bastards and praises unmitigated nature, Polixenes skillfully upholds the art of grafting:

> You see, sweet maid, we marry
> A gentler scion to the wildest stock,
> And make conceive a bark of baser kind
> By bud of nobler race. This is an art
> Which does mend nature — change it rather — but
> The art itself is nature. (IV iv 92–97)

Can anyone conceive of a more perfect definition of Shakespeare's theater? Is not the statue scene the exact translation of these lines in scenic terms? The fact that Polixenes tells a truth which he is about to deny when his own life and lineage are concerned does not mean it is false. Shakespeare has for a long time by indirections found directions out. An essential truth is here revealed, together with the contradiction that lies at the heart of most men, who often uphold ideas they do not put into practice. Behind the exuberance of the feast, with its dances and songs, there lies the ghost of death brandished by Polixenes as he is suddenly carried away by passion. In the grip of passionate anger, his judgment collapses, turning the happy comedy into tragedy. Polixenes' deeds do not follow his words and his wisdom is as illusory as the beauty of Antiochus's daughter. Pastoral nature alone is obviously not sufficient to regenerate human beings. A higher art partaking of nature itself is necessary to mend men and reach a truth which alone will make possible and credible the final reconciliation. It is as if Shakespeare tried to demonstrate how drama could reach the same goals, and even go beyond painting and literature in its imitation of reality. With Hermione's resurrection, drama does not merely reflect nature but tries to recreate it. We have gone from mimesis to *trompe-l'oeil*, from imitation to simulation.

The statue's final metamorphosis is produced with such care that Shakespeare's major concern cannot be doubted. In the scene where Giulio Romano is mentioned, everything is geared toward arousing desire and expectation and building up suspense. The reunion scene is described like a painting by a flabbergasted witness who lacks the words to tell what he has seen: "I make a broken delivery of the business" (V ii 9). The event is perceived at a distance through the emotional response of the characters. Shakespeare, long before Barthes, knew that the attempt to describe beauty was a tautological exercise and there was more eroticism and desire in indirect suggestion, in emphasizing the impossibility to describe than in taking the risk of a hyperbolic and incredible account. He appeals, as he always has, to the imagination of the audience on whom he pours a stream of words expressing amazement—"amazedness," "note of admiration," "a notable passion of wonder," and "I never heard of such another encounter, which lames report to follow it, and undoes description to do it" (V ii 55–57).

The scene itself is a kind of anamorphosis, in which language triggers emotions as powerfully as the reported passion of the actors. The oxymoron seems to be the only figure of style likely to render the paradoxical extremity of passion that is expressed in gesture language and dumb speech according to the witnesses. Shakespeare is not content to suggest wonder, he draws attention to the physical presence of the actors on the stage, to the double language, poetical and physical, of the stage, which enables him to go beyond the limits of both poetry and painting:

> There was casting up of eyes, holding up of hands, with countenance of such distraction that they were to be known by garment, not by favour. (V ii 46–49)

As often, it seems that Shakespeare is visualizing a painting. Which one? What revelation? What ecstasy? Pontormo comes to mind, or else Tintoretto, whose dramatic staging could not have left Shakespeare indifferent.

"Gentlemen" follow one another, each emphasizing the feeling of stupor in the presence of the improbable scene. There is a great confusion of senses, which recalls Bottom's when he attempts to tell his dream in *A Midsummer Night's Dream*. The Paulinian reference is more than ever appropriate in a play which has grace at its center, first as Hermione's special spiritual gift, as well as her mannerist elegance called *sprezzatura* by Castiglione. For the time being, one sees what one hears, one hears what one sees, but the scene remains inexpressible and the conclusion of this long description of the reunion is that it cannot be spoken.

There is a strange and curious irony in this telling what cannot be told and in stirring up the spectator's frustration through the hollow performance of a scene which he can only apprehend with his mind's eye. The conclusion of the story introduces with a metaphor the upcoming metamorphosis: "Who was most marble there changed color" (V ii 88), together with the statue and its remarkable creator.

After the emotional chaos of this scene (which it is of course preferable not to cut in the performances of the play), we are told that the characters have visited Paulina's art gallery, where they have seen many "singularities." Has anyone ever questioned this itinerary, which takes the characters from a cabinet of curiosities to a sculpture ascribed to Giulio Romano immediately after the naturalistic claims of the pastoral scene? The truth is that, contrary to many conventional ideas, nature alone is not sufficient to regenerate men.[27] A second modulation is necessary for art to improve nature and reach the superior reality which alone will make the final reconciliation possible and credible: the narrow definitions of tragedy and comedy must be overcome and transcended. The statue therefore provides the climax of the debate on art and nature begun earlier in the pastoral. It brings together the characters of the tragedy and of the comedy thanks to the charm of an unexpected apparition. Act five, scene three is built around *trompe-l'oeil*, developing the idea that art is a copy of life so accurate that Leontes, amazed at the likeness between the statue and the queen, believes she is breathing. Her veins and wrinkles, which surprise him at first, since they do not intimate the youth he was expecting, now offer such verisimilitude that Leontes perceives her breath and wants to kiss her. "What fine chisel / Could ever yet cut breath?" (V iii 78–79), he asks. No doubt the chisel of an artist so rare that even his nature is being questioned: "What was he that did make it?" (V iii 63) What? rather than Who? What is the artist made of, who can so perfectly mystify the eyes and create the appearance of life with a mere chisel?

The irony is, of course, that Shakespeare is here speaking of himself, of this art whose magic sometimes led him to believe, like Prospero, that he possessed divine powers. Wasn't it what was already suggested in Simonides's words? Isn't Shakespeare the artist who can exceed art, exceeding Giulio Romano himself in as much as his creation is superior to art and partakes of nature herself? "Be stone no more," commands Paulina, and the metaphor turns into a true metamorphosis. It is not art imitating life but suddenly life deceiving life itself. Esthetically, Hermione's tears are the marks of a style divorced from classicism, but they are also the symbols of art's lack, its powerlessness to *be* reality. Suddenly the rigid distinction which lies at the heart of the debate between art and nature is blurred and loses its relevance. Art is not what it seems to be in this play, since it is revealed to be nature — however, nature needs a lot of art in order to

---

[27] "Nature regenerates, even out of the slime of Nilus's mud or the long pastime of a winter's tale." Barbara J. Bono, *Literary Transvaluation* (Berkeley: University of California Press, 1984), 149.

mock art so well — especially if, as we can imagine, the boy actor playing Hermione is still just a "squeaking" boy.

Shall we conclude that all this is illusion and that Shakespeare's magic ends up in a powerless trick? I do not think so.

Shakespeare's visible play with genres and conventions is not merely a way to reveal his ingenuity. Manner for him is never without content. The statue's wrinkles, the suffering they indicate, give a density to the character that no statue possesses. In this masterful scene, it is life which works at the metamorphosis which, beyond art, leads to regeneration. Time is the vehicle of conversion; it is the force that brings about truth. It is the effective power, the dimension that visual and plastic arts can never possess. In the play, Time is the medium of metamorphosis and the metaphor which link gods and men, eternity and mutability, the symbol of life's course at the heart of creative nature:

> We are the craftsmen of our lives, we are the artists even whenever we choose, we keep molding from the matter that is given us by the past and the present, our heritage and circumstances, a unique figure: new, original, unpredictable, like the shape given by the sculptor to clay. (my translation)[28]

This quotation is particularly meaningful here: man is always absolutely free to mold time. Shakespeare's characters are never the helpless victims of a superior fate. Shakespeare did not believe in predestination. *The Winter's Tale* provides an answer to Pericles's ordeal. Hermione's resurrection cannot happen outside Time, her statue is after all *"th' argument of time"*[29] without which no metamorphosis exists. The appearance of Time as a character is paramount to the understanding of what happens next and no meaningful staging of the play can pass over Time too quickly. To use Bergson's image once again, the statue, which is suddenly revived, is the metaphor of the life which it took sixteen years for Leontes to mold again.

The king's morbid imagination had petrified Hermione, just as Pericles's disillusion aroused a vision of his statue-like daughter. Leontes's growing revival, his desire for redemption and his fancy awakened by Perdita, whose beauty calls her mother's image to mind, act like powerful revivers of inert nature. Time is suspended as dramatic action vanishes to leave

---

[28] Henri Bergson, "le possible et le réel," *La pensée et le mouvant* (Paris: PUF, 1969), 102. "Artisans de notre vie, artistes même quand nous le voulons, nous travaillons continuellement à pétrir avec la matière qui nous est fournie par le passé et le présent, par l'hérédité et les circonstances, une figure unique, neuve, originale, imprévisible comme la forme donnée par le sculpteur à la terre glaise."

[29] IV i 29 (my italics).

room for a minute observation of details: a miracle is being performed. Just as Lear bends over Cordelia's lips with a mirror to capture her breath, Leontes and his retinue are hanging on Hermione's lips, watching for the least perceptible movement, a breath, the tiny pulsing of a vein:

> See, my lord,
> Would you not deem it breathed, and that those veins
> Did verily bear blood? (V ii 63–65)

The sensuousness of this slow motion focuses the spectator's attention, who would not understand what's happening otherwise, and gives everyone, on stage and in the audience, time to become conscious of this passage between art and nature, between dream and reality, death and life. All senses are aroused in this magical moment enhanced by music. But to come back to Paulina, whose zeal seems to be Paul's own, it is not enough. She requires the spectators' faith — "It is required / You do awake your faith" (V iii 94–95) — since senses are deceivers, as Leontes's jealous crisis amply proved in the first part of the play, and faith alone, which is always born of judgment in the play, can impart all its meaning to this dramatic moment. Throughout the scene, the spectator, ignorant of Paulina's purpose, reacts with as much feeling and wonder as the characters. This suspension of disbelief is real and working. The moment you believe, things come true, and for the believer, there is indeed resurrection, were it for a fraction of time. It is easy to understand why this play was for so long put aside and misunderstood. A skeptical, materialistic audience could only see incoherent madness in it.

The masterful change worked by Shakespeare between *Pericles, Prince of Tyre* and *The Winter's Tale* is visible here. He substituted the Apostle Paul for the goddess Diana in Ephesus, insisted on the necessity of a faith, which Pericles obviously does not possess, and incorporated the narrative into the dramatic action, thus creating a *mise en abyme* of wonder. He brought together in the climax of the last act all the revelations, justified by Leontes's sixteen years' repentance. For his redemption is indeed a major element in the metamorphosis at work. We can all too easily understand Pericles's bitterness. He has been so ill-treated by fate that the recovery of his wife and daughter, even though moving, looks more like a whim of fortune than a necessary catharsis.

There is a magic of art which it shares with the sacred. When we are speaking of the theater, whose tools are flesh and bone, it is easier to measure the importance of the reflection at work in *The Winter's Tale*. Man needs the powers of art and nature in order to master his fears and his brutal force, to become wholly conscious of "un au-delà présent," says

Malraux,[30] a living afterworld which is right now. If Shakespeare mocks the genres and conventions of art, it is to assert the necessary interdependence of art and nature to create a higher, more spiritual reality.

It seems evident that in *The Winter's Tale*, Shakespeare reveals more than his virtuosity as a dramatist. He powerfully asserts his mastery of his art as well as his philosophy, as is confirmed by the following play, *The Tempest*, in which he goes on with questioning the respective value of art and nature and the meaning of a life which he felt was slowly taking leave of him. It is clear that he knew the artistic debates of his time, that he had a perfect mastery of the tools of critical judgment and would probably have enjoyed convincing his audience of the superiority of the theater over other arts in its ability to recreate life and lead its audiences to higher levels of spirituality. It is equally clear that the manner of his plays, which shares a lot of the attributes of *la Maniera*, is never superficial. It always goes together with a deep meditation on the matter which we call life. Concurrently, the author was always deeply conscious of the ephemerality of his art which was a paradox in itself. How could he ever expect to immortalize a thought, a creation, which had life's evanescence at its very center? The revelation which closes *The Winter's Tale*, Hermione's resurrection, possibly represents in the space of a moment, the quintessence of Shakespeare's art and spirituality.

THE TEMPEST: SHAKESPEARE'S FIREWORKS

Technically, *The Tempest* is Shakespeare's fireworks, the most daring *mise en abyme* of Shakespeare's art as a magician and entertainer. It's a kind of challenge too, as if he was on a quest to prove that he was the greatest and could really do anything he wanted. It is an example of mannerist drama, concentrating the expressive tensions, usually found in the design of the plays, within the main character's personality and in the moral questioning that dogs him throughout the play.

For twenty years Shakespeare has been questioning the legitimacy of kings and exploring the nature of authority, for twenty years he has been advocating patience and forgiveness as the only acceptable wisdom, exposing the arrogance of tyrants and the utter misery of bloody internecine war. In the last plays, he expands the time of his plots over years and generations, aware that the consequences of the decision of Henry VIII and England's own division would not be resolved in his lifetime. *The Tempest* pursues the guiding line of the tragicomedies featuring the inner debate of the exile as Providence gives him the opportunity to

---

[30] André Malraux, *Le Surnaturel* (Paris: Gallimard, 1977), 7.

revenge himself at last. For *The Tempest* is the story of a revenge which, as Prospero painstakingly organizes it, gradually loses shape and reason. The pardon that was a sudden decision in *Cymbeline* is here part of a line of reasoning which gradually leads Prospero to an inescapable truth: he cannot be the man he thinks he is — the virtuous man his beloved daughter admires — if he cannot subdue his own nature and conquer the temptation of vengeance.

Prospero has, like so many Shakespearean characters, a bucketful of resentment. His power has been usurped, he has been exiled twelve years, living in a cave in the wilderness like Belarius, deprived of almost everything except his books and his baby daughter, for whom he has been the most careful of schoolmasters. The play is therefore also part of the education of Miranda, whom Prospero tries to teach and impress with the most extravagant performances, such as the formidable storm that opens the play and must have left the audience dumbfounded.

They saw a tragedy occurring before their eyes, but perhaps first of all a drastic questioning of hierarchy. The sea, better than the forest, has the virtue of a leveler. Its storms offer the most potent metaphors to the idea of Providence, and to the man who escapes drowning, life does truly appear like a rebirth and a miracle.

On board, the Shipmaster is all powerful and the usual hierarchy does not apply: "What cares these roarers for the name of king?" asks the Boatswain, openly questioning the king's authority in such circumstances. The king is just a name, and under the name is a man like others — weak, sinful, powerless — a reality old Gonzalo brutally gets in his face like a wave as he is sharply rebuked by the Boatswain:

> You are a councillor; if you can command these elements to silence and work peace of the present, we will not hand a rope more. Use your authority. If you cannot, give thanks you have lived so long and make yourself ready in your cabin for the mischance of the hour, if it so hap. (I i 20–25)

Gonzalo's philosophy is unruffled and his reaction wittily points at the playwright's own daring: such breach of protocol, such saucy retort from a simple sailor to a king's counsellor, surely warranted hanging. Repeatedly, obliquely, Shakespeare reveals the superior courage and usefulness of simple men to the smooth running of the kingdom. The Shipmaster and the Boatswain are masters on board and the powerless nobility cuts a pitiful figure. But the elements are strongest and they are all about to drown. The scene ends in chaos and confusion. The dramatic effect must have been amazingly terrifying. This is the grand fortissimo opening of a tragedy whose beginning looks like an end. But water is a great purifier and out of the flood may rise a new order.

After this opening full of sound and fury, the tempo suddenly slows down into a sotto voce duet, as a father soothes his daughter's anguish. Prospero comforts her saying there is no harm done, strangely paraphrasing Paul's words to the passengers of the ship that takes him a prisoner to Rome and is shipwrecked on the coast of Malta "Not so much perdition as an hair" (see Acts 27:34 and Lk 21:18).

Thus, the tragedy was merely a show, the representation of itself, the play enacting its own meaning and power (as often in Shakespeare) in a *mise en abyme* which multiplies biblical echoes:

> Had I been any god of power, I would
> Have sunk the sea within the earth, or ere
> It should the good ship so have swallowed and
> The fraughting souls within her. (I ii 10–13)

Miranda's visionary prayer enlarges Prospero's stature to that of a divinity, whose power recalls those strange lines from the Book of Revelation: "and the earth opened her mouth, and swallowed up the flood which the dragon cast out of his mouth" (Rev 12:16). And the vision of "amazement" turns out to be true since Prospero reveals himself as the creator-stage-manager of this great show, with the ability to arouse storms and to alleviate them at will just for his daughter's sake, or so he says. For behind the appearances lies a troubled story of betrayal and exile which Prospero is at last impelled to unveil to his daughter. This peaceful interval provides the occasion for him to tell a tale many times begun and interrupted, the story of their arrival on this island. Suddenly turning into a kind of psychologist, Prospero probes Miranda's memory in order to give her back her identity and prepare her for her future. However, as the story unfolds, Prospero loses the equanimity and assurance that were his and grows more and more nervous and insistent, his speech constantly broken by expletives and worried calls to Miranda to be heedful and pay more attention. The foul play that he reveals to her has obviously not been rectified and the convoluted story reveals Prospero's not-altogether-clear conscience. He paints his love of liberal arts and his delight in secret studies as an unparalleled talent, which nonetheless kept him a stranger to his state. Confessing to his beloved daughter that, like a hermit, he neglected "worldly ends," thus giving free rein to his brother Antonio's love of power, is admittedly difficult, especially telling her how he failed her, how they were both expelled and sent out at sea in "a rotten carcass of a butt, not rigged, / Nor tackle, sail, nor mast" (I ii 146–47).

It is interesting to note that this was the exact destiny of Rudolf II of the House of Hapsburg in the spring of 1611, when, "tired of his brother's inactivity and culpable neglect of the realm," Rudolf's brother Matthias "marched on Prague where he was greeted in the old city as future King of Bohemia."[31] Rudolf II was renowned for his learning, vital interest in the arts, visual as well as occult, and his religious tolerance. But this of course could be variably interpreted:

> His Majesty is interested only in wizards, alchemists, kabbalists and the like, sparing no expense to find all kinds of treasures, learn secrets and use scandalous ways of harming his enemies. He also has a whole library of magic books. He studies all the time to eliminate God completely so that he may in future serve a different master.[32]

It is likely that he was in Shakespeare's mind when he created Prospero, as he seems to have been for several years already. The paradox is that the all-powerful magus (in his daughter's eyes), therefore, happens to be an irresponsible and deposed duke, whom his own daughter preserved, while divine providence landed them on an island already inhabited by two most contrasted characters: Ariel and Caliban, whom he subordinated to his will, a show of authority which he surely should have tried earlier on Antonio. What Shakespeare is telling us is that whatever you do, you can never make a completely fresh start. Memory, conscience, and other people's desire will always interfere with your plans. Life is a constant negotiation with oneself and others.

Miranda's questions, being encouraged, now threaten to embarrass her father, who has not worked his whole plot out yet. He is obviously improvising the action on the spur of the moment and puts Miranda to sleep in order to consult with Ariel concerning the situation. The long narrative scene is not at an end, as Prospero proceeds to remind protesting Ariel what he, Ariel, has been and whence he comes, how grateful he should be to Prospero after the witch Sycorax confined him a dozen years "into a cloven pine" for refusing to obey her. The irony, of course, lies in Prospero's own similar threat:

> If thou more murmur'st, I will rend an oak,
> And peg thee in his knotty entrails till
> Thou hast howled away twelve winters. (I ii 294–96)

---

[31] David Snelling, "Prospero on the Coast of Bohemia," in *Prospero. Rivista di Letterature Straniere, Comparatistica e Studi Culturali*, I (1994), 14. https://www.openstarts.units.it/entities/publication/16d8c447-62f4-48e8-8347-5d56af674aa3/details.

[32] R. J. W. Evans, *Rudolph II and His World*, 196. Proposition of the Archdukes in Vienna (1606).

He introduced himself as the witch Sycorax's antithesis, yet he speaks and acts like her, has been exiled like her, and will eventually acknowledge her "litter" as his own. The way he manipulates Ariel as well as his own daughter may accordingly seem a little disquieting. The idea that Prospero should represent white magic, whereas Sycorax dealt in black magic, would surely not have been a sufficient excuse to a man like Shakespeare, who had always taken care to avoid extremes and categories. He is more subtle than that. He is more likely to show us a man who, given certain circumstances, can actually become the reverse of what he pretends to be. Nobody is perfect, not even Prospero. Miranda being awakened, Prospero takes her for a visit to the other inhabitant of the island, Sycorax's son Caliban. Prospero uses him for menial tasks and cannot spare him in spite of the fact that Miranda resents him for being impervious to her kindness and instruction. Worse, he is more attracted to her body than to her mind. But wasn't it once again Prospero's responsibility for ignoring the ways of nature and lodging this male stranger with his own daughter?

After Ariel's appeal for liberty, it is now Caliban's turn to voice his protests and accuse Prospero of stealing his island and his freedom.[33] Prospero's life is by no means a peaceful one and this man who has acquired great powers seems to spend his time answering claims and warding off plots to undo him. If Prospero reflects, as has often been thought, Shakespeare's own psyche, it may hint at a reality hardly ever touched upon by critics, the fact that Shakespeare's job in those years had gradually been made difficult by rivals and other envious courtiers who probably desired nothing better than to get rid of him.[34] Prospero is not serene and for all his talents and protests, he does not seem to have found the detachment that wisdom requires. He is the last of Shakespeare's divided heroes, a character torn between virtue and vice, the temptation of retaliation or the will to pardon.

As for Miranda, she is immediately seduced by Ferdinand, ready to disobey her father, a fact of life that is always worrying for an affectionate father. Prospero, with his art and "spirits" that enable him to hold sway over all the people around him, suddenly finds himself facing an inescapable conclusion. He could at last revenge himself, but for this young couple, whose innocence he has to preserve and whose marriage seems the only conceivable way to restore peace. The creation of expressive tension has always been at the heart of Shakespeare's vision and here, once again, he

---

[33] Caliban has a serious claim and his linguistic criticism is sound. However, the argument of literacy would later be the seed of antislavery activism, which by the way seems to exculpate Prospero from any kind of racism. Prospero is still seeing the world in humanistic terms of improvement. Teaching Caliban would be step one on the ladder toward the spiritual world.

[34] See Asquith, chap. 15, "Silenced, 1610–1611," *Shadowplay*, 260–73.

manages to maintain the feeling of suspense throughout the play. Prospero's inner turmoil keeps the audience alert. He may take vengeance — and his threat to Ariel implies that he has the means to do so — or he may follow a quieter course for Miranda's sake. But until the very end, nobody, not even his dear spirit, knows how things may evolve. Anger is welling up in him, threatening to overwhelm his better self.

In the motley sample of humanity that suddenly reaches the island, we have a wide range of contrary reactions to destiny, from the most optimistic to the most dejected. They represent Prospero's enemies and Shakespeare's audience in a nutshell, the people he had set out to entertain and convince. Whereas there's no sign of abating in Gonzalo's faith in Providence, Alonzo even doubts Francisco's reassuring news concerning his son Ferdinand. Antonio and Sebastian display the arrogance and cynicism of two malcontents, who at no point reveal any empathy with their elders. Gonzalo's equanimity remains unruffled, yet he is quick to detect the lack of gentleness in his uncouth companions:

> My Lord Sebastian,
> The truth you speak doth lack some gentleness
> And time to speak it in. You rub the sore
> When you should bring the plaster. (II i 134–37)

Of all the characters, this old counselor is the kindest, but his idealism is mocked by the others, who believe there's neither goodness nor innocence in nature. His own utopia, an inverted mirror image of the world he knows, would strive to keep all creatures innocent and equal, though he would be ruling over them as their king. The paradox is not lost upon his detractors of course. Whether inspired by Thomas More or Montaigne, Gonzalo's commonwealth sounds a mere fantasy, which no man with a little knowledge of human nature would take seriously. The Golden Age, or any vision of Eden, where men would be naturally good and idle, like obedient children under the authority of a benevolent father, remained a literary projection of human desires, which Shakespeare obviously never really endorsed. For instance, Miranda, often performed as a very naïve, somewhat silly adolescent girl, is all too readily enthralled by the young man her father shows her. The fact that Prospero now has to invent a stratagem in order to keep them from getting to know each other too quickly is a piece of comedy reminding the audience of Friar Laurence trying to calm down Romeo and Juliet before their marriage rites.

More disturbing, however, are the plots immediately hatched by the survivors. Prospero has whispered orders to Ariel, whom we see, like Puck, manipulating the characters, discreetly putting them to sleep with music.

Antonio and Sebastian are now given a free hand to reveal themselves for what they truly are. They rush upon the occasion to contrive the death of Alonzo and his old counselor. But for Ariel's warning, the plot might have succeeded. The conspirators are caught in the act, yet manage to lie their way out of the situation. Good Gonzalo is not suspicious enough. Did Prospero hope that both malefactors would be apprehended by the king? If such was his desire, his plan misfired and none of the characters involved seems to be any wiser.

The farcical scene that follows provides an interesting mannerist relief while offering a rather cynical parody of the main plot. As Caliban, still grumbling and cursing his master, hides himself under his gabardine, Alonso's jester Trinculo takes him for a fish or some kind of monster, which, were he in England, would bring him ready money. Shakespeare is here mocking the contemporary fashion for monsters and marvels, which fascinated people to the detriment of more needy persons: "When they will not give a doit to relieve a lame beggar, they will lay out ten to see a dead Indian" (II ii 31–32), all the while winking at his audience, many of whom came primarily to see the monster Caliban! One remembers Shylock's despair at Jessica's readiness to sacrifice her mother's ring for a monkey, a subtle hint at the traditional rivalry of art and nature, which in mannerism were claimed to complement each other. The arrival of Alonso's drunken butler Stephano with a bottle of spirit shifts the argument from aesthetics to politics, unwittingly mocking Prospero's art (i.e., his spirit Ariel), as the butler uses wine like a spell on Caliban who is made to swear allegiance to him by kissing the bottle (i.e., "the book"). And while Caliban is poetically listing the wonders of the island to his new master, the jester is punctuating the scene with amazed expletives on this "very shallow," "weak," "credulous," "perfidious and drunken," "scurvy," "poor," "abominable" and most of all "ridiculous" monster for making "a wonder of a poor drunkard" (II ii 138–60). There is some Rabelaisian echo here[35] together with a wonderful grotesque tableau mimicking courtly protocol, as well as the colonists' way of cajoling Indians into accepting them. Shakespeare, who has been haunted all his life by the question of the legitimacy of power, here seems to debunk the question itself. Power is nothing here but a transient ability to charm, in love, in art, and in politics. Wonder is part of it, of course, and men seem likely to succumb to anything new and unexpected, even glittering garments on an invisible line. For all his art, Prospero knows that his power will last only the time of a magic spell,

---

[35] Rabelais, *Le Tiers Livre*, chap. 38, "ou Comment par Pantagruel et Panurge est Triboulet Blasonné," in which we are given up to 210 epithets to qualify this very famous Fool who inspired Verdi in *Rigoletto*.

which he has to use as best he can. Shakespeare-Prospero knows it too, who is trying a last time to enchant London audiences.

Among the many plots fomented behind Prospero's back, there is one that he secretly appreciates. His daughter, who incidentally reacts as did his brother Antonio in the past, is convinced that, while he is in his books, her father will not interrupt a secret meeting between her and Ferdinand:

> My father
> Is hard at study. Pray now, rest yourself.
> He's safe for these three hours. (III i 19–21)

She encourages Ferdinand to disobey Prospero's orders and completely forgets about his recommendations to herself. Their spontaneity and innocence are delightful to behold and far from the silliness of some performances. Like most Shakespearean girls, Miranda is direct and bold and does not hesitate to answer Ferdinand's unasked proposal: "I am your wife, if you will marry me" (III i 83).

Far from protesting, however, Prospero's heart is melting. His plan has hit the mark, yet he is past the age of innocence and cannot share their amazement. Has the magus lost his faith? The tone is strangely subdued and a little later, when he tries a last time to arouse wonder for the wedding of his children, he remains gloomy and out of sorts. Was Shakespeare alluding to events in his life? Were there people in the theater who knew the cause of such unease? It is indeed difficult to imagine that Prospero feared his enemies that much, they being in his power, and if he had really wanted vengeance, he could have drowned them all. More is obviously at stake! Caliban's iterative advice to Stefano smacks of censorship:

> There thou mayst brain him,
> *Having first seized his books*; (III ii 86–87)

> *Remember*
> *First to possess his books*, for without them
> He's but a sot as I am, nor hath not
> One spirit to command. (89–92)

> *Burn but his books* (93) (my italics)

Had Shakespeare been a victim of the king's watchers at last? Had some of his books been destroyed by Cecil's thugs? Had he, like Belarius in *Cymbeline*, been threatened in his properties? The success of the Stratford man must have made rivals envious, and if his enemies understood his indirections as we do, they might do their best to silence the man and subsequently erase as much as possible any document related to him. We can only wish we knew what books were instrumental to Shakespeare's art.

His power to amaze and leave his audience dumb with admiration is used forthwith on King Alonso's party, whose mouths are made to water at the vision of a banquet, which vanishes as they attempt to reach it. Ariel, as a harpy, then provides the moral of the dumb show, reviving past guilt and present griefs, and promises everlasting perdition unless they repent and amend their lives. Amazed, Alonso, who believes his son dead, is touched to the quick and wants to die, whereas distracted Sebastian and Antonio are trying to fight the visions with their swords. All of them now are in Prospero's power.

Meanwhile, Prospero proceeds to give his daughter to young Ferdinand, who has born the trials and vexations imposed by his father-in-law with a brave and pure heart. The reward is a most colorful masque in which Shakespeare no doubt rivaled Ben Jonson and his courtly entertainments, while subtly commenting on them. For Shakespeare, the virtue of those visions had meaning only in as much as they had moral consequences in reality. For him they could not be mere entertainment destined to flatter the king or the queen, but visions working wonder on the soul of the spectators and awakening their faith. The goddesses Ceres and Juno appear to bless the lovers and solemnize "a contract of true love." Yet Venus and her blind boy are expressly unwelcome. In his tragicomedies, Shakespeare more than ever values true and chaste love above all other passionate temptations — lessons that the father must have felt important to transmit to his daughters.

This "vanity" of Prospero's art, beautiful and symbolic though it is, is soon shaken by yet another threat against his life. Was Prospero under the spell of his own art that he forgot about the savage gang of Caliban? Or is he simply becoming tired and forgetful? He is suddenly brought back to the issue at hand, troubled and ill-tempered, apologizing to his son. The passage is probably the best known in all of Shakespeare's work, showing life as an "insubstantial pageant" destined to fade and disappear forever:

> Our revels now are ended. These our actors,
> As I foretold you, were all spirits, and
> Are melted into air, into thin air;
> And like the baseless fabric of this vision,
> The cloud-capped towers, the gorgeous palaces,
> The solemn temples, the great globe itself,
> Yea, all which it inherit, shall dissolve;
> And, like this insubstantial pageant faded,
> Leave not a rack behind. We are such stuff
> As dreams are made on, and our little life
> Is rounded with a sleep. (IV i 148–58)

The passage has often been turned into evidence of Shakespeare's agnosticism, which of course cannot be supported. While those beautiful lines do not seem to refer to Caliban's plot, Prospero's existential anguish at this point seems more related to his age and the gift he has just made of his daughter to another man, than to the enemies, which he has charged Ariel to neutralize. If we take Prospero to be an avatar of Shakespeare himself, those lines certainly reflect the sadness and disillusion of Shakespeare who foresaw the end of his theatrical career at this point, and it is difficult to separate them from what has just been said concerning a probable seizure of his books.

Action is resumed with Ariel's account of his tricks on Caliban and his gang and Prospero's order for more show, tempting the fools with mere glistening garments. Stefano and Trinculo immediately take the bait and even Caliban is appalled at the foolishness of his accomplices. The scene ends with the three plotters hunted by hounds and Prospero's evil charms. Ariel has been Prospero's faithful spirit and loyal servant throughout, his freedom repeatedly postponed. Now at last comes the climax of their endeavor with Ariel daring a personal comment on Prospero's power:

> *Ariel*: Your charm so strongly works 'em
> That if you now beheld them your affections
> Would become tender.
> *Prospero*: Dost thou think so, spirit?
> *Ariel*: Mine would, sir, were I human.
> *Prospero*: And mine shall. (V i 17–20)

For the first time in the play, this authoritarian man lets himself be influenced and listens to his own spirit's suggestion to choose the road to pardon:

> Though with their high wrongs I am struck to th' quick,
> Yet with my nobler reason 'gainst my fury
> Do I take part. The rarer action is
> In virtue than in vengeance. (V i 25–28)

It is time for a statement of affairs, and, remembering his achievements, Prospero for the first time in the play reveals himself as a true sorcerer, a magus who acquired huge powers over the elements and his fellow men. This Ovidian catalogue of wonders boasted by Medea, who could, like Prospero, work metamorphoses and resurrections, renders his ensuing renunciation all the more impressive. He could do wonders, yet somehow has decided to put an end to all this. The true and more amazing metamorphosis of course is that which he manages to work upon himself: choosing the path of reason and virtue against passion and vengeance. Ariel his better spirit, like a guardian angel, has whispered that much in his ear.

Prospero now reveals himself, forgives all of them — even though he knows that some may be unredeemable — and having retrieved his duke-dom from his brother, can now proceed to reveal his ultimate plans to Alonso. Alonso, the king of Naples, is still despondent, persuaded that his son Ferdinand died at sea. Prospero reproaches him for not seeking the help of patience, who, he is now proud to say, has helped him. And he is now ready to lie for the good cause, pretending that he too has lost his daughter. Pursuing the tale of his peregrination, Prospero, with a good sense of timing and of justice, gives Alonso, who's given back his dukedom, measure for measure. He discloses a scene of Ferdinand and Miranda playing chess.

The vision, called a "miracle" by Sebastian, appears like a window opened on the future, the trick of a magician, with the two young lovers not caught at dalliance, but significantly arguing about "a score of kingdoms" for which innocent Miranda would be ready to accept her husband's "wrangling." The revelation of the game of chess sums up all of Prospero's moods and decisions in the play in as much as it illustrates the relationship between will and destiny.[36] It also reveals the kind of humanistic education he has given his daughter, who may still be innocent of men, but already masters the art of diplomatic negotiation. She may be amazed at the beauty of the world she discovers, but Prospero knows that the newness of it will soon wear off. The trick is to substitute intelligence and knowledge for the emotional first vision in order to ensure its durability. In the game of chess, intelligence always has the upper hand over ignorance; the outcome does not owe anything to chance and it was favored in Elizabethan England precisely because it involved no gambling.

> At each stage of the game, the player is free to choose between several possibilities, but each movement will entail a series of unavoidable consequences, so that necessity increasingly limits free choice, the end of the game being seen, not as the fruit of hazard, but as the result of rigorous laws.
>
> It is here that we see not only the relationship between will and fate, but likewise between liberty and knowledge.... In other words, freedom of action is here in complete solidarity with

---

[36] Alphonsus the Wise, in his book on chess, relates how a king of India wished to know whether the world obeyed intelligence or chance. Two wise men, his advisers, gave opposing answers, and to prove their respective theses, one of them took as his example the game of chess in which intelligence prevails over chance, while the other produced dice, the symbol of fortuity.

foresight and knowledge of the possibilities; contrariwise, blind impulse, however free and spontaneous it may appear at first sight, is revealed in the final outcome as a non-liberty.[37]

Not only are the young people already well-equipped to rule their destiny, but Prospero's own game is now at an end. He ensured the future with Miranda's marriage to the soon-to-be king of Naples, bringing back peace between Naples and Milan in the process, even if this involves the loss of Milan as an independent power. Prospero can at last go back home where, he says, "every third thought shall be my grave," (V i 311) as he obviously has given up power and chosen a conclusion to his children's advantage.[38] In spite of his mercy, he knows that his brother is unredeemable and like a naughty child, can only be constrained by removing all temptation. However, to believe that this was Prospero's goal from the beginning is to forget about the rules of chess. Prospero, like Shakespeare himself, did his best with each opportunity presented to him. The young people might have disliked each other, just as some of the plots could have had different outcomes. During the length of the play, Prospero spends much of his time watching the game around him and deciding on his next move, when he feels he has an opening. Hence his moods and concerns when he feels things are not developing as he expected.

When all is concluded, Prospero keeps for himself the Epilogue, now begging the audience to release him from their spell, asking for their prayers and indulgence. Having relinquished his part as a magician, he is now an old man asking for leave to go. There is little doubt at this stage that Shakespeare and Prospero are one and the same, for as Stephen Greenblatt observes, "It is not Prospero but Shakespeare who has commanded old Hamlet to burst from the grave and who has brought back to life the unjustly accused Hermione. Shakespeare's business throughout his career had been to awaken the dead."[39] ♣

---

[37] Burckhardt Titus, "The Symbolism of Chess," *Studies in Comparative Religion* 3.2 (Spring 1969); www.studiesincomparativereligion.com.
[38] Who knows if Shakespeare's properties had not been threatened with seizure if he did not give up his line of thought? He may even have made his eldest daughter his principal heir to protect the property he had spent a lifetime to rebuild.
[39] Greenblatt, *Will in the World*, 376.

CONCLUDING THOUGHTS

*I*F STYLE MEANS ANYTHING, SHAKESPEARE'S WORK CAN-not be the work of a Calvinist. Its fanciful abundance and colors, its refusal of the straight line and of the narrowness of categories, its evident love of humanity in spite of all the latter's meanness and defects, its constant will to understand and forgive, all this and more gives us fair evidence of his position and beliefs. The best appellation for him might be that he was an Erasmian Catholic, always inclined to reconcile natural and revealed religion, emphasizing a middle way with a deep respect for traditional faith, piety, and grace. Erasmus, "the king of *but*,"[1] shared with Shakespeare the peculiar ability always to see both sides of a problem, which made him choose the *via media*, staying way away from extremes:

> The man who attacked both the Church and the Church's attacker at the same time, who urged that Luther be protected by the princes but refused to side with Luther, who placed Socrates in the same order of the blessed with St. Paul, obviously conceived that truth was rarely simple.[2]

Naturally, such apparent lack of commitment sometimes could appear weak, but in an absolutist regime like that of Lord Burleigh, to show a dissenting mind without being arrested required the agility of a conjuror and the secrecy of a cat. Shakespeare's mannerism was born out of necessity as much as taste and character. The division and chaos imposed on England by the rash and selfish decision of one monarch obviously sickened him. It was not simply the authoritarian whim of the king, who should have been an example to his people, it was the brutal denial of the soul of a whole nation, which left the people perplexed by a lie that passed for truth.

How could such a thing happen? How could the sin of a single man stain a whole nation? Young Shakespeare's earliest meditation on the subject appears to be *The Rape of Lucrece* in which Lucrece, trying to dissuade her rapist, launches into a long plea to Tarquin for honesty and self-respect, her words assuming the shape of an indictment against the arrogance and selfishness of those kings who forget the divine duties of their office. The question of the legitimacy of kings, the responsibilities involved in the act of ruling, were to haunt Shakespeare all his life. There is not a play where he does not question power, its requirements and its limits, in the State as well as in the family. The Tudors' divorce from the Church and the way

---

[1] Coined by Georges Duhamel, *Deux Patrons* (Paris: Hartmann Paul, 1937), 33.
[2] Kaiser, *Praisers of Folly*, 38.

they violently imposed their choice on the nation manifestly constituted a great betrayal of their duties as rulers. The Church had not only been raped and the monasteries dissolved, but the people had been abandoned, without any spiritual or medical succor, deprived of shelters for the poorest of them. Soon divisions and rivalries would create a gulf between those who remained loyal to the faith and those who seized on the opportunity to get rich by collaborating with the new power. In many instances, trust and friendship had been destroyed and lies had taken over.

If he missed many aspects of the old faith, which he kept reviving in his plays, Shakespeare nonetheless made friends with people who joined novel religions. We know that he lived in London among Huguenot exiles, and that Richard Field, who published his *Poems*, also provided books to him, related to classical literature and to more contemporary debates. If we read the allusion to Richard du Champs in *Cymbeline* correctly, this man, who should have been his religious enemy, was a dear friend of his.

AS IS OFTEN POINTED OUT, THE GUNPOWDER PLOT PROBABLY marked a turning point for Shakespeare. The rashness and extremism of the plotters ruined all hope of a more lenient policy toward Catholics. For indeed, all that Catholics were battling for at the end of the sixteenth century was freedom of conscience and recognition of their faith by the State. They could eventually have accepted the existence of a new religious settlement provided that Catholicism had been accepted as constitutive of the nation. This was essentially the Earl of Essex's stand,[3] the main reason why he was at odds with Cecil's government. Unfortunately he failed to touch the queen, who may herself have been manipulated by her ministers. His attempted riot failed and he was beheaded. After Elizabeth's death, the accession of James I brought a few years' reprieve and hope. James had much in common with Rudolf II and like him wanted harmony in his realm. But unfortunately "the Imperial embassy to London in 1605 to promote the toleration of the English Catholics was spoilt by the discovery of the gunpowder plot the same year."[4] It convinced the King that Catholics were indeed dangerous, and he should not grant them any recognition. In the years following that damnable event, Shakespeare, who had narrowly escaped,[5] went harsh and ironical. He now despaired of the Catholic cause and understood that there would be no improvement in their lot,

---

[3] Alexandra Gajda, *The Earl of Essex and Late Elizabethan Political Culture* (Oxford: Oxford Historical Monographs, Oxford University Press, 2012).
[4] David Snelling, "Prospero on the Coast of Bohemia," 13.
[5] His company had not only performed *Richard II* for the conspirators on the eve of Essex's riot, he also found himself related to those who had organized the Gunpowder Plot.

no improvement for his generation. It did not make him deny his faith, but he became more critical and moralizing and invested his hope in the new generation. His style naturally reflected his unease and questioning. What are generally called the *problem plays*, which include *Julius Caesar* and *Hamlet*, according to Maquerlot, correspond to his most cynical mannerism, in which little harmony emerges from the representation of disharmony. Hamlet may provide the truest expression of Shakespeare's disgust at the world of lies and spies in which he was caught. In *Macbeth, Othello*, and *King Lear* he would launch into an uncompromising exploration of evil, leaving little space for the working of grace and mercy. The presence of Lear's Fool in a tragedy, however, linked as he is with the aborted return of the beloved daughter and the posthumous redemption she works on her father, heralds a new vision of hope for Shakespeare, who has now discovered the essential presence of time in his art. (In his life too, for his daughters had now reached the age of marriage and as a father he had to let them go.)

In the kingdom of England, likewise, much was expected from young and gifted Prince Henry. Whether he would have been more enlightened than his father is difficult to say as he was swept away by typhoid fever before he reached manhood. Shakespeare's only consolation by then must have been his daughter Susanna's family. He liked John Hall, his son-in-law, and there may be much of Shakespeare in Prospero's attempt to provide for the future. Just as there may be much contemporary relevance in the threats endured by the exiled duke. Clare Asquith suggests that Shakespeare, now deprived of "the great patronage network of the Montague family," was silenced. After the death of Magdalen Montague in 1609, she writes, "Houses of members of the entourage were ransacked; manuscripts and books, among them the work of suspect poets and dramatists, became more vulnerable than ever to seizure."[6] Caliban's threat against Prospero's books may have been more than simple stage play. With the choice of Calvinistic George Abbot for the post of Archbishop of Canterbury in 1611, and until his fall from favor ten years later, a dark decade of oppression fell on all liberal-minded artists. Apart from Ben Jonson, who had openly renounced his Catholic faith, most major dramatists seem to have stayed on the bench during these years. The twilight of the stage lamented by Jonson in his 1623 homage to his friend was not caused by lack of talent but by the political climate.

It is important to stress the troubled period spanning Shakespeare's life in order to shed light on and to understand his particular *mannerism*.

---

[6] Asquith, *Shadowplay*, 262.

Mannerism as a style, even if not yet so named, was not unknown in the literary sphere and we generally accept the idea that young Shakespeare must have been influenced by his contemporary John Lyly, who had introduced a very ornate style of language using alliterations and antitheses, wordplay and other witticism, which was appreciated and imitated at court. Euphuism, just like marinism in France, were affected instances of mannerism, the matter remaining light and the language rather snobbish and disconnected from reality. If Shakespeare was influenced by Lyly, he soon outshone him. *Love's Labour's Lost* was a virtuoso piece showing that young Shakespeare had perfectly mastered verbal sparring and battles of wit. But it carried its own moral in its plot, and the way "to weed this wormwood" from Berowne's fruitful brain was, as he puts it "to move wild laughter in the throat of death," (V ii 821) surely the most extreme oxymoron that may be. Condemned to spend twelve months in a hospital where his merry wit could bring solace and cure the sick, he would learn what true art is about!

Shakespeare already had solace and cure in mind, and a very high idea of his talent, whose aim was not only to address all men rather than an elite courtly audience, but to solve the "intrinsicate" meaning of life, to create harmony out of the most radical oppositions and "to move wild laughter in the throat of death." There was matter in his mannerism and out of the inconstancies, illusions, and uncertainties of life, he meant to reveal truth, create wonder, and arouse faith. The books and the knowledge that helped create the success of Shakespeare's art remain a mystery to this day. Fortunately, his mention of Giulio Romano appears like a discreet vindication of his esthetical manner, which we can see maturing over the years. Surely, Shakespeare had read Vasari and had known the Italian Master for some time when he ventured to refer to him by name. *Romeo and Juliet* was early evidence of his mastery of what Eugene Green calls the Baroque Oxymoron in a subtle Counter-Reformation masterpiece. Like Giulio Romano, he could be said to be "learned, bold, sure, capricious, varied, abundant and universal."[7] Unfortunately such qualities aroused suspicion in a kingdom whose government had opted for Protestantism, and Shakespeare had to take even more precautions to disguise his Catholic sympathies in his plays. However, it seems that he was more and more daring as the years passed and the final revelation in *The Winter's Tale* only narrowly fell short of heresy. Hiding behind Paulina's precautions, as he was about to show no less than a resurrection on stage, Shakespeare feigned, as well as mocked, his enemies' comparisons of the Catholic Church with witchcraft. For a

---

[7] Vasari, *La vie des meilleurs peintres* vol. 2, book 7, 171.

few moments, the stage of the Globe must have been permeated with the sacredness of true faith, and the audience must have been awestruck, all the more if some perceived the allegorical references in Camillo and Paulina's characters, and in the inverted choice of Sicily and Bohemia.

Camillo and Paulina are good people, loyal and bold, healers and spiritual advisers both of them, pulling the strings of the plot after Leontes's demise, in order to restore peace in the realm and love among the former friends. If Paulina's name refers to Saint Paul, Robert. T. Morrison suggests Camillo's might point to contemporary Pope Paul V, whose name was Camillo Borghese.[8] Camillo is indeed spoken of as priestlike and holds for Leontes the role of confessor, until his king's madness forces him to exile himself with King Polixenes to Bohemia, where young Perdita is equally transported and saved from death by local shepherds. Bohemia, then, is a land of refuge, described by Edmund Campion in a letter to his fellow Jesuit, Robert Arden, as "a pleasant and blessed shore,"[9] which would be one more piece of evidence that Shakespeare, far from being "careless in detail," took great pains in multiplying precise but hidden references in his plays. He would rather bear the accusations of ignorance with equanimity than risk the life and work of his company. The most surprising is that Morrison's allegory fits rather well with the esthetic approach which I chose to privilege, and there is no doubt that Leontes's penitent progress culminating at the foot of a statue of his saintly Lady, under the guidance of another holy woman, smacks strongly of the old faith. We may never learn the true reasons that pushed Shakespeare to leave the stage and retire to Stratford while he was at the height of his powers, but the texts of his plays remain for us to probe. They prove wonderful, well-polished jewels whose intricacies and secrets are yet to be fathomed. Like Cleopatra, age cannot wither him, nor custom stale his infinite variety. He makes hungry where he most satisfies.

Annie-Paule de Prinsac
Vesvres, in Blessed Burgundy, France, in the year 2020

---

[8] For a complete allegory of the play, see Robert. T. Morrison, *A Tale Told Softly, Shakespeare's The Winter's Tale and Hidden Catholic England* (Scotts Valley, CA: CreateSpace, 2015). If the reference to Paul V is true, it is interesting to know that on September 22, 1606, he had expressly forbidden the Roman Catholics of England to take the new oath of allegiance imposed on them by King James I.

[9] Alfred Thomas, *A Blessed Shore: England and Bohemia from Chaucer to Shakespeare* (Ithaca: Cornell University Press, 2007), 168. Quoted by Morrison, 48.

ABOUT THE AUTHOR

ANNIE-PAULE MIELLE DE PRINSAC was assistant Professor at the University of Bourgogne (now retired). A musician, she first studied Elizabethan music and taught at the University of Sussex (England). She obtained a Sachs research scholarship at the University of Harvard, where she worked on Shakespeare's Last Plays, and followed her husband to Madagascar, where she taught at the University in Antananarivo. She later became a specialist in African American Literature at the French Academe with two books on Toni Morrison. She was a fellow of the Du Bois Institute at Harvard (Summer/Fall 2002). She has also written many articles on Shakespeare and African American literature (Morrison, Harriet Jacobs, Langston Hughes, E. J. Gaines).